ENGLISH EPISCOPAL ACTA

32

NORWICH 1244–1266

ENGLISH EPISCOPAL ACTA

GENERAL EDITORS: David M. Smith (1973– 2005)
Philippa M. Hoskin (2003 onwards)

1. LINCOLN 1067–1185. Edited by David M. Smith. 1980.

2. CANTERBURY 1162–1190. Edited by C. R. Cheney and Bridgett E. A. Jones. 1986.

3. CANTERBURY 1193–1205. Edited by C. R. Cheney and E. John. 1986.

4. LINCOLN 1186–1206. Edited by David M. Smith. 1986.

5. YORK 1070–1154. Edited by Janet E. Burton. 1988.

6. NORWICH 1070–1214. Edited by Christopher Harper-Bill. 1990.

7. HEREFORD 1079–1234. Edited by Julia Barrow. 1993.

8. WINCHESTER 1070–1204. Edited by M. J. Franklin. 1993.

9. WINCHESTER 1205–1238. Edited by Nicholas Vincent. 1994.

10. BATH AND WELLS 1061–1205. Edited by Frances M. R. Ramsey. 1995.

11. EXETER 1046–1184. Edited by Frank Barlow. 1996.

12. EXETER 1186–1257. Edited by Frank Barlow. 1996.

13. WORCESTER 1218–1268. Edited by Philippa M. Hoskin. 1997.

14. COVENTRY AND LICHFIELD 1072–1159. Edited by M. J. Franklin. 1997.

15. LONDON 1076–1187. Edited by Falko Neininger. 1999.

16. COVENTRY AND LICHFIELD 1160–1182. Edited by M. J. Franklin. 1998.

17. COVENTRY AND LICHFIELD 1183–1208. Edited by M. J. Franklin. 1998.

18. SALISBURY 1078–1217. Edited by B. R. Kemp. 1999.

19. SALISBURY 1217–1228. Edited by B. R. Kemp. 2000.

20. YORK 1154–1181. Edited by Marie Lovatt. 2000.

21. NORWICH 1215–1243. Edited by Christopher Harper-Bill. 2000.

22. CHICHESTER 1215–1253. Edited by Philippa M. Hoskin. 2001.

23. CHICHESTER 1254–1305. Edited by Philippa M. Hoskin. 2001.

24. DURHAM 1153–1195. Edited by M. G. Snape. 2002.

25. DURHAM 1196–1237. Edited by M. G. Snape. 2002.

English Episcopal Acta is a publication series of the British Academy.

The British Academy, established by Royal Charter in 1902, is the national academy for the humanities and social sciences, promoting, sustaining and representing advanced research. As an academy composed of senior scholars throughout the UK, it gives recognition to academic excellence and achievement, and plays a leadership role in representing the humanities and social sciences nationally and internationally. As a learned society, the British Academy seeks to sustain the health and promote the development of the various academic disciplines that make up the humanities and social sciences. And as a grant-giving body, the British Academy facilitates the research of individuals and groups of scholars.

More information can be found at *www.britac.ac.uk*

ENGLISH

EPISCOPAL ACTA

32

NORWICH 1244–1266

EDITED BY

CHRISTOPHER HARPER-BILL

Published for THE BRITISH ACADEMY

by OXFORD UNIVERSITY PRESS

Oxford University Press, Great Clarendon Street, Oxford OX2 6DP

Oxford New York
Auckland Cape Town Dar es Salaam Hong Kong Karachi
Kuala Lumpur Madrid Melbourne Mexico City Nairobi
New Delhi Shanghai Taipei Toronto

With offices in
Argentina Austria Brazil Chile Czech Republic France Greece
Guatemala Hungary Italy Japan Poland Portugal Singapore
South Korea Switzerland Thailand Turkey Ukraine Vietnam

Published in the United States
by Oxford University Press Inc., New York

British Library Cataloguing in Publication Data
Data available

Library of Congress Cataloging in Publication Data
Data available

Typeset by the editor
Printed in Great Britain
on acid-free paper by
Antony Rowe Limited,
Chippenham, Wiltshire

ISBN 978–0–19–726417–1

For Ruth
with love and gratitude for twenty-five years of support

CONTENTS

LIST OF PLATES

(between page lxiv and page lxv)

ACKNOWLEDGEMENTS

First I must thank my own university and the Arts and Humanities Research Council for funding a year of study leave which gave the opportunity for the completion of this volume. As always, I am grateful for the assistance of many archivists and librarians in the preparation of the edition. Thanks are expressed to all of those who have granted access to and permitted publication of documents in their ownership or custody, that is the authorities of all those repositories which are recorded in the list of manuscript sources, and most especially the Duke of Norfolk and the Marquess Townshend. Transcripts of Crown copyright material appear by permission of the Controller of Her Majesty's Stationery Office, and of manuscripts in the British Library by permission of the Trustees. All the archivists with whom I have had dealings have been unfailingly helpful, but I would like to thank most especially Dr John Alban and his staff at the Norfolk Record Office.

I have also received generous help from many fellow scholars in this field. Dr Michael Franklin at Cambridge and Dr Nicholas Karn at Oxford cheerfully checked for me transcripts made some years ago. Dr Martin Brett and Professor Brian Kemp have always been eager to discuss matters of mutual interest, and Professor Edmund King provided invaluable support. At my own institution I am extraordinarily fortunate in being able to draw upon the experience in their various fields and on the friendly advice of Professor Carole Rawcliffe, Mr Sandy Heslop Mrs Elizabeth Rutledge and Professor Nicholas Vincent. They, together with my other fellow medievalists Dr Stephen Church, Dr Lucy Marten and Dr Robert Liddiard, make the School of History at Norwich, under the benign leadership of Professor John Charmley, a congenial place in which to undertake this kind of scholarship. Most of all I am grateful to the successive general editors of the series, Professor David Smith and Dr Philippa Hoskin, for all the help they have given and care which they have shown, and supremely to Professor Christopher Brooke for the meticulous care which he has, over three volumes now, devoted to my work. Errors undoubtedly remain in abundance, but they are infinitely less numerous because of his selfless efforts.

My greatest debt, however, is to my wife, Dr Ruth Harvey who, despite the pressures of her own academic career, has been unstinting in her support for me and for my work for a quarter of a century. Her love and devotion could not be more appreciated, even if it may not always seem so, and the dedication of this book is a small token of my gratitude.

School of History   Christopher Harper-Bill
University of East Anglia,
Norwich

MANUSCRIPT SOURCES CITED

ORIGINAL CHARTERS OF THE BISHOPS OF NORWICH

Arundel Castle, Sussex, Duke of
Norfolk's muniments:
Hales ch. 104: *43*; Seething ch.
280: *106*
Cambridge, Jesus College muniments:
Gray 11, Caryl A7: *15*
Cambridge, King's College
muniments:
GBR 37: *112*
Canterbury, Dean and Chapter
Archives and Library:
Chartae Antiquae: C115/08: *1*;
C115/13: *139*
Dublin, Trinity College Library:
ms. 1208/374: *113*
Durham Cathedral muniments:
Misc. ch. 1515: *38*; 2. 13. Pont. 4:
39; Loc. 1: 25: *61*
Fakenham, Norfolk, Raynham Hall
muniments:
ex mss box 56: *35*
Ipswich, Suffolk R. O.:
HD1538/324/2 no. 184: *116*
London, British Library,:
Add. ch. 14676: *24*; Add. ch.
19278: *104*; Add. ch. 47959: *110*;
Add. ch. 47960: *111*
London, Guildhall Library:
ms. 25124/16: *Appx 1. 17*;
25124/18: *Appx 1. 18*; 25124/26:
81A
London (Kew), The National
Archives (formerly Public Record
Office):
C84/1/33: *60*
C85/130/1: *50*; /2: *49*; /3: *48*; /4:
53; /5: *51*; /6: *52*; /7: *56*; /8: *55*;

/9: *57*; /10: *58*; /11: *63*; /12: *65*;
/13: *64*; /14: *44*; /15: *46*; /16: *47*;
/17: *45*; /18: *155*; /19: *157*; /20:
158; /21: *160*; /22: *161*; /23: *163*;
/24: *164*; /25: *166*; /26: *167*; /27:
169; /28: *168*; /29: *170*; /30: *173*;
/31: *172*; /32: *171*; /33: *175*; /34:
177; /35: *174*; /36: *176*; /37: *178*;
/38: *179*; /39: *180*; /86: *54*; /89:
162
E40/14060: *153*; /14065: *76*;
/14072: *75*; /14114: *78*; /14118:
79; /14373: *2*; /14924: *80*;
/14927: *77*
E42/362: *74*
LR14/1107: *40*
SC1/7/205: *Appx 2. 43*
SC1/63/1: *165*
Norwich, Norfolk R. O.:
ms. 1392: *144A*; ms. Phillips 290:
118
DCN 31 (insert), *70*; DCN 43/44:
88; /45: *95*; /46: *98*; /47: *73*; /49:
185
NCR24b/1: *103*; /2: *138*; /3: *105*;
/4: *188*; NCR25b/604: *186*
Oxford, Bodleian Library:
Douce ch .(a. 1) 53: *187*
Norfolk ch. (a. 1) 54: *143*
Suffolk ch (a. 13) 1440: *3*
Sens, Musée de Sens:
Sens cathedral Trésor muniments
H26: *114*
Warwick, Warwickshire County R. O:
ms. CR 133/4: *Appx 2. 44*
Wells cathedral, Dean and Chapter:
charter 84: *61*

COPIES, TRANSCRIPTS AND MENTIONS OF CHARTERS OF THE BISHOPS OF NORWICH

Caen, Archives départmentales du
   Calvados:
   ms. H 32: *14*
Cambridge, Christ's College:
   Creake abbey muniments 7: *37,
   144*
Cambridge, Corpus Christi College:
   ms. E. P. R. 2: *102*
   ms. 16: *119*
Cambridge, Gonville and Caius
   College:
   ms. 36: *102*
Cambridge, King's College
   muniments:
   KER/638: *74*
Cambridge, Trinity College:
   ms.1245: *102*
Cambridge University Library:
   ms. I i. 3. 7: *102*
   ms.Gg iv 4: *Appx 2. 4*
   ms. Mm iv 19: *9*
   Ely Diocesan Records ms. G3/28:
   145
Canterbury, Dean and Chapter
   Archives and Library:
   Chartae Antiquae, C120: *17, 17A*; N1,
   89: *108*
   register A: *1, 17, 17A, 139*
Chelmsford, Essex R. O.:
   D/D By Q 19: *11, 41, 146–7*
Chichester, West Sussex R. O.:
   Ep VI/1/6: *33*
Dublin, Trinity College
   ms. E. 2. 22: *102*
Ipswich, Suffolk R. O.
   ms. HD 1538/345, no. 12: *124*
Lincoln Cathedral, chapter library:
   ms. C. 2. 9.: *102*
London, British Library:
   Addition Charter 7207: *Appx 2.*

17
   Additional Manuscripts: 4699:
   10A; 7096: *Appx 1. 2, 7, 11*;
   28564: *189A*; 34560: *122, 192*;
   40725: *7*; 46353: *134*; 61900: *37*
   Arundel Manuscript 221: *123*
   Cotton Manuscripts: Appx xxi:
   127–9; Claudius A xii: *9*;
   Faustina A iv: *120*; Galba E ii:
   42, 69–72, 181; Nero D i: *67–8*;
   Nero E vii: *195*; Titus C viii: *135,
   196–7, Appx 2. 19–20*; Vespasian
   E iii: *8, 126*
   Cotton Rolls: ii 19: *93, 108–9*; iv
   57: *181*
   Egerton Manuscripts: 3033: *16*;
   3137: *5–6A*
   Harley Charter 57 E 31: *Appx 2.
   23*
   Harley Manuscripts: 1708: *117*;
   2110: *15, 19–30, 143, Appx 2. 7–
   8*
   Stowe Charters: 292: *149*; 293:
   150; 294: *151*
London, Lambeth Palace Library:
   ms. 1212: *18*
   register of archbp Thomas
   Arundel: *18*
London (Kew), The National
   Archives:
   C53/57: *182*
   C54/67: *84, 125*
   CP25/1/157/70/907: *Appx 3. 5*;
   /157/71/927: *Appx 3. 6*;
   /157/71/934: *Appx 3. 7*;
   /157/78/1110: *Appx 3. 8*;
   /157/82/1207: *Appx 3. 9*;
   /214/19/6: *Appx 3. 1*; /214/19/23:
   Appx 3. 2; /214/19/27: *Appx 3. 3*;
   /214/19/28: *Appx 3. 4;*

PRINTED BOOKS AND ARTICLES CITED, WITH ABBREVIATED REFERENCES

Abingdon Chron.	J. Stevenson, ed., *Chronicon Monasterii de Abingdon*, 2 vols (Rolls Series, 1858)
Acta Stephani Langton	K. Major, ed., *Acta Stephani Langton Cantuariensis Archiepiscopi, A. D. 1207–1228* (CYS 50, 1950)
Anglia Sacra	H. Wharton, ed., 2 vols (London, 1691)
Ann. mon.	H. R. Luard, ed., *Annales monastici*, 5 vols (Rolls Series, 1864–9)
Banfield, T. G.	'A Descriptive Catalogue of the Seals of the Bishops of Norwich', *Norfolk Archaeology* 1 (1847), 305–23
BIHR	*Bulletin of the Institute of Historical Research*
Bk Fees	H. C. Maxwell-Lyte, ed., *Liber Feodorum: the Book of Fees commonly called Testa de Nevill*, 3 vols (London, 1920–31)
Blair, J	ed., *Minsters and Parish Churches: The Local Church in Transition, 950–1200* (Oxford University Committee for Archaeology, Monograph no. 17, 1988)
Blomefield, *Norfolk*	F. Blomefield and C. Parkin, *An Essay towards a Topographical History of the County of Norfolk*, 2nd edn, 11 vols (London, 1805–10)
Blythburgh Cartulary	C. Harper-Bill, ed., *Blythburgh Priory Cartulary* (Suffolk Record Society, Suffolk Charters 2–3, 1980–1)
BM Seals	W. de G. Birch, *Catalogue of Seals in the Department of Manuscripts in the British Museum*, 6 vols (London, 1887–1900)
Bracton's Notebook	F. W. Maitland, ed., *Bracton's Notebook: A Collection of Cases Decided in the King's Courts during the Reign of Henry the Third, Annotated by a Lawyer of that Time, seemingly by Henry of Bratton*, 3 vols (London, 1887)

BRUO   A. B. Emden, *A Biographical Register of the*
                                University of Oxford to A. D. 1500, 3 vols
                                (Oxford, 1957–9)
Bury Chron.   A. Gransden, ed., *The Chronicle of Bury St*
                                Edmunds, 1212–1301 (NMT, 1964)
Canterbury Professions   M. Richter, ed. (CYS 67, 1973)
Cautley, H. M.   *Suffolk Churches*, 5th edn (Woodbridge,
                                1982)
C. Ch. R.   *Calendar of the Charter Rolls*, 6 vols
                                (London, 1903–27)
CDF   J. H. Round, ed., *Calendar of Documents*
                                preserved in France...A.D. 918–1206
                                (London, 1899)
Cheney, C. R.   *English Synodalia of the Thirteenth Century*
                                (Oxford, 1941)
                                'Magna Carta Beati Thome: Another
                                Canterbury Forgery', BIHR 36 (1963) 1–26;
                                repr. in *Medieval Texts and Studies* (Oxford,
                                1973), 78–110
                                Notaries Public in the Thirteenth and
                                Fourteenth Centuries (Oxford, 1972)
                                Episcopal Visitation of Monasteries in the
                                Thirteenth Century, 2nd edn (Manchester,
                                1983)
Chibnall, M.   ed.,*Charters and Custumals of the Abbey of*
                                Holy Trinity, Caen (Records of the Social
                                and Economic History of England and
                                Wales, ns 5, 1982)
Chichester Chartulary   W. D. Peckham, ed., *The Chartulary of the*
                                High Church of Chichester (Sussex Record
                                Society 46, 1946)
Chron. Edward I   W. Stubbs, ed., *Chronicles, Edward I and*
                                Edward II, 2 vols (Rolls Series, 1882–3)
Chron. Maj.   H. R. Luard, ed., *Matthaeii Parisiensis*
                                Chronica Majora, 7 vols (Rolls Series,
                                1872–84)
Churchill, I. J.   *Canterbury Administration*, 2 vols (London,
                                1933)
Cirencester Cartulary   C. D. Ross and M. Devine, eds, *The*
                                Cartulary of Cirencester Abbey, 3 vols
                                (Oxford, 1964)
C. Lib. R.   *Calendar of Liberate Rolls*, 6 vols (London,
                                1917–64)

Cl. R.	*Close Rolls of the Reign of Henry III*, 14 vols (London, 1902–38)
Colvin, H. M.	*The White Canons in England* (Oxford, 1951)
CPL i	*Calendar of entries in the Papal Registers relating to Great Britain and Ireland 1198–1304*, ed. W. H. Bliss (London, 1893)
CPR	*Calendar of Patent Rolls* (London, 1891–)
Creake Abbey Cartulary	A. L. Bedingfield, ed., *A Cartulary of Creake Abbey* (Norfolk Record Society 35, 1966)
Crook, D.	*Records of the General Eyre* (Public Record Office Handbooks 20, London, 1982)
CRR	*Curia Regis Rolls...preserved in the Public Record Office* (London, 1922–)
C. & S.	*Councils and Synods, with other Documents relating to the English Church*, i, *A. D. 871–1204*, ed. D. Whitelock, M. Brett and C. N. L. Brooke, 2 parts; ii, *1205–1313*, ed. F. M. Powicke and C. R. Cheney, 2 parts (Oxford, 1964–81)
CYS	Canterbury and York Society
Davis, G. R. C.	*Medieval Cartularies of Great Britain* (London, 1958)
DB	*Domesday Book, seu Liber censualis*, 2 vols ('Record Commission', 1783)
DBM	R. F. Treharne and I. J. Sanders, eds, *Documents of the Baronial Movement of Reform and Rebellion, 1258–67* (OMT, 1973)
Delisle	L. Delisle and E. Berger, eds, *Receuil des actes de Henri II concernant les provinces francaises et les affaires de France*, 4 vols (Paris, 1909–27)
DKR	*Annual Reports of the Deputy Keeper of the Public Records* (London, 1915–)
W. Dugdale	*History of St Paul's Cathedral in London*, 2nd edn, ed. H. Ellis (London, 1818)
EEA	*English Episcopal Acta*, 1– (British Academy, 1980–)
EHR	*English Historical Review*
English Baronies	I. J. Sanders, *English Baronies: A Study of their Origins and Descent*, 1086–1307 (Oxford, 1960)

Eye Cartulary

V. Brown, ed., *Eye Priory Cartulary and Charters*, 2 vols (Suffolk Record Society, Suffolk Charters 11–12, 1992–4)

Fasti

D. E. Greenway, ed., *Fasti Ecclesiae Anglicanae, 1066–1300* by John le Neve, i- (London, 1968–)

Fines i, ii

B. Dodwell, ed., *Feet of Fines for the County of Norfolk (1198–1202)*; *Feet of Fines for the County of Norfolk (1202–15) and of Suffolk (1199–1214)*, PRS ns 27, 32 (1950–8)

First Register

H. W. Saunders, ed., *The First Register of Norwich Cathedral Priory* (Norfolk Record Society 11, 1939)

Foedera

T. Rymer and R. Sanderson, *Foedera, Conventiones, Litterae et cujuscumque generis Acta Publica*, ed. A. Clark and F. Holbrooke, 4 vols in 7 (Record Commission 1816–69)

Formulare Anglicanum

T. Madox, ed. (London, 1702)

Foundation of Walden

D. Greenway and L. Watkiss, eds, *The Book of the Foundation of Walden Monastery* (OMT, 1999)

Gesta Abbatum

H. T. Riley, ed., *Gesta Abbatum Monasterii S. Albani a Thoma Walsingham (A. D. 793–1401)*, 3 vols (Rolls Series, 1867–9)

Gervase

W. Stubbs, ed., *Gervase of Canterbury: Historical Works...*, 2 vols (Rolls Series, 1879–80)

Gibbs, M., and Lang, J

Bishops and Reform, 1215–1272 (Oxford, 1934)

Gray, A.

The Priory of St Radegund, Cambridge (Cambridge Antiquarian Society, 8°, 31, Cambridge, 1898)

Guala's Letters

N. Vincent, ed., *The Letters and Charters of Cardinal Guala Bicchieri, Papal Legate in England, 1216–1218* (CYS 83, 1996)

Harper-Bill, C.

'Battle Abbey and its East Anglian Churches', in *Studies in Medieval History presented to R. Allen Brown*, ed. C. Harper-Bill, C. J. Holdsworth and J. L. Nelson (Woodbridge, 1988), 159–72

'The Diocese of Norwich and the Italian Connection, 1198–1261', in *England and the Continent: Essays dedicated to the Memory*

of Andrew Martindale, ed. J. Mitchell
(Stanford, 2000), 75–89
'Above all these Charity': the Career of
Walter Suffield, Bishop of Norwich, 1244–
57', in *The Foundations of Medieval English
Ecclesiastical History: Studies presented to
David Smith*, ed. P. Hoskin, C. Brooke and
B. Dobson (Woodbridge, 2005), 94–110

Haughmond Cartulary U. Rees, ed., *The Cartulary of Haughmond
Abbey* (Shropshire Archaeological Society
and University of Wales Press, Cardiff,
1985)

HBC E. B. Fryde, D. E. Greenway, S. Porter and I
Roy, eds, *Handbook of British Chronology*,
3rd edn (Royal Historical Society, 1985)

Historia Minor F. Madden, ed., *Matthaei Parisiensis
Historia Minor*, 1067–1253, 3 vols (Rolls
Series, 1866–9)

HMC Various Collections Historical Manuscripts Commission, *Reports
on Manuscripts in Various Collections*, 8
parts (HMC, 1903–13)

HMC Wells Historical Manuscripts Commission,
*Calendar of Manuscripts of the Dean and
Chapter of Wells*, 2 vols (HMC, 1907–14)

HRH ii D. M. Smith and V. C. M. London, *The
Heads of Religious Houses: England and
Wales*, ii, *1216–1377* (Cambridge, 2001)

Hudson, W. 'The Norwich Taxation and the *Taxatio
Nicholai*', *Norfolk Archaeology* 17 (1910),
46–157

Jacob, E. F. 'A Proposal for Arbitration between Simon
de Montfort and Henry III in 1260', *EHR* 37
(1922), 80–2

Jocelin H. E. Butler, ed., *The Chronicle of Jocelin of
Brakelond* (NMT, 1949)

Jones, D. *St Richard of Chichester: The Sources for his
Life* (Sussex Record Society 79, 1995)

Kalendar R. H. C. Davis, ed., *The Kalendar of Abbot
Samson of Bury St Edmunds, and related
documents* (Camden Society 3rd series 84,
1954)

Kings Lynn D. M. Owen, *The Making of King's Lynn: A
Documentary Survey* (Records of the Social

	and Economic History of England and Wales, ns 9, 1984)
Lawrence, C. H.	*St Edmund of Abingdon* (Oxford, 1960)
Leiston Cartulary	R. Mortimer, ed., *Leiston Abbey Cartulary and Butley Priory Charters* (Suffolk Record Society, Suffolk Charters 1, 1979)
Letters of Innocent III	C. R. and M. G. Cheney, eds, *The Letters of Pope Innocent III (1198–1216) concerning England and Wales* (Oxford, 1967)
Lewes Cartulary: Norfolk Portion	J. H. Bullock, ed., *The Norfolk Portion of the Cartulary of the Priory of St Pancras at Lewes* (Norfolk Record Society 12, 1939)
Liber Eliensis	E. O. Blake, ed. (Camden Society 3rd series 92, 1962)
Llandaff Acta	D. Crouch, ed., *Llandaff Episcopal Acta, 1140–1287* (Publications of the South Wales Record Society 5, 1989)
Logan, F. D.	*Excommunication and the Secular Arm in Medieval England* (Toronto, Pontifical Institute of Medieval Studies, Studies and Texts 15, 1968)
Lunt, W. E.	*Financial Relations of the Papacy with England to 1327* (Medieval Academy of America, Cambridge, Mass., 1939)
Lyndwood, W.	*Provinciale, seu Constitutiones Anglie* (Oxford, 1679)
Maddicott, J. R.	*Simon de Montfort* (Cambridge, 1994)
Memorials of St Edmunds	T. Arnold, ed., *Memorials of St Edmunds Abbey*, 3 vols (Rolls Series, 1890–6)
Mon. Angl.	W. Dugdale, *Monasticon Anglicanum*, ed. J. Caley, H. Ellis and B. Bandinel, 6 vols in 8 (London, 1817–30)
Monumenta Franciscana	J. S. Brewer and R. Howlett, eds, 2 vols (Rolls Series, 1858–82)
MRH	D. Knowles and R. N. Hadcock, *Medieval Religious Houses: England and Wales*, 2nd edn (London, 1971)
Newington Longville Charters	H. E. Salter, ed. (Oxfordshire Record Society 3, 1921)
NMT	Nelsons Medieval Texts
Norwich Cathedral	I. Atherton, E. Fernie, C. Harper-Bill and A. H. Smith, eds, *Norwich Cathedral: Church, City and Diocese, 1096–1996* (London, 1996)

Norwich Cathedral Charters	B. Dodwell, ed., *The Charters of Norwich Cathedral Priory*, 2 vols (PRS ns 40, 46, 1974–85)
ns	new series
OMT	Oxford Medieval Texts
os	old series
Oseney Cartulary	H. E. Salter, ed., *Cartulary of Oseney Abbey*, 6 vols (Oxford Historical Society 89–91, 97–8, 101, 1929–36)
Oxenedes	H. Ellis, ed., *Chronica Johannis de Oxenedes* (Rolls Series, 1859)
Oxford DNB	*Oxford Dictionary of National Biography* (2005)
Pinchbeck Register	F. Hervey, ed., *The Pinchbeck Register*, 2 vols (Brighton, 1925)
Powicke, F. M.	*Henry III and the Lord Edward* (Oxford, repr. 1966)
PRS	Pipe Roll Society
Prynne, *Records* iii	W. Prynne, *The Third Tome of an Exact Chronological Vindication ...of the Supreme Ecclesiastical Jurisdiction of our...English Kings* (London, 1668)
PUE	W. Holtzmann, ed., *Papsturkunden in England*, 3 vols (Abhandlungen der Geschellschaft der Wissenschaften in Göttingen, phil.-hist. Klasse, Berlin, Göttingen, neue Folge 25 (1930–1); 3. Folge, 14–15 (1935–6), 33 (1952)
Ramsey Cartulary	W. H. Hart and P. A. Lyons, eds, *Cartularium monasterii de Rameseia*, 3 vols (Rolls Series, 1884–93)
Rawcliffe, C.	*Medicine for the Soul: The Life, Death and Resurrection of an English Medieval Hospital* (Stroud, 1999)
Reading Cartulary	B. R. Kemp, ed., *Reading Abbey Cartularies*, 2 vols (Camden Society 4th series 31–2, 1986–7)
Reg. Alex. IV	B. de la Roncière *et al.*, eds, *Les registres d'Alexandre IV (1254–61)*, 3 vols (Paris, 1902–59)
Reg. Bateman	P. E. Pobst, ed., *The Register of Willam Bateman, Bishop of Norwich, 1344–55*, 2 vols (CYS 84, 90, 1996–2000)

Reg. Clem. IV	E. Jordan, ed., *Les registres de Clément IV* (1265–68) (Paris, 1893–1945)
Reg. Giffard, Worcester	J. W. Willis Bund, ed., *Episcopal Registers, Diocese of Worcester: Register of Bishop Godfrey Giffard, September 23rd 1268 to August 15th 1301*, 2 vols (Worcestershire Historical Society 15, 1898–1902)
Reg. Gray	J. Raine, ed., *The Register, or Rolls, of Walter Gray, Lord Archbishop of York, with Appendices of Illustrative Documents* (Surtees Society 56, 1872)
Reg. Greg. IX	L. Auvray *et al.*, eds, *Les registres de Grégoire IX (1227–41)*, 4 vols (Paris, 1890–1955)
Reg. Hon. III	P. Pressutti, ed., *Regesta Honorii Papae III*, 2 vols (Rome, 1888–95)
Reg. Morton	C. Harper-Bill, ed., *The Register of John Morton, Archbishop of Canterbury, 1486–1500*, 3 vols (CYS 75, 78, 89, 1987–2000)
Reg. Urban IV	J. Guirard and S. Clémencet, eds, *Les registres d'Urbain IV (1261–64)*, 4 vols (Paris, 1892–1958)
Rites of Durham	J.T. Fowler, ed., *Rites of Durham ... written 1593* (Surtees Society 107, 1903)
Russell, J. C.	*Dictionary of Writers of Thirteenth-Century England* (London, 1936)
Rye, *Norfolk Fines*	W. Rye, ed., *A Short Calendar of the Feet of Fines for Norfolk* (Norwich, 1885)
Rye, *Suffolk Fines*	W. Rye, ed., *A Calendar of the Feet of Fines for Suffolk* (Ipswich, 1900)
St Benet of Holme	J. R. West, ed., *St Benet of Holme, 1020–1210* (Norfolk Record Society 2–3, 1932)
St Davids Acta	J. Barrow, ed., *St Davids Episcopal Acta, 1085–1280* (Publications of the South Wales Record Society 13, 1998)
Saunders, H. W.	'A History of Coxford Priory', Norfolk Archaeology 17 (1910), 284–372.
Saunders, H. W.	*An Introduction to the Obedientiary and Manor Rolls of Norwich Cathedral Priory* (Norwich, 1930)
Sayers, J. E.	'Canterbury Proctors at the Court of 'Audientia Litterarum Contradictarum', *Traditio* 22 (1962), 311–45; repr. in *Law and*

Records in Medieval England (London, 1988), ch. III
Papal Judges-Delegate in the Province of Canterbury, 1198–1254 (Oxford, 1971)
Original Papal Documents in England and Wales from the Accession of Pope Innocent III to the death of Pope Benedict XI (1198–1304) (Oxford, 1999)

Searle, E.   *Lordship and Community: Battle Abbey and its Banlieu, 1066–1531* (Toronto, Pontifical Institute of Medieval Studies, 1974)

Shinners, J. R.   'The Veneration of Saints at Norwich Cathedral in the Fourteenth Century', *Norfolk Archaeology* 40 (1987–89), 133–44

Sibton Charters   P. Brown, ed., *Sibton Abbey Cartularies and Charters* (Suffolk Record Society, Suffolk Charters 7–10, 1985–8)

Smith, D. M.   *Guide to Bishops' Registers of England and Wales* (Royal Historical Society, 1981)
'The "Officialis" of the Bishop in Twelfth- and Thirteenth-Century England: Problems of Terminology', in M. J. Franklin and C. Harper-Bill, eds, *Medieval Ecclesiastical Studies in honour of Dorothy M. Owen* (Woodbridge, 1995), 201–20

Spelman, *Concilia*   Spelman, H., *Concilia, decreta, leges in re ecclesiarum orbis britannici...ii (1066–1531)* (London, 1664)

Stoke by Clare Cartulary   C. Harper-Bill and R. Mortimer, eds, (Suffolk Record Society, Suffolk Charters 4–6, 1982–4)

Stubbs, W.   *Registrum Sacrum Anglicanum*, 2nd edn (Oxford, 1897)

Tanner, J.   *Notitia Monastica...* (London, 1744; repr. with addition by J. Naismith, Cambridge, 1787)

Taxatio   S. Ayscough and J. Caley, eds, *Taxatio Ecclesiastica Angliae et Walliae auctoritate Papae Nicholai IV circa 1291* (Record Commission, 1802)

Thesaurus NA   E. Martène and U. Durand, eds, *Thesaurus Novus Anecdotorum*, 6 vols (Paris, 1717)

VCH   *Victoria County History*

VN	W. E. Lunt, ed., *The Valuation of Norwich* (Oxford, 1926)
Warks. Fines i	E. Stokes *et al.*, eds, *Warwickshire Feet of Fines* i: *1195–1284* (Dugdale Society 11, 1932)
Wilkins, *Concilia*	D. Wilkins, ed., *Concilia Magnae Britanniae et Hiberniae, A. D. 446–1717*, 4 vols (1737)

OTHER ABBREVIATIONS

Add.	Additional
Appx	Appendix
archbp(s)	archbishop(s)
archdn(s)	archdeacon(s)
archdnry	archdeaconry
BL	British Library
Bodl.	Bodleian Library, Oxford
bp(s)	bishop(s)
Ch.	Charter
Ch. Ant.	Charta Antiqua
D. & C.	Dean and Chapter
fo.	folio
kt	knight
m.	membrane
misc.	miscellanea, miscellaneous
om.	omitted
pd	printed
repd	reprinted
R. O.	Record Office
s. -ex	late-century
s. -in	early-century
s. -med.	mid-century
ser.	series
TNA	The National Archives, Kew
Trans.	Transactions
transl.	tranlated, translation

INTRODUCTION

THE DIOCESE OF NORWICH

The development of the diocese, which comprised the counties of Norfolk and Suffolk and the half-hundred of Exning in Cambridgeshire, is outlined in a previous volume.[1] At the end of the thirteenth century the compilers of the *Taxatio Ecclesiastica* listed 1165 parishes, although it has been suggested that this was an underestimate and that the true total was 1349.[2] By the mid thirteenth century the four territorial archdeaconries of Norwich, Norfolk, Suffolk and Sudbury were long established.[3] For half a century there had been an official to aid the bishop in his non-sacramental functions and to deputise for him when absent,[4] and during the episcopate of William Raleigh, in 1241, there first occurs the official of the consistory, which implies that the court now sat regularly.[5]

Although the rapid multiplication of houses of monks, canons and nuns which had characterised the century and a half after the Norman Conquest had slackened in pace, the period covered by this volume saw the foundation of two nunneries, Marham and Flixton, both supported by the diocesan (85–7, 149–52), and the establishment by bishop Suffield himself of a major new hospital, St Giles in Norwich (103–7, 186–8).

By 1266 there were probably a dozen mendicant houses established in the diocese, but the impact of the friars is reflected in this collection only by bequests to them in Suffield's will, and by a reference to an episcopal confirmation for the Dominicans of Lynn (Appx 2. 35).

THE BISHOPS

WALTER SUFFIELD

Walter Suffield[6] was a member of a gentry family who held of the honour of Warenne the manor of Calthorpe (a toponymic used by some of his kinsmen) in north Norfolk;[7] in the 1220s the estate passed to his older brother Roger, whom Walter represented in the *curia regis*.[8] He probably studied first at Oxford, and

---

[1] *EEA* 6 pp. xxv–xxvi.
[2] Hudson, 'The Norwich Taxation' 69–70.
[3] *Fasti* ii 61–2.
[4] *EEA* 6 no. 336.
[5] *EEA* 21 Appx 2. 50A.
[6] For brief biographies, see BRUO 1813–14; Rawcliffe, *Medicine for the Soul* 18–33; Harper-Bill, 'Above all these Charity'.
[7] Blomefield, *Norfolk* iii 486–7; v 107; vi 514–5; xi 146–7, 176.
[8] *CRR 1225–26* no. 804.

later at Paris, where he graduated as doctor of canon law.[9] He was probably rector at some time of Somerton and Winterton, of Burgh in Flegg and one of the Suffolk Burghs, and of Great Snoring and Cressingham, 'to my poor parishioners' of which he made bequests in his will (138). In 1237 he acted as official *sede vacante* in Norwich diocese for archbishop Edmund of Abingdon,[10] and in his will he made reparation to those he had oppressed as official. He attested just one *actum* of bishop William Raleigh.[11]

He was obviously a member of St Edmund's friendship circle, and in his will the archbishop left him a cup, which he subsequently bequeathed to his own foundation of St Giles's hospital (138). Suffield also ultimately left twenty marks to the work which he had initiated on the saint's shrine at Pontigny.[12] His copy of the *Decretum* had come to him from master John of Uffington, a member of Edmund's *familia* and his proctor at the *curia*, called by Matthew Paris the most famous clerk in England.[13] Suffield in 1254 issued an indulgence for pilgrims to St Edmund's chapel at Bearpark (39), and one of his earliest episcopal *acta* is an indulgence for those praying at the tomb in St Paul's of Roger Niger, bishop of London, another reformer commonly reputed to be a saint (81). Suffield's closest association, however, was with St Richard Wich, St Edmund's chancellor and subsequently bishop of Chichester.[14] Their lives overlapped at may points: both were canon lawyers, they were consecrated as bishops within a month of each other; Richard was the main preacher of the crusade for the financing of which Walter was to be the principal collector. The bishop of Norwich granted an indulgence to benefactors of Chichester cathedral (32), and the bishop of Chichester dedicated Marham abbey in Norfolk, a foundation of the countess of Arundel which Suffield did much to stabilise (85–7).[15] Richard's biographer states that Walter became a better pastor through imitation of the saint, whose regard for him is obvious, as he was the only one of his episcopal colleagues whom he remembered in his will.[16] Eighteen months after Richard's death Walter made provision for his friend's soul by appropriating Mendlesham church to Chichester cathedral and reserving the rectorial income for the service of the future saint's tomb (33). Already before his elevation, Suffield moved in a milieu of sanctity which provided a model for his own episcopate.

The election of Suffield by the monks of Norwich took place shortly before 9 July 1244, when royal assent, and the restoration of temporalities eight days later, signified that Henry III had finally lost his long battle to prevent the

---

[9] *Cotton* 394..
[10] *CRR 1237–42* no. 318; cf. *Eye Cartulary* i no. 79.
[11] *EEA* 21 no. 132.
[12] For Edmund, see Lawrence, *St Edmund of Abingdon.*
[13] *BRUO* 1927–8; *Chron. Maj.* v 230.
[14] For an assessment and his *vita*, see Jones, *St Richard of Chichester;* for his *acta, EEA* 22 nos. 107–88.
[15] Jones, *St Richard of Chichester* 50.
[16] Ibid. 68, 165–6, *EEA* 22 no. 188.

translation of William Raleigh to Winchester.[17] In his will Suffield recognised the expense and trouble which the monks had incurred in the matter of his election, and the Winchester pipe roll for 1244–5 records the presence of the bishop-elect and prior of Norwich at Bishops Sutton and Alresford, and of Suffield at Farnham also.[18] A close relationship was obviously established, as Raleigh gave him a mitre and crozier (138) and again entertained him twice in 1246–7.[19] Suffield was with archbishop-elect Boniface of Savoy at Canterbury and Wingham from 25–27 October 1244, where he witnessed the elect's victory over the monks in the campaign initiated by St Edmund to enforce archiepiscopal rights over the cathedral chapter (18). In December 1244 he wrote to the prior and convent of Christ Church thanking them for the concession of the licence *alibi* (17); his election having been confirmed by the archbishop-elect at St Albans, he was consecrated in the priory church of Carrow at Norwich on 19 February 1245 by Fulk Basset, bishop of London and dean of the province,[20] and the following day, 20 February, as bishop, provided the *cautio* that his consecration outside the metropolitan church of Canterbury should not prejudice the future rights of the monks (17A).

Suffield was to have even more contact with the papacy than most of his episcopal colleagues. On his first visit to the *curia* as a bishop, to attend the Council of Lyons in summer 1245, he was one of a group of six bishops who undertook the collection of that subsidy sought by the pope since late 1244.[21] In the face of opposition and procrastination by the English government his colleagues reneged on their undertaking, and it was Suffield alone who eventually on 24 March 1246 wrote to the abbot and convent of St Albans (and doubtless to many other major churches), ordering the community to deliver their share of the taxation three weeks before Easter (119), although in the event further royal intransigence delayed payment until late 1246.

A far more onerous task was to fall on Walter's shoulders, foreshadowed by the mandate of Innocent IV in November 1250 to him and bishop Richard of Chichester to compel the English crusaders to set out on their expedition, on pain of ecclesiastical censure.[22] Before 6 May 1252 Suffield was added to the commission appointed by the pope to collect gifts and legacies for the furtherance of holy war and money paid for the redemption of crusading vows.[23] On 12 September 1253 he was mandated, together with John Climping, the new bishop of Chichester, and the abbot of Westminster, to assess and collect clerical taxation authorised by the pope, but to be paid to Henry III to finance his

---

[17] *EEA* 21 pp. xxxiv–xxxvii; *Fasti* ii 57.
[18] Winchester, Hampshire R.O., ms. 11M59/B1/18, m. 16d, 22d, 23.
[19] Ibid. ms. 11M59/B1/20, m. 3d, 26d.
[20] *Chron. Maj.* iv 261, 375, 378; *Ann. mon.* iii 166. No. 17A below confirms the date given in *Bury Chron.* 13, rather than 26 Feb., as recorded in the Waverley annals (*Ann. mon.* ii 336); cf. *Fasti* ii 57.
[21] For this levy, see *VN* 31–6; Lunt, *Financial Relations* 206–19, esp. 217–9; *C & S* II i 388–9
[22] *Chron. Maj.* vi 201–2; *EEA* 22 no. 186.
[23] Lunt, *Financial Relations* 440.

crusade, later diverted from the Holy Land to Sicily (63A). Suffield emerged as the senior partner of the triumvirate, to the extent that the reassessment of English ecclesiastical revenues rapidly became known as the Valuation of Norwich. He himself was allocated the dioceses of Norwich, Ely, Lincoln, Coventry and Lichfield, London (excluding the archdeaconry of London) and the entire northern province, being granted 500 marks for salary and expenses.[24] A few *acta* in this collection are a small reflection of the huge task to which he was committed (8, 16, 34, 82, 126, 133), and his itinerary in late 1254, extending to Durham, reveals the effort entailed for an elderly man who now wore a corset to contain his corpulence (138). Matthew Paris makes it clear that the bishop did not relish his task, and that his sympathies lay with the English clergy rather than pope or king.[25] The valuation, conducted by self-assessment, albeit backed by threats of excommunication and damnation, represented, perhaps unsurprisingly, a great underestimate of real income; a splendid example is provided by the fact that the cardinal and canonist Hostiensis received £80 *p.a.* from the canons of Walsingham for the farm of his church of East Dereham, which in 1254 was valued at only £48 13s 4d.[26] It is not surprising that pope and king were disappointed with the results achieved, and in May 1255 the new pontiff, Alexander IV, appointed archbishop Boniface and master Roland Masson, papal nuncio, to supersede the previous collectors.[27] In late summer 1255, however, Suffield, along with the abbot of Peterborough, was again instructed to execute the business of the cross, including collection of the tenth, as Masson's deputy;[28] so almost to the end of his life the bishop was burdened by the unwelcome duty of tax collection beyond the bounds of his own diocese.

On his second visit to the *curia* in 1248–9 Suffield, according to Matthew Paris, complained emotionally of the oppression of the English church, begging the pope to be merciful to the land which, above all others, was loyal to him. Most especially he complained of innumerable provisions, which sacrificed the interests of the most worthy native candidates to the incessant demands of papal nominees.[29] At least a dozen Italians can be demonstrated to have held parochial livings in the diocese of Norwich during Suffield's episcopate,[30] and a small group of his *acta* reveal the pressure placed on diocesan as well as religious houses by the demands of papal and curial *familiares* in search of enhanced income (27, 71, 78–9). Even the limitation of archiepiscopal rights of visitation and level of procurations came at the price of a levy of 6000 marks on non-exempt English churches, of which 4000 marks were destined for the papal *camera* (67–8).

---

[24] *VN* 52–3; *Chron. Maj.* vi 296–8; *CPR 1247–58* 164, 370, 377.
[25] *Chron. Maj.* v 451–2; *Gesta Abbatum* i 368.
[26] *VN* 399; TNA, E135/19151.
[27] Lunt, *Financial Relations* 259–60.
[28] Ibid. 275–6.
[29] *Historia Minor* iii 58.
[30] Harper-Bill, 'Diocese of Norwich and the Italian Connection' 82–8.

Suffield's dealings with pope Innocent IV were not, however, all unwelcome and burdensome. At the beginning of his episcopate, while at the Council of Lyons, he obtained papal ratification of his aim to ensure the provision of more and better endowed vicarages in parish churches in his diocese which were appropriated to religious (Appx 2. 1); this intent is reflected in many *acta*. Worthy Englishmen did in fact, among all the Italians, benefit from papal initiative; in October 1245 Suffield received a mandate to allow Thomas of Ingoldisthorpe, DCL and future bishop of Rochester, to hold an additional benefice with cure of souls in addition to his living of St Mary's, East Raynham.[31] In early 1248 Suffield submitted to the pope a question concerning legitimacy of birth, on which depended inheritance, which elicited from Innocent IV a very interesting decretal reminiscent of the rulings of Alexander III on marriage in the previous century (Appx 2. 13). In March 1249 the pope responded to Suffield's announcement in his presence that he intended to celebrate the long-delayed dedication of his cathedral church by granting an indulgence of one year and forty days to visitors on its anniversary (Appx 2. 16). The greatest benefit which bishop Walter obtained from the *curia*, however, in his own mind, was surely the confirmation by Innocent IV on 24 July 1251 of his foundation of the hospital of St Giles, which was taken under papal protection.[32] This confirmation was renewed on 10 March 1255 by Alexander IV, who in October 1257, after Suffield's death, confirmed the bishop's revised statutes for this house.[33]

Walter Suffield's personal relationship with king Henry III appears to have been good, in marked contrast to his predecessor William Raleigh, who had been harassed by the crown during the long-drawn out process of his translation to Winchester. He attested a few royal charters, particularly for East Anglian beneficiaries,[34] and was one of the arbiters, in 1252, for the assessment of Simon de Montfort's contested expenses in royal service in Gascony.[35] For his see he obtained at Christmas 1245 the grant of a weekly market and a fair in Easter week at his episcopal manor of Thornham, and seven years later the bishop and his successors were granted free warren on all their demesne lands, provided they did not lie within the royal forest.[36] The bishop was twice given royal protection, on going overseas, on pilgrimage to St Gilles en Provence in late 1248, and again in October 1253.[37] In May 1251 he was granted licence to make his will without any impediment, saving any debts he might owe to the king.[38] In August 1253 he received licence to hunt in the forests of Essex and in May 1256

---

[31] *Reg. Inn. IV* no. 1562; *CPL* i 222.
[32] Sayers, *Original Papal Documents* nos. 400–1.
[33] *Reg. Alex. IV* no. 254; *CPL* i 312; Norfolk R.O., DCN 43/48; cf. no. 107 below.
[34] *C. Ch. R. 1300–1326* 480; *1327–41* 50; *1257–1300* 315, 318, 402.
[35] *CPR 1247–58* 124.
[36] *C. Ch. R. 1226–57*, 289; 404.
[37] *CPR 1247–58* 28, 223.
[38] Ibid. 92.

was pardoned for taking four deer in the royal forest while on his way to court. The king made him gifts of deer in May 1254 and January 1257, and in his will Suffield bequeathed his pack of hunting dogs to his sovereign.[39] In June 1256 the bishop obtained respite of knighthood for three years for his nephew William (Appx 2. 32). The only recorded refusal of a request occurred when Henry in February 1255 personally rejected Suffield's claim to a monstrous fish which had been beached on land held by a young man who was his ward (Appx 2. 30).[40] Far more significantly, the greatest mark of royal favour and esteem was the king's invitation to preach at the translation of the Holy Blood relic to Westminster abbey in 1247;[41] the bishop was also personally invited in 1255 to the celebration of the feast of St Edward at Westminster, which the king himself could not attend.[42]

As diocesan, Suffield was apparently the first bishop of Norwich to signify the names of obdurate excommunicates to Chancery so that royal officers might be instructed to arrest them (44–58, 62, 64–5). In summer 1248 the bishop asked the king to liberate Bexwell church, described as 'occupied by the lay power', perhaps the consequence of an advowson dispute (Appx 2. 14). On the other hand, the pressure exercised on the episcopal administration is illustrated in the printed *curia regis* rolls for 1249–50. In the space of six months Suffield was required to produce three ecclesiastical judges – the official of the archdeacon of Sudbury and two incumbents who were presumably acting as rural deans – who had allegedly heard pleas concerning chattels which were not related to a last testament; the sheriff had reported that they had no lay fee by which they might be attached to answer for this incursion on royal jurisdiction.[43] In the case of the *persona* of West Bradenham, the bishop replied that, since he could not be traced within the diocese, he had sequestrated his ecclesiastical goods (Appx 2. 18). Suffield was also required to produce five clerks of Norwich, without lay fee, who had allegedly committed a breach of the peace by violent breaking and entering.[44] The diocesan, too, was instructed to institute a *persona* presented by a successful litigant following an assize of *darrein presentment*, provided he was suitable, to the church of Grundisburgh, the expenses of which business he mentioned in his will (138).[45] Such verdicts in the royal court were inviolable, in the case of the dispute in 1248 between St Benet of Holme and Stephen of Reedham over Scottow being maintained even in the face of a papal pronouncement, directed to Suffield, on the invalidity of the proceedings in the *curia regis* (70).[46] More routinely, there are recorded during Suffield's

---

[39] Ibid. 219; *Cl. R. 1253–54* 66; *Cl. R. 1254–56* 302; *Cl. R. 1256–59*, 20.
[40] Cf. Powicke, *Henry III and the Lord Edward* 334.
[41] *Chron. Maj.* iv 642–4; *Historia Minor* iii 58, 309.
[42] *Cl. R. 1254–56* 222.
[43] *CRR 1249–50* nos. 974, 1001, 2295.
[44] Ibid. no. 1317.
[45] Ibid. no. 2238.
[46] *Reg. Inn. IV* no. 4516; *CPL* i 255.

episcopate twenty- two royal presentations to benefices in the king's gift, in his own right or because of minority, forfeiture or vacancy (Appx 4). Beneficiaries include a learned member of the Lusignan family, a nephew of the Chancellor, the king's proctor at the papal *curia*, and the papal collector in England and his kinsman (Appx 4. 5, 7, 11, 17–8, 20–2), none of whom was any more likely than papal providees to be resident. The most interesting royal presentation, however, was that in 1246 of master Henry of Campden to Gosbeck church, because the manor was in the king's hands since Richard of Gosbeck, both lord of the manor and rector, had ravished the wife of William le Bretun and contracted marriage with her (Appx 4. 3).

Beyond Suffield's reception as diocesan of numerous royal writs, the crown constantly intervened in the practicalities of the collection of the taxation of the church in the king's dominions (31, 84, 125). The division of responsibilities between the papally-appointed collectors and the allocation of their expenses were made in May 1254 in consulation with the royal council,[47] and in approving their proposed procedure it was the king who instructed them to set the first term for payment at Michaelmas 1254, allowing that, if the whole subsidy could not be delivered then, further terms might be set with royal approval.[48] The king twice ordered the Dominicans and Franciscans to assist the collectors by preaching on the business of the Cross.[49] The crown instructed the collectors to ensure that that all those under vows, including crusading vows which could not conveniently be fulfilled, should contribute whatever they would have expended to the king's pilgrimage, granting them freedom from Jewish usury for five years and swift justice, in preference to others insofar as the law allowed.[50] In June 1254 Henry ordered from Gascony that the residue of 2200 marks assigned to his brother-in-law, William de Valence, when he took the Cross before the king himself, should be paid to him swiftly from the collectors' receipts.[51] This payment had been previously sanctioned by the pope, but when in late 1254 the king ordered Suffield to pay forty marks from his receipts to master Nicholas of Plympton, royal clerk, being a loan which he had secured to further the king's business, the bishop twice refused to pay out, considering this contrary to the papal ban on the use of any of the taxation before the launching of the crusade.[52] Eventually, after master Rostand Masson had been sent from the *curia* to take overall charge of collection, it was according to the royal mandate of 16 November 1255 that Suffield transferred to him 5500 marks for payment to Sienese merchants for the furtherance of the business of Sicily (Appx 2. 31).

Despite the demands of fiscal administration imposed upon him, Suffield appears to have been a very conscientious diocesan. Of his 142 recorded *acta*,

[47] *CPR 1247–58* 370.
[48] *Cl. R. 1253–54* 136–7.
[49] *CPR 1247–58* 337, 440.
[50] Ibid. 164.
[51] *Cl. R. 1253–54* 303–4, cf. Lunt, *Financial Relations* 437–8.
[52] *Cl. R. 1253–54* 69; *CPR 1247–58* 358.

twelve related to taxation matters, three to his consecration and profession, and one was a joint declaration with his fellow bishops. Of the remainder, eighteen were significations, which make their first appearance for this diocese. The residue of extant documents were issued at an average of ten a year, almost the exactly the same as for the former royal administrator Thomas Blundeville (1226–36).[53] Neither is the nature of the contents substantially different from that of the *acta* of his two immediate predecessors and his successor, all curialist bishops. There are, however, certain nuances which may indicate his personal interpretation of the sollicitude of pastoral care. In the majority (though far from all) of his grants *in proprios usus* he stipulated the immediate or subsequent taxation of a vicarage, and on other occasions he modified an earlier appropriation by insisting on provision for a vicar. Suffield was the first bishop of Norwich to licence a substantial number of chapels, both private and on monastic manors, for the celebration of mass. More than his predecessors or successors, he appeared eager to achieve arbitration and reconciliation in disputes over various matters, especially the receipt of tithes, rather than magisterially to pronounce judgement.

It is impossible to demonstrate with any certainty that the Norwich synodal statutes which are supplementary to those definitely issued by bishop William Raleigh should be attributed to Suffield, but it is notable that many of them, although of course reflecting earlier papal and provincial legislation, deal with matters also treated in his *acta*.[54] For example, the statute instructing that archdeacons should conduct an annual visitation but should demand only moderate procurations[55] is reflected in the concession which Suffield induced the archdeacon of Norfolk to make to the prior of Wymondham and the vicars of its appropriated churches, despite his previous victory over them at the papal *curia* (Appx 2. 19–20), and paralleled by the bishop's limitation of his own procurations (67). These near-contemporary statutes reflect too the concern shown in may of Suffield's *acta* to secure an adequate ministry in parish churches, particularly by the creation of vicarages in appropriated churches where none yet existed : rectors as well as vicars should be resident, and should be severely punished if they allowed wanton men to serve their cures; vicars not in holy orders must be ordained thereto before the next ember-day; the clergy should be distinguished from the laity by their sober dress, and if they transgressed in this they should be deprived of their livings. Those ordained in other dioceses should be carefully examined before institution to a benefice.[56]

---

[53] *EEA* 21 nos. 28–123.

[54] *C & S* II i 357–64 (statutes additional to those now securely attributed to bishop William Raleigh). These statutes are there dated, with a high degree of probability, 1240 × 1266, that is, within the episcopates of Raleigh, Suffield and Walton; cf. Cheney, *English Synodalia* 125–36. They were previously attributed to Suffield by Gibbs and Lang, *Bishops and Reform* 46, following Wilkins, *Concilia* i 731–6.

[55] *C & S* II i 360, no. 71.

[56] *C & S* II i 357–62, nos. 59–60, 64, 70–1, 73, 75, 83.

Suffield's veneration of the Eucharist, reflected in his nationalistically Christocentric sermon at Westminster in 1227 and by his gift to his own monks of a great silver cup in which to keep their chrystal reliquary containing the Holy Blood, is reflected in the diocesan statute that no leper or other person should ring a bell in a public street, except a priest carrying the host to the sick, so as to increase devotion.[57] It seems overall very probable that Suffield may be credited with far more than the one statute, relating to the testamentary rights of incumbents (102) which may attributed to him with complete certainty.

The most remarkable document of Suffield's episcopate is certainly his last testament, made on 19 June 1256 (138).[58] His most substantial legacy was to his own hospital foundation of St Giles, built for the remission of his sins and as a chantry for the salvation of his soul, which he had already endowed generously during his lifetime, imposing detailed regulations, most especially for the succour of the poor (103, 107).[59] His body was to be interred before the altar of the cathedral's Lady Chapel, which he himself had added to the east end as his other great building project.[60]

The will provides almost incidentally a survey of his household, for he was generous to all levels of servant, from junior kitchen staff to his most trusted clerks and chaplains. Among other bequests to nuns, mendicants and hospitals, and for the salvation of friends now deceased, what is most striking is the concern for the poor, needy and disadvantaged which is reiterated in clause after clause of the will, in which bequests are made to lepers, anchorites and the poor parishioners of many vills. This confirms Matthew Paris's notice of his exceptional charity, most especially manifested when in a time of great hardship he sold his plate to aid the destitute.[61]

There are various points in the will where Suffield appears to be repenting financial exactions in dubious circumstances, which might prejudice his salvation, and to be attempting restitution. It is interesting that Paris's one unfavourable mention of Suffield is his allegation that at the papal *curia* in 1249 he secured an infamous privilege allowing him to extort money from his diocese,[62] which is almost certainly a reference to the right of the bishop of Norwich to receive the first-fruits of benefices to which he had instituted new incumbents, secured by Pandulph from pope Honorius III,[63] which was still controversial at the end of the thirteenth century and was contested by

---

[57] *C & S* II i 361, no. 76.

[58] For more detailed treatment, see Harper-Bill, 'Above all these Charity' 104–10.

[59] For a fine study of the foundation and medieval history of the hospital, see Rawcliffe, *Medicine for the Soul*.

[60] Atherton, *Norwich Cathedral* 158–61. The Lady Chapel was demolished in the sixteenth century, after the Reformation.

[61] *Chron. Maj.* v 638.

[62] Ibid. v 80.

[63] *Reg. Hon. III* nos. 2257, 2456; *CPL* i 68, 71.

archbishops Pecham and Winchelsey.[64]

Suffield was active until the last months of his life. He was present at the consecration of episcopal colleagues at Canterbury on 7 January and at London on 11 March 1257. His last *actum* was issued at Hevingham on 25 April (6). It is likely that he attended an ecclesiastical council in London on 6 May, and was returning to his diocese when he died at Colchester on 19 May 1257 (Appx 5). He was soon, for a short time, locally venerated as a saint, although there is no record of any campaign for official canonisation.[65]

SIMON WALTON

Simon Walton[66] came originally probably from Walton Deyville in Warwickshire; in 1235–36 he appeared as plaintiff in a case concerning land at nearby Tysoe.[67] He first appears, as *magister*, in 1226,[68] and as a clerk of Osney abbey, from which he received a pension, in 1234.[69] It is almost certain that he had studied canon law at Oxford. In January 1237 he was granted protection on going overseas in the king's service, and in October 1241 was appointed royal proctor in a suit at the Roman *curia*.[70] He served as keeper of the temporalities of the see of Coventry and Lichfield in the long vacancy from December 1241 until March 1246.[71]

In spring 1246 he began his career as a royal justice. He served as a junior justice on eighteen of the eyres of Roger Thirkelby's circuit of 1246–49 and on three eyres headed by Henry of Bath in 1250–51. He acted as chief justice on twelve eyres between 1252–56, and when not itinerating, as a justice on the Bench at Westminster, sometimes as chief justice, between 1251–57.[72]

While serving as a judge he began the accumulation of property which continued after he became bishop. In 1246 he received the farm of the royal manor of Feckenham (Wo.), and in 1254 was granted the lease of the manor of Harvington (Wo.) by the prior and convent of Worcester, who had the previous year presented him to their church of Stoke Prior.[73] As bishop-elect he received royal confirmation of a sixteen-year lease by Fulk Fitzwarin of the manor of Tadlow (Ca.), and in 1260 he obtained for five years the manor of Assington (Sf.) as security for a loan.[74] At some time before 1261 he acquired the farm for

[64] *Reg. Winchelsey* ii 1179–80.
[65] Shinners, 'Veneration of Saints at Norwich Cathedral' 141.
[66] For brief biographies, see *BRUO* 1995–6; *Oxford DNB* (by Alan Harding).
[67] *Warks. F.of F.* i 106.
[68] *Cl. R. 1227–31* 117; he was engaged in litigation concerning land at Kinvaston (St.).
[69] *Oseney Cartulary* i 279; iii 42.
[70] *CPR 1232–47* 173, 265, 286.
[71] Ibid. 476; *CPR 1247–58* 147; *Cal. Lib. R. 1240–45* 395 (index); *Cl. R. 1237–42* 446, 488; *Cl. R. 1242–47* 84.
[72] Crook, *Records of the General Eyre* 18–19, 106–11, 118–21.
[73] *VCH Worcestershire* iii 114, 359, 389; *Ann. mon.* iv 442.
[74] *CPR 1247–58* 575; *CPR 1258–66* 41.

twenty-six years of the manor of Measham (Leics.), in which he and his tenant suffered some harassment (Appx 2. 41, 43). While bishop he purchased the wardship of James of Ellington (Appx 2. 37). Towards the end of his life he had consolidated his holdings in his own native territory; he held land at Walton Deyville, Loxley, Bradley and elsewhere, and had recently acquired the manor of Walton Mauduit from the earl of Warwick. These Midland estates he passed during his own lifetime to his son John, who had certainly been conceived before Simon entered into higher orders (Appx 2. 44–5).[75]

Walton was elected to the bishopric of Norwich on 4 June 1257.[76] The London annalist, perhaps hostile to him because of his record as royal justice and property speculator, accused him of imitation of his namesake Simon Magus, in that he paid 300 marks to the monks to secure their nomination.[77] It is unlikely, however, that a candidate so close to the king would need to resort to such bribery. Royal assent was given on 10 June, the temporalities restored to him on favourable terms before 11 August. He was consecrated at Canterbury on 10 March 1258. Another accusation against him can easily be dismissed. Matthew Paris states that soon after his election he sent messengers to the *curia* who by bribery obtained a dispensation that he might for four years retain all his former benefices, despite the wealth of his see.[78] It is clear, however, that he had very quickly resigned his church of Potton (Bd.), in the gift of St Andrew's priory, Northampton, and his portion of the church of Whittingham (Nb.), normally of the patronage of the bishop of Carlisle.[79]

From his election, as before, Walton was the recipient of marks of royal favour. On 13 August 1257, two days after the restoration of temporalities, the king by his special grace granted the bishop-elect the year's hay from the episcopal demesne.[80] On 11 December the crown conceded that he might levy the scutage due from his fees by his own bailiffs and answer to the king in the Exchequer.[81] In April 1262 Henry III granted eight oaks from the royal forest in Essex for the repair of the bishop's quay in London.[82] On a more personal level, in May 1259 and again in October 1260 Walton received gifts of three deer from the royal forest of Feckenham, and he was also granted pardons for hunting there, both before and after his consecration.[83] These inexpensive royal concessions, if intended as recognition of Walton's previous service as royal clerk and justice, were well rewarded by the bishop's record of loyalty to the

[75] The two Waltons were held of the earl of Warwick, Loxley of the prior of Kenilworth (*Reg. Giffard Worcs.* no. 1294).
[76] *Fasti* ii 57.
[77] *Chron. Edward I and II* i 50; cf. Gibbs and Lang, *Bishops and Reform* 91.
[78] *Chron. Maj.* v 648–9; Paris acidly adds that such concessions were now becoming common at the court of Rome.
[79] *CPR 1247–58* 574; *Reg. Alex. IV* no. 2281; *CPL* i 352.
[80] *Cl. R. 1256–59* 86.
[81] Ibid. 282.
[82] *Cl. R. 1261–64* 40.
[83] *Cl. R..1256–59* 77, 123; *Cl. R. 1259–61* 102; *Cl. R. 1261–64* 67.

king during the prolonged political crisis of the late 1250s and early 1260s, which in stark contrast to that of many of his episcopal colleagues, was exemplary.

In 1259, during negotiations leading to the formal sealing of the Treaty of Paris, Walton was on 15 May appointed as one of Henry III's ambassadors to king Louis IX, and again on 9 September he was granted protection on setting out as the king's envoy to France.[84] When on 27 March 1260 Henry wrote from St Omer to the justiciar ordering him to summon tenants-in-chief and their knights to London for 27 April, excluding those whom the king did not trust, among the bishops only Norwich, Salisbury and Exeter were included.[85] In summer 1260 Walton served as one of two royal representatives on the arbitration panel of six bishops appointed to investigate the king's charges against Simon de Montfort.[86] He was appointed, with the bishops of Salisbury and Worcester, as proctor for the prelates for the negotiation of clerical subsidies to the king, on 26 January 1261 and on a subsequent occasion.[87]

As relations between king and reformers declined, Walton was closely involved in every step of the campaign to emancipate Henry from the oaths and obligations which constrained his freedom of action. On 29 April 1261 pope Alexander IV commanded archbishop Boniface, Walton and John Mansell, treasurer of York (the last two certainly the king's nominees) to absolve certain prelates, magnates and others from oaths taken which were prejudicial to the royal authority, and eight days later another commission to the same three mandated them to use every endeavour to persuade the political classes of England to be faithful to their king.[88] The following year, on 25 February 1262, the same mandatories were appointed by pope Urban IV to absolve the king and queen and their sons from their oaths to observe certain statutes, ordinances and confederacies into which they had been coerced by a faction of the magnates, to the detriment of royal power;[89] and on 23 March Walton and Mansell were appointed executors of the pope's annulment of the Provisions of Oxford and of the penalties for non-compliance. In reaction to this, in June and July prominent royalists came under attack across England. Walton himself was forced to seek sanctuary at Bury St Edmunds (where on 27–8 July he issued nos. 170, 173); the Bury chronicler noted that 'the bishop of Norwich would have found no safe asylum had he not speedily fled to the liberty of St Edmund, for at this time that liberty was exceedingly precious in the eyes of the barons'.[90] An incidental reference in the Close Rolls reveals that Walton suffered confiscation of his personal estates until, by 20 August 1263, he had reluctantly taken an oath to

---

[84] *Cl. R. 1256–59* 477–8; *CPR 1258–66* 42.
[85] *Cl. R. 1259–61* 157–8.
[86] E.F. Jacob, 'A Proposal for Arbitration'; Maddicott, *Simon de Montfort* 197–8.
[87] *EEA* 29 nos. 122–3.
[88] Sayers, *Original Papal Documents*, nos. 645–6; *Foedera* I i 406; *DBM* 240–7, nos. 33–4.
[89] Sayers, *Original Papal Document* nos, 660–1; *Foedera* I i 416; *DBM* 248–51, no. 36.
[90] *Bury Chron.* 27.

observe the Provisions.[91] On 25 August, however, he was appointed as one of a commission of four to go to the ford of Montgomery on 30 September to make and receive amends for breaches of the treaty with Llewellyn ap Gruffyd.[92] It is probably in connection with this mission that he was on 15 September granted protection for one year from Michaelmas,[93] but he was back in his diocese on 12 December (193).

When in late summer 1264 the Montfortian government negotiated with the bishops, most of whom were its supporters, the grant of a tenth levied on all ecclesiastical benefices, it was obviously anticipated that Walton would be reluctant to comply by organising collection in his own diocese; a letter addressed to him outlined the urgent necessity, and the sheriff of Norfolk was instructed to visit him to emphasise the point.[94] On 3 December a writ directed to the bishop informed him that the council (nominally the king) was amazed that he had not yet collected and paid in the tenth, threatening distraint of the episcopal estates to the value of 700 marks if payment had not been made at London by 5 January 1265; but on 27 January a writ was issued to the sheriff ordering him to place the demand for the tenth in respite until mid-Lent.[95] The Montfortian government's mistrust of Walton was also signified when the writ of summons for a parliament to meet on 20 January 1265 was despatched to him thirteen days later than to all the other bishops.[96]

There is no evidence of any involvement by Walton in the momentous political events of 1265. He is not recorded to have ventured beyond his own diocese after August 1264, and then once only does he appear other than at his episcopal palace or manor-houses. On 29 September the pope ordered the legate Ottobuono to provide him with a coadjutor, on account of his age and weakness.[97] A royal grant of protection for one year, issued in December 1265, may signify his desire and intention to go on pilgrimage, but he died less than a month later, on 2 January 1266, 'in good old age', and was buried in the new Lady Chapel at Norwich cathedral.[98]

It is difficult to make a just evaluation of Walton's record as diocesan bishop. Like all his episcopal colleagues, he was subject to pressure both from the government at Westminster, which for most of his episcopate fluctuated between royal and baronial control, and from the papal *curia*. Fifteen recorded royal presentations to benefices were directed to him, including seven to livings in the gift of the vacant abbey of Bury St Edmunds (Appx 4). An instruction which was probably not unwelcome was that in Spring 1259 to desist from

---

[91] *Cl. R. 1261–64* 251.
[92] *CPR 1258–66* 227.
[93] Ibid. 277.
[94] *Cl. R 1261–64* 403–5; Powicke, *Henry III and the Lord Edward* 483 n. 2.
[95] *Cl. R. 1264–68* 82, 91.
[96] Ibid. 85, 88; cf. Powicke, *Henry III and the Lord Edward* 487; Maddicott, *Simon de Montfort* 317.
[97] *Reg. Clem. IV* no. 155; *CPL* i 430.
[98] *CPR 1258–66* 515; *Ann. mon.* iv 183; *Cotton* 141, 394–5; *First Register* 142.

harassment of the senior royal clerks John Mansell, Henry of Wingham and Walter of Merton, his former colleagues, with regard to contributions from their East Anglian livings to the Sicilian tenth, for which they had otherwise satisfied the king.[99] Less welcome may have been the order from the Montfortian government on 23 February 1265 that, in accordance with the council's policy, he should sequestrate the revenues of the church of Fakenham, held by Peter de Camberlato, an alien clerk who might be hostile to the kingdom, and place it in the hands of W. of Wortham, who held neighbouring benefices and was entirely trustworthy.[100]

Walton was not burdened, as had been Suffield, by the collection of taxation beyond his diocese. On 21 January 1262 pope Urban IV despatched to him, as to all English bishops, an urgent command to pay to Leonard, precentor of Messina, just appointed as general papal collector, a sum in proportion to his own resources to assist the *curia* in discharging debts to Roman merchants in pursuit of the business of Sicily; prelates were left free to decide what they would pay, and perhaps unsurprisingly there is no record of any payment made.[101] Walton did, however, respond to papal mandates relating to his diocese. He implemented the appropriation by pope Alexander IV of two parish churches to monastic houses, and taxed a vicarage in a third earlier appropriated by papal concession (141, 144–5). Amidst continued pressure on the richer livings of the diocese from Italian curial officials and their kin, the pope occasionally heeded native petitioners. In May 1261 pope Urban IV ordered Walton to find a benefice for John of Rudham, a poor clerk of his diocese;[102] in May 1263 the pope issued a notification of his collation to Adam of Canterbury, a papal chaplain, of the church of Bridgeham, vacant by the death in Rome of Landulph de Supino,[103] and in May 1264 instructed the bishop to make provision for master Walter of Lincoln, another poor clerk of his diocese, of some benefice in the gift of the monks of Eye, having satisfied himself as to his probity and subsequently ensuring that he maintained residence.[104]

Walton obtained from the *curia* for himself and his successors confirmation of the bishop of Norwich's right to receive the first year's revenue of benefices where no rector was in place at Easter (Appx 2. 39), and it was while he was an executor of the papal strategy to free Henry III from his domestic difficulties that the monks of Norwich obtained in January 1262 a general confirmation of their liberties and immunities.[105]

---

[99] *CPR 1258–66*, 8–9.
[100] *Cl. R. 1264–68*, 99–100.
[101] *Reg. Urban IV* no. 124; *CPL* i 382; cf. Lunt, *Financial Relations* 227–8.
[102] Sayers, *Original Papal Documents* no. 652.
[103] *Reg. Urban IV* no. 1737; *CPL* i 412.
[104] *Reg. Urban IV* no. 2005; *CPL* i 414.
[105] *Norwich Cathedral Charters* i no. 307.

Apart from significations of excommunication, of which there are twenty-two, there are extant thirty-five of Walton's *acta*. These show that, despite the political pressures on him, there is no calendar year in which he was totally absent from his diocese (Appx 5). It is noteworthy that of the fourteen *acta* recording the appropriation of parish churches, eight stipulated the taxation of a vicarage – a proportion almost the same as that for Walter Suffield. For his predecessor's hospital of St Giles he showed that care which had been requested in the founder's will, confirming its statutes, ratifying his grants and adding an indulgence for visitors and benefactors (186–8). Most remarkable, however, are the three recensions of the statutes for the recently established nunnery of Flixton (149–51), which if issued by a bishop who was not best known as a royal servant and a controversial political figure would be lauded as a splendid manifestation of episcopal concern for the pastoral care of those committed to his charge.

THE BISHOPS' OFFICERS AND *FAMILIA*

THE OFFICIAL

There are very few references in the *acta* to a named official. Master William of Horham occurs in May 1245 and December 1246 (20, 77). He had not appeared as a witness to episcopal *acta* before Suffield's succession, and first occurs in January 1245 (11), thereafter attesting on seven further occasions until February 1247 (109); twice, in April 1245, he is described as bishop's clerk (89, 108), and normally as *magister*. He was instituted on 30 March 1245 to the church of Banham, in the gift of St Mary's abbey, York, and its cell of Rumburgh (137). It is possible, from a reference in Suffield's will, that he was also *persona* of Grundisburgh (138). From October 1247 he held thirty acres of land of the bishop at Hoxne (Appx 3. 2). Horham first occurs as archdeacon of Suffolk on 11 September 1248 (13), and again twice in October 1248 (69, 118).[106] He witnessed nine episcopal *acta* as archdeacon, and last occurs on 24 October 1251.[107] The fact that William attested simply as *magister* once between his two occurrences as official (21) and once thereafter, in February 1247 (109), suggests that his office was not always noted, while the lack of reference to any other named oficial under Suffield may indicate that, like master Robert of Bilney under bishop Blundeville,[108] he continued to act as official after his appointment as archdeacon.

Under bishop Walton, master John of Alvechurch occurs as official. A native of a manor of the bishop of Worcester, who held land at Bromsgrove and Weston (Wo.), he was first noted as official of bishop Walter de Cantilupe of

---

[106] This predates the first reference given in *Fasti* ii 68.
[107] *Fasti* ii 68.
[108] *EEA* 21 p. xlv.

Worcester in 1242, when he was described as learned in the law.[109] In May 1245 a faculty was issued by the pope to the bishop to grant a dispensation to him to hold an additional benefice with cure.[110] In 1254 he was appointed to collect the king's dues from Churchdown and Oddington.[111] It was possibly through such occasional royal service that he had come to the attention of Simon Walton, by whom he was appointed official at Norwich, attesting as such on one occasion, which can be dated only 10 March 1258 × 8 December 1261 (197), but also possibly another *actum* with a corrupt witness list on 30 November 1257 (181). Alvechurch first occurs as archdeacon of Suffolk on 8 December 1261 (186); he only attests on one other occasion, 5 January 1264 (146), but in view of the paucity of witness lists to Walton's *acta*, this can hardly be used as an index of his attendance on the bishop. In August 1262 he was granted an indult by pope Urban IV: in addition to the churches of Hanbury (Wo.) and Wem (Sa.), which he had by papal sanction, and the archdeaconry, which he had acquired without dispensation, he might receive the church of East Harling (Nf.), which he currently held *in commendam*.[112] He was granted royal protection for travel overseas in September 1265[113] and last occurs on 3 September 1267.[114]

At some date, perhaps after Alvechurch's appointment to the archdeaconry, he was succeeded as official by Adam Walton, almost certainly a kinsman of the bishop, who had attested as *magister* on eight occasions, from November 1257 (181) to 25 October 1264 (187), and thence once only as official in May 1265 (184).

In Norwich diocese, apparently from the time of bishop William Raleigh, there was a distinction between the bishop's official and the official of the consistory, who presided in that court.[115] In 1241 and 1243 the latter office was exercised by master Hervey of Fakenham.[116] At the beginning of Suffield's episcopate Fakenham attests on eight occasions (six certainly and twice possibly in 1245), twice described as bishop's clerk (88–9), otherwise as *magister*; thereafter there is no recorded attestation, but he is a beneficiary of the bishop's will (138). He does, however, reappear as official of the consistory in the early years of Walton's episcopate, 1258 × 61 (197). It is possible that the system of dual officials lapsed in the first year of Suffield's episcopate, but certainly it was in place again within a few years, as the official and the official of the consistory were both to be involved in the appointment *sede vacante* of a new master of St Giles's hospital (103, 107).[117] Fakenham may not occur in the witness lists to

---

[109] *EEA* 13 p. xxxviii.
[110] *Reg. Inn. IV* no. 1273; *CPL* i 216.
[111] *Cl. R. 1254–56* 108.
[112] *Reg. Urban IV* no. 115; *CPL* i 382.
[113] *CPR 1258–66* 453.
[114] *CPR 1266–72* 102.
[115] *EEA* 21 p. xlvi.
[116] *EEA* 21 Appx 2. 50A; cf. ibid. pp. xl, lx.
[117] See D. M. Smith, 'The "Officialis" of the Bishop in the Twelfth and Thirteenth Centuries' 219.

Suffield's *acta* after 1245 (or at latest 1248) because he was outside the household, presiding regularly in the consistory court at Norwich. If so, he was making judgements there for a period of almost twenty years.

THE ARCHDEACONS

At Norwich, John of Ferentino, papal and royal servant,[118] who occurs last in January 1238, was succeeded eventually by master William Suffield, the bishop's brother. As *magister*, he attested seven *acta* between April 1245 (88, 108) and February 1246 (21–2, 91).

In October 1248 he was rector of Repps (118),[119] which living, with its annexed chapel of Bastwick, was subsequently granted to St Giles, Norwich; the hospital cartulary contains an undated note stating that the living was the personal gift of William, as *patronus et persona*, made in return for burial and perpetual commemoration there.[120] He was also involved in the acquisition for the hospital of St Mary's, South Walsham, which he confirmed on his brother's death after collusive litigation in the *curia regis*.[121] He first occurs as archdeacon of Norwich on 15 August 1248 (Appx 2. 15), and thereafter occurs very infrequently, attesting his brother's *acta* only twice (83; Appx 2. 25), and almost certainly one of his successor, on 30 November 1257 (181). He was probably dead by 8 December 1261, when bishop Walton appropriated to St Giles the church of Repps with Bastwick, with reservation of a vicar's portion for William of Rollesby for his lifetime (186).

Master Walter de Salerne, *alias* of London, first occurs on 7 January 1238 when, at the request of Christ Church Canterbury, he received a dispensation to hold an additional benefice with cure,[122] and was possibly in 1239 official of the bishop of Rochester.[123] He finally won his suit at the papal *curia* against Simon the Norman for the archdeaconry of Norfolk on 18 June 1244.[124] On 4 January 1245 he again received a dispensation to hold an additional benefice with cure.[125] He does not attest any of bishop Suffield's *acta*, nor was he a beneficiary of his will. His one occurrence, in the context of diocesan affairs, is his consent in June 1250 to the limitation of archidiaconal procurations levied on the appropriated churches of Wymondham priory and the exemption, in the case of default, of the monks themselves from sequestration of their revenues and of the parish churches from interdict (Appx 2. 20–1).[126] In 1252 he became prebendary of

[118] *EEA* 21 pp. xlvii–xlviii; *Fasti* ii 64.
[119] *CRR 1237–42* no. 356.
[120] Norfolk R.O., NCR 24/48 fos. 52v–53r.
[121] TNA, CP25/1/159/100/1658.
[122] *Reg. Greg. IX* no. 4406; *CPL* i 175.
[123] *Fasti* ii 66.
[124] *Reg. Inn. IV* no. 746; *CPL* i 210.
[125] *Reg. Inn. IV* no. 860; *CPL* i 211.
[126] This despite a verdict in his favour promulgated at the papal *curia* in June 1248 (*Reg. Inn. IV* nos. 4645–6; *CPL* i 258).

Rugmere in St Paul's following the death of master Richard of Wendover, the doctor, himself an intimate of bishop Suffield.[127] He was elected dean of St Paul's in April 1254, and six months later was dispensed to hold his archdeaconry in plurality, and on resignation thereof to hold a benefice of a similar value with the deanery.[128] He was provided by the pope to the archbishopric of Tuam on 29 May 1257, but after consecration at the *curia* he died in London in April 1258 before he could occupy his see.[129]

During the vacancy of the see following Walter Suffield's death, the crown conferred the archdeaconry of Norfolk on master Nicholas of Plympton. The son of Richard of Hagginton (De.),[130] he first occurs in royal service as king's proctor at the papal *curia* in May 1250.[131] In August 1250, described as papal subdeacon and clerk of Robert Passelewe, archdeacon of Lewes, he was granted an indult to hold, in addition to a canonry of the royal free chapel of Steyning (Sx), one other benefice with cure.[132] In January 1253 he was one of the proctors representing the king at the council of the province of Canterbury meeting at London, with power to appeal against its decisions if necessary.[133] In early June 1253 he was appointed as one of the royal proctors at the *curia* to seek graces and indulgences for the Holy Land subsidy, and to conduct other business.[134] In 1251, descibed as rector of Kingham (Ox.), he had received the first of many gifts from the king, six oaks and a fine robe; now, after his departure for the papal court in early July 1253, Henry III ordered that a benefice valued at eighty marks should be found for him.[135] On 24 September 1253, in an indult to receive an additional benefice with cure, he was described as papal clerk and nuncio to the king of England.[136] In February 1255 the king ordered that he should receive fifty marks a year at the Exchequer until the crown might make further provision for him, and by May 1256 he held land in chief at Gravesend.[137] In May 1255, described as papal subdeacon and chaplain and king's clerk, he received further indults to hold benefices with cure in plurality.[138]

In 1256–7 master Nicholas was heavily involved in the collection of the Holy land subsidy (now diverted to the business of Sicily). Master Rostand, the chief collector, on 8 June 1256 appointed him, together with Bernard of Siena and William of Lichfield, as his deputy while he was at the *curia* as the king's

[127] *Fasti* i 76.
[128] *Reg. Inn. IV* nos. 8115–6; *CPL* i 396.
[129] *Fasti* i 7; *HBC* 375.
[130] *CPR 1247–58* 168. That Hagginton is in Devon confirms that Nicholas's toponymic was Plympton rather than Plumpton, (as in Lunt, *Financial Relations*, index).
[131] *CPR 1247–58* 65.
[132] *Reg. Inn. IV* no. 4812; *CPL* i 261.
[133] *CPR 1247–58* 171.
[134] Ibid. 194–5, 197–8.
[135] *Cl. R. 1247–51* 478; *Cl. R. 1251–53*, 11; *CPR 1247–58* 234.
[136] *Reg. Inn. IV* no. 7021; *CPL* i 291.
[137] *CPR 1247–58* 399, 476.
[138] *Reg. Alex. IV* nos. 439, 506; *CPL* i 315, 317.

representative; they had custody of the money of the Cross, deposited at Westminster abbey.[139] They were involved in the collection of money pledged by English monasteries in bonds extorted by the bishop of Hereford, and on 18 February 1257 accounted for nearly 4000 marks received from the tenth and other contributions to the crusade.[140] In early summer 1257, as Henry III grew wary of his Sicilian commitments, Plympton was again a member of an embassy to the *curia*.[141] It was at this time, on 9 July, that he was appointed by the king, *sede vacante*, to the archdeaconry of Norfolk.[142] Not surprisingly, in view of his continued royal service, he does not attest any episcopal *acta*, although he would certainly have been well known to bishop Walton. In December 1257 he was granted an indult to hold a further benefice with cure, and a mandate was issued to three conservators to prevent any disturbance of his possession of any of his benefices; he was by this time a canon of Exeter cathedral.[143]

Plympton largely disappears from view for the next four years, but in July 1262 he accompanied the king to France as a negotiator of the proposed process of arbitration of English domestic disputes by Queen Margaret.[144] On 13 March 1264, as the king from his base at Oxford prepared for confrontation, Plympton was appointed, along with the bishop of Lichfield, as king's proctor to seek out Simon de Montfort and his adherents and negotiate with them, preliminary to the meeting which they arranged at Brackley.[145] He last occurs in a Norwich charter dated 20 October 1264, and was probably dead by August 1267, when his successor as archdeacon of Norfolk first occurs.[146]

In the archdeaconry of Suffolk, between the tenure of William of Horham and John of Alvechurch, treated above as officials, came the occupancy of master William of Dunton, who does not appear previously as a witness from the household and who occurs only twice, witnessing a papal judge-delegate judgement in December 1257,[147] and one episcopal *actum* (197). He is otherwise totally obscure. At Sudbury, master William of Clare, who had acted as bishop Raleigh's official and had been advanced to the archdeaconry by December 1242,[148] continued as archdeacon throughout Suffield's episcopate, and was still alive, although not called archdeacon, in August 1258.[149] His official was master Edmund of Walpole (Appx 2. 4). His first known successor, master Thomas of Ingoldisthorpe, does not occur until July 1266, after the death of bishop

---

[139] *CPR 1247–58* 498–500, 521.
[140] Ibid. 517, 587.
[141] Lunt, *Financial Relations* 278, n. 8.
[142] *Fasti* ii 66.
[143] *Reg. Alex. IV* nos. 2364–5; *CPL* i 353.
[144] *CPR 1258–66* 219–20.
[145] *CPR 1258–66* 307–8.
[146] *Fasti* ii 66–7.
[147] *Eye Cartulary* i no. 98.
[148] *EEA* 21 p. xlvi.
[149] *Fasti* ii 70.

Walton.[150]

THE *FAMILIA*

A valuable insight into the composition of bishop Suffield's *familia* is provided
by his last testament (138). As his executors he chose two kinsmen, his nephew
Walter,[151] and master Hamo of Calthorpe, whom he had appointed as the first
master of St Giles's hospital,[152] and also a layman, Geoffrey of Loddon, who in
1242 was seneschal of the cathedral priory.[153] Alongside these he nominated four
of his own clerks, obviously those most trusted amongst his *familiares* still alive.
From William of Pakenham, the bishop believed, 'nothing but death could
separate him'. He was bequeathed a silver cup and a psalter, and was exhorted to
benefit Suffield's soul. He attested eleven *acta* between February 1246 (21, 91)
and August 1252 (43), in five of which he was described as clerk, and on four
recorded occasions he represented the bishop in litigation in the *curia regis*
(Appx 3. 5–8), where he also acted as proctor for Roger, the bishop's brother.[154]
In March 1256 he received an annual pension of 2s from the church of St Peter,
South Lynn, the rector of which was master John of Ingoldisthorpe on the death
or resignation of either party, the whole church should pass to the other (80). By
July 1268 the vicarage had been consolidated with the *personatus*, and
Pakenham was rector; he was sufficiently affluent that, when the church was in
ruins because of flooding, he could in 1271 afford to provide a new site and
rebuild it, guaranteeing to the prior and convent of Lewes the *ius patronatus*.[155]
A William of Pakenham, junior, was a minor beneficiary of Suffield's will, and a
John of Pakenham, unusually for a man who was not *persona*, obtained from
Castle Acre priory the farm of the demesne tithe of Fouldon (Appx 2. 7).
William himself does not occur as a witness in *acta* of bishops Walton or
Scarning.
       William of Whitwell, 'faithful and dear' to the bishop, was an executor and
was bequeathed an image of the Blessed Virgin Mary, a painted tablet, two
books of sermons, the bishop's 'great belt' and the cup from which he drank with
its paten (138). He attests on fourteen occasions from February 1247 (109) to
June 1254 (87), four times described as clerk and once, probably in error, as
magister (Appx 2. 8). There is no record of any benefice held by him. Giles of
Whitwell, chaplain, almost certainly a kinsman, witnessed three *acta* between
April 1251 and June 1254 (43, 83, 87), is almost certainly that Giles the chaplain
who also received a generous bequest, including a psalter.

---

[150] Ibid.
[151] *Reg. Alex. IV* no. 2363; *CPL* i 353. He was in Dec. 1257 rector of Great Cressingham, Suffield and
Snoring.
[152] Rawcliffe, *Medicine for the Soul* 251.
[153] *Norwich Cathedral Charters* i no. 203.
[154] TNA, CP25/1/157/71/936.
[155] TNA, E40/14923; *Lewes Cartulary: Norfolk Portion* nos. 173–4.

Another executor, master Hugh of Corbridge, was bequeathed a bible and a cup with a stand. He attests four times, twice in 1246 described as clerk (9, 77), and then not until June 1254, when he was *magister* (87). It is very probable that he had been studying at university in the interim, and it is quite possible that he was the same master Hugh who later, in 1269, supported the Oxford Dominicans in the controversy with the Franciscans on the observance of evangelical poverty.[156] The final executor, William of Witchingham, clerk, received a cup and stand and £5; he attested on only three occasions, between 1248–54 (43, 69, 87).

Among others who both attest *acta* and are beneficiaries of Suffield's will, the most notable is master Robert de Insula, archdeacon of Colchester, who received a ring.[157] He was, in fact, the most frequent of all witnesses, attesting on twenty-one occasions between August 1248 (37) and June 1254 (87). It seems that for six years he was often in attendance on a bishop who was not his own diocesan, and there is no obvious explanation for this. Master Adam of Bromholm was dead by the time bishop Walter made his will, in which it is noted that he had purchased from Adam's executors his theology books. He attested eleven times between January 1245 (11) and April 1246 (9), and once thereafter in October 1248 (94). Shortly before 22 March 1245 he was instituted to the church of St Gregory, Sudbury (110), and by August 1246 he was rector of Heveningham (Appx 2. 6). He was probably dead by 25 June 1252, when a new rector was instituted to Sudbury (111).

William, clerk of the bishop's chapel, received in his will £2 and a book of canticles which had belonged to John Bigod, late rector of Settington (Nb.), for whom Suffield had written a testimonial to the archbishop of York (Appx 2. 12). The clerk of the chapel may well have been William of Ludham, clerk, who attested eight *acta* between April 1246 (9) and August 1252 (43); it is unlikely to have been William of Acle, whose three datable attestations are all in October 1248 (69, 94, 118). The only man described as bishop's chaplain is John of Holkham (9), elsewhere called clerk (22), who attested eleven *acta* between February 1246 (91) and April 1251 (83). Also described simply as chaplain was Thomas of Tew (Ox.), who attested on seven occasions between December 1246 (77) and April 1251 (83), and is probably a kinsman of that master Robert of Tew who was a frequent witness of bishop John de Gray's *acta*;[158] he is probably the same man as Thomas the chaplain, who attested three times in 1247 × 48 (12–13, 94), and is possibly the Thomas, rector of Homersfield, who occurs once only, in December 1249, in an *actum* not relating to his own locality (26); but equally the rector of Homersfield might be Thomas of Walcott, once described as bishop's clerk (88), often as clerk, who attests fifteen times between February 1246 (110) and August 1252 (43), and who was instituted to Castle Acre priory's

---

[156] *BRUO* 484.
[157] For him see *Fasti* i 19–20.
[158] *EEA* 6 p. xlvi.

church of Fulmodestone in February 1251 (27); or even, though less likely, Thomas of Eccles, bishop's clerk, two attested twice in April 1245 (89, 108), or Thomas le Bigod, bishop's clerk, probably kinsman of the earl of Norfolk, who attested on five occasions in 1245 (11, 88–9, 108, 136). Another scion of a noble family and bishop's clerk was Richard de Riboeuf, who also witnesses in 1245 (11, 20, 88–9, 108). In that same year occur all four attestations of Henry of Bottisham, bishop's clerk (11, 20, 88–9), who is probably the same man as Henry, *persona* of Beeston, who occurs once in the same year (108). Adam of Worstead, described simply as *dominus*, occurs six times in the early years of Suffield's episcopate, before October 1248 (12–13, 20, 91, 118, 136).

Among these obscure witnesses there occurs one more prominent figure, master Lawrence of Somercotes, who attests on three occasions between May 1245 and February 1247 (9, 20, 109). He was a papal subdeacon by 1243 and was provided by Innocent IV to a prebend of Chichester.[159] He was presumably a kinsman of Robert of Somercotes, *auditor litterarum contradictarum* in 1238 and the following year created cardinal deacon of St Eustace.[160] Subsequently, Lawrence acted as official of bishop Wich of Chichester. In 1254, after St Richard's death. he was appointed as one of the commissioners entrusted with the crusading tenth in Ireland (84, 125). He wrote a treatise on episcopal elections,[161] completed in July 1254, which work has led to the plausible suggestion that his mind lay behind the complex arrangements for the election of a master of St Giles's hospital (103, 107), which later had to be simplified.[162]

Others named in Suffield's will, who were probably members of his *familia* in the later years of his episcopate (for which there are few witness lists) are master Nigel, Matthew the chaplain and William of Foston, clerk. John the clerk was *scriptor* of the bishop's clerk. Daniel of Beccles, who was charged with the distribution of various alms, Philip the bishop's sequestrator, and Geoffrey and Hugh de Camera may have been clerks or laymen (138).

Suffield's will, with its bequests to so many of his servants, provides a snapshot of the substratum of the episcopal household – for the provision of food and drink, a butler, cook, saucer, a brewer and his boys and two ewerers, and also a fisherman and a skinner; a watchman and two messengers, a groom, a smith and a farrier, four carters and the keeper of the packhorse for the bishop's bed; a laundress; two named pages, as well as the boys of the household. Suffield also remembered his servants (or sergeants) at London, Bacton and Wicks Bishop, his seneschal at Lynn and the warreners of all the episcopal manors. His intimacy with his domestics is perhaps revealed both by the provision for commemoration of his deceased servants, and by his use in this formal document of nicknames, such as 'sleepy Robert' and 'bare Scot' (138).

---

[159] *EEA* 22 p.lvi and refs. there given.
[160] Sayers, 'Canterbury Proctors' 325 n. 7.
[161] *Tractatus seu summa de electionibus episcoporum*, ed. A. von Wretscke (1907).
[162] Rawcliffe, *Medicine for the Soul* 28.

There are extant only eleven witness lists to the *acta* of bishop Simon Walton. Of these ten are attested by master Adam of Walton, who became official towards the end of the episcopate. Master Stephen of Strumpshaw, once described as bishop's seneschal (184), attests on seven occasions, as does master John of Worcester, once described as chancellor (184). A certain John was clerk of the bishop's chapel. Robert, probably of Wolvercote,[163] occurs as witness on six occasions, and was granted by the bishop the wardship of an heir (Appx 2. 37). Only three other witnesses occur more than once – John of Norwich (three times), master John of Wixoe (twice), and John Thebauld, a layman (five times).

CONTENTS OF THE *ACTA*

CONFIRMATIONS

Among other confirmations there is one long and detailed *pancarte* for Castle Acre priory (184). Other, less detailed general confirmations were issued listing various categories of posessions of the cathedral priory, its cellarer, and of St Paul's hospital (88–9, 97, 100, 108). Confirmations of specific possessions were issued in favour of Blythburgh priory (7), Castle Acre (26), the Dominicans of Lynn (Appx 2. 35), Norwich cathedral priory (95) and Sibton abbey (124); and also for the Norman houses of Bec (3, confirming the verdict of papal judges-delegate), the two abbeys of Caen (14, 142) and Savigny (148) – these are perhaps an indication of the anxiety of these houses, now 'alien', about their English possessions. A group of confirmations were cast in the form of an *inspeximus* of a charter of the bishop's predecessors, sometimes recited (25, 101, 108, 188), otherwise simply mentioned (13, 20, 26, 124); also inspected and recited were a charter of king Henry II (4), an archiepiscopal grant for Pontigny (114), an indult of pope Alexander IV (141), a charter of a bishop of Ely relating to a church in Norwich diocese (116), and three charters of laymen, one being the foundation charter of a chantry established by bishop Suffield's kinsman and one relating to the lands of the church of Repps, destined to swell the endowment of that bishop's foundation of St Giles (43, 118, 153).

GRANTS

There are a few charters recording grants on the episcopal demesne, or the confirmation of lands purchased, for various servants of the bishops (73, 144A, 190, 194A). Bishop Suffield confirmed a third part of the tithe of assarts at Thorpe to St Paul's hospital, and by a further grant extended this to clearances yet to be made (108–9). The most significant grant, however, was that by Simon

---

[163] For the extraordinary number of variations of his toponymic, some of which bear little relationship to each other, see index *s. n.*; East Anglian scribes seem to have been unacquainted with this place.

Walton to the burgesses of Bishop's Lynn of the right of electing a mayor (182), although this was far from the end of the intermittent but long-running series of disputes between the bishop and the ruling elite of the town.[164]

NEW FOUNDATIONS

The Cistercian female abbey of Marham, was founded by Isabelle, widow of Hugh d'Albini, earl of Arundel, and was consecrated on 24 February 1249 or 1250 by Richard Wich, bishop of Chichester. In Sept. 1251 Suffield granted the nuns right of burial in their own cemetery, and the freedom to bury lay persons who were not parishioners of the two churches of Marham, appropriated to Westacre priory (85–6). Three years later the diocesan sanctioned the transfer to the nuns of the demesne tithes of the manor (87).

Flixton priory, for Augustinian canonesses, was founded in 1258 by Margery, widow of Bartholomew of Creake; the following year bishop Walton dedicated a cemetery, although the church was not yet built, and issued certain statutes supplementary to the Rule of St Augustine (149); these were revised in December 1261, when a chantry was established for the soul of the founder (150); further additions followed in March 1263 (151), including the provision that the house should be visited annually by the bishop's senior confessor within the Norwich chapter. In 1265 Walton appropriated Dunston church to the priory (152). The bishop was showing especial concern for this nunnery years before the founder resigned the patronage of the house to bishop Middleton and his successors.

St Giles's hospital was the great project of Suffield's episcopate; traditionally founded in 1249.[165] There are extant two sets of statutes; it is impossible to date these firmly, but the original series (103) was probably issued before 24 July 1251, when pope Innocent IV confirmed the foundation; the second version (107) was inspected and confirmed by pope Alexander IV a few months after the founder's death, and subsequently by bishop Walton (188). The complement of the hospital was to be a master, four (active) priests, with a deacon and subdeacon, and in addition three or four (nursing) sisters, all following the rule of St Augustine, although not wearing the habit of that order. The house was to provide permanent refuge for all poor infirm priests of the diocese who were broken by age or bedridden.There were to be at least thirty beds for the use of the infirm poor, without any charge, until they should recover. Seven poor scholars were to have a daily meal on schooldays, and thirteen poor men were to be fed on a daily basis, and thirteen extra whenever the bishop visited; there was to be a distribution of bread every S aturday between 25 March and 15 August to as many poor who presented themselves, and a box from which the passing poor might receive alms. The statutes contain detailed regulations for

---

[164] *King's Lynn* 34–7.
[165] For much fuller discussion, see Rawcliffe, *Medicine for the Soul*, esp. ch. 1 and Appx. 1.

liturgy and conduct, and very convoluted rules for the election of a new master, which were subsequently simplified by bishop Scarning. Various other *acta* detail specific grants to the new hospital . On 1 Oct. 1251 the founder confirmed the site of the house, other possessions in Norwich and its appropriated churches (105); four months earlier he had recorded the appropriation of Cringleford church (104), and two years later that of Seething, in an *actum* which also made provision for the liturgical and charitable commemoration of his obit in the cathedral (106) . In 1261 bishop Walton appropriated the church of Repps with its chapel of Bastwick, granted by William Suffield, the archdeacon, just after his brother's death (186). At Repps no vicarage was established, and it was specified that the hospital might appoint chaplains to serve the cure, and the same was in fact the case at Cringleford. The vicarage originally stipulated at Seething was jettisoned in 1264 (187).

CHAPELS

A new category of *acta*, foreshadowed only once in 1243,[166] comprises licences for the establishment of chapels, all issued by Walter Suffield rather than his successor. Permission was granted for chapels or chantries within religious houses (6A, 85–6, 150) and chapels in the manor houses of monastic estates (10–A, 113, 115) and in the residences of prominent lay persons (2, 40, 42, 112, 121). In the case of his kinsman Roger of Hales, bishop Suffield inspected the foundation charter (43). In all other cases he was most careful to safeguard the rights and revenues of the parish church, and the clauses designed to guarantee these became almost common form.

APPROPRIATION

Six churches were appropriated to the new hospital of St Giles (103–7, 186–7); five churches and a mediety to the cathedral priory (94, 98, 100, 184); but in general it is a case of individual additions to the resources of houses which had already received many of their churches *in proprios usus*. On rare ocasions appropriation might be immediate, effected on the resignation or death of the current incumbent; for example, when Yaxley church was appropriated to Eye in 1264 (146–7), and in the same year Besthorpe was granted in its entirety to Wymondham, an appropriation which for some reason was opposed by the abbot of St Albans (196–7). At the other extreme, some appropriations were not put into effect for decades. For example, Kempstone had originally been granted to to Castle Acre *in proprios usus* by John of Oxford, 1188 × 98,[167] but in 1227 bp Blundeville had instituted a new *persona;*[168] only in 1246, half a century after the

---

[166] *EEA* 21 no. 137A.
[167] *EEA* 6 nos. 199–200.
[168] *EEA* 21 no. 41.

original appropriation, was it made effective and a vicarage ordained (21–2). At Methwold, too, John of Oxford and John de Gray had granted the church to Castle Acre after the death or resignation of master Thomas,[169] and although bishop Blundeville renewed this appropriation in 1235,[170] John of Vercelli was now incumbent rector, and he was still alive in 1246; even Suffield's reiteration of the appropriation in 1249 (26) does not appear to have taken immediate effect. The norm, however, was that appropriation should be put into effect on the death or resignation of the present rector. The process was normally obviously the result of negotiation between religious houses and the diocesan, although on two occasions, at Pakenham for the monks of Bury and at Gately for the canons of Creake, bishop Walton simply put into effect grants *in proprios usus* by the pope (141, 144). In some cases a transitional arrangement was made; at Barmer the church was appropriated to Coxford on the resignation in 1252 of William of Syderstone, the rector, but he was to retain until his death or resignation the free lands of the church, in return for a very small farm rendered to the canons (36). Creake abbey was to receive 8 marks a year from the incumbent of St Martin's, Quarles, now from 1248 styled vicar, but after his departure the canons were to take the full income of the church apart from a vicarage to be taxed by the bishop (37), and the same house was awarded 20s a year by bp Walton, to be paid by the current rector of Gately, pending full appropriation on his departure (144). Somewhat strangely, a rector was to remain *persona* at Cavenham even after the church was appropriated to Stoke by Clare in 1254 (129).

Increasingly in this period some reason is given for appropriation – probably put into the bishop's mind by the beneficiaries. Suffield reiterated the appropriation of Neatishead to St Benet's in consideration of the dangers and misfortunes by which the monks were afflicted, and the great loss that they had sustained in relation to that church (72). Mendlesham church was appropriated to Chichester cathedral in 1254 specifically to finance the chantry and annual obit of Suffield's friend bishop Richard Wich (33). Hemblington church was appropriated to the cathedral priory in 1248 because of the daily increase of religious observance by the monks (94), and the appropriation of Toftrees to Lewes in 1246 was justified by a paean of praise for the virtues of the Cluniac order (77). The monks of Eye were instituted in 1247 to the rectory of Playford so that its revenues might support the repair and maintenance of their conventual church (41). Hospitality and the alleviation of poverty were often cited: Great Hautbois church was appropriated to the canons of Coxford in 1245 for the maintenance of hospitality (35), all the fruits of Horning church, except for five marks given to the infirmarer, were from 1248 to be distributed to the poor at St Benet's abbey gate (69, 181), and Sibton abbey in 1263 received full possession of St Peter's church, Cransford, for the maintenance of guests and the poor, formerly received cheerfully by the monks at a time when hospitality was

---

[169] *EEA* 6 nos. 199–200.
[170] *EEA* 21 no. 48.

threatened by the sterility of the land (193). When Seething church was appropriated to St Giles's hospital, ten marks was to be diverted from its revenues to the cathedral almoner (106). Blickling, a church recently burdened by pensions to papal provisors, was in 1265 appropriated to the monks of Norwich for the use of the cellarer, for the improvement of the food for guests (184). When in 1251 Suffield confirmed the appropriation of Little Witchingham to Longueville priory, he insisted that the monks' proctor should each Ash Wednesday distribute two seams of peas to the poor of the parish (83).

There are two notable cases when grants *in proprios usus* by the bishops were totally ineffective. In 1246 bishop Suffield readjusted the respective portions of the monks of Bury and the vicar of Woolpit, (10), appropriated on papal authority by John de Gray.[171] After prolonged disputes between monks and vicar, the incumbent in the early fourteenth century called himself, and was locally considered to be, the rector. Thomas Blundeville had appropriated Scottow church to St Benet's in March 1232 and twenty months later had ordered that the monks should be inducted into corporal possession,[172] but in 1249, in compensation for its loss by judgement of the royal court, Suffield appropriated to them the church of Woodbastwick (70).

On three occasions Suffield created a perpetual benefice for religious within churches of which they held the advowson. In 1245 eight marks were detached from Banham church, two for Rumburgh priory and six for its mother house of St Mary's York (136–7); the ladies of Nuneaton were granted a perpetual benefice of ten marks in the church of St Gregory's Sudbury, on account of their poverty and especially the deficiency of their vestments (110–11). In 1245 Suffield augmented Stoke by Clare's pension of 10s from Rede church, transforming it into a benefice of 50s, until vacated by the present rector, when it should be appropriated; this was done in consideration of the monks' merciful works in the provision of hospitality and aid for the poor (127).

VICARAGES

In a few cases, as a sign of particular favour, the bishop allowed a parish to be served by chaplains appointed and removable by the corporate rector. This was the case with all the churches appropriated to bishop Suffield's hospital of St Giles, with the exception of Seething, and even here the vicarage was suppressed in 1264 (187). The canons of West Dereham were permitted by Suffield to fulfil the parochial functions of the church in which they were founded by their own chaplains, so that no occasion might be given for the reduction of their renowned hospitality (134). Bishop Walton allowed the poor nuns of Flixton to serve Dunston church by their own chaplains (152), and made the same concession to

---

[171] *EEA* 6 no. 335.
[172] *EEA* 21 nos. 66–7.

the monks of Rumburgh at St Michael's, South Elmham (191). The monks of the cathedral priory were not required to make provision for vicarages by Suffield at Hemblington (94) or by Walton at Blickling (184).

Such concessions were, however, rare, and Suffield at the beginning of his episcopate laid down a programme when he reported to Innocent IV that there were churches in his diocese held by religious or others where either no vicarage had been taxed or one had been taxed in an inappropriate manner, asking for papal authorisation to correct this situation (Appx 2. 1). He believed that the diocesan should take personal responsibility in this sphere: when in January 1248 he discovered that the vicarage at Walden abbey's church of Chippenham had been taxed by the official rather than the bishop, he proceeded, almost as a matter of principle, to make a new taxation (132). At Crimplesham, appropriated to Stoke by Clare, he noted disapprovingly that although there were various portions carved out of the church's income, no vicarage had been ordained there (128). Worstead church had been appropriated to the cathedral priory by Thomas Blundeville in 1227, with provision for a vicarage, and he had inducted the monks into possession in 1235;[173] now in 1246, when he instituted a vicar, Suffield made a very detailed taxation of a vicarage (98–9).

The bishops sought to establish a reasonable balance between the interests of the appropriating body and the vicar. To the vicar of St James, Castle Acre, who had hitherto received a knight's corrody and 10s *p.a.*, Suffield in 1246 allocated a sum which would give him some independence from the monks (23), while at Wymondham parish church, at the institution of a new vicar in 1251, he augmented the previous endowment of the vicarage by the grant of a monk's corrody, so that he might better keep residence (135). His adjustment of the vicar's income at Upton, however, was apparently in favour of the canons of Butley (13), and when making provision for the maintenance of vicars in the churches of Hempstead and All Saints, Wicklewood, granted to the cathedral priory by his predecessors, Suffield stipulated that the vicarages should not be burdensome to the monks (95).

Following the practice of his thirteenth-century predecessors, in a few cases Suffield reserved to the diocesan the selection of incumbents. The bishop was to collate to the vicarage of Mendlesham, appropriated to the dean and chapter of Chichester (33), while the monks of Longueville were obliged to present to the bishop his own nominee for the vicarage of Little Witchingham (83). Episcopal nomination of the rector of St Gregory's Sudbury was also a condition of the ladies of Nuneaton receiving a benefice within that church (110–11). More unusually, in the resolution of a dispute between them, while Robert de Scales ceded the advowson of South Raynham to the nuns of Blackborough, he and his heirs were to retain presentation to the vicarage (6).

---

[173] *EEA* 21 nos. 86–93.

INSTITUTIONS

Very few institutions are extant, and where these are recorded it is normally because they are to the vicarage of a church which had only recently been appropriated (22, 99, 147, 196), or when a benefice had been created within a church for the religious who were patrons (137) or the vicarage had been augmented (135). The letters of institution to Herringby church (30), as other letters of institution to Castle Acre churches from the late twelfth century, suggests that the issue of such written testimony to new incumbents had now become habitual, as was certainly the case in Lincoln diocese.[174]

By far the most interesting *acta* relating to appointment to livings reflect the growing practice of papal intervention, which placed great pressure on the diocesan as well as on religious houses. In 1249 the newly instituted rector of a mediety of Walpole was obliged to pay a pension to Henry de Monticello, whom bishop Suffield had intended to institute there after receiving a papal mandate to make provision for him; the rector, moreover, had also to make a large contribution to the pension due from the monks of Lewes, patrons of the living, to a papal chaplain who had resigned another of the priory's livings (78–9). In 1252 the new incumbent of Potter Heigham, presented by St Benet's, was to pay a pension to the Roman clerk to whom the church had been collated by the papal nuncio in England (71). In 1252, too, bishop Suffield attempted to extricate himself from the burden placed on the episcopal church of Blickling to pay a large annual pension to a papal nominee by instituting him to Castle Acre's church of Fulmodestone, to which the monks had already presented a clerk; the complicated arrangements eventually agreed to make some financial provision for both these men whilst instituting to the living itself an episcopal clerk (27–8) provide a splendid example of the forces which compelled even a very conscientious diocesan bishop to treat benefices as financial commodities – as did indeed the canon law of the church.

SETTLEMENT OF DISPUTES

There are twelve extant notifications by the bishop of his resolution of disputes between two parties relating to parishes, revenues or rights within his diocese. In addition, there are six records of such compositions issued by one or both of the parties and sealed with the bishop's seal. In one case, agreement had been reached between the monks of Lewes and the rector of Sculthorpe over contested tithes, and the composition between them was subsequently submitted to Suffield for approval and, if necessary, amendment; the bishop did, indeed, modify the agreement (75). More often, however, it appears that the bishop attempted to act as judicial arbiter in long running disputes where reconciliation had appeared

---

[174] D. M. Smith, *Guide to the Bishops' Registers of England and Wales* (Royal Historical Society, 1991) 105–8.

impossible and the parties eventually submitted to his judgement – for example, *tandem nobis mediantibus inter eos sub forma subscripta pax exstitit* (5), *tandem post altercationes...nobis mediantibus...lis inter eos mota amicabiliter quievit* (11), *nos qui universorum pacem et quietam desideramus...eos ad pacem sub hac forma reduximus et concordiam* (123).

Half of the recorded adjudications, a total of nine, related to disputed tithes; seven of these cases were disputes betwen a religious house and a local incumbent in whose parish the monastery claimed demesne tithes. Most usually the religious leased the tithes to the *persona* and his successors for a fixed annual farm (24, 75, Appx 2. 15, 25). At Marsham the bishop judged that, although two-thirds of the tithe of the episcopal demesne pertained to the cathedral prory, the current vicar, because of his particular merits, might hold them for his lifetime for 5s *p.a.*(93). The canons of Butley were to pay the rector of Stoke Ash 30s *p.a.* for the demesne tithe of sir Robert of Kenton (11), and the monks of Sibton granted the rector of Heveningham (an episcopal clerk) and his successors nine acres and a toft in compensation for tithes there (Appx 2. 6). Castle Acre also leased two-thirds of the demesne tithes of Houghton-on-the-Hill to the canons of Coxford (Appx 2. 8) and two-thirds of the Freville demesne tithes at Fouldon to John of Pakenham, probably a kinsman of an episcopal *familiaris* (Appx 2. 7). Usually payment of the annual farm was to be made in two instalments at the Easter and Michaelmas synods, and should the farmer of the tithes default at any term (sometimes with a few days grace) the penalty varied from immediate forfeiture of the tithes, with an obligation nevertheless to pay arrears of the farm, down to payment of compensation for expenses and inconvenience. In almost all cases the parties submitted to the bishop's jurisdiction in this matter and to his imposition of excommunication and interdict, without need for formal judicial process, and renounced all legal means by which they might appeal against the episcopal decision.

Other cases in which the bishop adjudicated or arbitrated involved the advowsons of South Raynham (5) and Ashby in Lothingland (92), in both of which the successful claimant agreed to a measure of compensation for their rivals' loss; interestingly, in the South Raynham case the parties were required to ratify the agreement by making a final concord in the *curia regis*. Two cases concerned a benefice in, or pension from, a church, claimed by a monastery. At Heveningham, St Neots priory was induced to abandon its claim to a 'new' annual benefice of three and a half marks in return for twelve acres of the church's free land, from which tithes were to be paid to its appropriated church of Ubbeston (120); while at Woolpit the monks of Bury pardoned the vicar twenty-five marks out of forty marks arrears in their pension, on condition that he should submit to the bishop's summary jurisdiction in case of future default in payment (Appx 2. 42). Three cases involved lawful presentation to and rightful incumbency of churches. At St Michael's Fincham there had been a double presentation by the monks of Castle Acre, and the bishop decreed that the incumbent should pay a pension to the disappointed candidate until he or his nominee should be in possession of a benefice worth twenty marks *p.a.* (29). The other two cases involved the consequences of papal intervention in the appointment to parochial livings (71, 78); in neither case did the papal candidate obtain the living, but in both he was to be financially compensated therefrom until he should obtain a suitable benefice. Finally, the bishop rejected the claim of the vicar of Hacheston that the canons of Hickling should in any way be responsible for the maintenance of the chapel there (66), and oversaw the surrender to Sibton abbey of possessions misappropriated by Robert of Darnford, who submitted himself to the jurisdiction of the bishop and his official to guarantee his future good conduct (133).

INDULGENCES

Suffield issued indulgences of the maximum number of forty days for St Giles, on that saint's feast (107), for Chichester cathedral at the behest of his friend bishop Wich (32) and for those making an offering at the tomb of St Cuthbert or the Galilee at Durham (38); thirty days for the fabric fund of St Paul's cathedral (81A), following a previous grant of unspecified length for the same cause and for visitors to the tomb of bishop Roger Niger (81); twenty-five days for benefactors of St Radegund's nunnery in Cambridge (15); twenty days (along with many other bishops) for Reading abbey (117); at the end of his life he granted some remission to visitors of the newly discovered tomb of St Alban (Appx 2. 33). Walton issued a further indulgence of forty days for St Giles (188), one of twenty days for Pinley priory in his native Warwickshire (189A), and almost certainly one for benefactors of Salisbury cathedral, at the dedication of which he was present (Appx 2. 38).

SIGNIFICATIONS OF EXCOMMUNICATION

These constitute the largest category of documents in this collection. The practice of reporting, or signifying, to the royal chancery the names of those persons obdurately excommunicate for more than forty days, with a request that the king should act to bring about their capture, originated in the early years of Henry III's reign and became standard procedure in most dioceses in the mid thirteenth century.[175] Written significations commence in Norwich diocese almost certainly in 1245; between then and 1266 there are extant forty-two significations; no. 159, a reference in the Close Rolls, demonstrate that not all significations now survive as originals, although it is impossible to know how many are missing. Ninety-five persons were signified to Chancery, two of them on two separate occasions. The majority of the significations, twenty-four, contain only one name; ten contained two or three names, and seven, four to six names; in addition there is the wholesale excommunication and signification of

---

[175] F. D. Logan, *Excommunication and the Secular Arm* 23–4

thirteen laymen of Shouldham (58). Those denounced included a prior, eleven rectors, five chaplains, a *magister* and three clerks. Among seventy-five laypeople, there were four knights, and only four women. There is one notification to the crown of the absolution of a person previously signified (169). It is frustrating that only once is the reason for excommunication even implied, in the case of the signification of the executors of a last testament (177).

TAXATION

A group of documents provides some evidence, although 'only in dim outline'[176] of the process of clerical taxation for Henry III's crusade, initially to the Holy Land and then to Sicily. In the king's dominions beyond England the collectors appointed deputy commissioners. In Ireland the archbishop of Dublin and John de Frosinone, who acted as papal collector in Scotland and Ireland, were reinforced by the despatch, after consultation with the king, of master Lawrence of Somercotes, who was given overriding control of collection and allocated £100 *p.a.* expenses (84, 125). Other unnamed, and apparently unwilling, deputies were appointed for the Channel Islands and Gascony (31).

Within England they appear to have appointed no deputy collectors, despite royal permission that they might do so.[177] Assessment and collection was made the responsibility within each deanery of the rural dean and a group of associates (34, 126), and cathedrals and religious houses were entrusted with self-assessment, conducted by a committee drawn from the community (8, 16, 82). The assessors were threatened with excommunication in case of fraud or laxity (as were those who bore false witness to them concerning the value of their own benefices); but if they faithfully fulfilled their task, they were promised the remission of penance earned by all those giving aid to the Holy Land (126).

The collectors had published their commission in London on 4 July 1254 (63A), and the king had hoped for collection of the first year's tenth by Michaelmas.[178] Suffield's mandate to the rural dean of Chipping Norton was dated 18 July 1254 (34) and those to St Paul's London, Burton abbey and the dean of Christianity of Stafford (82A, 8, 126) were probably despatched in late summer or early autumn; but the mandate to Canons Ashby priory was dated as late as 11 November, with 14 December as the date for return of the assessment (16), and a second mandate needed to be addressed to St Paul's, with the assessment only being returned to Suffield on 10 February 1255 (82B).

---

[176] Lunt, *Financial Relations* 261.
[177] *CPR 1247–58* 373.
[178] *Cl. R. 1253–54* 123–6.

DIPLOMATIC OF THE ACTA

INVOCATIO

Only three *acta* have an invocation – the two versions of the statutes of St Giles's hospital, in which the Angelic Salutation is followed by invocation of the Trinity (nos. 103, 107), and bishop Suffield's will, in which invocation of the Trinity is preceded by a cross (no. 138).

INTITULATIO

As elect, both bishops styled themselves *miseratione divina* (or *divina miseratione*) *Norwicensis electus*. As bishop, out of 123 examples Suffield used the title *Dei gratia Norwicensis episcopus* on sixty-eight occasions (55% of the total); on twenty-five occasions (20%) the appellation was *miseratione divina Norwicensis episcopus*, and once only *Dei miseratione episcopus Norwicensis*. *Miseratione divina* (or once only, *eiusdem*) occurs in fourteen *acta*, of which twelve are significations addressed to the king. *Permissione divina Norwicensis episcopus* is used on ten occasions, three of which are notifications to the crown and four times the episcopal title is supplemented by *negotii crucis a sede apostolica deputatus*. In his will, and in two documents issued jointly with his fellow collectors of the subsidy, the style is simply *Norwicensis episcopus*. In two instances, both *acta* in favour of St Giles (103, 105), and therefore manifestations of his search for personal salvation, Suffield added to his title *indignus* or *licet indignus*. It is worth noting that two recensions of no. 89 have *miseratione divina* and *Dei gratia*; and that in nos. 101–2, issued on the same day for the same beneficiary, different titles are used.

Of fifty-two extant examples for Simon Walton, *miseratione divina* (or *divina miseratione*, or *miseratione eiusdem*) *Norwicensis ecclesie minister humilis* (or *humilis minister*) occurs on twenty-five occasions, but twenty-two of these are significations directed to the king. Otherwise, *Dei gratia Norwicensis episcopus* occurs on twelve occasions, *divina miseratione* (or *miseratione divina*) *Norwicensis episcopus* on eleven, and *divina permissione Norwicensus episcopus* twice. Again, no. 194 in different recensions has *divina miseratione* and *divina permissione*.

INSCRIPTIO

Of those *acta* addressed universally, the vast majority for both bishops have variants of 'to all the faithful of Christ (*or* all the sons of holy mother church) who shall see (*or* inspect) or hear these present letters (*or* writing)', or 'to whom these present letters (*or* writing) may come; such variants occur in ninety-five of Suffield's *acta* and in twenty-three of Walton's. Only on one occasion *sciant presentes et futuri quod nos* was used (105), and once *noverit universitas vestra* (150). No.86 has simply *hec est ordinatio*, and in nos 103 and 107, the two versions of the St Giles statutes, the *inscriptio* is replaced by an *invocatio*.

In *acta* addressed specifically to individuals or groups, except for one document issued by Suffield as elect (17), the bishop's title precedes the *inscriptio*. In all *acta* addressed to the king, however, an obsequious address comes before the bishop's title.

SALUTATIO

In *acta* addressed universally the most common greeting was *salutem in Domino sempiternam* (seventy-two instances, 58%). *Salutem in Domino* occurs on twenty-eight occasions (22.5%); *salutem eternam in Domino*, or *eternam in Domino salutem* twenty times (16%). The simple *salutem* occurs three times, twice in jointly issued *acta*, and *salutem et benedictionem* once.

In *acta* addressed specifically to named individuals and groups, other than the king, *salutem, gratiam et benedictionem* occurs on four occasions, and *salutem* and *salutem sempiternam* once each. In notifications addressed to king Henry III, Suffield habitually used *salutem in eo qui dat salutem regibus*, and once only *salutem et quicquid honoris et reverentie*. For Walton the norm was *salutem cum omni reverentia, obsequio et honore*, which occurs, with four very minor variations, twenty-three times, with once only *salutem et debitam cum omni honore et ferventi dilectione reverentiam*.

ARENGA

Thirty-one *acta* have pious preambles; of these twenty-one are in favour of Benedictine houses, and four for the new hospital of St Giles, Norwich. Seventeen dwell upon the special episcopal obligation to religious communities, and five on the virtues of the religious life – particularly notable is the fulsome praise of the Cluniac order in no. 77. In the authorisation of the establishment of a chapel at a monastic manor-house it is emphasised that the religious should be segregated from the laity (115). Twice the duty to provide hospitality is stressed (109, 186), and once how pleasing to God is the construction of churches (41). Alms, bishop Walton observes, remedy the consequences of sin (143). There is great merit in visiting the threshold of saints (81A), and the virtues of particular saints are extolled (38–9). Two *arengae* focus on the fragility of human memory (18, 188), and two are insistent that the founder's intentions should be observed in perpetuity (103, 107). In a synodal statute bishop Suffield stresses that, although unworthy of episcopal ofice, he is anxious to foster good practice and eliminate bad (102).

On twenty-one occasions the *arenga* is a complete sentence, followed by phrases such as *hinc est, cum igitur, nos igitur, quocirca* or *proinde*. In ten instances the arenga is a dependent clause, often introduced by *cum*, normally running into the *dispositio*, but twice followed by a notification clause.

NOTIFICATIO

The notification clause was still common, with fifty-nine instances, although certainly not near universal, as it had been under bishop John of Oxford, 1175–1200.[179] The most common form, with twenty-six instances, is *noverit universitas vestra*, either with the accusative and infinitive or with *quod* and a dependent clause. *Noveritis* occurs eleven times, variants on *universitati tenore presentium notum fiat* (*notum facimus, volumus esse notum, innotescat*) eight times, *ad universorum* (or *omnium*, or *universitatis vestre*) *notitiam volumus pervenire nos* nine times, with four other forms occurring once only. Normally the notification followed the salutation, but twice (7, 197) occurs after the *arenga*.

NARRATIO AND DISPOSITIO

By virtue of the many different categories of business dealt with in the *acta*, there is such great variety in the core of the texts as to make generalisation almost impossible. In sixteen *acta* the merits or misfortunes of the religious house which is the beneficiary are recounted. In four cases the immediate past history of a parish church (36, 79, 106, 128) and once of customary rights (14), is recalled. Mention is made of grants by the bishop's predecessors, by lay donors and, an innovation in the mid thirteenth century, of apostolic mandates and the consequences of their implementation (27, 78, 144, 187). On one occasion the bishop described how he had discovered defects in the ordination of a vicarage (132). As evidence increases for the intervention of the bishop as arbitrator, in fourteen *acta* there is a narrative of the development of a dispute, most usually concerning tithes, but twice relating to the complications arising from dual presentation to a benefice (29, 71). In one important instance, practically the whole *actum* is a narrative of archbishop-elect Boniface's actions to impose his will on the chapter of Christ Church, Canterbury, as witnessed by Walter Suffield (18).

The *narratio* was normally followed by the *dispositio*, which was the reason for the issue of the *actum*. In a few instances this is extremely long, for example the two recensions of the statutes for St Giles's hospital (103, 107) and the three versions of the observances to be followed at newly-founded Flixton priory (149–51). Rather shorter were the provisions made for the new nunnery at Marham (85–7). In the grant of Mendlesham church to Chichester cathedral were included regulations for the chantry of St Richard, which the appropriation was intended to finance (33). The terms of tenure of the chaplain of a chantry established in the nunnery of Blackborough were outlined (5, 6A).

---

[179] *EEA* 6 pp. lxvi–lxvii.

There is only one full-scale general confirmation of listed possessions, for Castle Acre priory (143), but there are shorter ratifications of various categories of possession for the cathedral priory (88–9, 97, 100). A synodal statute relating to the last testaments of incumbents survives as an *actum* addressed generally (102), and regulations concerning visitation and procurations were directed to the rural deans of the diocese (67–8). Among the more common categories of document, the resolution of disputes, especially concerning tithes, sometimes involved the parties' submission, in the event of infringement, to the bishop's judgement without formal judicial process and the renunciation of all potential legal remedies which might be invoked to circumvent this. As the authorisation of private chapels became more common, the clauses employed to guarantee the rights of the parish or mother church approached common form. Grants *in proprios usus* occasionally detailed new interim arrangements to last until the departure of the current incumbent (36–7, 186), or regulated the purposes for which revenues should be used (41, 69, 181). The taxation of a vicarage within an appropriated church could vary from the provision that one should be established in the future, through the stipulation that it should be decent, suitable or adequate, to a synopsis of the constituent revenues of rectory and vicarage, or even a very detailed account of these (98, 197).

Clauses reserving the rights, honour or dignity of the church of Norwich and of the bishop and his successors occur in twenty-six *acta*, as does reference in thirteen documents to the consent of the prior and convent of the cathedral chapter (in addition to the twenty-four *inspeximus* and confirmation charters issued by prior and chapter, to which there is once only a reference within the episcopal *actum*).

INSPEXIMUS

The charter by which a previous *actum* or *acta* was inspected, and normally recited, which came into frequent usage in the episcopate of John de Gray (1200–14) continued to be used in the mid thirteenth century. Of seventeen such charters (twelve of Suffield, five of Walton), twelve recited the text(s) inspected, five (all of Suffield) merely made reference to them. In eight cases the word *inspeximus* follows the *salutatio*, in nine the *notificatio* is followed by *nos inspexisse*. Nine of such charters inspect *acta* of the bishop's predecessor(s), four the deeds of lay beneficiaries (including one of king Henry II (4)). Other documents inspected are a papal indult (141), a notification by papal judges-delegate (3), a charter of the bishop of Ely (116) and, in a joint *inspeximus* and confirmation with bishop Richard of Chichester, documents relating to Pontigny abbey's possession of the church of Romney in Kent (114).

INJUNCTIO

The injunctive clause was confined to mandates directed to subordinates. Of eight instances, four relate to Suffield's delegation of his authority as *executor negotii crucis* to local subordinates (8, 16, 34, 126), and one to his earlier responsibility for the raising of papal taxation (119). Two commands to the rural dean of Hingham, relating to the limitation of procurations (67–8) are the surviving examples, preserved by Matthew Paris, of mandates presumably sent to every rural dean of the diocese.

While the numerous notifications of decisions made by the bishop as arbitrator do not contain an injunctive clause, they were by their nature injunctions.

SANCTIO

Although infrequent, the sanction clause occurs more often than in the period 1215–43. This is possibly due to the increasing use of excommunication as a sanction as the thirteenth century progressed – which is reflected also in the threat of that censure against those who might break the terms of bishop Suffield's verdicts as arbitrator. Of *sanctio* clauses in the proper sense, one occurs in Walton's general confirmation for Castle Acre priory (143), another in the second statutes for St Giles's hospital (107), and a third in a diocesan staute (102). Three more sanction clauses relate to the safeguarding of the rights of a parish church when a chapel was established within its bounds (2, 40, 112).

CORROBORATIO

The majority of *acta* addressed generally, excluding indulgences, have a corroborative clause. In *inspeximus* charters, there are almost as many different forms as there are *acta*. In other grants, concessions and confirmations by far the most common form is: *in cuius rei testimonium huic* (or *presenti*) *scripto sigillum nostrum apponi fecimus* (or *duximus apponendum*), of which there are eighty-one instances, in nine of which there is reference also to the appending of the chapter seal, and in three cases of other seals. There are seven instances (three for Suffield, four for Walton) of a corroboration clause beginning *et ut*, or *ut autem*, or *ut igitur*, with no measure of standardisation thereafter. In seven *acta* there is no corroborative clause where one might be expected (37, 85, 95, 100, 108, 127, 137).

In addition to documents attested by the prior and chapter of the cathedal (103, 107) and by the whole synod (102), forty-five *acta* have a witness list; of these ten are in favour of the cathedral priory and five for Castle Acre. Seventy-two *acta* which might, by the convention of the mid-thirteenth century, have had a witness list (that is, excluding mandates, significations and indulgences) in fact do not. It is interesting that no. 101, for the cathedral priory, has a witness list, but no. 100, issued on the same day for the same beneficiary, does not.

ESCHATOCOL

At the conclusion of episcopal *acta* a dating clause was now the norm, although not invariable; fourteen texts, including two originals (73, 103) do not have a date. The dating clause normally includes the place of issue; in 123 *acta* this is expressed by *apud* and the accusative, in 27 documents by the locative case. Alternatives are *die synodi...in ecclesia sancte Trinitatis* (in a synodal statute, 102); *in capitulo* (103, 107); and *in manerio* (145). Three *acta*, of which two are originals, have no place-date (104, 146, 166).

A precise date is usually given, although in one case only the year (95) and in another month and year only (17). The day and month is normally expressed according to the Roman calendar; in seventeen *acta*, however, the liturgical calendar was used; of these, five occur under Suffield and twelve (of which five are significations) under Walton. In roughly half the dated *acta* (seventy-eight instances, forty-five under Suffield and thirty-three under Walton), dating was by the year of grace. In forty-four cases (forty Suffield, four Walton) the pontifical year was used; and in thirty-four cases (twenty-four Suffield, ten Walton) the two forms of dating were combined.

As in the previous volumes, there are inevitably problems relating to the calculation of the year, by either method. As regards pontifical year, however, there are sufficient examples to indicate that it was habitually reckoned from the day of consecration rather than of election. Of *acta* dated by both methods, and in which it is irrelevant whether the new year started at Christmas or the Annunciation, nos. 38, 72, 87, 94, 99–102, 124, 142–3, 187–8, 191, 195 all demonstrate daring from the consecration – all of these would be a year later in the pontifical cycle if dated from election.

Turning to the calculation of the year of grace, nos. 26, 30, 70, 79–80, 146 and 175, ranging in date from 27 December to 6 March, and all dated by the pontifical year and year of grace, demonstrate that the new year did not commence on Christmas day (or, a remote possibility, 1 January), but on the feast of the Annunciation, 25 March. Nos. 27–8, for Castle Acre, were obviously issued on the same day, 24 February, and since it can be established that Suffield was consecrated on 19 February (rather than 26 February) 1246 (17A), the eighth year of his pontificate, to which no. 28 is dated, must be 1252 by the modern reckoning, rather than the 1251 of no. 27. In a few cases the commencement of the year at the Annunciation can be corroborated by the historical context. Bishop Suffield's *cautio* (17A), dated 20 February, cannot be 1244 by modern usage, since royal assent to his election was not given until 9 July 1244.[180] The bishop's lettter to the abbey of St Albans concerning papal taxation (119) was certainly sent on 24 March 1246, rather than 1245 as written in the text.[181] The notification to the king of the election of new prior of St Peter and St Paul,

---

[180] *Fasti* ii 57.
[181] Lunt, *Financial Relations* 216.

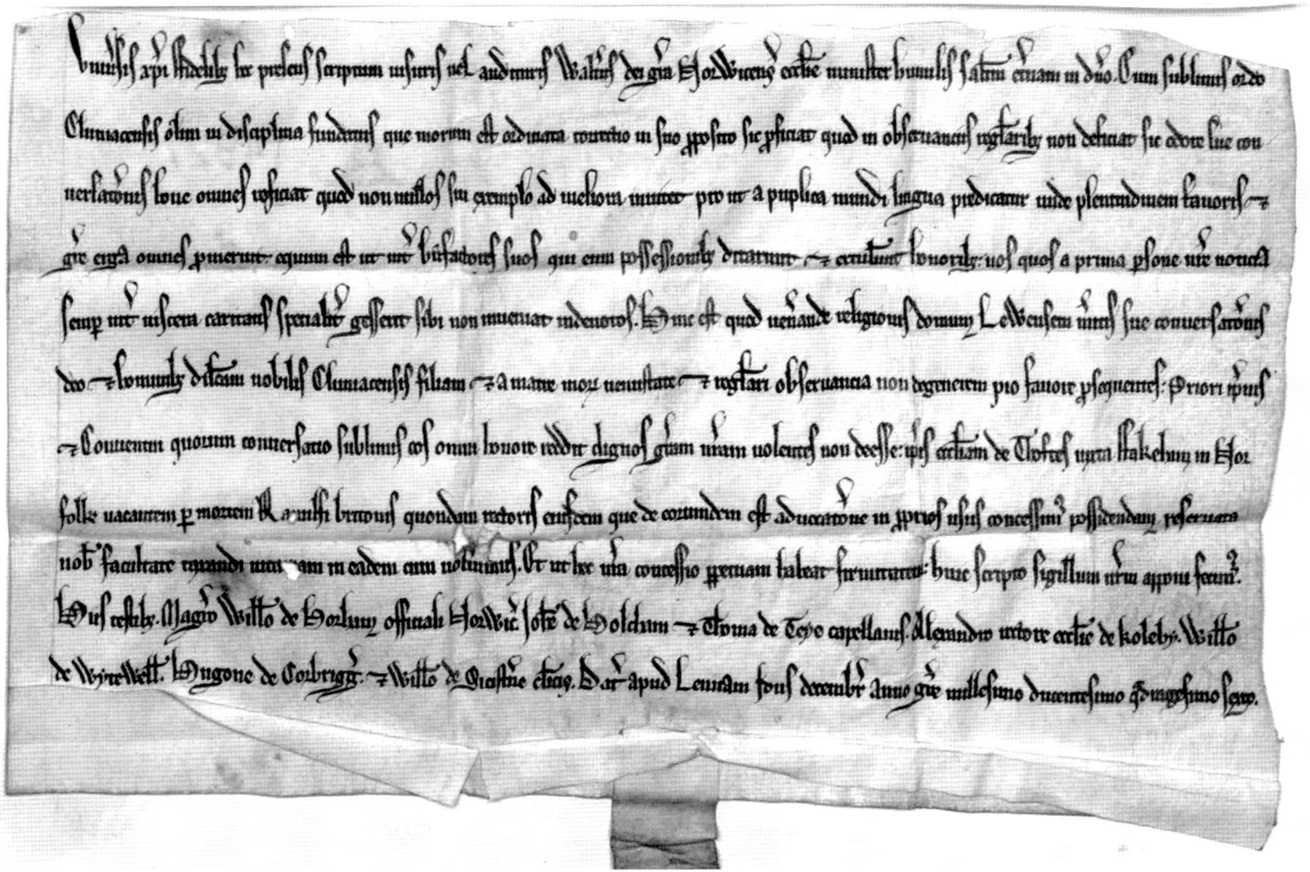

The National Archive no.138

PLATE I

PLATE II

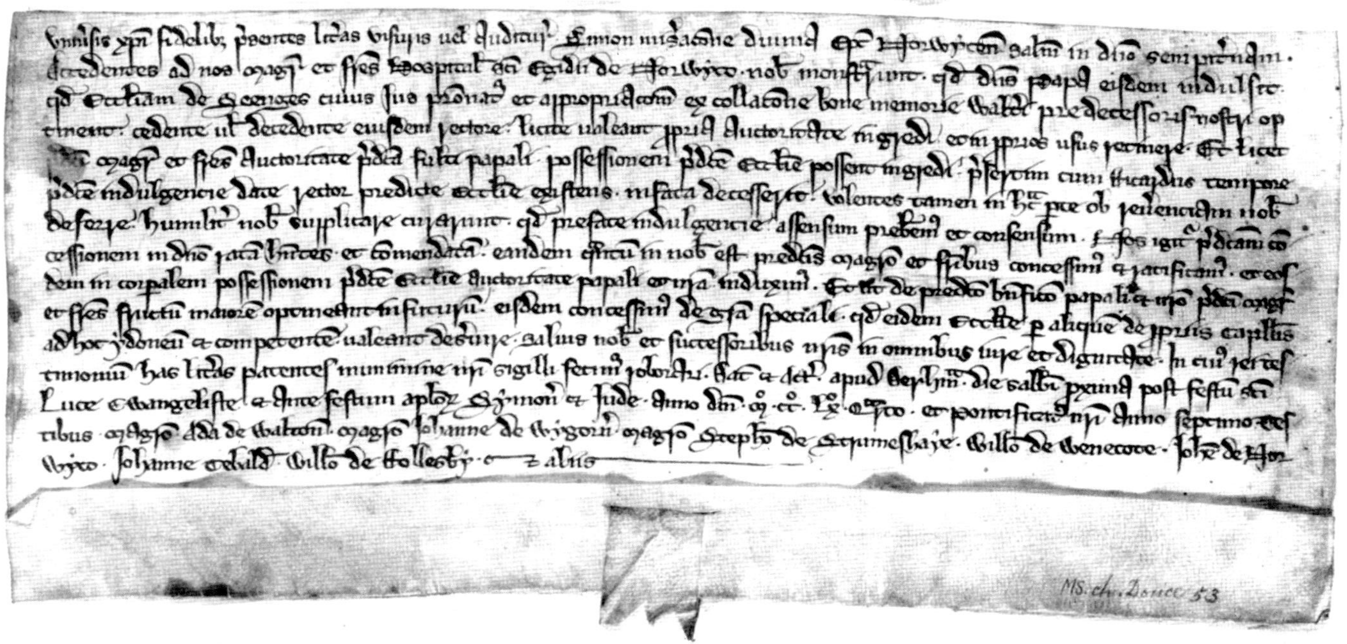

Bodleian Library, Oxford

no.187

PLATE III

Suffolk Record Office, Ipswich   no.116

Norfolk Record Office   no.185   no.188

PLATE IV

Ipswich (60) is demonstrated by royal records to have been written on 15 January 1252.[182]

There is only one apparent exception to the reckoning of the year of grace by the Annunciation. No. 11, issued by Suffield as bishop-elect, must be reckoned from Christmas, as if by the Annunciation the date would be 2 January 1246, by when he had been consecrated for over ten months. It may be simply that he and his clerks were as yet unfamiliar with habitual practice of the episcopal chancery

VALEDICTION

The valediction had fallen into disuse in *acta* addressed universally. It occurs twice in letters addressed to other ecclesiastics (34, 119), and may have been omitted in such communications which are extant only as copies in cartularies or chronicles. In *acta* addressed to the king a valediction is almost universal, although omitted twice (162, 177). The simple *valete* occurs once (169), but in all other cases there are variations on the theme of 'long live the king'. There are many variants for reference to the royal person – most commonly *regia maiestas*, but also *excellentia regia*, *vestra potestas regia*, *serenitas vestra*, *vestra perspicitas*, *celsitudo regia* and *reverenda dominatio vestra*.

FORMAT AND SCRIPT

There is a small group of large documents – confirmations for Pontigny and Castle Acre (114, 143), two recensions of the statutes for St Giles (103, 188), and bishop Suffield's last testament (138). The average dimensions of these are 407 × 380 mm (including turn-up).The three handsome *inspeximus* charters by prior Roger and the convent of Norwich of bishop Walton's statutes for Flixton priory (149–51) indicate that the episcopal *acta* themselves must have been impressive documents.

Of the remainder of extant originals, excluding significations, the majority are in such a format that the vertical measurement of the parchment (including turn-up) is between half and two-thirds of the horizontal measurement. In only four cases is the vertical measurement less than half that of the horizontal (15, 35, 74, 104), and in one case only (73) is the vertical measurement greater than the horizontal. As for significations of excommunication, and two other notifications to the king, these are uniformly elongated strips of parchment, the average measurement of which is 165 × 53 mm.

As for script, it is difficult for an editor who is not an expert palaeographer to make any intelligent comments. Of Suffield's extant original *acta*, nos. 75 and 77, produced for Lewes priory within three days of each other, appear to be in the same hand, while the three extant originals for the cathedral priory (88, 95,

---

[182] *HRH* ii 396.

98) are written in different hands – not surprisingly, since they span eleven years. It is perhaps more significant that a group of five *acta* produced between March and May 1245 (2, 35, 40, 88,110) are all apparently written by different scribes. As for bishop Walton's *acta*, nos. 186–8, for the hospital of St Giles, all appear to be in the same hand, which may also have produced no. 143, for Castle Acre priory, while his other three extant originals, nos. 144A, 153, 185, all appear to be written by different scribes. The significations of excommunication, which were certainly produced by episcopal clerks, are again written in several different hands during each episcopate. As for beneficial *acta*, it is impossible to say with any certainty that any two *acta* for different beneficiaries were written by the same scribe. The similarity of the hands of all the *acta*, however with the exception of Appx. 1. 19, suggests the standardised style of the episcopal chancery.

SEALING

In beneficial *acta*, the normal means of affixing the seal was by parchment tag passed through a single slit cut through the two thicknesses of parchment of the turn-up at the foot of the document. Nos. 70 and 73 now have no turn-up, but this has almost certainly cut off. In only one case, no. 103, the first statutes for St Giles, was the more complex means of sealing by tag utilised, with two parallel incisions through the turn-up and a third on the crease.[183] In two cases certainly, and one probably, the seal was attached by cords; two of these instances were prestige documents – the general confirmation for Castle Acre priory (143) and the confirmation of the St Giles statutes (188); a confirmation of an individual grant to the small priory of Mountjoy at Haveringland (153) is more surprising. One *actum* is exceptional; Appx 1. 19, which was issued either by Suffield or his predecessor William Raleigh, is sealed on the tongue, with a tie. There is no similar extant example for either bishop, although this was the method always used for the sealing of significations of excommunication and other short notifications to the king.

Whereas in the previous two episcopates, most sealings were in green wax,[184] there was now no such uniformity, with seals produced in natural wax, or varnished light or dark brown, dark green or red, with no obvious pattern. A number of *acta* bear evidence of sealing with more than one seal. In most cases the episcopal seal is partnered by that of the prior and convent of Norwich (3, 73, 103, 111), to which once is added that of the hospital of St Giles (106). No. 78 bore the seals of parties to a complex agreement, no. 114 that of bishop Richard of Chichester, and bishop Suffield's will (138) those of his seven executors. Of bishop Suffield's seal, there are seven reasonable impressions affixed to *acta*,

---

[183] For descriptions of the two methods of sealing with tag, see *EEA* ii pp. xlvi–xlvii.
[184] *EEA* 21 p. lxxii.

and two good detached examples,[185] as well as twelve fragments of various sizes. The seal is a pointed oval, measuring approximately 76 × 43 mm. It bears a conventional full-length representation of the bishop standing upon a platform, dressed in mass vestments, a pastoral staff in his left hand and his right hand raised in benediction. The background is diapered faintly with a double reticulated pattern, lozengy with a small indistinct quatrefoil in each space; there is to the left of the bishop's head a small crescent, and a small estoile (star) to the right. In the field to either side are small carved openings containing on the left a bull's head, on the right a lion's head. Below the platform is a representation of the cathedral. The legend is + WALTERUS: MISERATIONE: DIVINA: NORWICENSIS: EPISCOPUS. The counterseal is a smaller pointed oval, approximately 51 × 28 mm. It depicts Christ in glory, enthroned, lifting His right hand in benediction. In the field on either side is an estoile. At the base, under a trefoiled arch, to the left, the bishop is kneeling in prayer. The legend is + HOC TE TORMENTO: REDIMI WALTERE: MEMENTO, which might be thought more appropriate to an image of the crucifixion.

Of bishop Walton's seal, the only fine example is attached to no. 185.[186] It is a pointed oval, measuring approximately 63 × 43 mm. It too bears a full-length representation of the bishop, standing in mass vestments, blessing and holding a crozier. He is set against a diapered background, between an estoile to the right and a crescent moon to the left, and the figure is set beneath an unsupported canopy carrying gabled structures. A worn impression of his counterseal is affixed to no. 188. It measures 50 × 33 mm., and the legend is indecipherable. It appears to show, beneath an unsupported canopy, an enthroned figure. Below, under a trefoil arch, to the left is the bishop, praying. The most likely identification of the main figure is the Blessed Virgin Mary, since there is a protusion of wax above the left knee suggesting that it supports another form, that is, the infant Jesus. Since the dedication of the cathedral is to the Trinity, it might be suggested that this could be an indication of Walton's personal devotion to Mary.

EDITORIAL METHOD

This edition follows the method of other volumes in the series, as laid down in detail in the fourth volume.[187] A list of regularly used abbreviations is provided. Originals are given the letter A, with duplicate originals described as A[1] and A[2]. Copies are described as B, C *etc.* Where an original is extant, it has not normally been collated with copies, but where there survive only transcripts, these have

---

[185] *BM Seals* nos. 2024–5.
[186] I am grateful to my colleague Mr T. A. Heslop for this descripton of Walton's seal, which has not previously been properly catalogued.
[187] *EEA* 4 pp.xlii–xliv.

been collated and most variants noted – and most especially this principle has been applied to personal and place names. Modern punctuation has been applied throughout, and *c/t* and *u/v* have been standardised according to modern usage.

All extant *acta* are published in full, with the exception of documents already printed in other volumes of this series. Where the text of an *actum* has been lost, but it is certain that a charter or letter once existed, a description is included in the main series of texts, the number being prefixed by an asterisk.

Within each episcopate, the *acta* are printed in alphabetical sequence according to beneficiary or addressee, or the person or corporation primarily affected by judicial decisions. Under each beneficiary documents have normally been arranged in chronological order, except where two or more *acta* refer to the same matter. The majority of these *acta* are dated. Where they are not, or where the date in the text is not precise, the dating limits are placed in square brackets after the caption; and where these are narrower than the dates of the pontificate, they are justified in the notes appended to individual documents. The modern practice of beginning the year on 1 January has been used throughout.

WALTER SUFFIELD

1. Profession

Profession of obedience made to Boniface [of Savoy], archbishop-elect of Canterbury. [Norwich, 19 February 1245]

A = Canterbury D. & C., Ch. Ant. C115/108. No endorsement, approx. 100 × 47 mm.
B = Canterbury D. & C. register A (prior's register) fo. 268r. s. xiv med.
Pd from A and B in *Canterbury Professions* no. 181.

Ego Walterus Norwicensis ecclesie electus promitto canonicam obedientiam et debitam subiectionem sancte Cantuariensi ecclesie et Bonifacio eiusdem ecclesie electo et successoribus suis canonice substituendis, et ego Walterus subscribo. +

For date, see no. 17A.

2. Philip Basset

Concession, with the consent of Nicholas son of Warin Joel, perpetual vicar of Soham, that he may have a chantry in the chapel at his residence there. The chaplain who is to minister therein shall, on his first arrival and in the presence of the vicar or his chaplain, swear on the holy gospels that he will surrender all oblations and offerings on the day of receipt or the next day to the mother church, and that he will not admit any parishioners to confession or to any other sacrament, unless their death is imminent. The chapel shall be subject to the mother church, in token whereof Basset shall, when resident, go with his household to the mother church to pray at Christmas, Easter, the Assumption of the Blessed Virgin Mary and the [dedication] feast of the church, and shall offer at high mass the customary oblations. Sentence of excommunication is promulgated against any who may seek to undermine or evade the terms of this concession. Norwich, 21 April 1245

A = TNA, E40/14373. Endorsed: Saham (s. xiii); approx. 192 × 112 + 11mm.; parchment tag, fragment of seal, light brown wax, counterseal.

Omnibus Cristi fidelibus ad quos presens scriptum pervenerit Walterus Dei gratia Norwicensis episcopus salutem eternam in Domino. Noveritis nos, de voluntate et consensu Nicholai filii Warini Ioel perpetui vicarii ecclesie de Saham, domino Philippo Basset cantariam in capella in curia sua de Saham constructa concessisse sub hac forma, videlicet quod capellanus in ea ministraturus in primo suo adventu, presente vicario matricis ecclesie vel suo capellano, iurabit inspectis sacrosanctis ewangeliis quod omnes oblationes ac obventiones undecumque eidem capelle obvenientes matrici ecclesie eadem die qua percipiuntur vel proxima sequenti integre et absque diminutione restituet, et quod nullum parochianum matricis ecclesie ad confessionem sive aliquod aliud sacramentum ecclesiasticum admittet, nisi periculum mortis immineret. Erit siquidem prefata capella matrici ecclesie subiecta, et in signum subiectionis prefatus miles unacum familia sua ad matricem ecclesiam accedet diebus infrascriptis, videlicet die nathale Domini et die Pasche, assumptionis beate Marie et festivitatis ecclesie, cum debitis et consuetis oblationibus ad magnam missam, si ibidem fuerit prefatam ecclesiam veneraturus. Nos vero omnes illos qui aliquid in huius nostre concessionis preiudicium sive fraudem machinaverint sive fieri procuraverint sententia excommunicationis innodamus. In cuius rei testimonium presenti scripto sigillum nostrum apponi fecimus. Dat' apud Norwicum .xi. kalendas Maii pontificatus nostri anno primo.

> Soham was a royal manor granted in 1203 to Hubert de Burgh; when in 1227 he was created
> earl of Kent, he was confirmed in hereditary possession of the manor, to be held by the service
> of one knight's fee. The crown seized Soham in 1232 when Hubert was deprived of the
> justiciarship and his earldom, but it was restored to him on his pardon on 20 May 1234. Within
> four months he rewarded Philip Basset, who in 1233 had helped free him from captivity in
> Devizes castle, by granting him 176 acres of his demesne at Soham, with lordship over
> numerous tenants holding 465 acres there (*C.Ch.R.* 1226–57 195). Around 1242 each lord of
> Soham held his part for the service of half a knight's fee, Hubert holding in chief and Philip of
> Hubert (*Bk Fees* ii 924). In the mid thirteenth century Basset enlarged his estate by purchase,
> and in 1262 obtained from John de Burgh a lease for his own lifetime of the Burgh manor (*VCH
> Cambridgeshire* x 500). Shortly before this license for a chantry was granted Basset had, in
> Lent 1245, been appointed one of the proctors of the universitas Angliae at the forthcoming
> Council of Lyons (*C & S* II i 392, 402). For a brief conspectus of his career, see Oxford *DNB*.

3. Abbey of Le Bec-Hellouin

Inspeximus *and confirmation of the settlement before the priors of Bentley and Harmondsworth, papal judges delegate, in 1247 [25 December 1246 × 24 March 1248], of a dispute between the monks, represented by William de Guineville, their special proctor, and Walter, rector of Great Wratting, concerning various tithes which the monks used to and should receive in that parish. After proceedings had progressed some way, eventually an amicable composition was reached between the parties, whereby Walter and his successors as rector shall in the monks' name receive these tithes and all else which the monks had or should have in that parish from the demesne of Peter of Tolworth, even if these other revenues are not from that demesne, excepting however anything which may subsequently be conferred on the monks in this parish from another demesne, rendering to the monks or their assigns at Stoke [by Clare] twenty-eight shillings a year in two instalments at the feasts of the Purification of the Blessed Virgin Mary and the Nativity of St John the Baptist;*

and if any rector should default in payment at these terms, the monks may enter freely into possession of these tithes without contradiction or impediment, suffering no civil or canonical penalty on this account; or if they so prefer they may prosecute the rector for recovery of the money, since this composition is for the utility of the parish church rather than of the monks. Norwich, 29 April 1248

A = Bodl. ms. Suffolk ch. (a. 13) 1440. Endorsed: Magna Wratting Norwic' dioc' de portione decimarum (s. xiii); approx. 270 × 120 + 12 mm., two slits, fragment of parchment tag through left, seals missing.

Omnibus hoc scriptum visuris vel audituris Walterus Dei gratia Norwicensis episcopus salutem in Domino. Litteras priorum de Benetleya et de Hermodesworth iudicum a domino papa delegatorum inspeximus in hec verba: Omnibus Cristi fidelibus ad quos presentes littere pervenerint de Benetleia et de Hermodesworth priores iudices a domino papa delegati salutem. Universitatem vestram volumus non latere quod cum olim anno Domini M° CC° XL° septimo coram nobis auctoritate apostolica questio verteretur inter abbatem et conventum Becci ex parte una et Walterum tunc rectorem ecclesie de Magna[a] Wratting' Norwicensis diocesis ex altera super quibusdam decimis quas dicti monachi percipiebant et percipere debebant in dicta parochia de Wratting', dictis monachis causam agentibus per fratrem Willelmum de Guinevill' procuratorem eorum generalem tunc temporis habentem specialem componendi potestatem, et aliquamdiu processum esset in causa, tandem inter partes super predictis decimis amicabilis compositio intercessit sub hac forma: quod dictus W. rector vel eius successores qui pro tempore fuerint nomine dictorum monachorum dictas decimas unacum omnibus aliis quas percipiebant tunc temporis dicti monachi vel percipere debebant in dicta parochia de Wratting' de dominico Petri de Thaleword, etiam sinon alia fuerint de eodem dominico provenientia, exceptis dumtaxat si que dictis monachis de alio dominico inposterum conferantur in eadem parochia, inperpetuum possidebunt, reddendo inde annuatim dictis monachis vel eorum assignato apud Stokes viginti et octo solidos sterlingorum bone et legalis monete ad duos anni terminos, ad purificationem beate Marie virginis quatuordecim solidos et ad nativitatem beati Iohannis Baptiste quatuordecim solidos, ita tamen quod si W. rector vel aliquis successorum suorum in dicte pecunie solutionem ultra quam debuerit cessaverit, liceat dictis monachis dictarum decimarum absque aliqua contradictione vel impedimento, nulla propter hoc eis pena civili vel canonica infligenda, libere ingredi possessionem, vel si maluerint contra dictos rectores agere ad dictam pecuniam nomine decimarum consequendam, cum in utilitate ecclesie parochialis potius quam dictorum monachorum hec[b] compositio sit provisa. In cuius rei testimonium tam signa nostra quam signa partium presentibus litteris apponi fecimus. Dat' anno Domini M° CC° XL° VII°. Nos igitur dictam compositionem ratam habentes et acceptam, eam presenti scripto et sigilli nostri et sigilli capituli nostri Norwicensis appositione roboravimus. Dat' apud Norwicum .iii. kalendas Maii anno dominice incarnationis M° CC° XL° VIII°.

^a Mangna A   ^b huius A

For litigation between Bec and various Suffolk rectors from whose parishes the monks claimed tithes, see *EEA* 21 no. 125. The Wratting case had commenced before 26 July 1245 (Sayers, *Papal Judges Delegate* 318–9). In 1254 Bec's portion of £1 8s was assigned to the prior of Ruislip, the church itself was valued at £6 13s 4d, and the prior of Hatfield Regis had a portion of 10s (*VN* 440). There was further litigation in 1259–60, when on 2 January before papal judges delegate at London the rector recognised his obligation to Bec's pension of £1 8s and to arrears of £6 6s, which he would pay to the subprior of Stoke by Clare as proctor of the monks of Bec (Windsor D & C mss, Great White Book, pp. 229–30), and in 1291 Bec's portion, now assigned to the prior of Ogbourne, had been reduced to £1, while the church was valued at £8 (*Taxatio* 121b).

4. Biddlesden Abbey

Inspeximus *of a charter of king Henry II [1154 × 62] by which he confirmed the gift to the monks by Ernald de Bosco of the manor of Biddlesden, three carucates called 'Marieland' in Syresham, all the land of Whitfield and Dodford, all the land of Westcott, and the land of Osbert de Wanci and William of Holbeach, that is 'Blakeham', and all else which they had been given in alms or had purchased, granting them himself exemption from various obligations and exactions.*

Snoring, 25 March 1251

A= BL ms Harl. ch. 84 D 6. Endorsed: Confirmatio Henrici regis secundi patris domini Iohannis regis de manerio de Bitlesdena et de tribus carucatis terre in Siresham que vocatur Marielond et totam terram de Witfelde et de Doodforde et totam terram de Wescoote et terram Osbarthi de Wancy et Willelmi de Holebeck, scilicet Blakeham cum omnibus pertinentiis (s. xiii); de Bytlesden', ponatur in shefio eiusdem (s. xvi); pressmark; approx. 230 × 110 + 25 mm.; fragment of seal, natural wax, counterseal.
Pd (royal charter only) in Delisle, no. lix.

Omnibus Cristi fidelibus presentes litteras visuris vel audituris Walterus miseratione divina Norwicensis ecclesie minister humilis salutem in Domino sempiternam. Noverit universitas vestra nos inspexisse cartam domini H. regis patris domini Iohannis regis, non viciatam, non cancellatam nec in aliqua sui parte abolitam, sigillo eiusdem domini H. regis signatam, de confirmationibus et libertatibus monachis et monasterio de Bittlesden concessam in hac forma: H. rex Anglie et dux Normannorum et Aquitan' et comes Andeg' archiepiscopis, episcopis, comitibus, baronibus, iusticiariis, vicecomitibus, omnibus amicis et fidelibus suis Normann' et Anglie salutem. Sciatis me concessisse et confirmasse donationem illam quam Ernoldus de Bosco fecit Deo et monachis de ordine Cisterciensi de manerio de Bettlesdena cum omnibus appenditiis suis, ad fundendam ibidem abbatiam ordinis Cisterciensis, et de tribus carucatis terre in Syresham que vocatur Marieland et quicquid ad eas pertinet, et terram totam de Whitefeud et de Doddeford et quicquid ad illas pertinet, et totam terram de Westcote, et terram Osberti de Wancy et Willelmi de Holebek, scilicet Blakeham et quicquid ad illas pertinet. Et confirmo omnia illa que eis in elemosina date sunt vel que ipsi mercati sunt. Quare volo et firmiter precipio quod supradicti monachi prefatas terras bene et in pace, libere et quiete et honorifice teneant et habeant in perpetuam elemosinam, in bosco et in plano, in pratis et pascuis et omnibus aliis rebus et locis, cum omnibus libertatibus et liberis consuetudinibus eisdem terris pertinentibus, sicut alie ecclesie eiusdem ordinis sive in Anglia sive in Normann' melius et liberius tenent. Et volo et firmiter precipio ut sint quieti de shiris et hundredis et placitis et querelis et occasionibus et auxiliis et operationibus et murdris et danegeldis et omnibus aliis geldis et hidagiis et tolnetis et omnibus consuetudinibus corone mee pertinentibus. Et precipio quod monachi qui ibidem Deo serviunt bene et in pace, libere et quiete, teneant quieti et soluti omni servitio seculari, ne quis aliquando inde consuetudinem ullam requirat. Testibus: Thoma cancellario, R. comite Cornubie, comite Leycestr', Roberto de Dunstanvill' et aliis. In cuius rei testimonium huic presenti scripto sigillum nostrum apponi fecimus. Dat' apud Naringes .viii. kalendas Aprilis anno gratie millesimo ducentesimo quinquagesimo primo et pontificatus nostri anno septimo.

Henry II's charter (BL ms Harl. ch 84 C 4) may be dated December 1154 × August 1158; it will be no. 229 in the forthcoming new edition by N. Vincent and others. It is not clear why bp Suffield was asked to inspect this document. It was presumably not in his capacity as papal tax assessor, since he does not use the title *negotii crucis executor a sede apostolica deputatus*. The most likely explanation is that the unidentified 'Blakeham' ('Blacaham' in *Regesta* iii no. 104) is Great or Little Blakenham, in Suffolk, although there is no other extant documentation relating to any possessions of Biddlesden there.

5. Blackborough Priory

Notification that, when a dispute arose between Robert de Scales, the patron, and the prioress and convent concerning the advowson of the church of South Raynham and various other matters, eventually by the bishop's mediation peace was made between them in the following form: the nuns quitclaimed to Robert and his heirs all right which they had in the advowson of the church of Sandon [Ess.] and also the right of receiving annually one mark from that church, so that Robert and his heirs should present to that church at every vacancy, with no reclamation by the nuns. Robert quitclaimed to the nuns the church of South Raynham, granted to them by his father, to be converted in proprios usus, *to which the bishop's consent has been obtained, saving a vicarage to be taxed by him within moderation, to which Robert and his heirs should present a suitable* persona. *The nuns should in perpetuity maintain a chaplain to celebrate every day in their house at the altar of the Blessed Virgin Mary for the souls of Robert, Clementia his wife and his ancestors and successors, and this chaplain is to be presented to Robert and his heirs and to take a canonical oath thus to celebrate. If at any time a chaplain should cease to so celebrate through the negligence or fault of the nuns, they have pledged that the bishop, archdeacon or [rural] dean, at the discretion of Robert and his heirs, may sequestrate the fruits of the church until due recompense is made for the celebration omitted. If a chaplain should be removed for legitimate cause, his substitute should similarly be presented to Robert and his heirs and take an oath. For greater security, Robert promised that he would make a charter concerning this concession of the church to the nuns, and that anything in it might be amended by the bishop, who undertook for the nuns that they would make a charter concerning their concession to Robert, in which likewise any necessary amendment should be made by the advice of their friends and of the bishop. Both parties swore that they would have all these matters corroborated by a chirograph made in the* curia regis *before the justices, and the bishop will ensure that this is done.*   London, 27 March 1257

B = BL ms. Egerton 3137 (Blackborough cartulary) fos 187v–188r. s. xiii ex. C = ibid fos. 188v–189r (*inspeximus* by official of Norwich, 24 March 1289).

Universis Cristi fidelibus Walterus miseratione divina episcopus Norwicensis salutem in Domino sempiternam. Universitati vestre volumus esse notum quod cum inter dominum Robertum de Scal' patronum domus monialium de Blakebergh nostre diocesis ex una parte ac priorissam et moniales dicte domus ex altera super advocatione ecclesie de South Reynham nostre diocesis et super quibusdam aliis coram nobis suborta esset materia questionis, tandem nobis mediantibus inter eos[a] sub forma subscripta pax exstitit[b] reformata, videlicet quod priorissa et moniales predicte totum ius quod habuerunt in advocatione ecclesie de Sandon' Londoniensis diocesis, necnon et ius quod habuerunt percipiendi annuatim unam marcam de eadem ecclesia, dicto Roberto de Scal' et heredibus suis remiserunt inperpetuum et quietum clamaverunt, ita quod idem Robertus et heredes sui libere et absolute ad eandem quotiens vacaverit valeant presentare, non obstante reclamatione monialium predictarum. Dictus vero Robertus advocationem ecclesie predicte de South Reynham, quam quondam Robertus de Scales pater dicti Roberti per cartam suam ipsis monialibus in puram et perpetuam elemosinam concesserat et carta sua confirmaverat, eisdem concessit et de se et heredibus suis inperpetuum quietam clamavit ecclesiam antedictam earum propriis usibus applicandam, ac de voluntate nostra super hoc petita et optenta applicatam perpetuis temporibus applicandam, salva in eadem vicaria per nos moderate taxanda, ad quam prefatus Robertus et heredes sui nobis et successoribus nostris personam ydoneam presentabunt, qui ad eorum presentationem debebit admitti. Dicte etiam moniales quemdam capellanum qui in domo sua de Blakebergh singulis diebus missam in honore beate Marie pro anima dicti Roberti, Clementie uxoris sue et animabus antecessorum et successorum suorum ad altare beate Marie celebrabit perpetuis temporibus sustentabunt, idemque capellanus sic[c] celebraturus dicto Roberto et heredibus suis presentabitur et de celebrando secundum formam canonicam prestabit iuratoriam cautionem. Quod si quandoque per negligentiam vel etiam culpam dictarum monialium idem capellanus in celebratione debita cessaverit, obligarunt se moniales predicte quod episcopus Norwicensis qui pro tempore fuerit vel archidiaconus [fo. 188r] vel etiam decanus loci, quemcumque horum iidem

Robertus et heredes sui elegerint, fructus dicte ecclesie libere valeat sequestare et tam diu sub sequestro suo tenere quousque de celebratione ipsa omissa vel etiam pretermissa pro animabus predictorum debita recompensatio sit impensa. Et si dictus capellanus ob aliquam causam legitimam a dicta domo debeat amoveri, alius qui loco suo succedet dicto Roberto et suis heredibus ut superius dictum est presentabitur et de celebrando cavebit. Ad plenam insuper et perpetuam securitatem premissorum memoratus Robertus fideliter promisit se cartam suam super concessione de prefata ecclesia de South Reynham facturum monialibus antedictis, in qua carta cum facta fuerit si aliquid fuerit emendandum de nostro consilio et provisione fideli liberaliter faciet emendari; nosque pro illis monialibus manucepimus illud idem, quod videlicet eidem cartam facient de premissis sibi concessis, in qua cum facta fuerit si aliquid remanserit emendandum de consilio amicorum suorum et nostra fideli provisione faciemus totaliter emendari. Insuper a partibus fideliter est promissum quod omnia premissa per cyrographum in curia domini regis coram iustitiis facient roborari, et nos hoc idem fideliter procurabimus et fieri faciemus. In cuius rei testimonium ad instantiam predictarum partium huic scripto sigillum nostrum duximus apponendum. Dat' London' sexto kalendas Aprilis anno incarnationis dominice millesimo CC^mo quinquagesimo septimo et pontificatus nostri anno tertiodecimo.

[a]eas B, C [b]etitit B [c]si B

In a final concord reached before the king's justices at Norwich on 26 July 1228 the prior of Castle Acre, defendant, quitclaimed to Robert de Scales and Thomas of Ingoldisthorpe, claimants, the whole advowson of South Raynham; they in return granted to the monks residing at Norman's Burrow in South Raynham 40s rent in that vill (fo. 186v of B). The advowson of the church of St Martin was granted to the nuns by Robert son of Roger de Scales, for the salvation of himself and Alice his wife, in the year of grace 1249 (ibid., fo. 185v). Robert son of Robert confirmed his father's grant, renouncing any resort to civil or ecclesiastical law even if, with the bp's consent, the nuns should appropriate the church, saving to himself and his heirs presentation to the vicarage to be taxed therein (ibid.). A further charter of Robert son of Robert records his concession of the advowson of the church, for the souls of himself and Isabelle, now his wife (ibid. fo. 187r). A charter of the prioress and convent records the undertaking, at the bp's mandate, that since Robert has confirmed to them the rights in South Raynham church granted by his father, they will maintain a chaplain to pray for him and Clementia his (presumably second) wife (ibid. fo. 188v). The exemplification by mr J. of Ferriby, the official, made on 24 March 1289, was because the condition of the documents had deteriorated through frequent use.

6. Blackborough Priory

Notification that, since he has granted to the nuns in proprios usus *the church of South Raynham, at the petition of the lord Robert de Scales, son and heir of the late lord Robert, of whose advowson the church was, saving a vicarage to be taxed by the bishop, to which Robert and his heirs should present at each vacancy, he has taxed a vicarage therein in this manner: the vicar shall have all the altarage of the church with all pertaining thereto, excepting the free land of the church with all its appurtenances and the free tenants of the church with their rents, services and all other appurtenances, and also escheats, and except also for the tithes of hay and of land sown with any sort of grain, which the nuns shall have in perpetuity. The vicar shall discharge all the ordinary obligations of the church, and extraordinary burdens shall be borne by nuns and vicar pro rata. The vicar shall each year on 29 December pay the nuns half a mark for a pittance, and on that day in perpetuity the obit of the lord Robert and his successors shall be celebrated.* Hevingham, 25 April 1257

B = BL ms. Egerton 3137 (Blackborough cartulary) fo. 187r (149r). s. xiii ex. C = ibid. fo. 187r–v (149r–v) (*inspeximus* by prior Simon and the convent of Norwich, 2 May 1257).

Universis Cristi fidelibus Walterus miseratione divina episcopus Norwicensis salutem in Domino sempiternam. Cum ecclesiam de South Reynham nostre dioceses dilectis in Cristo filiabus priorisse et conventui monialium de Blakebergh caritatis intuitu et etiam ad piam petitionem[a] domini Roberti de Scalis filii et heredis quondam domini Roberti de Scalis, de cuius patronatu ecclesia ipsa fuit, concesserimus in[b] proprios usus perpetuis temporibus possidendam, salva vicaria in eadem per nos taxanda ad quam dictus Robertus et heredes sui quotiens vacaverit nobis et successoribus nostris libere presentabunt, nos vicariam ipsam duximus sic taxandam: quod vicarius quicumque pro tempore fuerit in eadem habeat totum alteragium ipsius ecclesie cum omnibus ad illud provenientibus et etiam pertinentibus quoquomodo, exceptis libera terra eiusdem ecclesie cum omnibus suis pertinentibus, necnon et liberis[c] tenentibus ecclesie sepedicte cum eorum redditibus, servitiis et omnibus aliis suis pertinentiis et etiam eschaetis, exceptis etiam decimis feni et terrarum quocumque genere bladi semitarum, que omnia dictis monialibus libere inperpetuum remanebunt. Et idem vicarius omnia onera dictam ecclesiam contingentia, ordinaria videlicet, sustinebit; extraordinaria vero ab utrique[d] agnoscantur pro rata. Solvet insuper idem vicarius dictis monialibus annuatim dimidiam marcam argenti ad pitanciam die beati Thome archiepiscopi in natali, quo die obitum dicti domini Roberti et antecessorum et successorum suorum perpetuis temporibus solempniter facient annuatim. In cuius rei [e-][testimonium presenti scripto sigillum nostrum fecimus apponi].[-e] Dat' apud Hevyngham septem kalendas Maii pontificatus nostri anno tertiodecimo et anno Domini millesimo CC[mo] quinquagesimo septimo.

[a] petitionem *omitted* B, C   [b] et in B, C   [c] libere B, C   [d] utriusque B, C   [e-e] *omitted* B, C

See no. 5 above.

6A. Blackborough Priory

Notification that, in the presence of the bishop and also of the lord Robert de Scales, the nuns have solemnly undertaken to maintain in their house for all time

a chaplain, who shall every day celebrate a mass of the Blessed Virgin Mary for the souls of Robert, his ancestors and successors. The chaplain shall be chosen by the nuns and presented to Robert and his heirs, in whose presence he shall swear to fulfil this service. If the chaplain should be removed from the house because of incontinence or other dishonourable conduct, or because of perjury committed in failing to discharge this service, this should be done by mutual consent of Robert and his heirs and of the nuns, and if there is disagreement between them on this matter, he should, if there is due cause, be removed by the diocesan or the official. After his removal another should be appointed in the same manner and swear a similar oath, and this should be the case whenever there is a replacement. If, on the removal or the death of the chaplain, the nuns fail to choose a replacement and present him within a month to Robert and his successors at South Raynham, if they are there or nearby, then in that instance Robert and his heirs shall choose the chaplain and present him to the bishop. Sealed by the bishop, and also with the common seal of the prioress and convent.

Hevingham, 25 April 1257

B = BL ms. Egerton 3137 (Blackborough cartulary) fos. 188r–189v. s. xiii ex.

Universis Cristi fidelibus Walterus miseratione divina episcopus Norwicensis salutem in Domino sempiternam. Constitutis in presentia nostra domino Roberto de Scalis et priorissa et monialibus de Blakebergh, obligarunt se firmiter priorissa et moniales predicte quod perpetuis temporibus habebunt et etiam sustinebunt quemdam capellanum in domo sua de Blakebergh, missam in honore beate Marie virginis gloriose pro anima dicti Roberti et animabus omnium antecessorum et successorum suorum diebus singulis celebrantem; qui capellanus per moniales electus dicto Roberto et heredibus suis presentabitur et in ipsius vel heredum suorum presentia iuramentum prestabit quod fideliter, prout est ordinatum, servitium faciet antedictum. Quod si capellanus ipse propter incontinentiam vel aliam inhonestatem, vel etiam eo quod convictus fuerit legittime de periurio commisso pro servitio ipso non facto, a domo ipsa debeat amoveri, hoc de consensu fiat et consilio utriusque, tam videlicet dicti domini Roberti et heredum suorum quam etiam monialium predictarum; quod si super huiusmodi amotione inter ipsos dissentio exoriatur, per diocesanum qui pro tempore fuerit vel etiam officiarium loci, ratione licita, amoveatur; quo amoto, loco ipsius alius substituatur, qui sub forma prescripta dicto Roberto et heredibus suis presentabitur et iuramentum prestabit, et sic fiet de singulis substituendis ibidem. Et si contingat quod, amoto vel etiam mortuo capellano ipso, moniales ipse alium infra mensem eligere neglexerint et domino Roberto et heredibus suis apud Southreynham, si ibidem vel ibi prope fuerint, presentare, si per ipsas steterit quo minus presentetur, tunc Robertus memoratus et heredes sui ea vice eligent capellanum et episcopo presentabunt. Et ne hoc iudicium valeat inposterum revocari, [fo. 189v] tam sigillum nostrum quam et commune sigillum dictarum priorisse et monialium presentibus est appensum. Actum apud

Hevyngham septimo kalendas Maii pontificatus nostri [anno] tertiodecimo et anno Domini millesimo CC^{mo} quinquagesimo septimo.

See no. 5 above.

7. Blythburgh Priory

Confirmation for the canons of the great and lesser tithes of Roger de Wymplis and of all his men in the vill of Thorington and of two-thirds of the great tithe of the whole fee of Roger de Money in Stoven and Wickham [Market], which they have by the concession and alms of their predecessors.

[19 February 1245 × 19 May 1257]

B = BL ms. Add. 40725 (Blythburgh cartulary) fo. 55r–v. s. xiv ex. C = ibid. fo. 55v (*inspeximus* by prior Simon and the convent of Norwich).
Pd from B and C in *Blythburgh Cartulary* ii no. 421.

Omnibus sancte matris ecclesie filiis ad quod presens scriptum pervenerit Walterus Dei gratia Norwicensis episcopus salutem in Domino. Cum ex officio pastorali nos deceat de grege nobis commisso sic esse solicitos ut sicud ei spirituale triticum erogare tenemur, ita subditis nostris et viris maxime religiosis qui vel minus sufficienter sunt fundati vel qui pia fidelium largitione victui necessaria competenter minime sunt assecuti providere debeamus, ut quod ex donis sibi subvenientium sunt adepti secura tranquillitate possideant et per nostre sollicitudinis amminiculum maiora melius et facilius adquirant, ad universitatis vestre volumus notitiam pervenire nos, considerata sacre religionis honestate que in domo de Blybur tam laudabiliter quam habunde^a Dei gratia vigere dinoscitur, pensataque facultatum tenuitate quas possident hii qui in eadem divino famulatui perseveranter intendunt, omnes decimas Rogeri de Wymplis et omnium hominum suorum tam maiores quam minutas in villa de Thoritone et decimas duarum garbarum de toto feodo Rogeri de Money in Wycham et in Stowene quas habent ex collatione et elemosina predecessorum suorum eisdem canonicis duximus misericorditer confirmandas. Et ut hec nostra confirmatio maiorem optineat firmitatem, eam presentis scripti serie et sigilli nostri appositione corroboravimus. Hiis testibus: magistro Roberto de Insula archidiacono Colcestrie,^b magistro Willelmo.

^a habude B   ^b B *ends here*

For the Wymplis, or Thorington, family see *Blythburgh Cartulary* i 15–16; for the Money family, ibid. 12–13, and for a confirmation of these tithes by Roger de Money, ibid. ii no. 403.

8. Burton Abbey

Mandate, issued as executor of the business of the cross appointed by the apostolic see, to the subprior and those of the chapter under oath that, whereas they had lately sworn to make an estimate, free from fraud, of all the immovable possessions of their house, greater and lesser, excluding the revenues of their parish churches, which are to be estimated by the rural deans, and except for revenues in the king's hands during a vacancy, they should now, in obedience to the apostolic see and under oath, make a full estimate and commit it to writing, fully and clearly, in sealed letters patent.   [Summer – Autumn 1254]

> B = BL ms. Cotton Vesp. E iii (Burton chronicle) fo. 46r. s.xiii ex.
> Pd from B in *Ann. mon.* i 326–7.

Walterus permissione divina episcopus Norwicensis etc. discretis viris subpriori de Burthonia et iuratis de capitulo salutem in Domino. Cum sacramentum nuper prestiteritis super estimatione omnium bonorum immobilium ad ecclesiam vestram spectantium, maiorum et minorum, absque fraude facienda, exceptis proventibus ecclesiarum parochialium quas habetis, qui per decanos debent estimari, et exceptis bonis que sunt in manu domini regis tempore vacationis, vobis in virtute obedientie qua sedi apostolice tenemini et sub religione sacramenti prestiti iniungimus quatenus, in hac parte fideliter vos habentes, que sit iusta estimatio omnium bonorum vestrorum supradictorum in scriptis fideliter redigatis, et illam estimationem plene, plane et dilucide per literam patentem sigillo capituli signatam, nobis habere faciatis ad diem et locum infrascriptos. Damus etc. Contradictores etc. Consulimus etc. Predictas autem estimationes etc. ut supra.

> For the form of this letter, see no. 126 below. The collectors published their commission in London of 4 July 1254 (63A), and the king had hoped for collection of the first year's tenth by Michaelmas (29 September); but the mandate to Canons Ashby priory (16) was not delivered until 11 November 1254. For other similar letters, see nos 34, 82, 126. See also intro. p. lviii.

9. Bury St Edmunds Abbey

Notification that, with the consent of his cathedral chapter and of the abbot and convent of St Edmunds, he has taxed a vicarage in the church of Woolpit, which is appropriated to the abbot and convent. The vicar shall receive all the revenues of the church, in great and lesser tithes, oblations, free land and all other appurtenances, saving to the monks an annual pension of twenty marks, to be paid in equal instalments at the two Ipswich synods. The vicar shall discharge all customary obligations of the church, including those to bishop and archdeacon. The abbot and convent have accepted this taxation, notwithstanding prior custom or any documents hitherto obtained from any source. They shall present freely to the vicarage whenever it falls vacant.   Thorpe, 12 April 1246

B = CUL ms. Mm iv 19 (register of *vestiarius*) fo. 144r (later addition). s. xiii med. C = BL ms.
  Cotton Claud. A xii (hostiller's register) fo. 87r–v (10r–v, 84r–v). s. xv in.
Pd from C in *Memorials of St Edmunds* iii 81–2.

Omnibus Cristi fidelibus has litteras visuris vel audituris Walterus Dei gratia
Norwicensis episcopus eternam in Domino salutem. Noveritis nos de consensu
capituli nostri in ecclesia de Wlpet,[a] venerabilibus viris abbati et conventui de
sancto Eadmundo[b] appropriata, vicariam de consensu dictorum abbatis et
conventus in hunc modum taxasse, videlicet quod vicarius dicte ecclesie qui pro
tempore fuerit percipiet omnia ad dictam ecclesiam[c] pertinentia seu undecumque
provenientia, in decimis maioribus et minoribus,[d] oblationibus, libera terra et
omnibus aliis ad dictam ecclesiam quocumque modo pertinentibus, salvis
supradictis abbati et conventui viginti marcis annuis nomine pensionis a vicario
eiusdem ecclesie qui pro tempore fuerit ad duos terminos solvendis, videlicet ad
unam synodum de Gipewico[e] decem marcis et ad aliam synodum decem marcis.
Sustinebit etiam dictus vicarius omnia onera[f] eiusdem ecclesie episcopalia,
archidiaconalia et omnia alia debita et consueta. Dicti autem abbas et conventus
hanc nostram taxationem, non obstante aliqua consuetudine prius habita, non
obstantibus etiam aliquibus instrumentis a quocumque prius obtentis,
acceptaverunt et ei expresse consenserunt, salva dictis abbati et conventui futuris
temporibus libera presentatione ad dictam vicariam quotienscumque eam vacare
contigerit. In cuius rei testimonium presenti scripto sigillum nostrum et sigillum
capituli nostri fecimus apponi. Hiis[g] testibus: magistro Laurentio de Sumercote,[h]
magistro Ada[j] de Bromholm,[k] domino Iohanne de Holcham capellano nostro,
Willelmo de Pakeham, Hugone de Correbrigg,[l] Willelmo de Ludham clericis.
Dat' apud Thorp pridie idus Aprilis anno gratie millesimo ducentesimo
X°L sexto.[m]

  [a] Wolpet C   [b] Edmundo C   [c] quocumque modo pertinentibus *deleted* B   [d] et C
  [e] Gyppewyco C   [f] honera B   [g] His C   [h] Somerton C   [j] Adam B   [k] Bromholme C
  [l] Corbrigge C   [m] millesimo CC^mo quadragesimo sexto C

For a summary of the earlier history of Woolpit church, see *EEA* 6 no. 335. In 1211 the church
was appropriated to the monks by bp Gray by authority of an indult of pope Alexander III; the
vicar was to have an annual income of 10 marks (£6 13s 4d) (ibid. nos. 325–6). Despite bp
Suffield's taxation, which was presumably designed to augment the value of the vicarage, it
was in 1254 valued at only £2, while the monks' portion was assessed at 20 marks (£13 6s 8d)
(*VN* 425). On 17 March 1261 the vicar acknowledged before bp Walton that he was two years
in arrears with payments of the monks' pension, but the monks, out of compassion for his
straitened circumstances, reduced these arrears from 40 marks to 15 marks, and he promised
henceforth to make payment in full (below, Appx 2. 242). In 1291 the vicar's portion was
assessed at the increased valuation of 10 marks, and the monks' portion was divided between
obedientiaries, the infirmarer and pittancer receiving £6 each and the hostiller £1 6s 8d (*Taxatio*
119b). In 1325 the pension had again fallen into arrears by two years, and on this occasion there
was resort to formal litigation, the monks appealing to Rome, and for tuition to the court of
Canterbury, against Roger Chauncelere, who is described as rector rather than vicar, and who
adopted an aggressive rather than apologetic tone. From the testimony of one witness, Woolpit
had reverted to the status of a rectory more than forty-one years before, that is before 1284,
when he had first known a rector whom he had not seen instituted, but who is described as the
first rector; afterwards he had seen two rectors instituted, and they had all paid the pension,

until Chauncelere refused to render it to 'country bumpkins' (*rusticis*) (*Memorials of St Edmunds* iii 84–96, 105–112, a long account of the preliminary pleading). In 1331 a new rector recognised his obligation to pay the pension, as did his successor in 1346, after a protestation saving the rights of his rectory (ibid. 96–101). There was, however, a further dispute as to liability in 1402, when again the arrears amounted to two years; these were halved by agreement after litigation in King's Bench (ibid. 101–5).

10. Bury St Edmunds Abbey

Licence for the monks to celebrate divine office in their chapel at Pakenham whenever any of them may be present there.   [Great] Barton, 15 March 1251

B = TNA, DL 42/5 (cellarer's cartulary) fo. 55v (36v). s. xiii ex.

Omnibus etc. Walterus Dei gratia Norwicensis episcopus salutem. Noverit universitas vestra nos viris venerabilibus monachis sancti Eadmundi in capella curie eorum de Pakeham, cum aliquis eorum ibidem[a] fuerit, divina celebrandi liberam in Domino concessisse facultatem, salvis in omnibus ecclesie matricis indempnitate et nostre Norwicensis ecclesie dignitate. In cuius rei testimonium huic scripto sigillum nostrum fecimus apponi. Dat' apud Berton' idibus Martii anno Domini M°CC° quinquagesimo.

[a] ibidem *om.* B

The manor of Pakenham was valued at £40 13s 9d in 1268 (*VN* 541). In 1291 the cellarer's temporalities there were assessed at £62 14s 0½d (*Bury Chron.* 108). For the parish church, see no. 141 below.

10A. Bury St Edmunds Abbey

Licence for the monks to celebrate divine office in their chapel at Stanton whenever any of them may be present there.   [Great] Barton, 15 March 1251

B = BL, Add. ms. 4699 (Bury register of Stanton evidences) fo. 10v. s. xiii ex.

Omnibus Cristi fidelibus presens scriptum visuris vel audituris Walterus Dei gratia Norwycensis episcopus salutem in Domino sempiternam. Noverit universitas vestra nos viris venerabilibus monachis sancti Edmundi in capella infra septa curie eorum de Stanton sita, cum aliquis eorum ibidem fuerit, divina celebrandi liberam in Domino concessisse facultatem, salvis in omnibus ecclesie matricis indempnitate et nostre Norwycensis ecclesie dignitate. In cuius rei testimonium presenti scripto sigillum nostrum fecimus apponi. Dat' apud Berton' idibus Martii anno Domini millesimo CC^{mo} quinquagesimo.

Stanton was a manor of the chamberlain, assessed at £4 for the tenth in 1254 and at £10 10s 3d in 1291; the almoner and the hospital of St Saviour also had revenues there (*Bury Chronicle* 43–4, 105, 110).

11. Butley Priory

Confirmation by the bishop-elect of agreement between the canons of Butley on one part and William, rector of Stoke [Ash], on the other, concerning the demesne tithes of Robert of Kenton, knight, in Debenham and Kenton. The canons asserted that by the common law [of the church] the tithes pertained to the churches of Debenham and Kenton, the rector that they pertained to his church of Stoke [Ash] which had been in possession thereof from time immemorial. Eventually, through the bishop's mediation and with the consent of the monks of Eye, patrons of Stoke [Ash], it was resolved that the canons should receive the said tithes in perpetuity and without contradiction, but should pay the rector thirty shillings a year in two instalments at the Suffolk synods, on pain of twenty shillings for the bishop's use if at any term payment should not be made; and if eight days after any synod and after a third demand the canons have not paid that instalment, then they shall forfeit these tithes, which shall be assigned to the rector. Both parties under oath bound their successors to the observance of this composition, and the bishop pronounced sentence of excommunication against any who might contravene it. Sealed by the bishop, the two priors and the rector.   Ipswich, 2 January 1245

B = Essex R. O., D/DBy. Q19 (Eye priory cartulary) fo. 30r–v. s.xiii ex.
Pd in *Eye Cartulary* i no. 49.

Walterus miseratione divina Norwicensis electus universis Cristi fidelibus presens scriptum visuris vel audituris salutem eternam in Domino. Notum vobis facimus quod cum[a] inter priorem et conventum de Buttele ex una parte et magistrum Willelmum rectorem ecclesie de Stok' ex altera super decimis de dominico Roberti de Kenigtun' militis in villa de Debeham et de Kenigtun' questio esset suborta, dictis priore et conventu proponentibus prefatas [fo. 30v] decimas ad ecclesias suas de Debeham et de Kenigtun' de iure communi pertinere, supradicto rectore in contrarium asserente easdem decimas ad ecclesiam suam de Stok' spectare et eandem ecclesiam in possessione illarum decimarum extitisse a tempore a quo non extat memoria, tandem post altercationes hinc inde et intermedia habita nobis mediantibus, interveniente etiam consensu prioris et conventus de Eya patronorum dicte ecclesie de Stok', lis inter eos mota amicabiliter quievit et in forma perpetue pacis est consensum in hunc modum: videlicet quod dicti prior et conventus de Buttel' sine aliqua contradictione recipient dictas decimas perpetuo et pacifice possidebunt. Solvent autem iidem prior et conventus de Buttele supradicto rectori ecclesie de Stok' et eius successoribus inperpetuum triginta solidos annuatim, videlicet in synodo Pasche Gipewic' quindecim solidos et in synodo sancti Michaelis quindecim solidos, sub pena viginti solidorum ad opus domini Norwicensis episcopi si aliquis terminus pretereat insolutus; et si post lapsum octo dierum post synodum memorati prior et conventus de Buttele tertio requisiti ac congrue interpellati supradictam pecuniam non solverint, ex tunc cadent a possessione dictarum decimarum prefato rectori et eius successoribus assignanda. Hanc autem compositionem fideliter observare predictus rector tam pro se quam pro suis successoribus corporali prestito sacramento firmiter promisit, supradicti autem prior et conventus ad eandem compositionem inperpetuum observandam per procuratores ad hoc specialiter datos corporali iuramento interveniente se obligaverunt. Nos autem predictam compositionem auctoritate Norwicensis ecclesie confirmavimus, et omnes illos excommunicationis sententia innodamus qui contra eam inposterum aliquid attemptaverint. In cuius rei testimonium una cum[b] predictis prioribus et eorum conventibus de Buttel' et de Eya necnon et supradicto rectore ecclesie de Stok' huic scripto sigilla nostra apposuimus. Acta sunt hec coram nobis apud Gipewicum quarto nonas Ianuarii anno Domini M⁰ CC⁰ X⁰L V⁰. Testibus: magistro Herveo de Fakeham, domino Thoma le Bigot, magistro Willelmo de Horham, magistro Ada de Bromhelm, domino Roberto de Beccles canonico Cicestr', Ricardo de Ribof et Henrico de Bodekesham clericis, magistro Willelmo Ponscum, Willelmo de Bramford capellano.

[a] cum *interlined* B   [b] cum *repeated, first expunged* B

For a brief history of Stoke Ash church, see *Eye Cartulary* ii 49–50. The reason for the rector's interest in these tithes is unclear, but probably stems from the fact that Robert Malet, who gave Stoke Ash church to his foundation at Eye, also held portions in the churches of Debenham and Kenton (*DB* ii 305a-b, 326a).

12. Butley Priory

Grant to the canons in proprios usus *of the church of St Peter, Little Worlingham.*   [24 February 1247 × 11 September 1248]

B = Bodl. ms. Suffolk ch. (a. 2) 190 (*inspeximus* by prior Simon and convent of Norwich, 11 September 1248). s.xiii med.
Pd in *Leiston Cartulary* no. 154.

Omnibus Cristi fidelibus ad quos presens scriptum pervenerit Walterus de Suffeld Dei gratia Norwicensis episcopus salutem in Domino. Ad omnium volumus notitiam pervenire nos causa Dei et religionis favore concessisse, dedisse et presenti carta confirmasse ecclesie sancte Marie de Buttel' et canonicis ibidem Deo servientibus, in puram et perpetuam elemosinam et in proprios usus perpetuo possidendam, ecclesiam de Parva Werlingham sancti Petri cum omnibus ad eam pertinentibus, salva in omnibus et per omnia reverentia et obedientia sancte Norwicensis ecclesie. Et ut hec nostra concessio, donatio et carte nostre confirmatio perpetuam optineat firmitatem, eam presenti scripto [et] sigilli nostri munimine corroboravimus. Hiis testibus: magistro Willelmo de Horham archidiacono Suff', magistro R. de Insula archidiacono Colecestr', magistro Herveo de Fakeham, Adam de Wrthested', Willelmo de Whithewell', Thoma capellano et aliis.

Mr William of Horham occurs without title in the bp's retinue on 24 February 1247 (no. 21 below; *Fasti* ii 68).

Domesday Book (ii 283) records two and a half churches in Worlingham. The present church is dedicated to All Saints. The site of St Peter's was in 1975 rediscovered during road making, just inside the parish boundary of North Cove, with which it was consolidated, being abandoned soon after 1474 (Cautley, *Suffolk Churches* 435). In both 1254 and 1291 it was valued at £2 (*VN* 461; *Taxatio* 118).

13. Butley Priory

Notification that the bishop has inspected the charter of William Raleigh, his predecessor, concerning the taxation of the church of Upton, from which he has learned that of the eighteen acres in the vill pertaining to the church which master Hugh of Upton is to hold by special concession of the canons, half should after his death go to increase the vicar's portion. Considering, however, the canons' religion, honest life and devout preoccupation with divine service, and also their hospitality and charity, he now by episcopal authority assigns the said eighteen acres after master Hugh's death to the canons' portion, and ordains that they shall each year, on the feast of St Margaret, pay five shillings to the vicar for the time being.   [24 February 1247 × 11 September 1248]

B = Bodl. ms. Suffolk ch. (a. 2) 190 (*inspeximus* by prior Simon and convent of Norwich, 11 September 1248). s. xiii med.
Pd in *Leiston Cartulary* no. 154.

Universis Cristi fidelibus ad quos presens [scriptum] pervenerit Walterus de Suffeld' Dei gratia Norwicensis episcopus salutem in Domino. Ad universorum notitiam volumus pervenire nos cartam venerabilis patris Willelmi de Raleheg predecessoris nostri super taxatione vicarie ecclesie de Upton' confectam inspexisse, ex cuius tenore perpendimus octodecim acrarum terre in villa de Upton ad dictam ecclesiam spectantium quas magister Hugo de Upton de prioris et conventus de Buttele concessione speciali possidebit, medietatem post dicti magistri decessum vicarii qui pro tempore fuerit accrescere debere portioni.[a] Vero dictorum prioris et conventus religionem, honestatem et assiduam in obsequiis divinis devotionem, necnon hospitalitatem et caritatis largitatem attendentes, dictas octodecim acras post decessum dicti magistri Hugonis eorundem prioris et conventus portioni quam habent in dicta ecclesia episcopali auctoritate intuitu caritatis totaliter assignamus, concedimus et confirmamus, ita tamen quod dicti prior et conventus quinque solidos sterlingorum post decessum dicti magistri vicario qui pro tempore fuerit annuatim die sancte Margarete in perpetuum persolvent. Et ut hec nostra assignatio, concessio et confirmatio perpetuam optineant firmitatem, eas presenti scripto et sigilli nostri appositione corroboravimus. Hiis testibus: magistro Willelmo de Horham archidiacono Suff', magistro Roberto de Insula archidiacono Colecestr', magistro Herveo de Fakeham, Adam de Wrthestede, Willelmo de Whitewell, Thoma capellano et aliis.

^a portione B

Mr William of Horham occurs without title in the bp's retinue on 24 February 1247 (no. 21 below; *Fasti* ii 68).

In 1254 the church, and in 1291 the canons' portion apart from the vicarage, was valued at £16 13s 4d, and in 1254 the vicarage was assessed at 13s 4d (*VN* 366; *Taxatio* 78b).

14. Caen, Abbey of Holy Trinity

Confirmation for abbess Johanna and the convent of a benefice of five and a half marks, payable in instalments at the two Norwich synods, which from times long past they have been accustomed to receive in the church of Horstead.

Terling, 26 March 1245

> B = Caen, Archives dép. du Calvados, H 32 (cartulary of English possessions of the abbey). s. xiii ex.

Universis Cristi fidelibus has litteras visuris vel audituris Walterus miseratione divina Norwicensis episcopus eternam in Domino salutem. Etsi votivum sit nobis singulis religiosis nos reddere gratiosos, ipsis gratia prosequi speciali que in sexu fragili constitute et Deo venerabiliter famulantur. Cum Iohanna dilecta in Cristo filia abbatissa et conventus de Cadomo a multis retro temporibus quinque marcas et dimidiam ad duas synodos Norwicenses solvendas in ecclesia de Horsted nostre diocesis percipere consueverint, nos dictis abbatisse et conventui, quas ob religionis sue favorem insuper et multimodam earundem probitatem intra viscera gerimus caritatis, gratiam volentes facere specialem, dictum beneficium eis auctoritate pontificali perpetuo confirmamus. In cuius rei testimonium presenti scripto sigillum nostrum duximus apponendum. Datum apud Terling' .vii. kalendas Aprilis anno Domini millesimo ducentesimo quadragesimo quinto.

> The manor of Horstead was confirmed to the nuns in 1131 by King Henry I as a gift of his brother William Rufus (*Regesta* ii no. 1692). The nuns' benefice or portion in the church was valued at 5 marks (£3 13s 4d) in 1291, when the residue of the church was recorded at £13 6s 8d; the profits of the manor received by the nuns were then estimated at £20 10s 6½d (*Taxatio* 78b, 100). For surveys of the manor, see Chibnall, *Charters and Custumals of the Abbey of Holy Trinity, Caen* 36, 51–5. According to the list of abbesses (ibid. 139–40), the abbess in 1245 was not Johanna, but Juliana de Saint-Sernin, who did fealty for the English lands in 1237, occurs in 1261 and died not later than 1266. There were probably two abbesses called Johanna in the period from 1183 to 1230.

15. Cambridge, St Radegund's Priory

Indulgence of twenty-five days of enjoined penance granted to contributors to the building of the priory church or the upkeep of the nuns, to be valid in perpetuity.

Cambridge, 13 August 1254

> A = Jesus College Cambridge muniments, Gray 11, Caryl A7. No endorsement; approx. 154 × 59 + 11 mm., badly stained; parchment tag, seal missing.

Pd (calendar) in Gray, *The Priory of St Radegund, Cambridge* 79.

Omnibus Cristi fidelibus ad quos presentes littere pervenerint Walterus miseratione divina Norwicensis episcopus salutem in Domino sempiternam. De Dei omnipotentis misericordia et gloriose virginis Marie omniumque sanctorum meritis confidentes, omnibus parochianis nostris et aliis quorum diocesani hanc nostram indulgentiam ratam habuerint qui de bonis sibi a Deo collatis ad constructionem seu sustentationem ecclesie et monialium sancte Radegundis in Cantebrig' aliqua pie contulerint subsidia caritatis viginti et quinque dies de iniuncta sibi penitentia misericorditer relaxamus pre-[sent]ibus[a] perpetuis temporibus duraturis. Dat' apud Cantebrig' idus Augusti anno Domini MCCL quarto et pontificatus nostri anno decimo.

[a] Reading conjectural

The church of St Radegund's priory largely survives as the chapel of Jesus College, Cambridge.

16. Canons Ashby Priory

Letter, as executor of the business of the crusade, to the cellarer, sacrist and sworn men of the chapter, to the effect that, since he recently received from them a sworn undertaking that they would provide an assessment of the income from the priory's rents, lands and other immoveable goods, except for the revenues of its parish churches, which are to be assessed by the rural deans, he enjoins them, in virtue of obedience, to reduce this estimate to writing, to be delivered to him or to his representative at St James's abbey, Northampton, on 14 December. He warns them to render a true account, notwithstanding previous estimates, lest subsequently others may find them to have been untruthful, and thus to have incurred the sentence of excommunication promulgated by the apostolic see against those wittingly reducing or not paying the tenth.

Sulby, 11 November 1254

B = BL ms. Egerton 3033 (Canons Ashby cartulary) fo. 7v (13v). s. xiii ex.

Walterus permissione divina Norwicensis episcopus, negotii crucis executor a sede apostolica deputatus, discretis viris celerario et sacriste de Esseby et iuratis de capitulo salutem in Domino. Cum nuper a vobis sacramentum recepimus super estimatione proventuum vestrorum terrarum, reddituum, censuum et omnium aliorum bonorum vestrorum immobilium ad ecclesiam vestram spectantium, maiorum et minorum, absque fraude facienda, exceptis proventibus ecclesiarum parochialium quas habetis, qui per decanum debent estimari, vobis in virtute obedientie qua sedi apostolice tenemini et sub religione sacramenti prefati iniungimus quatinus in hac parte fideliter vos habentes que sit estimatio omnium bonorum vestrorum supradictorum in scriptis fideliter redigatis et illam estimationem plene, plane et dilucide per scripturam sigillo capituli vestri sigillatam nobis habere faciatis ad diem et locum infrascriptos. Consulimus insuper ad vestram salutem et communem liberationem quod in taxationibus faciendis sic diligentes et veraces sollicitudine et facto vos habeatur, non obstantibus aliquibus taxationibus prehabitis, ne ex postfacto alii facta vestra et dicta scrutantes vos inveniant a via veritatis manifeste declinasse et in sententiam excommunicationis incidisse, quam per sedem apostolicam in omnes illos qui scienter in dicta decima subtrahenda vel non solvenda fraudem commiserint promulgari demandatur. Predictas autem estimationes in scriptis fideliter redactas nobis vel certo nuntio nostro sigillo capituli vestri signatas in abbatia sancti Iacobi iuxta Norhampton in crastino sancte Lucie habere faciatis. Dat' apud Suleby .iii. Idus Novembris anno gratie M° CC° L° quarto.

See intro., p. lviii.

17. Canterbury, Christ Church Cathedral Priory

Letter, as bishop-elect, thanking the prior and convent for the grant of licence that he might be consecrated elsewhere than in their cathedral church, anywhere he might wish other than in his own cathedral, with the promise that no prejudice shall arise therefrom to their church. Terling, December 1244

B = Canterbury D. & C. register A (prior's register) fo. 76v. s. xiv med. C = ibid., Ch. Ant. C120 (roll of *cautiones*) m. 7. s. xv in.

Viris venerabilibus et discretis priori et conventui sancte Trinitatis Cantuariensis Walterus miseratione divina Norwicensis electus salutem eternam in[a] Domino. Quoniam de gratia speciali nobis concessistis extra ecclesiam vestram ubicumque voluerimus, nostra ecclesia excepta, consecrari, anime[b] nostre gratias referimus quas valemus firmiter,[c] promittentes quod occasione huius libere concessionis vestre nullum vobis vel ecclesie vestre inposterum preiudicium generabitur. In cuius rei testimonium has litteras nostras vobis fecimus patentes. Dat' apud Terlinghe anno Domini M° CC° XLIIII° mense Decembris.

[a] in *interlined* C   [b] gratie B   [c] firmas C

The venue for the consecration of the suffragans of Canterbury had recently, but only from the late twelfth century, been a highly contentious issue, largely because it was associated in the monks' minds with the plans of the archbps to establish a secular collegiate church. In 1191 the Canterbury chronicler records that the papal legate was persuaded that consecration should not take place other than in Christ Church (*Gervase* i 487). Archbp Stephen Langton, however, had consecrated four suffragans in his cathedral church (and none after 1219), compared with fifteen consecrated elsewhere. The issue came to a head in 1235, when archbp Edmund consecrated the new bps of Lincoln (Robert Grosseteste) and St Asaph at Reading; the monks obtained a pledge from the archbp that consecration of bps *alibi* was only permissible with their consent, and on 20 November 1235 they obtained papal confirmation of this right (*Reg. Greg. IX* no. 2840; *CPL* i 149). However, when Edmund was at the *curia* to defend the archbp's rights against the monks, he obtained, on 14 April 1238, a papal indult allowing him to consecrate bps outside Canterbury when urgent need so dictated, notwithstanding his own concession to the monks, twice confirmed by the pope (*Reg. Greg. IX* no. 4339; *CPL* i 192). It was around this time too, on 17 May 1238, that the pope informed the legate Otto in England that the archbp had sought permission to found and endow a collegiate church (at Maidstone), but that the monks' proctors, predictably, vehemently opposed this (*Reg. Greg. IX* no. 4345; *CPL* i 173). It was probably in the early stages of this conflict with their archbp that the monks produced the *Magna Carta Beati Thome*, of which clause IX refers to the monks' right to insist on consecration of suffragan bps in their church. It is highly likely that Robert Grosseteste had seen this spurious charter of Becket before his consecration in June 1235, and there is a definite reference to it in the *libellus* of the monks presented to papal judges delegate, which was drawn up before 10 May 1236. For a full discussion of this dispute, and an edition of the main texts, see C.R. Cheney, 'Magna Carta Beati Thome: another Canterbury Forgery', *BIHR* 36 (1963), 1–26; repr. *Medieval Texts and Studies* (Oxford 1973), 78–110, where for consecrations, see pp. 88–9, 91, 95–6. Coming so soon after the consecration by the pope of a new archbp, Boniface of Savoy, on 15 January 1245, the site of Suffield's consecration was obviously a matter of some importance, and the form adopted, of a request for consecration *alibi*, granted by the monks of Canterbury on condition that a *cautio* safeguarding their rights was issued by the new bp, became the norm. In fact, the last bp of Norwich to have been consecrated at Christ Church was Everard in 1121 (*EEA* 6 370–1,373, 375; *EEA* 21 178, 180). There was further contention between archbp and monks on this issue in 1284, under archbp Pecham. For later practice, see *Canterbury Administration*, i 273–5, where evidence is cited that payment was made for the licence *alibi*.

17A. Canterbury, Christ Church Cathedral Priory

Pledge by the bishop that the licence granted by the prior and convent that he might be consecrated elsewhere than in their cathedral church, that is at Carrow outside Norwich, should in no way redound to their prejudice in future as regards the consecration of suffragans of their metropolitan church.

Norwich, 20 February 1245

B = Canterbury D. & C. register A (prior's register) fo. 76v. s. xiv med. C = ibid., Ch. Ant. C120 (roll of *cautiones*) m. 7. s. xv in.

Walterus Dei gratia Norwicensis episcopus venerabilibus viris priori et capitulo ecclesie Cristi Cantuariensis salutem in Domino. Cum in[a] metropolitana ecclesia vestra Cantuariensi eiusdem suffragenei munus consecrationis a longe retro temporibus consueverint optinere, et vos de gratia vestra speciali, ob quasdam causas que vobis ad hoc pro nobis plurimum inducebant, concesseritis nobis ad instantiam nostram extra ecclesiam vestram Cantuariensem, scilicet apud Karhowe extra Norwicum, consecrari, nos, qui prefatam ecclesiam Cantuariensem tamquam metropolitanam nostram in omnibus revereri[b] volumus ac devotum obsequium impendere eidem optamus, volumus et protestamur quod occasione consecrationis nostre apud locum predictum celebrate nullum vobis aut ecclesie vestre Cantuariensi circa consecrationes suffraganeorum ipsius ecclesie preiudicium generetur inposterum, sed omnia iura, consuetudines et possessiones que in consecrationibus suffraganeorum Cantuariensis ecclesie habere dinoscimini vobis sint salva et illesa. In cuius rei testimonium sigillum nostrum huic scripto apponi fecimus. Dat' anno Domini M° CC^{mo} XLIIII° apud Norwicum decimo kalendas Martii.

^a in *om.* B   ^b venereri C

This letter is crucial in determining the date of Suffield's consecration. Since it is issued as bp, rather than bp-elect, the date of 26 February 1245 given in the Waverley annals (*Ann. mon.* ii 336), as preferred in *Fasti* ii 57, cannot be correct. It is almost certain that the consecration was celebrated (as stated in *Chron. Bury* 13) on 19 February 1245, and that this cautio was issued the following day. Suffield was consecrated by Fulk Basset, bp of London, in the absence abroad of archbp Boniface (Stubbs, *Reg. Sacr. Angl.* 41; *Chron Maj.* iv 261, 378).

18. Canterbury, Christ Church Cathedral Priory

Notification that the bishop has caused to be recorded the actions of B[oniface], archbishop-elect of Canterbury, in his cathedral church, which he himself witnessed. When the elect came to the chapter, all the officials surrendered their offices, and those who had them their keys, which he took back to his own chamber and handed to one of his lay servants. As regards appointment of the prior, he commanded those present in chapter, on pain of excommunication, that they should nominate no person through grace or favour, but only if they should believe him to be suitable. All then left the chapter, and he asked each monk individually whom he considered most suitable, and he himself wrote on tablets what each said, so that nobody might know what was said or by whom; but a monk sitting some distance away wrote down the names of those examined and those nominated, by means of signs and figures, as an aide-memoire for the elect, who alone knew the meaning of this code. Boniface then departed, and that night in his chamber at Wingham, in the presence of his council, he read aloud the monks' depositions and discussed whom he might elevate to the priorate, with more regard to his own perception and to the good of the house than to the statements. Having decided with his council to appoint Nicholas of Sandwich, next day he returned to chapter and nominated and appointed him; he then rose, began to chant 'Miserere mei Deus', entered the church and installed the prior. As regards the appointment of officials, he summoned to his chamber the prior and some monks chosen by himself and discussed appointments, and then once more entered chapter and nominated and appointed whom he wished to the obediences. Some, including the subprior, he restored of his own volition to their former offices; and at this time he appointed prior, subprior, precentor, cellarer, chamberlain, sacrist and internal and external penitentiaries. These things were done at Canterbury on 25 October 1244 and the two days following. In witness whereof both the bishop and the archdeacon of Canterbury, who saw all this, have appended their seals, as they did to the writings of the archbishop-elect and to the monks' statements. [19 February 1245 × 1248]

B = Lambeth Palace Library, ms. 1212 (register of the see of Canterbury) fos. 58v–59r (pp. 112–13). s. xiii ex. C = ibid., register of archbp Thomas Arundel, fo. 15r. s. xv in.
Pd from C in *Anglia Sacra* i 174–5.

Omnibus presentes litteras inspecturis Walterus miseratione divina Norwycensis episcopus salutem in Domino. Quoniam humane fragilitatis tam infirma est conditio quod ea que in presenti vita aguntur a memoria cito decidunt, et non perraro oblivionis tenebris obumbrantur, quedam que per venerabilem fratrem B. Dei gratia Cantuariensem electum in ecclesia Cantuariensi fieri vidimus ad perpetuam eius rei memoriam in scriptis duximus annotanda. In primis vidimus ipsum ingredi capitulum, quo omnes officiales sua deposuerunt officia, et qui claves habebant eas eidem reddiderunt, et vidimus prefatum dominum electum deferre claves ipsorum usque ad cameram suam et eas tradere cuidam laico servienti suo seculari. In creatione prioris sic procedebat: in primis omnibus de conventu in capitulo presentibus inhibuit in virtute obedientie et sub pena excommunicationis ne quis eorum quemquam sibi nominaret gratia vel favore nisi quem crederet ydoneum ad regimen prioratus. Post hec, omnibus exeuntibus capitulum, omnes sigillatim requisivit, interrogando unumquemque sic: quid tibi videtur magis ydoneus ad regimen prioratus; et ipsemet electus propria manu in tabulis[a] scribebat dicta singulorum, ita quod nullus monachus quid a quo diceretur prescire valeret. Verum quidam monachus sedens a remotis scribebat nomina examinatorum et personas nominatas, nunc per signa, nunc per figuras, prout idem electus in animo concipiebat. Quid tamen sibi volebant illa signa vel figure nullus sciebat nisi ipse electus solus. Post hec, omnibus sic examinatis, vidimus electum recedere, et eadem nocte prefatus electus apud Wengham in camera sua, nobis et aliis quos volebat presentibus, excluso monacho Cantuariensi, dicta sic examinatorum sibi et suo consilio legebat, et quem vellet priorem preficere tractabat, non multum innitens examinationi sed potius sue proprie conscientie et utilitati domus. Et cum iam ordinasset cum suo consilio de Nicholao de Sandwich creando in priorem, in crastino reversus est ad capitulum et eum eis nominavit et prefecit priorem, et statim surgens et incipiens 'Miserere mei Deus', ingressus ecclesiam ipsum priorem installavit. Post hec, volens de creatione officialium tractare, iussit in camera sua ad se venire priorem et alios monachos pro sua voluntate, et ibidem de personis preficiendis[b] tractavit cum eis, et postea ingressus est capitulum, et quem volebat ad hanc vel illam nominabat obedientiam et officium committebat eidem. Quosdam etiam prout volebat ad priora officia restituebat, suppriorem scilicet et alios, et hac una vice omnes infrascriptos creavit et prefecit: priorem, suppriorem, precentorem, celerarium,[c] camerarium, sacristam, penitentiarios extra et intra. Hec siquidem acta fuerunt apud Cantuariam[d] die martis proxima ante festum apostolorum Symonis et Iude et duobus diebus sequentibus anno Domini M° CC° XLIIII°.[e] In huius rei testimonium nos et archidiaconus Cantuariensis, qui omnia premissa vidimus et tractavimus, signa nostra apponi fecimus, scripta etiam que fecit dominus electus et monachus cum examinarentur monachi similiter signavimus.

[a] talibus C   [b] preficiendorum B, C   [c] cellarium C   [d] Cant' B   [e] millesimo CC° XLIIII° C

Between bp Suffield's consecration and the death of Simon Langton, archdn of Canterbury, in 1248. Relations between archbp Edmund and the monks had not been harmonious, and they had been engaged in almost continual litigation during his pontificate. It was almost certainly at this time, in 1235 or 1236, that the *Magna Carta beati Thome* was fabricated. The tension between archbp and chapter was exacerbated by Edmund's resurrection of the plan to found and endow a secular collegiate church, now to be at Maidstone, formally announced in May 1238 at the *curia* when he was seeking confirmation of the concord reached with the monks, which was favourable to the archbp and which the monks' proctors now repudiated. In the meantime, suspicion of forgery by the monks of documents to support their case led the pope to order his legate in England, cardinal Otto, to investigate. As a result of the legate's enquiries prior John of Chetham in autumn 1238 resigned his office into the legate's hands and left the cathedral priory to become a Carthusian; two other monks were also removed. In November 1238 archbp Edmund, at the convent's request, entered the chapter to supervise the election of a new prior, but his deposition of the subprior provoked the monks to walk out of chapter. In response to this insult the archbp suspended the community from sacred functions, but the monks ignored this sentence, against which they appealed, and in January 1239 they elected a new prior, Robert de la Lee, without the archbp's consent. He excommunicated first the group which had elected Lee, and then the whole convent. An effort by the legate to effect reconciliation was fruitless, and this acrimonious dispute was ended only by the archbp's death on 16 November 1240 at Pontigny, probably on his way to the *curia*. Cardinal Otto absolved the chapter from Edmund's sentence so that the election of a new archbp could proceed; before papal confirmation of this absolution on 6 March 1241, on 1 February the chapter elected Boniface of Savoy, and this election was eventually confirmed by pope Innocent IV in Autumn 1243. Boniface came to England for some months in 1244, the temporalities of the see being restored between 27 February and 1 May, and his pallium despatched on 2 April, although he was consecrated later, on 15 January 1245, by the pope at Lyons. Robert de la Lee resigned as prior, last occurring on 9 October 1244, and the actions carefully recorded in this actum are the first manifestation of Boniface's campaign to restore the rights of the see of Canterbury. The removal and appointment of monastic officials below the level of prior ran counter to cl. 5 of the *Magna Carta beati Thome*, which represents the monks' aspirations in the 1230s, this clause harking back to a dispute when archbp Baldwin appointed a cellarer and sacrist in 1187. There is an account of the dispute in *Gervase* ii 131–202, and a modern summary in C.H. Lawrence, *St Edmund of Abingdon* 163–8; see also C.R. Cheney, 'Magna Carta Beati Thome'; *Fasti* ii 11; *HRH* ii 27.

19. Castle Acre Priory

Incomplete actum relating to the hermitage at Slevesholm.

[19 February 1245 × 19 May 1257]

B = BL ms. Harley 2110 (Castle Acre cartulary) fo. 7r (later addition). s. xv.

Omnibus Cristi fidelibus ad quos presens scriptum pervenerit Walterus Dei gratia Norwicensis episcopus salutem eternam in Domino. Cum dilectus filius frater Iohannes monachus in hermitorio de Slevesholm infra limites parochialis ecclesie de Methelwold....

The island site of St Mary, Slevesholm, at Methwold, was granted to Castle Acre by William de Warenne, 1222 × 26. It ceased to be occupied between 1351 × 74, so the bp must be Suffield, rather than Walter Lyhart (1446–72) (*MRH* 102).

20. Castle Acre Priory

Inspeximus *and confirmation of charters of bishops John I, John II and Thomas [Blundeville], his predecessors, by which they granted to the monks the churches of St Mary Magdalene, Wiggenhall, and Kempstone with all their appurtenances, saving honourable and sufficient provision for vicars who shall minister therein.*

Gaywood, 8 May 1245

B = BL ms. Harley 2110 (Castle Acre cartulary) fo. 131v (125v). s. xiii med.

Universis Cristi fidelibus ad quos presens scriptum pervenerit Walterus Dei gratia Norwicensis episcopus salutem in Domino. Noverit universitas vestra nos inspexisse cartas Iohannis primi et Iohannis secundi et Thome, predecessorum nostrorum, in quibus continetur quod ipsi concesserunt priori et monachis de Castelacra ecclesiam sancte Marie Magdalene de Wigehale [et] ecclesiam de Kemestun cum omnibus ad dictas ecclesias pertinentibus, salva honesta et sufficienti sustentatione vicariorum qui in eisdem ecclesiis ministrabunt. Nos vero, dictas concessiones et confirmationes ratas et gratas habentes, easdem auctoritate episcopali confirmamus. In cuius rei testimonium presentibus sigillum nostrum apponi fecimus. Dat' apud Geywde .viii. idus Maii pontificatus nostri anno primo. Testibus: magistro Willelmo de Horham officiali, magistro Laurentio de Sumercote, magistro Willelmo de Suthfeld, domino Ada de Wrdested', magistro Ada de Bromhom, Ricardo de Ribof, Henrico de Bodekesham et aliis.

The *acta* cited are probably *EEA* 6 nos. 199–200 (both of bp John of Oxford; there is no extant charter of bp John de Gray relating to these churches), and *EEA* 21 44, by which bp Blundeville appropriated the church to the monks and taxed a vicarage on 18 December 1228.

21. Castle Acre Priory

Grant to the monks in proprios usus *of the church of Kempstone, which is of their advowson, saving a vicarage to be taxed by the bishop, to which whenever it is vacant the monks shall present a suitable clerk.*   Rollesby, 9 February 1246

B = BL ms. Harley 2110 (Castle Acre cartulary) fo. 131v (125v). s. xiii med.

Universis Cristi fidelibus has litteras visuris vel audituris Walterus miseratione divina Norwicensis episcopus eternam in Domino salutem. Noverit universitas vestra nos caritatis intuitu dilectis filiis priori et conventui de Castellacra ecclesiam de Kemestun', que de ipsorum est advocatione, in proprios usus concessisse, salva vicaria per nos taxanda ad quam quotienscumque eam vacare contigerit dicti prior et conventus nobis et successoribus nostris clericum idoneum presentabunt, salvis etiam in omnibus episcopalibus consuetudinibus et nostre Norwicensis ecclesie dignitate. In cuius rei testimonium presenti scripto sigillum nostrum duximus apponendum. Hiis testibus: magistro Willelmo de

Horham, magistro Willelmo de Suffeud, magistro Ada de Bromhom, Willelmo de Pakeham, Willelmo de Sidesterne, Roberto de Glemham capellano, Thoma de Walcot' et aliis. Dat' apud Rollesbi .v. idus Februarii pontificatus nostri anno primo.

> For the original grant by bp John of Oxford, to take effect when the church was next vacant, see *EEA* 6 nos 199–200; a new *persona*, by which is probably meant rector, had however been instituted by bp Blundeville in December 1227 (*EEA* 6 no. 41).

22. Castle Acre Priory

Admission, at the presentation of the monks, of Walter of Castle Acre, priest, to the vicarage of the church of Kempstone, with cure of souls. The vicarage shall consist of all the altarage, a certain manse, all the free land of the church, all the tenement which Sewal and Agnes hold of that land, the tithes of peas and beans and all other appurtenances of the church, saving to the monks the residual portion of the great tithe. The vicar shall discharge all the customary episcopal and archidiaconal obligations of the church.   North Elmham, 19 February 1246

> B = BL ms. Harley 2110 (Castle Acre cartulary) fos 131v–33r (125v–).[1] s.xiii med.

Omnibus Cristi fidelibus has litteras visuris vel audituris Walterus miseratione divina Norwicensis episcopus eternam in Domino salutem. Noveritis nos dilectum filium Walterum de Castelacra presbiterum ad vicariam ecclesie de Kemestun' ad presentationem dilectorum filiorum prioris et conventus de Castelacra admisisse eique curam animarum commississe, salvis in omnibus episcopalibus consuetudinibus et nostre Norwicensis ecclesie dignitate. Consistit autem dicta vicaria in toto alteragio, in quodam manso, in tota libera terra ipsius ecclesie, in toto tenemento quod tenent Sewal et Agnes de ipsa terra, in decimis pisarum et fabarum et in omnibus aliis ad dictam ecclesiam pertinentibus, salva dictis priori et conventui residua portione decimarum maiorum. Sustinebit autem dictus vicarius omnia onera episcopalia et archidiaconalia debita et consueta. In cuius rei testimonium presenti scripto sigillum nostrum duximus [fo. 133r] apponendum. Hiis testibus: magistro Willelmo de Suffeld, magistro Adam de Bromholm, domino Iohanne de Holkam clerico, Willelmo de Pakeam, Drogone de Castelacra clerico, Hugone de Corebrig' et aliis. Dat' apud Northelmam .xi. kalendas Martii pontificatus nostri anno secundo.

> [1] Fo. 132 is an half-page insert; the second numeration ends here.

> Kempstone church was valued at £2 13s 4d in 1254, and in 1291, appropriated to Castle Acre and including the vicarage, at £4 (*VN* 381; *Taxatio* 79b).

23. Castle Acre Priory

Notification that when a dispute arose between the monks and John of Walton, vicar of the church of St James, Castle Acre, the vicar asserting that his vicarage had been assigned certain portions and rents of the church, the monks maintaining that from the foundation of the church the vicarage had consisted of a knight's corrody and ten shillings, the bishop eventually induced them to a peaceful settlement in the following terms. The monks shall receive all the tithes, great and lesser, and the obventions of the altarage, with no deduction. John shall while vicar receive as his vicarage ten marks a year in two instalments at the two Norwich synods, and shall claim no more, except a penny from the Christmas oblation, a penny at Easter and a penny at St James's day. This ten marks he shall receive for discharging on his own the burden of ministry in the church and paying the synodals. He also took a corporal oath, in the bishop's presence, that he would be faithful to the monks in all things, collecting the tithes and obventions and delivering them to the monks without deduction. If he should, with the bishop's licence, delegate a chaplain to celebrate divine office for him, that chaplain shall take a similar oath. On the death or resignation of the present vicar the former right of the monks in the church shall be restored.

North Elmham, 28 April 1246

B = BL ms. Harley 2110 (Castle Acre cartulary) fo. 131v (125v). s. xiii med.

Omnibus Cristi fidelibus has litteras visuris vel audituris Walterus miseratione divina Norwicensis episcopus eternam in Domino salutem. Cum orta esset dissensio inter priorem et conventum de Castelacra⁻ᵃ ex una parte⁻ᵃ et Iohannem de Walton' vicarium ecclesie sancti Iacobi de Castelacre ex altera super eo quod dictus I. asserebat dictam vicariam sub certis portionibus et redditibus dicte ecclesie sibi fuisse assignatam, dictis vero monachis in contrarium asserentibus dictam vicariam a prima fundacione dicte ecclesie in uno corredio unius militis et decem solidis annuis extitisse, tandem post multa intermedia eosdem ad hanc formam pacis reduximus, videlicet quod dicti monachi omnes decimas et obventiones tam maiores quam minores totius ecclesie et alteragium absque diminutione aliqua integraliter percipient. Dictus vero I. suo perpetuo percipiet nomine vicarie tantummodo .x. marcas annuas ad duas sinodos Norwic' equis portionibus sibi solvendas, nec ultra dictas .x. marcas in dicta ecclesia sibi aliquod vendicabit preter .i. denarium de oblatione die natalis Domini et .i. denarium die Pasche et .i. denarium die sancti Iacobi. Percipiet autem dictus I. dictas .x. marcas pure et libere, sustinendo solummodo honus ministrandi in dicta ecclesia et synodalia solvendi. Insuper autem corporali iuramento inspectis sacrosanctis coram nobis prestito promisit se dictis monachis fidelem in omnibus futurum in decimis et obventionibus cum diligentia debita colligendis et eisdem monachis cum omni integritate et absque diminutione aliqua fideliter solvendis. Et si de licentia nostra capellanum ad celebrandum divina sibi subrogaverit, idem capellanus simile prestabit iuramentum. Decedente vero vel recedente dicto vicario, salvum sit ius pristinum dictis monachis in ecclesia memorata. In cuius rei testimonium presenti scripto sigillum nostrum duximus apponendum. Dat' apud North Elmam .iiii°. kalendas Maii pontificatus nostri anno secundo.

ᵃ⁻ᵃ interlined B

The parish church of Castle Acre was valued at £16, and the vicarage at £3 6s 8d, in 1254 (*VN* 383); in 1291 the valuations were £17 6s 8d and £4 13s 4d respectively (*Taxatio* 80b).

24. Castle Acre Priory

Notification that when a conflict arose between the monks and the persona *of the church of Gresham over two-thirds of the tithe of the demesne of the late lord Richard son of William Branche in Gresham, eventually the parties, with the consent of the lord Peter Branche, the patron, submitted to the bishop's ordinance. He, having considered the cases of both parties and taken the advice of men learned in the law, has decreed that the rector and his successors should hold these tithes of the monks at a perpetual farm of eighteen shillings a year, to be paid in equal instalments at the two Norwich synods. If at any term payment is not made within eight days, unless the rector be prevented by just and evident cause, he shall at the simple complaint of the monks or their agent be compelled by the diocesan bishop, with only one warning, without formal judicial process and by sentence of interdict and excommunication, to make the payment due within fifteen days of that monition, and in addition to pay forty shillings as compensation for damages, interest and expenses incurred by the monks, all legal remedies available to one failing to make payment being in this case invalid. Drawn up in the form of a chirograph, sealed by the bishop, the parties and the patron.* [24 February 1247 × February 1253]

A = BL ms. Add. ch. 14676. Endorsed: Compositio de decimis de Gresham (s. xiii), Gresham (s. xv); indented chirograph, approx. 200 × 148 mm., four slits, tags and seals missing.
B = BL ms. Harley 2110 (Castle Acre cartulary) fo. 134v (127v). s. xiii med.

Universis sancte matris ecclesie filiis presentes litteras visuris vel audituris Walterus Dei gratia episcopus Norwicensis salutem in Domino sempiternam. Ad universitatis vestre notitiam volumus pervenire quod cum orta esset dissensio coram nobis inter priorem et conventum de Castelacra ex una parte et personam ecclesie de Gresham ex altera super duabus partibus decimarum provenientium de dominico quondam domini Ricardi filii Willelmi Branche in villa de Gresham, quas dicti Acrenses ad eos pertinere dicebant, tandem post multa intermedia predicte partes, interveniente consensu domini Petri Branche patroni ecclesie de Gresham, se super dictis decimis ordinationi nostre totaliter summiserunt. Nos igitur, auditis et pensatis rationibus partium, de consilio iurisperitorum sic duximus ordinandum: quod dictus rector et eius successores teneant dictas decimas ad perpetuam firmam de dictis Acrensibus pro octodecim solidis argenti eis annuatim a dictis rectoribus ad duas synodos Norwic' pro equalibus portionibus solvendis, ita videlicet quod si dictus rector vel aliquis successorum suorum in solutione dicte pecunie ultra octo dies post lapsum alicuius terminorum cessaverit, nisi iusta et evidenti causa fuerit prepeditus, rector qui in solutione cessaverit ad simplicem querelam vel interpellationem dictorum Acrensium vel eorum certi nuntii per episcopum loci qui pro tempore fuerit, unica monitione premissa, sine cause cognitione et strepitu iudiciali, per interdicti et excommunicationis sententias compellatur solvere dictis Acrensibus infra quindecim dies post amonitionem sibi factam pecuniam illa vice non solutam, et insuper quadraginta solidos nomine recompensationis dampnorum, interesse et expensarum que pro dicta pecunia suo termino non soluta recuperanda dicti Acrenses fecerint vel habuerint, circumscriptis omni exceptione, cavillatione, appellatione et omni iuris auxilio que non solventi competere possint in hac parte. Huic autem ordinationi nostre et in scriptis in modum cyrographi redacte et coram dictis partibus et patrono pupplicate eedem partes et patronus ipsam ordinationem nostram expresse acceptantes sigilla sua unacum sigillo nostro ad perpetuam eius firmitatem apposuerunt. Hiis testibus: magistro Roberto de Insula archidiacono Colecestr', magistro Willelmo de Horham archidiacono Suff', magistro Iohanne de Pagrave, domino Iohanne de Holcham capellano, Thoma de Walecote clerico et aliis.

Mr William of Horham occurs without title in the bp's retinue on 24 February 1247 (21). Mr Robert de Insula's successor as archdn of Colchester had ceased to occupy his previous position as archdn of Essex by February 1253 (*Fasti* i 20).

In 1254 the church was valued at £3 6s 8d and in 1291 at £4 13s 4d; in both assessments the monks' portion of 18s is recorded (*VN* 392; *Taxatio* 86).

25. Castle Acre Priory

Inspeximus *and confirmation of the grant by bishop Thomas to the monks* in proprios usus *of the church of St Mary Magdalene, Wiggenhall, and the ordination of a vicarage therein [EEA 21 no. 44]. With regard to the tithe of turves, the vicar shall receive from this either four shillings or twelve thousand turves, as the monks may choose.* North Elmham, 13 April 1248

B = BL ms. Harley 2110 (Castle Acre cartulary) fo. 133r. s. xiii med.

Omnibus Cristi fidelibus presens scriptum visuris vel audituris Walterus Dei gratia Norwicensis episcopus salutem in Domino sempiternam. Inspeximus cartam bone memorie domini Thome de Blonvilla predecessoris nostri in hec verba: [*EEA* 21 no. 44]. Hanc igitur concessionem et donationem gratam habentes et ratam auctoritate nostra confirmamus, et specialiter decimam totius turbe illius parochie, ita tamen quod pro tempore vicarius habebit annuatim .iiii^{or}. solidos de decima predicta vel .xii. miliaria de dicta decima, quod predictorum dicti prior et monachi elegerint, per manus eorundem percipienda. In cuius rei restimonium presenti scripto sigillum nostrum fecimus apponi. Dat' apud Northelmam idibus Aprilis pontificatus nostri anno quarto.

Margin: non ostendatur (s. xv).

The church was valued in 1254 at £10 13s 4d and the vicarage at £4 (*VN* 382); in 1291 the respective valuations were £16 and £4 13s 4d (*Taxatio* 80).

26. Castle Acre Priory

Notification that the bishop has inspected charters of bishops John I, John II and Thomas, his predecessors [EEA 6 nos 199–200, 343; EEA 21 no. 48], from which he has learned that the church of Methwold was granted to the monks in proprios usus and that this grant was confirmed by the chapter of Norwich. This he too confirms, saving an honourable and sufficient vicarage to be taxed by him when he so wills, to which when it is vacant the monks shall present a suitable persona.   Marham, 27 December 1249

B = BL ms. Harley 2110 (Castle Acre cartulary) fo. 133r–v. s. xiii med.

Omnibus Cristi fidelibus presens scriptum visuris vel audituris Walterus Dei gratia Norwicensis episcopus salutem in Domino sempiternam. Noverit universitas vestra nos cartas venerabilium predecessorum nostrorum Iohannis primi, Iohannis secundi et Thome plenius inspexisse, ex quarum tenore perpendimus ecclesiam de Melewd' dilectis filiis [fo. 133v] priori et conventui de Castelacra esse collatam in proprios eorundem usus inperpetuum convertendam, dictamque collationem confirmatione capituli nostri Norwicensis invenimus esse munitam. Nos igitur tam collationem predictam quam confirmationem ratam habentes et firmam, utramque auctoritate pontificali duximus confirmandam, salva honesta et sufficienti vicaria per nos cum voluerimus in eadem taxanda, ad quam cum vacaverit dicti prior et conventus nobis et successoribus nostris personam ydoneam presentabunt, salvis etiam episcopalibus consuetudinibus et nostre Norwicensis diocesis ecclesie dignitate. In cuius rei testimonium presenti scripto signum nostrum fecimus apponi. Hiis testibus: magistris Roberto et Willelmo de Colecestria et de Suffolc' archidiaconis, Thoma rectore ecclesie de Humeresfeld, Willelmo de Witewell', Roberto rectore ecclesie de Prilleston', Willelmo de Ludham et aliis. Dat' apud Marham .vi. kalendas Ianuarii anno Domini M° CC° XLIX° et pontificatus nostri anno quinto.

John of Oxford and Thomas Blundeville had both stipulated that a vicarage should be taxed within the church. In 1235, however, John of Vercelli was rector, and he was still alive in 1251 when bp Suffield was ordered by the pope to protect him in his benefices in Norwich diocese (*Reg. Inn. IV* no. 4993; *CPL* i 266). The church was valued at £21 6s 8d in 1254 and, appropriated to Castle Acre, at £22 13s 4d in 1291; Lewes priory had a portion of £2 (*VN* 388; *Taxatio* 88).

27. Castle Acre Priory

Notification that whereas the bishop wished provision to be made, according to apostolic mandate, in the church of Fulmodestone with the chapel of Croxton, of the monks' advowson, of Petrinus the clerk, son of the noble Hugh Blanch of Lavagna, to whom by the terms of that mandate the bishop himself and the church of Blickling, of his patronage, are bound in the sum of forty marks until provision should be made for him of a benefice valued at forty marks, eventually after much discussion the monks committed the church and chapel to the bishop's ordinance, and master John of Palgrave freely renounced his presentation by the monks thereto. Taking account of all the circumstances, the bishop has ordained that now, and on other occasions when there is a vacancy, a suitable persona *shall be admitted at the monks' presentation; and that as long as the bishop and his church are obligated to Petrinus, so shall this church remain obligated and the rector for the time being shall, for the exoneration of the bishop and his church of Blickling, pay thirty marks to Petrinus until provision is made by the bishop of him to a benefice worth forty marks, according to the papal mandate, so that on his death, resignation or provision as specified, the church and chapel shall be free in perpetuity of this payment of thirty marks. Realising, moreover, that the sick and frail of the convent have few and meagre resources from which they may be restored to health in the infirmary, in addition to the monks' customary and long-established receipt of forty shillings, which he confirms, he assigns to the infirmary in perpetuity ten marks a year to be received in equal instalments at the two Norwich synods from the rector for the time being as a perpetual annual benefice, payment commencing at the Michaelmas synod 1252, excommunication being pronounced against any person who may threaten the existence of this benefice or withdraw or threaten payment of the ten marks or commit fraud therein. From this ten marks, however, master John, who was presented to the church, shall receive five marks until provision is made by the monks for him or for another of his choice of a benefice worth twenty marks or more, according to the tenor of his charter that this provision should not be of a vicarage; and when such provision is made and he or his nominee has peaceful possession of such a benefice, the said ten marks shall be converted in full to the use of the infirmary. The monks, accepting this ordinance, presented to the bishop Thomas of Walcott, clerk, whom he instituted according to the form of this ordinance. Sealed by the prior and convent, master John, Thomas of Walcott and the bishop.*

North Elmham, 24 February 1252

B = BL ms. Harley 2110 (Castle Acre cartulary) fo. 135r–v (128r–v). s. xiii med.

Omnibus Cristi fidelibus presens scriptum visuris vel audituris Walterus Dei gratia Norwicensis episcopus salutem in Domino sempiternam. Noverit universitas vestra quod cum de mandato sedis apostolice Petrino clerico nato nobilis viri Hugonis Blanch' de Lavagna, qui nos et ecclesiam nostram et ecclesiam de Bliclingh' de nostro patronatu in .xl. marcis habebat obligatam donec eidem in beneficio ecclesiastico ad valentiam .xl. marcarum iuxta tenorem mandati apostolici fuerit provisum, in ecclesia de Fulmodestun' cum capella de Croxton de patronatu prioris et conventus monachorum Acrensium^a vellemus providere, tanden post multa intermedia prior et conventus ipsam ecclesiam cum capella nostre ordinationi commiserunt, magistro Iohanne de Pagrave de presentatione de eo facta^b ad beneficia premissa sponte cedente. Nos igitur, pondatis circumstantiis universis, sic duximus ordinandum: quod ad dictorum Acrensium presentationem nunc et alias cum vacaverit dicta ecclesia persona ydonea admittatur; et quod prefata ecclesia semper maneat obligata quamdiu nos et dicta ecclesia fuerimus dicto P. obligati, et eius rector qui pro tempore fuerit ad nostri et ecclesie nostre de Bliclingh' exonerationem solvat .xxx. marcas dicto P. donec eidem in beneficio .xl. marcarum secundum [fo. 135v] tenorem mandati apostolici fuerit per nos provisum, ita quod eo decedente vel recedente vel eidem proviso ut predictum est, prefata ecclesia cum capella a prestatione annuarum .xxx. marcarum libera maneat imperpetuum. Insuper etiam, attendentes infirmos et debiles conventus ecclesie Acrensis paucos et exiles redditus habere de quibus in infirmaria possint honeste recreari, .x. marcas preter solitam et antiquam prestationem .xl. solidorum, quam approbamus et confirmamus, eidem infirmarie perpetuis temporibus assignamus, approbamus et concedimus, percipiendas ad duas synodos Norwic' pro equalibus portionibus per manus rectoris ecclesie de Fulmodestun' quicumque fuerit de bonis ipsius ecclesie nomine annui et perpetui beneficii, incipiente predicta solutione in synodo sancti Michaelis anno Domini M° CC LII°, excommunicantes omnes qui ipsos super ipso beneficio inquietabunt vel molestiam sive gravamen^c inferent vel dictas .x. marcas annuas ab usibus infirmarie subtrahent, minuent vel aliquo modo contra nostram ordinationem fraudabuntur; hoc salvo, quod ex hac expressa nostra ordinatione de predictis .x. marcis magister Iohannes, qui ad ipsam ecclesiam cum capella fuerat presentatus, quinque marcas percipiet donec eidem vel alicui de suis per ipsos Acrenses in beneficio .xx. marcarum vel amplius, secundum tenorem carte sue quod non sic vicaria fuerit provisum; et cum sibi vel alicui de suis fuerit provisum et alter ipsorum beneficium pacifice fuerit assecutus, dicte .x. marce in usus infirmarie integritaliter ut premissum est convertantur. Hanc autem nostram ordinationem prefati prior et conventus acceptantes Thomam de Walecote clericum nobis presentaverunt, quem secundum ordinationis memorate formam admisimus et rectorem in ecclesia de Fulmodestun' cum capella instituimus. In huius rei testimonium dicti prior et conventus, magister I. et Thomas de Walecote huic scripto signa sua unacum signo nostro apposuerunt. Actum apud Northelm' .vi. kalendas Martii anno gratie M CC LI°.

^a Acrensensium B   ^b Pagrave presentationi de eo facte B   ^c gravamen *interlined* B

Pope Innocent IV was himself a member of the comital family of Lavagna. What is strange in these complex arrangements is the relatively low value of the livings involved. Fulmodestone is valued at £10, to which two mss add 'de quibus prior de Castelacra xiii m; idem prior 1 m' (*VN*

420); the 13 marks comprise the pension of 10 marks for the infirmary here granted , in addition to the ancient pension of 3 marks granted by bp John of Oxford (*EEA* 6 no. 188). Blickling was valued at £10, 'sine portione P. de Lama' (probably a pension to another provisor) (*VN* 367). Despite undervaluation of benefices in 1254, neither church could have found the sum of £26 13s 4d which the bp was required to provide for Petrinus, nor even the £20 expected from Fulmodestone towards that pension. It can only be supposed that first the bp, then the monks of Castle Acre, provided the bulk of the pension from their own general funds, and that the bp's increase of the monks' pension from the church was some recompense for this. For mr John of Palgrave, see no. 29 n. below. Thomas of Walcott was a member of the bp's *familia*.

28. Castle Acre Priory

Notification that when the monks committed to the bishop's ordinance the church of Fulmodestone with the chapel of Croxton, of their advowson, among other things he ordained that, of the ten marks assigned to the monks' infirmary to be paid by the rector for the time being from the goods of the church as a perpetual annual benefice, master John of Palgrave should receive five marks a year in two instalments at the Norwich synods, until provision should be made for him or his nominee of a benefice worth twenty marks or more, according to the terms of his charter so that he should not be provided with a vicarage. When provision has been made, so that he or his nominee has peacefully secured a benefice, the said ten marks should be rendered in full to the infirmary. Sealed by the prior and convent, who consent, and by the bishop. North Elmham, 24 February 1252

B = BL ms. Harley 2110 (Castle Acre cartulary) fo. 135v (128v). s. xiii med.

Omnibus Cristi fidelibus presens scriptum visuris vel audituris Walterus Dei gratia Nortwicensis episcopus salutem in Domino sempiternam. Noverit universitas vestra quod cum prior et conventus de Castelacra ecclesiam de Fulmodestun' cum capella de Croxetun' vacantes, que de eorum patronatu esse noscuntur, ordinationi nostre commisissent, nos inter cetera que in instrumento ordinationis nostre continentur ordinavimus quod de .x. marcis quas infirmarie ipsorum Acrensium perpetuis temporibus assignavimus per manus rectoris ecclesie de Fulmodestun', quicumque fuerit, de bonis ipsius ecclesie nomine annui et perpetui beneficii percipiendas, magister Iohannes de Pagrave percipiat annuatim .v^{que}. marcas per manus dicti rectoris ad duas synodos Nortwic' pro equalibus portionibus, donec eidem I. vel alicui de suis per ipsos Acrenses in beneficio .xx. marcarum vel amplius secundum tenorem carte sue quod non sic vicaria fuerit provisum, et cum sibi vel alicui de suis provisum fuerit et alter ipsorum beneficium pacifice fuerit assecutus, dicte .x. marce in usus infirmarie integritaliter ut premissum est convertantur. Hanc autem ordinationem nostram prefati prior et conventus acceptantes huic scripto sigillum suum unacum sigillo nostro apposuerunt. Actum apud Northelmham .vi. kalendas Martii anno pontificatus nostri anno octavo.

See no. 27.

29. Castle Acre Priory

Notification that when a dispute was heard before the bishop between master John of Palgrave and master Geoffrey of Dereham, at different times presented by the monks to the church of St Michael, Fincham, eventually patrons and presentees resigned all right stemming from these presentations on this occasion and submitted to the bishop's ordinance, which he made thus: that master Geoffrey should hold the church as rector for his lifetime, and should pay to the monks the customary pension of a mark a year at the two Norwich synods, and at the same time and place he shall pay to master John six marks a year from the revenues of the church as a simple benefice. If master John or his accredited proctor is not present there, master Geoffrey should for his discharge deposit the money with the sacrist in the treasury at Norwich, to be paid to master John or his proctor. If at any term master Geoffrey should fail to make payment within fifteen days, then as penalty the pension shall be increased by four marks. Each of master Geoffrey's successors in the church shall be bound to the same payment, with the same penalty clause, until provision is made by the monks of master John or anyone nominated by him to an ecclesiastical benefice worth twenty marks or more and he or anyone at his nomination has entered into secure possession of that benefice, as is more fully contained in the instrument which he has from the monks. When such provision is made, or on the death or resignation of master John, payment of the pension shall cease. The penalty clause shall be applicable not from the time of delivery of the ordinance, but only from the date of these present letters. Sealed by the prior and convent, by Robert archdeacon of Colchester and by the bishop.

Thornham, 20 December 1252 (ordinance); Lambourne, 21 October 1253 (notification)

B = BL ms. Harley 2110 (Castle Acre cartulary) fo. 135r (128r). s. xiii med.

Universis Cristi fidelibus presentes litteras[a] inspecturis Walterus miseratione divina Norwicensis episcopus salutem in Domino sempiternam. Ad omnium notitiam volumus tenore presentium pervenire quod cum inter dilectos filios magistros Iohannem de Pagrave et Galfridum de Derham, ad ecclesiam sancti Michaelis de Fincham a priore et conventu Acrensibus diversis temporibus presentatos, mota fuisset querimonio coram nobis, tandem predictis presentantibus et presentatis totum ius quod habebant in sua presentatione seu ex ea resignantibus illa vice et se pure, simpliciter, absolute ordinationi nostre supponentibus, taliter duximus ordinandum: quod dictus magister G. ipsam ecclesiam habeat et possideat in suo perpetuo tamquam rector ipsius. Solvat autem ipsis priori et conventui .i[am]. marcam singulis annis in duabus synodis Norwic' solite pensionis; prefato vero magistro I. solvat eisdem terminis et loco .vi. marcas de bonis eiusdem ecclesie nomine beneficii simplicis annuatim; quod si forsan idem magister I. termino et loco personaliter non intersit nec aliquis certus assignatus ipsius cui possit pecunia secure persolvi, ipse magister G. ad

sui liberationem pecuniam consignet et deponat in thesaurario Norwic' penes
loci sacristam ipsi magistro I. vel eius certo assignato solvendam. Siquidem idem
magister G. solutionem pecunie non fecerit in aliquo termino prout superius est
expressum nec infra .xv. dies sequentes, extunc singulis terminis nomine pene in
.iiii^or. marcis dicta pensio augeatur, et fiat solutio de .x. marcis sicuti de sex est
contentum. Eandem etiam pensionem et eodem modo cum sua pena faciat
successor eiusdem G. in ipsa ecclesia quicumque pro tempore fuerit in eadem
quousque prefato magistro I. vel alicui de suis quem ipse nominaverit in
beneficio ecclesiastico .xx. marcarum vel amplius ab ipsis Acrensibus fuerit
provisum, et ipse vel aliquis de suis pacificam ipsius beneficii possessionem
adeptus fuerit, quod in instrumento quod habet de dictis Acrensibus plenius
continetur. Sic provisione completa seu per decessum vel recessum ipsius I.,
cesset pensio et prestatio memorata. Volumus autem ordinando quod pensionis
augmentatio loco pene non a tempore ordinationis facte sed a data presentium
incipiat locum habere. In cuius rei testimonium et probationem consensus nos
ordinationi presenti unacum sigillis dictorum Acrensium et magistri Roberti
archidiaconi Colecestr' signum nostrum duximus apponendum. Actum
ordinationis ipsius apud Thornham manerium nostrum .xiii. kalendas Ianuarii
pontificatus nostri anno .viii. Dat' presentium apud Lamburn .xii°. kalendas
Novembris pontificatus nostri anno .ix°.

ª litteras *interlined* B

The church of St Michael, Fincham (where there was also a church of St Martin) was valued in
1254 at £10, and the portion of the prior of Castle Acre at £3 6s 8d (*VN* 410). Mr John of
Palgrave attested charters for Lewes priory (*Lewes Cartulary: Norfolk Portion* nos. 19, 143,
145) and occurs frequently as a witness in the Castle Acre cartulary (BL ms. Harley 2110). He
had been presented to, but eventually merely received a pension from, Fulmodestone church
(nos. 27–8 above). He was rector of Ryston, and died as such on 6 May 1254 (*Lewes Cartulary:
Norfolk Portion* no. 64). Mr Geoffrey of Dereham was on 22 December 1257 granted by pope
Alexander IV an indult that he might hold one benefice in addition to the three which he now
had, and on resigning any might accept another (*Reg. Alex. IV* no. 2433; *CPL* i 354). He may
have been of the same family as the mr Geoffrey of Dereham who acted as datary from 1203–5
for bp John de Gray (*EEA* 6 p. xlvi).

30. Castle Acre Priory

*Admission, at the presentation of the monks, of Walter of Foston, clerk, to the
church of Herringby, with cure of souls, saving to the monks the customary
annual pension of forty shillings.*   Coxford, 26 February 1256

B = BL ms. Harley 2110 (Castle Acre cartulary) fo. 133v. s. xiii med.

Omnibus Cristi fidelibus presentes litteras inspecturis vel audituris Walterus
miseratione divina episcopus Nortwicensis salutem in Domino sempiternam.
Noveritis nos ad presentationem dilectorum filiorum prioris et conventus de
Castelacra dilectum in Cristo filium Walterum de Focestun' clericum ad

ecclesiam de Haringebi admisisse eidemque curam animarum eiusdem commississe, salvis in omnibus episcopalibus consuetudinibus et sancte Nortwicensis ecclesie dignitate, salvis etiam dictis priori et conventui annua pensione de eadem ecclesia .xl. solidorum debita et consueta. In cuius rei testimonium presentibus sigillum nostrum duximus apponendum, Dat' apud Kokesford' .v. kalendas Martii anno Domini M° CC° LV° et pontificatus nostri duodecimo.

For the appropriation of the church by bp John of Oxford, see *EEA* 6 no. 202; this was confirmed by bp Thomas Blundeville in 1233 (*EEA* 21 no. 46); the pension was raised from 20s to 40s by bp William Raleigh in 1240 (ibid. no. 128). In 1254 the church was valued at £5, with the prior of Castle Acre having an annual pension of £2 (*VN* 376); in 1291 the church was assessed at £5 6s 8d (*Taxatio* 79).

'Focestun' is probably Foston, *alias* Fodderston, an extinct parish now within the parish of Shouldham Thorpe, Nf., rather than Foxton, Ca. (*Reg. Bateman* i no. 429n.).

*31. Channel Islands And Gascony

Mandate sealed by the bishop, the bishop of Chichester and the abbot of Westminster, to the commissioners in the Channel Islands and Gascony, transmitting to them the papal mandate for the collection of a tenth of ecclesiastical revenues. [Before 22 June 1254]

Pd in *Cl. R.* 1253–54 77–8.

Mentioned in a royal writ addressed to the two bps and the abbot, dated 22 June 1254: 'quia commissarii qui sunt in Insulis regis et in Vasconia super collatione decime proventuum ecclesiasticorum regi concessorum in subsidium terre sancte non adhibent fidem mandato nec sigillis W. et I. Norwycensis et Cycestrensis episcoporum nec abbatis Westmonasteriensis, nec volunt mandatum suum exequi donec inspexerint autenticum...'.

The king ordered the collectors that they should send a pair of those latest duplicate letters which master Nicholas of Plympton (Plumton'), king's clerk (subsequently appointed *sede vacante* to the archdnry of Norwich), had obtained from the *curia* concerning the collection of the tenth, which he had recently handed over to them, and deliver them to him or his accredited messenger for transmission to the king in Gascony.

*32. Chichester Cathedral

Indulgence of forty days remission of enjoined penance to those visiting the cathedral church or giving alms thereto. [2 April 1247 × April 1248]

Mentioned only as similar to the indulgence granted by Fulk Basset, bp of London, dated 23 May 1247.
Pd (calendar) in *Chichester Chartulary* no. 83.

The bp of London's indulgence follows that of bp Richard Wich of Chichester, dated 2 April 1247, in granting remission to those of his diocese and of other dioceses whose bps ratified his grant who visited the cathedral on the feasts or within the octaves of Pentecost, Holy Trinity and St Faith, or who made a contribution to the fabric fund (*EEA* 22 no. 130). Bp Basset also promised that such benefactors should also participate in the spiritual benefits of his own cathedral and other churches of his diocese (*Chichester Chartulary* no. 79). In April 1248 bp Wich extended to inhabitants of Chichester diocese the benefits of indulgences granted by the bps of London, Winchester, Salisbury, Bath and Wells, Exeter, Norwich and Carlisle (*C. & S.* II i 420–1; *EEA* 22 no. 132). For the poor state of the fabric of the cathedral in the mid thirteenth century, see Jones, *St Richard of Chichester* 17.

33. Chichester Cathedral

Grant to the dean and chapter in proprios usus *of the church of Mendlesham, which is of their advowson, to take effect on the death or resignation of the present incumbent. They shall receive as the* personatus *two thirds of the great tithe and shall have the buildings appurtenant to the church, in order that they may fund and maintain a priest at the tomb of the late bishop Richard [Wich] of Chichester, whom they shall pay eight marks a year. They shall also keep two candles continually burning at the tomb, for which they shall pay twelve marks, and they shall pay five marks for the keeping of his anniversary, of which at least two marks shall be distributed to the poor; beyond this, the cardinals and the boys of the choir shall have two marks a year. All of this shall be paid from the fruits of the church of Mendlesham, and the remainder of their portion used for the good of the community according to the discretion of the chapter. The vicar shall have the third part of the tithes and all the altarage for his maintenance and that of another chaplain and the ministers of the church, and he shall discharge all customary dues of the church and contribute according to his portion to extraordinary obligations. The bishop and his successors shall collate the vicarage whenever vacant to a suitable* persona, *who shall swear to maintain residence. The vicar shall also have all the free land of the church with rents, rendering in perpetuity to the dean and chapter those three marks a year which the abbot and convent of Battle used to receive when patrons. Excommunication shall be pronounced against transgressors of this ordinance unless they amend their ways within eight days. Both dean and chapter and vicar are bound to observance on pain of withdrawal of their revenues from the church without judicial process. Of his special grace, the bishop concedes that the dean and chapter shall not be bound by reason of this church to attend his diocesan synods, saving the obedience and reverence due to his office and to the church of Norwich.*   Terling, 22 October 1254

B = West Sussex R. O., Ep VI/1/6 (Liber Y, Chichester cathedral cartulary) fo. 112r–v. s. xiii med.

Pd (calendar) in *Chichester Chartulary* no. 251.

Omnibus presentes litteras visuris vel audituris Walterus Dei gratia Norwicensis episcopus salutem in Domino sempiternam. Altissimus ecclesie fundator, sternens per ordinem lapides eius fundensque eam in saphiro ac iaspide et lapidibus sculptis,[1] futuras professionum diversitates ordinumque varietates ac diversas vite meritorum regulas varietate lapidum prefiguravit; inter quas nobilis Cicestrensis ecclesia, in qua per decanum et canonicos ipsius ecclesie sub habitu regulari nomen Ihesu Cristi venerabiliter colitur [et] veneratur, lausque Dei, beate Virginis et omnium sanctorum in altum dedicatur et celebratur, non immerito commendatur. Nos igitur, summo desiderio affectantes in ipsa ecclesia, in qua etiam gleba corporalis[a] gloriosi pontificis Ricardi eiusdem ecclesie quondam episcopi revisit[b] et requiescit, divinum cultum augmentare et ad laudem et honorem ipsius patris aliquam prerogativam honoris atque beneficii in ipsa transducere ad decorem, de ecclesia de Mendlesham nostre diocesis, cuius ecclesie prefati decanus et canonici vere sunt patroni, et quam ecclesiam[c] idem decanus et capitulum nostre ordinationi per suas litteras patentes, prout in eisdem sigillo capituli signatis continetur, commiserunt, sic duximus ordinandum, videlicet quod, vacante dicta ecclesia de Mendlesham per mortem sive resignationem eorum[d] qui eam tenent in presenti, prefata ecclesia in usus proprios cedat capituli in hunc modum, videlicet quod prefatum capitulum nomine personatus percipiat duas partes omnium garbarum et omnium maiorum decimarum ad ipsam ecclesiam pertinentium, cum edificiis ad dictam ecclesiam spectantibus. Insuper or-[fo. 112v] dinamus quod decanus et capitulum unum inveniant et preficiant sacerdotem perpetue in loco quo requiescit venerabilis pater antedictus divina celebrantem, et eidem singulis annis octo marcas ad eius victum et sustentationem persolvant terminis competentibus ab ipsis statuendis. Preter hec dicti decanus et capitulum iugiter et continue omni tempore invenient duos cereos eius tumbam ardentes, ad quod opus et onus .xii. marcas persolvent. Insuper solvent .v. marcas die anniversarii sui ad eius anniversarium faciendum, et fiet distributio illarum .v. marcarum secundum ordinationem decani et capituli, proviso tamen quod pauperes Cristi ex hac summa ad minus habeant .ii. marcas. Preter hec cardinales et pueri de choro .ii. marcas percipient annuatim. Et harum predictarum, scilicet .viii., .xii., .v. et .ii. marcarum, solutio fiet singulis annis fideliter et sine contradictione de bonis ecclesie de Mendlesham decano et capitulo assignatis. Totum residuum portionis eis assignate cedet in utilitatem communitatis secundum piam et discretam ordinationem ipsius capituli. Vicarius autem qui pro tempore fuerit tertiam partem decimarum et omnia pertinentia ad alteragium ad sui sustentationem et alterius capellani qui cum eo erit et ministrorum ecclesie pleno iure habebit, et sustinebit omnia onera debita et consueta; inconsueta vero et extraordinaria pro sua parte sustinebit. Quotienscumque siquidem ipsa vicaria vacaverit, nos et successores nostri ipsam persone idonee conferemus, qui vicarius personalem se facturum residentiam in institutione sua iurabit. Volumus insuper et ordinamus quod idem vicarius habeat totam liberam terram cum redditibus, solvendo annuatim .iii. marcas, quas percipere consueverunt abbas et conventus de Bello de ecclesia memorata dum erant patroni, decano et capitulo inperpetuum. Nos autem omnibus qui hanc nostram fideliter servabunt ordinationem Dei largimur benedictionem; transgressoribus vero et non observantibus Dei damus maledictionem, nisi infra .viii. dies se correxerint. Insuper reservamus nobis et successoribus nostris potestatem compellendi tam decanum et capitulum quam vicarium per subtractionem proventium ipsius ecclesie de plano et sine strepitu iudiciali ad huius nostre ordinationis observationem. Concedimus etiam de gratia speciali pro nobis et successoribus nostris eidem decano et capitulo ut ad sinodos nostras occasione predicte ecclesie eis appropriate venire minime valeant compelli, salva tamen obedientia et reverentia nobis et successoribus nostris et ecclesie nostre Norwicensi debitis et consuetis. In cuius rei testimonium presentibus sigillum nostrum duximus apponendum. Dat' apud Therlyng .x. kalendas Novembris anno Domini M° CC° LIIII.

[1] Cf. Rev. 21 : 19.

[a] corporalis *interlined* B   [b] *reading uncertain*   [c] ecclesiam *interlined* B   [d] eorundem B

The advowson of Mendlesham, one of that group of East Anglian churches granted to Battle abbey by William Rufus, was granted to Chichester cathedral by abbot Ralph on 26 September 1248; this was done apparently on the initiative of bp Richard Wich (*Chichester Chartulary* nos. 249, 903 (34)); the gift was probably made as a token of the concord established between Battle and its diocesan only thirteen years before, after prolonged conflict (Searle, *Lordship and Community* 96–8). The appropriation was authorised eighteen months after bp Wich's death by a friend who was devoted to his memory (Jones, *St Richard of Chichester* 165–6). In 1254 the church was valued at 40 marks (£26 13s 4d), 'de quibus pensio magistri de Feryng, 30 m.' (*VN* 429). In 1291 the church was valued at £22 and the vicarage at £12 (*Taxatio* 123b).

At Hilary 1261 an action brought by Roger of Lewknor against Nicholas of Lewknor for the manor of Mendlesham with appurtenances, including the advowson, ended in a final concord by which Nicholas was to hold for life, but thereafter manor and appurtenances were to revert to Roger and his heirs; the dean and chapter of Chichester laid claim to the advowson (TNA, CP25/1/214/26/43). At Hilary 1270 Peter of Burgate sued the dean and chapter for the advowson, but by a final concord recognised it to be their right, for which he received from them payment of 60 marks (TNA, CP25/1/214/30/2).

34. Chipping Norton Rural Deanery

Mandate, issued as executor of the business of the cross appointed by the apostolic see, to the [rural] dean and his [named] associates, that whereas at a meeting of the clergy at Eynsham he has by apostolic authority promulgated sentence of excommunication against those who, by withholding or failing to pay a tenth of their ecclesiastical revenues, wittingly commit fraud, he now orders them, on pain of suspension, to publish this sentence and to order all rectors and vicars, on pain of excommunication, that they should without fraud and in accordance with their consciences present to them an estimate of their ecclesiastical revenues. If it seems expedient so to do, they should in accordance with their oath make further enquiries, and should then commit their estimate to writing, sealed with their seals, which should on 2 August in the church of St James, Northampton, be delivered to the subprior, to be forwarded to the bishop or his agent. They should themselves retain a copy. They are empowered to compel all within the deanery to give their testimony under oath. He imposes this office on them for the remission of their sins, granting by apostolic authority that they shall be participants in the relaxation of penance indulted to those contributing to the Holy Land subsidy. The dean, moreover, since he has with others sworn to further the business of the cross, should make full enquiry into legacies in aid of the Holy Land, and hand the results of this to the bishop's agent. He should also show obedience and offer assistance to those coming to preach the crusade. Eynsham, 18 July 1254

B = Oxford, Bodl. ms. Dep. C 392 (Circencester abbey cartulary, formerly Vestey mss, Stowell Park) fo. 128r–v (119r–v, pp. 245–6, 255–6). s. xiii med.
Pd from B in *Cirencester Cartulary* ii 407–8, no. 458.

Walterus permissione divina Norwicensis episcopus, negotii crucis executor a sede apostolica deputatus, dilectis sibi in Cristo decano de Nort', Iohanni rectori ecclesie de Certell', Roberto vicario de Sipton', W. rectori ecclesie de Spillesbr' et magistro I. rectori ecclesie de Cerceden', salutem in Domino sempiternam. Cum nos,[a] convocato capitulo vestro[b] et clero universo coram nobis apud Eynesham, sententiam excommunicationis in genere auctoritate apostolica promulgaverimus in omnes illos qui, vel in subtrahenda decima proventuum suorum ecclesiasticorum tam maiorum vel minorum vel non solvenda, scienter fraudem commiserint, vobis mandamus in virtute obedientie sub pena suspensionis iniungentes quatinus, hanc sententiam publicantes, singulis rectoribus et vicariis sub pena excommunicationis antedicte iniungatis ut iustam suorum proventuum ecclesiasticorum estimationem absque fraude vobis plene exprimant et manifestent iuxta sue conscientie veritatem. Vos siquidem, sub sacramento nobis prestito, tam ab ipsis rectoribus [et] vicariis, si presentes fuerint, quam ab aliis prout melius videritis expedire, plenius inquiratis veritatem, videlicet que sit iusta estimatio tam maiorum quam minorum et ipsam iustam estimationem, in scriptis fideliter redigentes signatam sigillis vestris, in crastino beati Petri ad vincula in ecclesia beati Iacobi Norhampton' absque ulteriori dilatione tradatis subpriori custodiendam et nobis vel nuntio nostro litteras nostras differenti fideliter restituendam. Transcriptum autem penes vos[c] retineatis et salvo custodiatis. Damus autem vobis omnibus et singulis vestrum plenam potestatem compellendi ad iurandum omnes et singulos pro veritate vobis in hac parte manifestanda, prout melius videritis expedire. Hoc siquidem officium vobis in remissionem peccatorum iniungimus, concedentes vobis auctoritate sedis apostolice ut relaxationis indulte subvenientibus in terre sancte subsidium participes efficiamini in Domino. Insuper tu, fili decane, qui de negotio crucis fideliter exequendo una cum supradictis sacramentum prestitisti corporale, super legatis in terre sancte subsidium plenius inquiras veritatem et quod inveneris in scriptis redigas et requisitus gerenti vices nostras in hac parte habere facias. Hac etiam venientibus predicare crucem et ex parte ecclesie missis iuxta formam mandati nostri obedias et reverenter eisdem assistas ac devote. Valete. Dat' apud Eynesham .xv. kalendas Augusti anno Domini M° CC° LIIII[to].

[a]vos B   [b]nostro B   [c]vos interl. B

The incumbents addressed are those of Churchill, Shipton-under-Wychwood, Spelsbury and Sarsden, all in the deanery of Chipping Norton. The deanery lay within the circuit of the abbot of Westminster (*Cirencester Cartulary* ii no. 457). See intro. p. lviii.

35. Coxford Priory

Grant to the canons in proprios usus, *for the maintenance of hospitality, of the church of Great Hautbois, which is of their advowson.*   Coxford, 1 May 1245

> A = East Raynham, Raynham Hall mss box 56. Endorsed: conf' ecclesie de Haub'; Hugh of Mursley's notarial sign (s. xiv in); approx. 165 × 60 + 12 mm.; parchment tag, fragment of seal, black wax, counterseal.
> B = Norfolk RO, ms. SUN/8 (Coxford cartulary) fo. 56v. s. xiii ex. C = ibid. (*inspeximus* by prior Simon and the convent of Norwich).
> Pd (partial calendar) in Saunders, 'Coxford Priory', 312.

Omnibus Cristi fidelibus ad quos presens scriptum pervenerit Walterus Dei gratia Norwicensis episcopus salutem in Domino sempiternam. Etsi omnium religiosorum speciali pululemur dilectione, illos tamen maiori tenemur prosequi beneficio qui in nostra diocesi constituti hospitalitatis causa seipsos eviscerant et depauperant. Cum igitur dilecti filii prior et conventus de Cokesford, operibus misericordie intendentes, hospitalitatis gratiam cunctis se insignes reddant et pauperibus undique ad eos confluentibus congrue subsidia administrent, nos insufficientie sue subvenire volentes, ecclesiam de Magna Hauboys, que de eorum est advocatione, illis in proprios usus concessimus possidendam, salvis in omnibus episcopalibus consuetudinibus et nostre Norwicensis ecclesie dignitate. In cuius rei testimonium hoc presens scriptum fieri fecimus et sigillo nostro muniri. Dat' apud Cokesford kalendas Maii pontificatus nostri anno primo.

> For the earlier history of the church, see *EEA* 6 no. 82. It was valued at £3 6s 8d in 1254 and £4 in 1291 (*VN* 366; *Taxatio* 82b).

36. Coxford Priory

Notification that when William of Syderstone, once rector of Barmer, of the canons' advowson, after he had acquired a benefice in the church of Hindringham, by the bishop's advice resigned his church into his hands, and the prior and convent committed the church on this occasion to the bishop's disposition, he, considering on the one hand the merits in regular observance and hospitality of the canons, but on the other that they had recalled William from the schools at the beginning of his studies to the service of the church, in which he had faithfully remained for almost seven years, whereby he had sacrificed learning and time, of which nothing is of more value; perceiving too the good will felt for him by the canons and their intention to offer suitable remuneration for the service of the church and considering that the modest benefice which William has in the church of Hindringham does not suffice for his honourable maintenance and that the revenues of the church which he has resigned are small, after some days has ordained that the canons shall have the church of Barmer in proprios usus, *in such manner that William shall have the free land of the church and the fruits, paying to the canons as a farm one mark a year in equal instalments at the two Norwich synods, although the fruits are of far greater value. After his death or resignation the prior and convent shall have all the fruits of the church with its free land, saving the honourable maintenance, to be ordained by the bishop or his successors, for a vicar to minister therein.*

Weasenham, 8 December 1252

B = Bodl. ms. Norfolk ch. (a. 1) 73 (i) (*inspeximus* by prior Simon and the convent of Norwich, 23 July 1254) s. xiii med. C = Norfolk R. O., ms. SUN/8 (Coxford cartulary) fo. 57r. s. xiii ex. D = ibid. (as B).

Omnibus Cristi fidelibus ad quos presens scriptum pervenerit Walterus Dei gratia episcopus Norwicensis salutem in Domino sempiternam. Noverit universitas vestra quod cum dilectus filius Willelmus de Sydestern[a] aliquando rector ecclesie de Bermere, que est de advocatione dilectorum filiorum prioris et conventus de Cokesford,[b] post adeptum beneficium in ecclesia de Hindringham[c] ad consilium nostrum dictam ecclesiam in manus nostras resignasset et dicti prior et conventus eandem ecclesiam ea vice ordinationi nostre commississent, nos pensatis ex una parte meritis dictorum prioris et conventus in laudabili observantia regulari et in gratia hospitalitatis copiose pro viribus suis, item attendentes ex altera parte quod olim prior et conventus de Cokesford[b] qui tunc fuerunt memoratum Willelmum a scolis in primordio sui profectus in obsequium ecclesie sue vocaverunt, in quo fideliter stetit et laudabiliter per septem annos vel fere, unde forte iacturam eruditionis et temporis, qua nulla maior incurreret[d], item percipientes erga eundem dictorum prioris et conventus voluntatem bonam et gratiosam et ad gratam obsequii ecclesie eorundem inpensi remunerationem paratam, attendentes etiam quod modicum beneficium quod habet in dicta ecclesia de Hindringham[c] ad honestam ipsius sustentationem non sufficit et quod tenuis sit et exilis in proventibus supradicta ecclesia quam resignavit, de memorata ecclesia post aliquot dies taliter duximus ordinandum, videlicet concessimus quod ad hospitalitatem dicte domus de Cokesford[b] augmentandam prefatam ecclesiam de Bermere habeant in usus proprios eiusdem prioris et conventus, ita tamen quod idem Willelmus liberam terram eiusdem ecclesie habeat et ipsius ecclesie fructus suo perpetuo percipiat, solvendo singulis annis dictis priori et conventui nomine firme unam marcam argenti in duabus synodis Norwicensibus pro equalibus portionibus, licet iidem fructus multo maioris valoris existant, et post eius decessum vel recessum omnes fructus ecclesie predictos cum libera terra habeant iidem prior et conventus, salva honesta sustentatione vicarii qui in ea pro tempore ministrabit per nos vel successores nostros perpetuo ordinanda,[e] et salvis in omnibus episcopalibus consuetudinibus et nostre Norwicensis ecclesie dignitate. In cuius rei testimonium huic scripto sigillum nostrum fecimus apponi.

Data[f] apud Weseham .vi. idus Decembris anno Domini millesimo CC° L°
secundo et pontificatus nostri anno .viii°.

[a] Sidesterne C   [b] Cok' C, D   [c] Hyndryngham B   [d] incurrebat B, C   [e] ordinandi C, D   [f] Act'
C,D

In 1254 Barmer church was valued at £6 and the prior of Coxford's portion at 13s 4d; in 1291
the church was assessed at £6 13s 4d; Binham priory had a portion of 6s (*VN* 420; *Taxatio* 89b).
In 1326 bp Ayreminne appropriated Barmer to the canons referring back to bp Suffield's actum
(Bodl. ms Norfolk ch. 73 (ii)). The vicar's portion at Hindringham was valued in 1254 and 1291
at £5; the church was assessed at £26 4s 7d in 1254 and at £23 6s 8d in 1291 (*VN* 373; *Taxatio*
81b).

37. Creake Abbey

Grant to the canons in proprios usus *of the church of St Martin, Quarles, so that
at present they shall receive as the* personatus *eight marks a year at the two
Norwich synods from Martin the vicar, who shall have all the revenues of the
church as his vicarage and shall discharge all the ordinary obligations, others
being shared by vicar and canons according to their portions. After his death or
resignation they shall have possession of the whole church, saving a vicarage to
be taxed by the bishop or his successors.*   Thornham, 21 August 1248

B = Cambridge, Christ's College, Creake abbey muniments 7 (*inspeximus* by prior and convent
    of Norwich, 14 December 1267). s. xiii ex. C = BL ms. Add. 61900 (Creake abbey
    cartulary) fo. 44r–v (47r–v). s. xiv in. D = ibid. fos. 44v–45r (47v–48r). s. xiv in.
Pd (transl.) from C and D in *Creake Abbey Cartulary* nos. 137–8.

Omnibus Cristi fidelibus ad quos presens scriptum pervenerit Walterus Dei gratia
Norwicensis[a] episcopus salutem in Domino sempiternam. Ad universorum
notitiam volumus pervenire nos intuitu caritatis et religionis favore dilectis filiis
abbati et conventui sancte Marie de Prato iuxta Crek' ecclesiam sancti Martini de
Quarsles[b] in usus proprios concessisse, ita quod in presenti recipient octo marcas
annuas de eadem nomine personatus in duabus sinodis Norwicensibus[c] per
manum Martini vicarii, qui omnes fructus et[d] proventus dicte ecclesie percipiet
nomine vicarie et inde omnia onera consueta et debita sustinebit, et alia pro rata
portionum suarum ipse vicarius et canonici sustinebunt. Post eius autem
decessum vel recessum eis totam ecclesiam in usus proprios concessimus
perpetuo possidendam, salva vicaria per nos vel successores nostros taxanda,
salvis etiam episcopalibus consuetudinibus et nostre ecclesie Norwicensis[a]
dignitate. Hiis testibus:[e] magistro Roberto de Insula archidiacono Colecestr' et
aliis. Dat' apud Thornham .xii. kalendas Septembris pontificatus nostri anno
quarto.

[a] Norwycensis C, D   [b] Quarles C; Qwarles D   [c] synodis Norwycensibus C, D   [d] et *om.* C   [e]
C, D *end here*

The advowson of the church had recently been granted to the canons by John of Quarles
(*Creake Abbey Cartulary* no. 132). In April 1248 Abbot William successfully sued Nicholas,

son of John of Quarles, in the *curia regis* on a plea of warranty of charter for a parcel of land and the advowson; Nicholas acknowledged the canons' right and was received into confraternity (ibid. no. 145). The canons were inducted into corporal possession of the church on 28 May 1248 (ibid. no. 139, where wrongly dated 1249, incorrect whether the pontificate is dated from election or consecration); thus this actum was formally issued after induction. In 1254 the *personatus*, held by the abbot, was valued at 8 marks (£5 6s 8d) and the vicarage at £1 (VN 374). A vicarage was taxed, on the authority of bp Roger Scarning, by mr Thomas of Deopham, his clerk, on 20 January 1274 (*Creake Abbey Cartulary* no. 148). In 1291 the church, appropriated to the canons and apart from the vicarage not subject to the tenth, was listed at £5 (*Taxatio* 81).

38. Durham Cathedral Priory

Indulgence of forty days remission of enjoined penance to all those of his diocese, and to others whose diocesans ratify this grant, who, contrite and confessed, visit and pray at the feretory of St Cuthbert or the Galilee chapel and there make an offering. Durham, 8 September 1254

> A = Durham Cathedral Muniments, Misc. Ch. 1515. Endorsed: Walterus Norwicensis episcopus .xl. dies visitantibus feretrum sive galileam, anno M° CCLIIII° (s. xiii); approx. 175 × 114 + 23 mm.; parchment tag, seal, brown wax, counterseal.

Omnibus Cristi fidelibus ad quos presens scriptum pervenerit Walterus Dei gratia Norwicensis episcopus salutem in Domino sempiternam. Inter preclaros Cristi confessores quorum presentia corporalis Anglicane patrocinatur ecclesie, beatus Cuthbertus non mediocre sanctitatis preconium dinoscitur optinere, nec immerito laudibus humanis attollitur cuius meritis infirmi sanitatis gratiam consecuntur, cuius caro carie carens et prorsus integra perseverans dormientem potius quam mortuum preservare videtur. Membra namque beati viri incorrupta penitus manere non solum venerabilis Bede presbiteri scriptura testatur, verum etiam quamplurium sanctorum asserunt testimonia, et ipsius sacratissimi corporis translatio evidentissime comprobavit. Nos igitur, tanti confessoris considerante insignia, de Dei misericordia, gloriose virginis Marie, sancti Cuthberti omniumque sanctorum meritis confidentes, omnibus parochianis nostris et aliis quorum diocesani hanc nostram indulgentiam ratam habuerint, si de peccatis suis vere contriti fuerint et confessi, qui ad feretrum confessoris antedicti sive ad galileam ecclesie eiusdem devotionis et orationis advenerint ac de bonis sibi a Deo collatis ad prefatum feretrum sive ad galileam aliquid cum devotione attulerint, de iniuncta sibi penitentia quadraginta dies misericorditer inperpetuum relaxamus. Dat' Dunelm' .vi. idus Septembris anno Domini M CC L quarto et pontificatus nostri anno decimo.

> The Galilee chapel was constructed by bp Hugh du Puiset and had been completed by 1174 × 1189, by which date it housed an altar dedicated to the Blessed Virgin; see R. Halsey, 'The Galilee Chapel', in *Medieval Art and Architecture at Durham Cathedral* (BAA, 1980) 59–79. By 1279 it was already being used for sessions of the bp's court (*EEA* 29 no. 231), and by the fourteenth century was the regular site of the consistory court. On 29 January 1255, and again on 30 January 1256, bp Walter Kirkham of Durham granted remission of forty days penance to

those who visited the shrine of St Cuthbert to pray and make an offering, confirming forever all indulgences in favour of the feretory granted by other bps; among those which he had inspected was that of bp Suffield (ibid. nos. 72, 74), which is listed in the mid sixteenth century in *Rites of Durham* 151.

39. Durham Cathedral Priory

Indulgence of thirteen days remission of enjoined penance to all those of his diocese, and to others whose diocesans ratify this grant, who, contrite and confessed, visit and pray at the chapel dedicated to St Edmund of Canterbury at Bearpark. Durham, 8 September 1254

> A = Durham Cathedral Muniments 2. 13, Pont. 4. Endorsed: Indulgentia .xiii. dierum concessa W. Norwycense episcopo omnibus causa devotionis vel orationis accedentibus ad capellam fundatam in honore sancti Edmundi episcopi in Beurepayre; pressmark (s. xiii); pressmark (s. xv); approx. 143 × 92 + 15 mm.; parchment tag, seal, brown wax, counterseal.

Omnibus sancte matris ecclesie filiis ad quos presentes littere pervenerint Walterus Dei gratia Norwicensis episcopus salutem in Domino sempiternam. Beati patris Eadmundi Cantuariensis ecclesie presulis dum adhuc a nobis cerneretur in terris vita gloriosa, miracula etiam que per ipsum a Domino fiunt, ad ipsius sancti laudem excollendam et divulgandam nos compellunt et inducunt. Nos ex dispensatione nobis credita Cristi fidelibus non solum erogare artum verbi Dei verum etiam ad eterne messionis manipulos recolligendos animos ipsorum excitare debitores nos recognoscentes, de Dei misericordia, gloriose virginis Marie necnon et gloriosi confessoris antedicti omniumque sanctorum meritis confisi, omnibus parochianis nostris et aliis quorum diocesani hanc nostram ratam habuerint indulgentiam, si de peccatis suis vere contriti fuerint et confessi, qui ad capellam de Beurepeir in eiusdem sancti honore dedicatam causa devotionis vel orationis advenerint, de iniuncta sibi penitentia sive penalitate eis pro commissis debita tresdecim dies in conspectu altissimi relaxamus. Dat' Dunelm' .vi. idus Septembris anno Domini M CC L quarto.

> Bearpark, or Beaurepaire, was a manor of the prior, where he frequently resided at no great distance from his convent. It was also used as a monastic rest-house, where meat might be eaten. Its 400 acres of grazing land were used in part for the prior's stud-farm of horses, and the manor was a source of coal for the cathedal priory. In the late middle ages it was 'one of the greatest country seats in northern England' (R.B. Dobson, *Durham Priory 1400–1450* (Cambridge, 1973) 95–8). On 30 January 1256 bp Walter Kirkham of Durham granted forty days remission of penance to those who visited the chapels at Bearpark dedicated to the Blessed Virgin, St Edmund and St Catherine, ratifying all indulgences issued by other bps (*EEA* 29 no. 73).

40. Agnes l'Enveyse

Notification that, with the consent of the prior and convent of Pentney, the bishop has conceded to her for her lifetime a free chantry in the chapel of her house at Chediston. The chaplain who is to minister there shall on his first arrival swear on the Gospels, in the presence of the vicar of the mother church or his chaplain, that he will render all oblations and obventions given at the chapel without any deduction to the mother church within a day of receipt, and that he will not admit any parishioner to confession or any other sacrament unless they are in danger of imminent death. The chapel shall be subject to the mother church, and in token of this subjection the lady, if present there, and her household shall attend the parish church at Christmas, Easter, the Assumption of the Blessed Virgin Mary and the church's [dedication] feast, offering the customary oblations at high mass. Excommunication is pronounced against any who may act contrary to the terms of this concession. On Agnes's death the chapel and administration [of the sacraments] shall be suspended.

Pentney, 6 May 1245

A = TNA, LR14/1107. Endorsed: De capella de Chetestan (s. xiii med.); approx. 172 × 88 + 15 mm.; parchment tag, fragment of seal, natural wax varnished dark green, counterseal.

Omnibus Cristi fidelibus ad quos presens scriptum pervenerit Walterus Dei gratia Norwicensis episcopus salutem in Domino. Noveritis nos, de voluntate et consensu dilectorum filiorum prioris et conventus de Panten', karissime in Cristo filie domine Agneti le Enveyse quoad vixerit liberam cantuariam in capella in curia sua de Chetestan constructa concessisse sub hac forma, videlicet quod capellanus in ea ministraturus in primo suo adventu, presente vicario matricis ecclesie vel suo capellano, iurabit inspectis sacrosanctis evangeliis quod omnes oblationes et obventiones matrici ecclesie eadem die qua percipiuntur vel proxima sequenti integre et absque diminutione restituet, et quod nullum parochianum matricis ecclesie ad confessionem sive aliquod aliud sacramentum ecclesiasticum admittet, nisi periculum mortis imineret. Erit siquidem prefata capella matrici ecclesie subiecta, et in signum subiectionis prefata domina unacum familia sua ad matricem ecclesiam accedet diebus infrascriptis, videlicet die natalis Domini et die Pasche, Assumptionis beate Marie et festivitatis ecclesie, cum debitis et consuetis oblationibus ad magnam missam, si ibidem fuerit prefatam ecclesiam veneratura. Nos vero omnes illos qui aliquid in huius nostre concessionis preiudicium sive fraudem machinati fuerint sive fieri procuraverint sententia excommunicationis innodavimus. Decedente vero dicta domina, predicta capella ipso iure sit suspensa sine spe administrandi in ea. In cuius rei testimonium presenti scripto sigillum nostrum apponi fecimus. Datum apud Panten' .ii. nonas Maii pontificatus nostri anno primo.

The parish church of Chediston was appropriated to the Augustinian canons of Pentney (*Taxatio* 118b). Agnes l'Enveyse was the widow of William l'Enveyse and daughter and heir of William of Drayton (*Bk Fees* iii 212). In 1242–3, with Thomas son of Baldwin, Roger

Lestrange and Reginald of Dunham she held a fee of the Ria honour of Hockering in Scarning, West Walton and Wolterton (ibid. ii 909).

Her own charter acknowledging these terms for her chapel is witnessed by mr William Suffield and mr William of Horham (TNA, LR14/1121). Provision was made for the soul of William l'Enveyse, and for the discharge of his debts, in bp Suffield's will (no. 138 below).

41. Eye Priory

Grant to the monks in proprios usus, *for the repair and maintenance of their conventual church, for which they lack resources, of the church of Playford, of which they hold the advowson. The revenues shall not be converted to any other use unless for a specific cause approved by the bishop and the monastic chapter, after which even then they shall revert to their former use.* Bacton, 11 May 1247

B = Essex R. O., D/DBy. Q 19 (Eye cartulary) fos. 30v–31r. s. xiii ex.
Pd in *Eye Cartulary* i no. 50.

Omnibus Cristi fidelibus has litteras visuris vel audituris Walterus Dei gratia Norwicensis episcopus salutem in Domino sempiternam. Cum ea que ad ecclesiarum [fo. 31r] constructionem pio conferuntur affectu in conspectu altissimi suavius redoleant et luculentius eluceant inter opera caritatis, et ecclesia dilectorum in Cristo filiorum prioris et conventus de Eya, opere sumptuoso nobiliter inchoata, frequenti et continua indigeat reparatione ad quam ipsorum non suppetunt facultates, ipsis ad ecclesie sue constructionem et perpetuam sustentationem ecclesiam de Plaiford, in qua ius optinent patronatus, in proprios usus assignamus, statuentes ne quis inposterum contra nostram voluntatem et assignationem eandem[a] in alios usus convertere presumat, nisi certa causa interveniente a nobis et suo capitulo specialiter approbata, qua cessante dicte ecclesie proventus in pristinos usus cedere volumus et precipimus. In cuius rei testimonium presenti scripto sigillum nostrum duximus apponendum. Dat' apud Baketon' .v. idus Maii pontificatus nostri anno .iii°.

[a] eosdem B, *probably to agree with* proventus *below.*

The advowson of Playford was disputed in the late 1220s and 1230s by Alan of Withersdale (*EEA* 21 no. 58). In 1268 Eye's right was once more disputed in the *curia regis*, unsuccessfully, by Thomas of Clare, then lord of the manor (*Eye Cartulary* ii no. 392). In 1254 the church was valued at £16 13s 4d, in 1291, presumably after the establishment of a vicarage which is not taxed, at £8 (*VN* 452; *Taxatio* 117b). For a brief history of the church, see *Eye Cartulary* i 48.

42. Reginald Le Gros

Notification that, with the consent of the abbot of St Benet of Holme, patron of the church of Stalham, and of the rector thereof, the bishop has conceded to the lord Reginald le Gros, knight, and his heirs a perpetual chantry in the chapel of his house at Stalham. The chaplain who is to celebrate there shall on his first arrival swear on the Gospels, in the presence of the rector or his proctor, that he will render all oblations at the chapel to the mother church within a day of their receipt, and that he will not admit any parishioner to confession or any other sacrament, unless they are in danger of imminent death. The chapel shall be subject to the mother church, and in token of this subjection the knight and all his household shall, if present, go to the parish church of Stalham at Christmas for three masses, and high mass at Easter, Pentecost, the Assumption of the Blessed Virgin Mary and the feast of the church's dedication, offering the due oblations. If the chaplain should prove contumacious in any of these matters, the chapel shall be suspended until satisfaction is made to the mother church.

Thornage, 28 June 1247

B = BL ms. Cotton Galba E ii (St Benet cartulary) fo. 49r (20r). s. xiii ex.

Omnibus Cristi fidelibus has litteras visuris vel audituris Walterus Dei gratia Norwicensis episcopus salutem in Domino sempiternam. Noverit universitas vestra nos de consensu dilecti filii abbatis sancti Benedicti de Hulmo, ecclesie de Stalham patroni, pariter et eiusdem ecclesie rectoris, domino Reginaldo le Gros militi et heredibus suis perpetuam cantariam in capella in curia sua apud Stalham sita concessisse sub hac forma, videlicet quod capellanus in eadem ministraturus in primo suo adventu, presente rectore matricis ecclesie vel suo procuratore, inspectis sacrosanctis evangeliis corporali sacramento se astringet quod omnes oblationes dicte capelle undique provenientes eo die quo percipiuntur vel proximo die sequenti matrici ecclesie fideliter et absque ulla diminutione restituet, nec aliquem parochianum matricis ecclesie ad confessionem vel ad aliud sacramentum ecclesiasticum, nisi mortis periculo iminente, recipiet. Erit siquidem prefata capella matrici ecclesie subiecta, et in signum subiectionis prefatus miles et heredes sui cum tota familia sua, si ibidem fuerint, diebus infra notatis ad matricem ecclesiam accedent, scilicet die natalis Domini ad tres missas, diebus vero Pasche, Pentecostes, Assumptionis gloriose virginis et festi ecclesie ad magnam missam, ipsam debitis oblationibus veneraturi. Quod si capellanus qui ibidem fuerit in aliquo premissorum rebellis extiterit, capella sit ipso vice suspensa donec matrici ecclesie per ipsum fuerit satisfactum. In cuius rei testimonium presenti scripto sigillum nostrum duximus apponendum. Dat' apud Thorneg' .iiii. kalendas Iulii pontificatus nostri anno tertio.

Reginald le Gros in 1242–3 held one knight's fee in Sloley, Lammas, Scottow and Tuddenham of the Ria honour of Hockering (*Bk Fees* 910); he was thus a neighbour of the bp's own family.

43. Hales in Loddon, Chapel of St Andrew

Inspeximus and confirmation of a charter of Roger of Hales, knight, by which he endows the chapel in perpetuity for two chaplains and their successors, who shall each day celebrate two masses, one of the Blessed Virgin Mary and the other pro defunctis. *The endowment is detailed. One chaplain shall be warden.*

He shall be presented by sir Roger and his successors to the bishop, and shall swear an oath to act in good faith with regard to spiritualities, divine office and temporalities, and he shall choose a colleague who is suitable, at the peril of his soul. These chaplains shall be perpetual, and shall not be removed without manifest and reasonable cause. On the death of the warden, sir Roger or his heirs shall present another suitable chaplain as aforesaid, who shall be admitted without difficulty; and if he or his heirs should be negligent in such presentation, the diocesan may appoint on that occasion, saving their rights at future vacancies. Warranty is granted.   [? Great] Snoring, 25 August 1252

A = Arundel Castle, duke of Norfolk's muniments, Hales ch. 104. Endorsed: Carta de fundatione capelle sancti Andree (s. xv); approx. 360 × 185 + 20 mm.; three slits, parchment tag through central slit, fragment of bp's seal, brown wax.

Omnibus Cristi fidelibus presens scriptum visuris vel audituris Walterus Dei gratia Norwicensis episcopus salutem in Domino sempiternam. Noverit universitas vestra nos cartam domini Rogeri de Hales militis inspexisse in hec verba: Sciant presentes et futuri quod ego Rogerus de Hales filius Walteri de Suffeld concessi, dedi et hac presenti carta mea confirmavi Deo et beate Marie et omnibus sanctis et capelle sancti Andree site prope regiam viam que se extendit a viridi planicie de Hales versus Herewellestun' et duobus capellanis et eorum successoribus qui in dicta capella divina inperpetuum celebrabunt, videlicet unam missam cotidie de gloriosa virgine Maria et aliam pro defunctis, totum gardinum meum quod abbuttat super ipsam capellam, et iacet inter terram Willelmi de Vernon' et fossatum alterius gardini mei, quantum habet in longitudine et latitudine, cum toto fossato et quinque pedibus extra fossatum versus aquilonem, et totam illam peciam terre que iacet inter dictam capellam et regiam viam que se extendit versus Herewelleston' cum tota latitudine a terra Willelmi de Vernon' versus austrum usque ad fossatum versus aquilonem, cum toto fossato quod se extendit a viridi planicie usque ad boscum meum, cum quinque pedibus extra fossatum, et duas acras terre mee in villa de Hales que abutant super viridem planiciem de Hales que fuerunt Alani villani, et unam acram que iacet iuxta illas acras versus austrum que fuit Wulvive Fanne, et unam acram ad capud ipsius terre versus orientem de feudo Alani de Hekingham, et novem acras terre in Vilaynestoft que iacent iuxta mesuagium quod fuit Walteri villani versus austrum, et duas acras terre que iacent iuxta viam que extenditur de Hales usque monasterium de Kirkeby versus occidentem, et octodecim acras terre que iacent iuxta ipsam viam versus orientem, et duas acras terre in campo de Hales que vocantur Brunlingwong', et unam parvam peciam terre que vocatur Waterrode, et unam peciam que vocatur Ravenesrod, et unam peciam que vocatur Haldenesrode, et duas pecias que vocantur Dallemeresrodes, et totam peciam que iacet iuxta mesuagium quod fuit Roberti de Grinvillies versus occidentem, quantum se extendit in longitudine et latitudine, et duas acras terre apud Gosemere, et dimidiam acram in Lodnebreche que iacet iuxta terram Ade le Bucmongere versus orientem, et unam acram et unam rodam in Herewellestun' que vocantur Sharpescroft, et unam acram et unam rodam in Herewellestun' que vocantur Trolondescroft, et duos denarios annui redditus quod Editha Trolond michi debuit pro domo sua sita ad capud ipsius terre, et quinque acras terre in villa de Raveningham que iacent ante mesuagium quod fuit Odonis Fridai et abutant super viam qua pergitur usque Tungate versus austrum, et unam acram terre apud Kecmilne, et duas acras terre et dimidiam in una pecia et tres rodas in alia pecia que iacent inter boscum Thome filii Roberti et mesuagium quod fuit Roberti de Bosco, et unam acram que vocatur Shoteshomesacre, et quatuor acras prati in prato meo de Elingham quod vocatur le Parc, scilicet ad capud versus orientem, et duas acras turbarii sub domo Roberti filii Philippi, et totum boscum meum de Brom qui iacet iuxta mesuagium Alani de Stanstede versus austrum, et Petrum secatorem cum toto tenemento suo quod de me tenuit et cum tota sequela sua, et Stephanum Lewine cum toto tenemento suo quod de me tenuit et cum tota sequela sua, et homagium et servitium Warini de Pastun'[a] cum toto tenemento suo quod de me tenuit in villa de Nortun', et unum denarium redditus quem Reginaldus God michi debuit, et quatuor solidos et octo denarios annuatim percipiendos de redditu quem Margareta quondam uxor Henrici Dom et Thomas filius eius michi annuatim debuerunt pro terra quam de me tenuerunt in villa de Nortun', et quatuor solidos annuatim percipiendos de redditu Willelmi Herbert, et homagium et servitium Thome filii Walteri de Hales cum toto tenemento suo quod de me tenuit, et totum iuncarium meum quod habui in villa de Hadescho in marisco qui vocatur Kirkemers, et totum mariscum meum de Nortun' qui vocatur Milnehowemers, et totum mariscum qui iacet inter ipsum mariscum et mesuagium Thome filii Henrici Dom, cum omnibus pertinentiis ad predictos mariscos et pratum et boscum pertinentibus, habenda et tenenda predictis capellanis et eorum successoribus et capelle predicte in liberam, puram et perpetuam elemosinam inperpetuum. Erit autem unus capellanus custos ipsius capelle et omnium bonorum mobilium et immobilium ad ipsam capellam pertinentium, et episcopo loci per me sive per heredes meos presentabitur, qui se fideliter in spiritualibus divinisque officiis et temporalibus habiturum iurabit, sociumque sibi assumet in periculo anime sue quem divino cultui domuique credit fore idoneum. Erunt autem perpetui isti capellani nec absque causa manifesta et rationabili ammovebuntur. Decedente vero custode, ego sive heredes mei alium capellanum idoneum presentabimus, ut supradictum est, qui absque difficultate admittetur. Et si ego vel heredes mei in presentatione predicta facienda negligenter fuerimus, volo et concedo pro me et heredibus meis quod liceat loci diocesano illa vice custodem in capella predicta de capellano idoneo preficeret, salva michi et heredibus meis presentatione de alio capellano facienda cum idem in fata discesserit. Et ego Rogerus de Hales et heredes mei warantizabimus, adquietabimus et defendemus predictis capellanis et eorum successoribus et capelle predicte omnes predictas terras, redditus et tenementa cum omnibus pertinentiis contra omnes inperpetuum. In huius autem rei testimonium huic scripto una cum sigillo domini Norwicensis et de Norwico et de Laungel' capitulorum sigillum meum apposui. Hiis testibus: domino

Willelmo Aages, domino Willelmo de Senges, domino Waltero de Senges, domino Iohanne de Lodnes, Willelmo filio Rogeri de Brom, Rogero filio Walteri de Raveningham, Roberto de Hulmo, Willelmo de Vernon', Ricardo filio Walteri de Cadamo, Rogero de Dicleburg', Stephano filio Alani de Mundham, Roberto Bil, Andrea Wascelin et multis aliis. Nos autem dictam donationem, concessionem et providentiam ratam habentes, eam auctoritate pontificali confirmamus. Hiis testibus: magistro Roberto de Insula archidiacono Colecestr', Thoma de Theya capellano, Willelmo de Whitewell', Willelmo de Pakeham, Thoma de Walkote et Willelmo de Ludham clericis, Egidio de Whitewell', Willelmo de Ditton', Willelmo de Wichingham et aliis. Dat' apud Snaring' .viii. kalendas Septembris anno Domini millesimo ducentesimo quinquagesimo secundo.

ᵃ *Probable reading, small hole in ms.*

The chapel was situated at Hales Hall, to the south of Loddon and within that parish, rather than the separate parish and vill of Hales, to the south-south-east of Loddon.

Roger of Hales was certainly a kinsman of the bp, but is to be distinguished from Roger of Suffield, the bp's brother, since they were engaged in litigation against each other in 1225–26 (Rye, *Norfolk Fines* 40, no. 184). Roger of Hales's father, Walter of Suffield, with Oliva his wife and William his son, was before 11 July 1202 granted by Cecily of Norton all her part of Loddon and 'Milnehoemes' in Norton Subcourse, which is mentioned in Roger's charter above (*Fines* i no. 381). Roger of Hales was himself dead by 1267–68, when Roger son of Walter of Hales brought an action against Matilda, his widow (Rye, *Norfolk Fines* 102, no. 1526).

In 1277 × 1278 the official of the bp of Norwich conducted a judicial enquiry into the status of the chapel, here called the chapel of sir Roger of Hales's manor of 'Wrantishaghe' in Loddon, following a recent episcopal visitation, during which Thomas Dune claimed to have been instituted to the chapel, although he had never been admitted by the bp; this appeared to be to the prejudice of the mother church of Loddon and its vicar, in that he had administered the sacraments to the parishioners and to others and had received their offerings, to the danger of their souls. Dune claimed to have been collated to the chapel by sir Roger without the consent of the diocesan, on the strength of an undated concession by the abbot and convent of Langley, to whom Loddon church was appropriated, allowing him freely to institute chaplains to the chapel of St Andrew of 'Wrantishaghe' without contradiction by the canons; these chaplains might receive all offerings at the chapel, together with the lesser tithes; the servants of the lord living in their own dwellings must render all due and customary offerings to the mother church, and receive the sacraments there, and the chaplains, in token of their subjection, shall each year pay to the mother church all offerings received by them on Easter Sunday and the feast of St Andrew, and themselves offer two candles of one pound weight; they should not celebrate nor receive payment for anniversary or memorial masses for the parishioners of Loddon. The official adjudged this concession to be invalid, since no such rights might be conveyed, nor chaplain instituted, nor divine service conducted, without the diocesan's permission, nor the sacraments celebrated without the vicar's consent. In future there should be no chaplain instituted without licence of bp and vicar, and all offerings received up to now should be restored to the vicar (Norfolk R. O., Reg. 2/4, fo. 156v, noted in *Reg. Bateman* no. 1919; a sixteenth-century addition, dated 24 May 1277, but since mr J. de Ferriby describes himself as official of bp William (Middleton), who was not elected until 24 February 1278 following the death of bp Roger Scarning on 22 January 1278, this is possibly in error for 24 March 1277/8.)

44. Henry III, king of England

Notification addressed by the bishop-elect to Henry III asking that he bring secular authority to bear on Walter, rector of Great Fakenham, who has remained excommunicate for more than forty days.   Thorpe, 19 January 1245

A = TNA, C.85/130/14. No endorsement, approx. 155 × 50 mm., tongue torn away.

Venerabili domino H. Dei gratia regi Anglie, domino Hibern', duci Normann' et Aquit' et comiti Andeg', Walterus miseratione divina Norwicensis electus salutem et quicquid potest honoris et reverentie. Quia Walterus rector ecclesie de Magna Fakenham, claves ecclesie contempnens, pertinaciter perseveravit in excommunicatione per quadraginta dies et amplius, vestram excellentiam duximus exorandam quatinus ipsum secundum consuetudinem terre vestre capi facientes quod vestrum est in hac parte exequimini. Valeat excellentia regia per tempora longa. Dat' apud Torp' .xiiii. kalendas Februarii anno confirmationis nostre primo.

45. Henry III, king of England

Notification addressed to Henry III asking that he bring secular authority to bear on Hamo of Cressingham, who has remained excommunicate for more than forty days.   [19 February 1245 × 19 May 1257]

A = TNA, C.85/130/17. No endorsement; approx. 147 × 57 mm., tongue torn away.

Excellentissimo domino H. Dei gratia illustri regi Angl', duci Normann', comiti Andegav' et Aquitan', domino Ybern', W. miseratione divina Norwicensis ecclesie minister humilis salutem in eo qui dat salutem regibus. Noverit excellentia vestra regia Hamonem de Cressingham nostre diocesis propter eius manifestam offensam et contumaciam auctoritate nostra excommunicationis sententia esse innodatum, ac eundem Hamonem in prefata sententia, claves ecclesie pertinaciter contempnendo, per quadraginta dies et amplius perseverasse. Quapropter magnificentie vestre regie supplicamus quatinus ipsum Hamonem, quem Dei timor ab errore non revocat, faciatis secundum regni vestri consuetudinem approbatam quousque absolutionis beneficium meruerit optinere potestate regia coherceri. Valeat excellentia vestra per longa tempora. Dat' apud.[a]

[a] A ends here

The earliest extant signification from Norwich diocese is dated 19 January 1245 (no. 44 above). Nos. 45–7 have the year missing because of damage. Since no significations survive from the episcopate of William Raleigh, it is assumed that they were issued by Suffield, but it is possible that they are of Raleigh's time. For the dates of the first significations from the various dioceses, see Logan, *Excommunication and the Secular Arm* 23–4, n. 44.

46. Henry III, king of England

Notification addressed to Henry III asking that he bring secular authority to bear on Richard of Attlebridge, who has remained excommunicate for more than forty days.   Norwich, 26 July [1245 × 1256]

A = TNA, C.85/130/15. No endorsement; left hand side missing, remains approx. 120 × 46 mm.

[Egregio ac magnifico][a] domino H. Dei gratia illustri regi Angl', domino Ibern', duci Norm', Aquit' et comiti Andeg', W. miseratione [divina Norwicensis ecclesie] minister humilis salutem in eo qui dat salutem regibus. Quia Ricardus de Attlebrig de comitatu [Norfolc' sententia excommunicationis in-][a]nodatus per quadraginta dies et amplius in ipsa sententia perseveravit, claves ecclesie contemp-[nendo, vestre magnificentie][a] dignum duximus supplicandum quatinus cohercionem quam regia celsitudo contra tales exercere [contra ipsum iubeat exerceri][a]. Valeat regia maiestas vestra per tempora longiora. Dat' apud Norwicum .vii°. kalendas Augusti ... .

[a] *Conjectural reading*

See no. 45.

47. Henry III, king of England

Notification addressed to Henry III asking that he bring secular authority to bear on Ranulf de Rosei, who has remained excommunicate for more than forty days.   Terling, 20 October [1245 × 1256, probably 1247]

A = TNA, C.85/130/16. No endorsement; approx. 140 × 48 mm., bottom left hand corner torn away.

Excellentissimo domino suo H. Dei gratia illustri regi Anglorum, domino Hybern', duci Norm', Aquit' et comiti Andeg', W. miseratione divina Norwicensis ecclesie minister humilis salutem in eo qui dat salutem regibus. Regie celsitudini tenore presentium significamus quod Ranulfus de Rosey, nostra auctoritate excommunicationis [sent]-entia innodatus, in ea per quadraginta dies et ultra stetit pertinaciter, claves ecclesie contempnendo. Quapropter [vestram maiestatem egr][a] –egiam imploramus quatinus contra eum, quem Dei timor non revocat ab errore, vestre regalis potentie auxilium [iubeatis inferri. Vestra][a] crescat potestas regia diu duratura. Dat' apud Terling .xii. kalendas Novembris anno... .

[a] *Conjectural reading*

See nos. 45 above and 53 below.

48. Henry III, king of England

Notification addressed to Henry III asking that he bring secular authority, by the agency of the sheriff of Suffolk, to bear against Ralph of Waldingfield, knight, and Richard of Pulham, chaplain, who have remained excommunicate for more than forty days. 24 March 1246

A = TNA, C.85/130/3. No endorsement; approx. 175 × 70 mm.; tongue and tie, fragment of seal, light brown wax.

Excellentissimo domino suo H. Dei gratia regi Angl', domino Hybern', duci Norm', Aquit' et comiti And' Walterus permissione divina Norwicensis episcopus salutem in eo qui dat salutem regibus. Vestre excellentie declaramus Radulfum de Waldingefeud' militem et Ricardum de Pulham capellanum propter multiplices et manifestas contumacias[a] suas excommunicatos fuisse et per quadraginta dies et amplius, contemptis ecclesie clavibus, in eadem excommunicatione pertinaciter perdurasse. Cum igitur sacrosancta ecclesia non habeat ultra quid faciat et talium contumaciam expediat per brachium seculare puniri, maiestatem regiam humiliter imploramus quatinus quod vestrum est contra huiusmodi contumaces vicecomiti Suff', in cuius balliva morantur, exequi demandetis. Valeat serenitas vestra per tempora longiora. Dat' nono kalendas Aprilis pontificatus nostri anno secundo.

[a] contumacies A

49. Henry III, king of England

Notification addressed to Henry III asking that he bring secular authority to bear against Hugh Gernegan, knight, Ralph son of William and Hugh his brother, and Richard son of William Bonsergaunt, of Mendlesham, Sf., who have remained excommunicate for more than forty days. Broome, 10 August 1246

A = TNA, C.85/130/2. No endorsement; approx. 180 × 58 mm., tongue and tie, seal missing.

Egregio et magnifico domino domino H. Dei gratia illustri regi Anglie, domino Hibernie, duci Normannie et Aquitanie et comiti Andegavie Walterus miseratione divina Norwicensis ecclesie minister humilis salutem in eo qui dat salutem regibus. Cum dominus Hugo Gernegan miles, Radulfus filius Willelmi, Hugo frater eius et Ricardus filius Willelmi Bonsergaunt de Mendlesham in comitatu Suffolchie per quadraginta dies et amplius in sententia excommunicationis, claves ecclesie contempnendo, perseveraverunt, regie celsitudini vestre humiliter supplicandum duximus et devote quatinus cohercionem quam regia maiestas contra tales exercere consuevit contra predictos iubeat inferri. Valeat regia maiestas in Domino per tempora longa. Dat' apud Brom .iiii. idus Augusti anno Domini M° CC° XL sexto.

50. Henry III, king of England

Notification addressed to Henry III asking that he bring secular authority to bear on Luke of St Edmunds, chaplain, of the county of Suffolk, who has remained excommunicate for more than forty days.

[14 September × 15] October 1246

A = TNA, C.85/130/1. No endorsements. Approx. 181 × 30 mm., bottom left corner, probably with tongue, torn away, no evidence of sealing.

Egregio et magnifico domino, domino H. regi Angl', domino Hib', duci Norm' et Aquit' et comiti And', Walterus permissione divina Norwicensis ecclesie minister humilis salutem in eo qui dat salutem regibus. Cum Lucas de sancto Eadmundo, capellanus de comitatu Suff', per xl dies et amplius, claves ecclesie contempnendo, in sententia excommunicationis pertinaciter perseveraverit, regie celsitudini vestre humiliter duximus supplicandum et devote quatinus cohercionem quam regia maiestas contra tales exercere consuevit celsitudo vestra contra eundem iubeat inferri. Valeat maiestas regia in Domino per tempora longa. Dat' apud ......ᵃ Octobris anno Domini Mᵒ CCᵒ XL sexto.

ᵃ *Document torn at this point.*

51. Henry III, king of England

Notification addressed to Henry III asking that he bring secular authority to bear upon Geoffrey Laundel, chaplain, and Henry, rector of Wiggenhall, who have remained excommunicate for more than forty days.

[25 March 1247 × 24 March 1248]

A = TNA, C.85/130/5. No endorsement; approx. 168 × 44 mm.; tongue torn away; badly stained.

Egregio ac magnifico domino H. Dei gratia illustri regi Angl', domino Hybern', duci Normann', Aquit' et comiti And', Walterus miseratione eiusdem Norwicensis ecclesie minister humilis salutem in eo qui dat salutem regibus. Cum Galfridus Laundel capellanus et Henricus rector de Wigehaul de comitatu Norfolch', claves ecclesie pertinaciter contempnendo, per quadraginta dies et amplius in sententia excommunicationis perseveraverunt, vestre duximus supplicandum magnificentie quatinus districtionem quam contra tales regia maiestas consuevit exercere celsitudo vestra inferri iubeat in eosdem. Valeat excellentia vestra semper in Domino. Dat' apud .... XLᵒ septimo.

52. Henry III, king of England

Notification addressed to Henry III asking that he bring secular authority to bear upon Walter son of Gilbert of Colville, who has remained excommunicate for more than forty days. Thetford, 9 April 1247

A = TNA, C.85/130/6. No endorsement; approx. 140 × 54 mm.; left-hand bottom corner torn away.

Egregio et magnifico domino H. Dei gratia illustri regi Anglie, domino Hybernie, Acquit' et comiti Andeg', Walterus miseratione divina Norwicensis ecclesie minister humilis salutem in eo qui dat salutem regibus. Cum Walterus filius quondam Gilberti de Kolevill', claves ecclesie contempnendo, per quadraginta dies et amplius in sentencia excommunicationis perseveravit, celsitudini vestre humiliter supplicandum duximus et devote quatinus districtionem quam regia maiestas vestra contra tales exercere consuevit celsitudo vestra contra eundem iubeat inferri. Valeat regia maiestas vestra per tempora longiora. Dat' apud Theford .v°. idus Aprilis anno Domini millesimo ducentesimo quadragesimo septimo.

53. Henry III, king of England

Notification addressed to Henry III asking that he bring secular authority to bear against Ranulf de Rosei, rector of Rockland [St Mary], and Nicholas Nel, rector of Walpole, who have remained excommunicate for more than forty days. London, 16 September 1247

A = TNA, C.85/130/4. No endorsement; approx. 182 × 60 mm.; tongue torn away.

Egregio et magnifico domino H. Dei gratia illustri regi Angl', domino Hybern', duci Norm' et Aquit', comiti And', Walterus permissione divina Norwicensis ecclesie minister humilis salutem in eo qui dat salutem regibus. Vestre notum facimus excellentie Ranulfum de Roseie rectorem ecclesie de Rokelond et Nicholaum Nel rectorem ecclesie de Walpole de comitatu Norfolc' per quadraginta dies et amplius, claves ecclesie contempnendo, pertinaciter in sentencia excommunicationis perseverasse. Quapropter dominationi vestre humiliter supplicandum duximus et devote quatinus districtionem quam regia maiestas contra tales exercere consuevit contra dictos Ranulfum et Nicholaum celsitudo vestra iubeat exerceri. Valeat regia maiestas vestra semper in Domino. Dat' London' .xvi. kalendas Octobris anno Domini millesimo ducentesimo quadragesimo septimo.

54. Henry III, king of England

Notification addressed to Henry III asking that he bring secular authority to bear upon Adam of Heacham, who has remained excommunicate for more than forty days.   Hertford, 7 March 1248

A = TNA, C.85/130/86. No endorsement; approx. 135 × 50 mm., tongue torn away.

Egregio ac magnifico domino H. Dei gratia illustri regi Angl', domino Hybern', duci Normann', Aquit' et comiti And', Walterus miseratione eiusdem Norwicensis ecclesie minister humilis salutem in eo qui dat salutem regibus. Vestra noverit excellentia Adam de Heccham de comitatu Norfolc', claves ecclesie pertinaciter contempnendo, in sententia excommunicationis per quadraginta dies et amplius perseverasse. Quapropter vestram imploramus magnificentiam quatinus districtionem quam regia maiestas vestra contra tales exercere consuevit celsitudo vestra inferri iubeat in eundem. Valeat regia maiestas semper in Domino. Dat' apud Hertford nonis Martii anno Domini M° CC° quadragesimo septimo.

55. Henry III, king of England

Notification addressed to Henry III asking that he bring secular authority to bear on Roger of Badingham, rector of Easton [Bavents], who has remained excommunicate for more than forty days.

Terling, [26 March 1248 × 9 March 1249]

A = TNA, C.85/130/8. No endorsement; approx. 146 × 40 mm., tongue and bottom left corner torn away.

Egregio ac magnifico domino H. Dei gratia illustri regi Angl', domino Hibern', duci Norm', Aquit' et comiti Andeg', Walterus miseratione divina Norwicensis ecclesie minister humilis salutem in eo qui dat salutem regibus. Quia Rogerus de Bading', rector ecclesie de Eston de comitatu Suff', claves ecclesie pertinaciter contempnendo, per quadraginta dies et amplius in excommunicationis perseveravit sententia, regie magnificentie humiliter supplicamus et devote quatinus districtionem quam regia maiestas contra tales consuevit exercere celsitudo vestra inferri iubeat in eundem. Valeat regia maiestas vestra semper in Domino. Dat' apud Terling' .vii. ....ᵃ anno Domini millesimo ducentesimo quadragesimo octavo.

ᵃ *Approx. eight letters missing.*

Reckoning the year beginning at the Annunciation, possible dates range from vii kalends March 1248 to vii Ides March 1249.

56. Henry III, king of England

Notification addressed to Henry III asking that he bring secular authority to bear upon William of Dunton, chaplain, who has remained excommunicate for more than forty days. Thornham, 1 June 1248

A = TNA, C.85/130/7. No endorsement; approx. 158 × 50 mm., tongue and tie, residual remains of wax.

Egregio ac magnifico domino domino H. Dei gratia illustri regi Angl', domino Ibernie, duci Norm' et Aquit' et comiti And', Walterus miseratione divina Norwicensis ecclesie minister humilis salutem in eo qui dat salutem regibus. Quia Willelmus de Dunton capellanus de comitatu Norfolch', claves ecclesie pertinaciter contempnendo, per quadraginta dies et amplius in excommunicationis perseveravit sententia, celsitudini vestre humiliter supplicamus et devote quatinus districtionem quam regia maiestas vestra contra tales exercere consuevit in ipsum inferri vestra iubeat excellentia. Valeat regia maiestas vestra semper in Domino. Dat' apud Thornham kalendis Iunii anno Domini M° CC° XL° octavo.

57. Henry III, king of England

Notification addressed to Henry III asking that he bring secular authority to bear on Roger of Heacham, Adam son of Roger, Peter atte Lane, Nicholas son of Jocelin and Stephen atte Lane, of the county of Norfolk, who have remained excommunicate for more than forty days. Dunham,[1] 23 August 1249

A = TNA, C.85/130/9. No endorsement; approx. 165 × 65 mm., tongue and tie.

Egregio ac magnifico domino H. Dei gratia illustri regi Angl', domino Hybern', duci Norman', Aquit' et comiti And', Walterus miseratione divina Norwicensis ecclesie minister humilis salutem in eo qui dat salutem regibus. Quia Rogerus de Heccham, Adam filius Rogeri, Petrus atte Lane, Nicholaus filius Goscelini et Stephanus atte Lane de comitatu Norfolc', claves ecclesie pertinaciter contempnendo, per quadraginta dies et amplius in excommunicationis sententia perseverarunt, dominationem vestram humiliter rogamus et devote quatinus districtionem quam contra tales regia consuevit exercere maiestas celsitudo vestra inferri iubeat in eosdem. Valeat regia maiestas vestra semper in Domino. Dat' apud Dunham .x°. kalendas Septembris anno Domini M° ducentesimo quadragesimo nono.

[1] Probably Dunham or Downham Market, Nf., or Santon Dunham, Sf.; but possibly Downham, Ca., or Downham, Ess.

58. Henry III, king of England

Notification addressed to Henry III asking that he bring secular authority to bear on Adam Talbot and Samson his brother, Alan, Adam's servant, Alan of Shouldham, Geoffrey the deacon, Geoffrey the smith, Matthew son of Matilda, Roger Brun, William Hogger, Hugh Swen, Richard the cobbler, Richard Erl and Robert Cusin of Shouldham, who have remained excommunicate for more than forty days. Gaywood, 15 December 1252

A = TNA, C.85/130/10. No endorsement; approx. 190 × 40 mm., tongue missing.

Egregio ac magnifico domino H. Dei gratia illustri regi Angl', domino Hybern', duci Normann', Aquit' et comiti And', Walterus miseratione divina Norwicensis ecclesie minister humilis salutem in eo qui dat salutem regibus. Quia Adam Talebot, Samson frater eius, Andreas serviens dicti Ade, Alanus de Shuldham, Galfridus diaconus, Galfridus faber, Mattheus filius Matildis, Rogerus Brun, Willelmus Hogger, Hugo Sweyn, Ricardus sutor, Ricardus Erl et Robertus Cusin de Shuldham de comitatu Norfolch', claves ecclesie pertinaciter contempnendo, per quadraginta dies et amplius in sententia excommunicationis perseveraverunt, dominationi vestre humiliter supplicamus et devote quatinus districtionem quam regia maiestas vestra contra tales exercere consuevit celsitudo vestra inferri iubeat in eosdem. Valeat regia maiestas vestra semper in Domino. Dat' apud Geywud .xviii. kalendas Ianuarii anno Domini millesimo CC° L° secundo.

59. Henry III, King of England

Notification of the vacancy of the priory of St Peter and St Paul, Ipswich.
[Shortly before 29 December 1252]

Mention of letters of the bp in the licence to elect granted on 29 December 1252 to the canons, in the persons of Nicholas of Ipswich and Thomas of Naughton, canons, who had been sent to the king with the bp's letters and letters patent of the convent.
Pd in *CPR 1247–1258* 169.

The vacancy was caused by the death, resignation or removal of William of Colneis; for the election of Nicholas of Ipswich, see no. 60; see also *HRH* ii 396.

60. Ipswich, Priory of St Peter and St Paul

Notification to king Henry III that he has examined and confirmed the election of Nicholas of Ipswich, canon, as prior, and request that the king should fulfil his part in this matter. London, 15 January 1253

A = TNA, C84/1/33. No medieval endorsement; approx. 164 × 62 mm.; tongue torn away, seal missing.
Pd (calendar) in *DKR* v Appx. ii no. 559.

Excellenti et magnifico domino H. Dei gratia regi Angl', domino Hybern', duci Norm', Aquit' et comiti Andag', Walterus permissione divina Norwicensis ecclesie minister humilis salutem in eo qui regibus dat salutem. Electionem de Nicholao de Gypeswico canonicum in domo sancti Petri de Gypeswico nuper celebratam examinavimus prout decuit diligenter et ipsam de consilio nobis assidentium plurimum peritorum duximus confirmandam. Quapropter regiam celsitudinem affectuose rogamus quatinus quod ad vos pertinet in hac parte benignitate solita impendatis. Valeat vestra perspicuitas per tempora longa in Domino diu duratura. Dat' Lond' .xviii. kalendas Februarii anno Domini M CC L° secundo.

> Royal assent to the election of Nicholas, the subprior, was recorded on 8 January, before bp Walter's formal notification, and again on 15 January 1253 (*CPR 1247–1253* 170, 172); cf. *HRH* ii 396.

61. Henry III, king of England

Joint document, issued in the king's presence, with B[oniface of Savoy], archbishop of Canterbury, F[ulk Basset], bishop of London, H[ugh of Northwold], bishop of Ely, R[obert Grosseteste], bishop of Lincoln, W[alter de Cantilupe], bishop of Worcester, P[eter d'Aiguieblanche], bishop of Hereford, W[illiam of York], bishop of Salisbury, W[alter Kirkham], bishop of Durham, R[ichard Blund], bishop of Exeter, S[ilvester Everdon], bishop of Carlisle, W[illiam of Bitton I], bishop of Bath and Wells, L[awrence of St Martin], bishop of Rochester, and T[homas de Waleys], bishop of St David's, notifying excommunication of those infringing the great charter and the forest charter.

Westminster, 13 May 1253

A¹ = Wells D. & C., charter 84. Dorse inaccessible; approx. 332 × 116 + 23 mm.; two parchment tags remain, one small fragment of green wax.

A² = Durham D. & C., ms. Loc. 1: 25. No endorsement; approx. 333 × 117 + 24 mm.; twelve parchment tags, seals missing.

Pd from A¹ in *Foedera* I i 289; *C & S* II i 477–8 (listing many other mss.); also pd in *Ann. mon.* i 305–6; (calendar) *EEA* 13 no. 94; 29 no. 94; 30 no. 108; *St David's Acta* no. 121 (listing other printed versions).

This ratification of Magna Carta came at the end of two years of negotiations between the English prelates and the king concerning the granting of a tax to fund his proposed crusade. *St David's Acta* no. 121 notices variant readings for the date of 14 and 15 May. Similar ratifications had been made in 1225 and 1237 (Powicke, *King Henry III and the Lord Edward*, 367–8, 36–7, 153–4).

62. Henry III, king of England

Notification addressed to Henry III asking that he bring secular authority to bear on Lawrence Pall, Reginald le Mercer and Nicholas Lek of Walsham [le Willows], who have remained excommunicate for more than forty days.

London, [14 September × 15 October, possibly 13 October] 1254

A = TNA, C.85/130/11. No endorsement; approx. 176 × 42 mm., tongue and tie torn away.

Egregio ac magnifico domino H. Dei gratia regi Angl', domino Hybern', duci Normann', Aquit' et comiti And', Walterus miseratione divina Norwycensis ecclesie minister humilis salutem in qui regibus dat salutem. Cum Laurentius Pall, Reginaldus le Mercer et Nicholaus Lek de Walsham, laici de comitatu Suff', in sententia excommunicationis, claves ecclesie contempnendo, per quadraginta dies et amplius pertinaciter perseveraverunt, egregie celsitudini vestre duximus humiliter supplicandum quatinus choercionem quam regia maiestas contra tales exercere consuevit contra predictos excommunicatos iubeatis inferri. Valeat celsitudo regia per tempora longiora. Dat' London' [.iii. Idus]ᵃ Octobris anno Domini Mᵒ CCᵒ Lᵒ quarto.

ᵃ *Reading uncertain*

*63. Henry III, King of England (Council)

Letters of the bps of Norwich and Chichester and the abbot of Westminster to the king's council, notifying its members who remained in England that in levying the tenth of the incomes of ecclesiastical benefices conceded to the king as a subsidy for the Holy Land they would adopt the following procedure, by which they firmly believed that they could act effectively, that is by the promulgation of sentence of excommunication against all ecclesiastical persons who fraudulently fail to provide a true estimate of their incomes, after the deduction of necessary expenses, and if with good reason they suspect anyone of underestimating their benefices, by eliciting the truth by examination under oath of both them and their neighbours. [c. 17 May 1254]

Pd in *Cl. R. 1253–54* 135–6.

Mentioned in a royal letter to the three prelates, 28 May 1254: 'Cum nuper consilio nostro commoranti in Anglia per litteras vestras significaveritis quod in inponenda decima proventuum beneficiorum ecclesiasticorum regni nostri nobis a sede apostolica in subsidium terre sancte concessa formam subscriptam provideritis, per quam creditis et firmiter tenetis vos posse procedere, videlicet quod per sententiam excommunicationis promulgande in omnes personas ecclesiasticas qui iustam proventuum suorum estimationem, expensis tantum necessariis deductis, fraudulenter occultabunt, et si aliquos suspectos merito habueritis quod sua beneficia minus plene estimaverint per sacramentum ipsorum vel vicinorum suorum rei veritatem plenius eruendo...'.

The date is that of the meeting of the collectors with the king's council, when the allocation of their respective circuits was determined (Appx 2. 27; *CPR 1247–58* 188).The king's letter, dated 28 May 1254, informs the collectors that he approves this procedure and instructs them to set the first term of payment around Michaelmas next; if the subsidy cannot be delivered at one term, they should set further terms for payment, to be approved by him (See Lunt, *Financial Relations* 257, *CPR 1247–58*, 370, 377).

63A. Henry III, King of England

Notification, with J[ohn Climping], bishop of Chichester and R[ichard de Crokesle], abbot of Westminster, reciting the mandate of pope Innocent [IV], dated at Assisi, 12 September 1253, that, since the archbishops and bishops of England have not responded to his mandate that a tenth of ecclesiastical revenues should be collected for payment to the king for three years before his passage to the Holy Land, and as the king has sworn to undertake this journey within two years of 24 June next, they should by papal authority enforce collection within the kingdom and other lands subject to the king, notwithstanding any papal indult. The revenues thus collected should be deposited in safe places until the king embarks on his enterprise, and until then nothing should be disbursed without the express permission of the apostolic see.

London, 4 July 1254

B = BL ms. Cotton Nero D i (Liber additamentorum of Matthew Paris) fo. 123v. s. xiii med. C (papal letter only) = Rome, Vatican Library, papal registers 23, register of Innocent IV 3, fo. 20, no. 169).

Pd from B and C in *Chron. Maj.* 6 296–7, no. 147.

Omnibus Cristi fidelibus ad quod presentes litere pervenerint Walterus et Iohannes miseratione divina Norwicensis et Cicestrensis episcopi et Ricardus abbas Westmonasteriensis, salutem in Domino. Mandatum domini pape nobis directum, non cancellatum, non abolitum, non in aliqua sui parte vitiatum, suscepimus in hec verba: Innocentius episcopus,[a-]servus servorum Dei[-a], venerabilibus fratribus Norwicensi et Cicestrensi episcopis ac dilecto filio abbati Westmonasteriensi Londoniensis diocesis, salutem et apostolicam benedictionem. Pro parte carissimi in Cristo filii nostri Anglie regis illustris fuit propositum coram nobis, quod cum nos olim venerabiles fratres nostros, universos archiepiscopos [et] episcopos per regnum Anglie constitutos, rogandos duxerimus attentius et monendos, nostris eis dantes literis in mandatis, ut, quod decima ecclesiasticorum proventuum eiusdem regni, quam ipsi regi pro terre sancte subsidio duximus per triennium concedendam ante suum passagium [b-] posset colligi, eidem[-b] regi concederent liberaliter et libenter, ipsi preces, monita et mandata nostra surdis auribus pretereuntes[c] hactenus id facere non curarunt. Cum igitur prefatus rex, sicut asseritur, proposuerit a festo beati Iohannis Baptiste proximo futuro usque ad biennium, iuramento ad hoc prestito, transfretare, [d-]discretioni vestre per apostolica scripta[-d] mandamus quatinus per vos vel per alios dictos archiepiscopos et episcopos aliosque ecclesiarum prelatos et ceteras personas ecclesiasticas eiusdem[e] regni et aliarum terrarum eiusdem regis ut eidem concedant quod ex tunc huiusmodi decima colligata, monitione premissa auctoritate nostra, sublato cuiuslibet appellationis obstaculo, compellatis, non obstante si eis vel ipsorum aliquibus a sede apostolica sit indultum quod interdici, suspendi vel excommunicari [f-] non possint [nisi] per literas apostolicas plenam et expressam ac de verbo ad verbum facientes de indulto huiusmodi mentionem,[-f] et constitutione de duabus dietis edita in concilio generali. Volumus autem[g] quod in tutis locis dicta pecunia[h] fideliter deponatur, assignata eidem regi pro prefate terre subventione cum iter arripuerit[j] transmarinum, ita quod nichil interim sumatur vel extrahatu[k] exinde absque mandato sedis apostolice speciali. Quod si non omnes his exequendis poteritis interesse, duo vestrum nichilominus exequantur. Dat' Asisii, .ii.[l] idus Septembris, pontificatus nostri anno .xi. Nos igitur tenorem mandati predicti fecimus solempniter publicari, et in testimonium huius rei sigillis nostris presentem scripturam duximus muniendam. Datum London' .iv. nonas Iulii anno gratie M° CC° LIV.

[a-a]om. B   [b-b]colligendam   [c]transeuntes C   [d] om. C   [e]ipsius C   [f-f]etc. usque mentionem C   [g] autem om. B   [h]decima C   [j]arripuit C   [k]subtrahatur C   [l]ii om. B

See intro., p. xxix–xxx, lviii.

64. Henry III, king of England

Notification addressed to Henry III asking that he bring secular authority to bear on Roger Heved of 'Aldeburg',[1] who has remained excommunicate for more than forty days.   Blofield, 20 July 1255

A = TNA, C.85/130/13. No endorsement; approx 165 × 48 mm., tongue torn away.

Egregio viro ac domino magnifico H. Dei gratia illustri regi Angl', domino Hybern', duci Normann', Acquit' et comiti Andegav', Walterus miseratione divina episcopus Norwycensis salutem in eo qui regibus dat salutem. Quia Rogerus Heved de Aldeberg' nostre diocesis excommunicatus iam per .xl. dies et amplius in excommunicationis sententia pertinaciter perseveravit, claves ecclesie contempnendo, celsitudini vestre humiliter duximus supplicandum quatinus cohercionem quam regia potestas contra tales exercere consuevit in eum fieri iubeatis. Valeat in Domino vestra regia serenitas per tempora longiora. Dat' apud Blafeud' .xiii. kalendas Augusti anno gratie M° CC° L° quinto.

[1]Aldborough, Nf., or Aldeburgh, Sf.

65. Henry III, king of England

Notification addressed to Henry III asking that he bring secular authority to bear on Roger Lorkin, Geoffrey Ballard, William Crudde of Ipswich, William

brother of Geoffrey of Barsham, Ralph of Groton and Cecilia of 'Sandhil', of the
county of Suffolk, who have remained excommunicate for more than forty days.
Wicks Bishop, 20 January 1256

A = TNA, C.85/130/12. No endorsement; approx. 172 × 50 mm., parchment tongue, tie torn
away.

Egregio ac magnifico domino H. Dei gratia illustri regi Angl', domino Hibern',
duci Norm', Acquit' et comiti And', Walterus miseratione divina Norwicensis
ecclesie minister humilis salutem in eo qui regibus dat salutem. Quia Rogerus
Lorkin, Galfridus Ballard, Willelmus Crudde de Gipwico, Willelmus frater
Galfridi de Bercham, Radulfus de Grotene et Cecilia de Sandhil de comitatu
Suff', claves ecclesie contempnendo, in sentencia excommunicationis per
quadraginta dies et amplius perseverarunt, regie celsitudini vestre duximus
humiliter supplicandum quatinus coercionem quam regia maiestas contra tales
exercere consuevit contra dictos excommunicatos iubeat inferri. Valeat celsitudo
vestra regia per tempora longiora. Dat' apud Wikes .xiii. kalendas Februarii anno
gratie M° CC° L° quinto.

66. Hickling Priory

Notification that when a dispute was brought before him between the canons and
the vicar of Hacheston as to who should bear the cost of serving the chapel of
Hacheston, he ordained that the vicar should bear in entirety the burden of
serving both the mother church and the chapel.   Ipswich, 14 May 1245

B = Bodl. ms. Tanner 425 (Hickling cartulary) fo. 10v. s. xiii med.

Omnibus Cristi fidelibus ad quos presens scriptum pervenerit Walterus Dei gratia
Norwicensis episcopus salutem in Domino. Cum inter priorem et conventum de
Hykel' et vicarium de Hachestune quis honus deserviendi capelle de Hachestune
sustinere deberet coram nobis questio verteretur, nos super premissis decrevimus
quod dictus vicarius tam honus deserviendi matrici ecclesie quam dicte capelle
totaliter sustinebit. In huius rei testimonium huic scripto sigillum nostrum apponi
fecimus. Valete in Domino. Dat' apud Gypewic' pridie idus Maii pontificatus
nostri anno primo.

The church was valued at £12 in 1254 and at £13 6s 8d in 1291; there is no separate reference
to a vicarage (*VN* 466; *Taxatio* 117).

67. Rural Dean of Hingham

Mandate to the [rural] dean of Hingham, relating that he has received a
mandate of R[obert], bishop of Lincoln, F[ulk], bishop of London and W[illiam],
bishop of Bath and Wells, which he is sending to him for inspection and

transcription; by the authority of which he orders him and all subject to him, in virtue of obedience and under threat of canonical penalty, that when archdeacons or others to whom pertains the office of visitation come to them in person to conduct visitation, they shall receive them honourably with the number of riders specified in the decree of the [Third] Lateran Council [c.4], and should provide for them victuals to the value of seven shillings and sixpence, or that sum in money if they prefer, in the knowledge that if the visited render more in victuals or money or the visitors receive more, or if they give them anything for visitation when they do not visit, the bishop will punish him by his own agency or that of the conservators, according to the form of the foresaid constitution. In lesser churches, moreover, where because of the insufficiency of possessions visitors have by custom received less, they shall receive what has been customary, until the bishop shall ordain otherwise. The bishop himself, when God willing he visits in the future, will be content with victuals to the value of thirty-one shillings and ten pence or that sum in money, or less according to the resources of the place. London, 2 February 1253

B = BL ms. Cotton Nero D i (Liber additamentorum of Matthew Paris) fo. 110r. s. xiii med. Pd in *Chron. Maj.* vi 231–2.

Walterus Dei gratia Norwicensis episcopus dilecto filio decano de Hengam salutem, gratiam et benedictionem. Mandatum venerabilium patrum R. Lincolniensis, F. Londoniensis et W. Wellensis et Bathoniensis episcoporum recepimus, quod vobis transmittimus inspiciendum et transcribendum, eadem auctoritate vobis et omnibus subditis vestris in virtute obedientie et sub pena canonica districtius mandantes et precipientes quod cum archidiaconi vel alii ad quos officium visitationis pertinere dinoscitur personaliter ad vos causa visitandi accesserint, ipsos cum numero equitaturarum in constitutione Lateranensi proviso honeste recipiatis, et victualia usque ad summam septem solidorum et sex denariorum secundum communem estimationem, vel ipsam numeratam pecuniam prout maluerint, ministretis eisdem, pro certo scituri quod si plus in pecunia vel victualibus persolveritis sive ipsi plus receperint, seu ipsis non visitantibus quid nomine visitationis prestiteritis, nos tam solventes quam recipientes per nos vel per ipsos conservatores antedictos secundum formam constitutionis antedicte puniemus. In ecclesiis autem minoribus, ubi propter bonorum insufficientiam minorem quantitatem percipere consueverunt, percipiant ut solebant, donec cum ipsis communiter aliter ordinaverimus. Nos autem, cum in locis que, favente Domino, in posterum visitabimus, in victualibus usque ad summam .xxxi. solidorum et .x. denariorum secundum communem estimationem, vel ipsa pecunia et minori, secundum loci facultates, volumus esse contenti. Datum London' quarto nonas Februarii pontificatus nostri anno octavo.

Similar mandates were almost certainly despatched to all the rural deans of the diocese. In 1250 archbp Boniface of Savoy encountered widespread opposition to his metropolitical visitation of his province, the bishops of which appealed to Rome (*Chron. Maj.* v 186–8; *Abingdon Chron.* 7–8). Eventually in 1252 pope Innocent IV pronounced in favour of the archbp's right to conduct such a visitation (*Reg. Inn. IV* nos. 5670–2), but eleven weeks later wrote to the bps of Lincoln, London and Bath and Wells detailing the maximum procurations to be levied in future by any prelate, and appointing them conservators in this matter (*Ann. mon.* i 300–1); the letter instructed that procurations 'in victualibus et necessariis' should not exceed the sum or value of four marks (£2 13s 4d). On 28 February 1254 the pope repeated this order, apparently giving it universal force (*Reg. Inn. IV* no. 7314).

A Norwich diocesan statute, one of a number supplementary to those probably promulgated by bp William Raleigh, 1240 × 1243, but before *c.* 1266, records an episcopal injunction to the archdns that they should conduct annual visitation of churches but should demand only moderate procurations, and inhibits the suspension of churches where procurations were not paid (*C. & S.* II i 361–2, no. 81).

68. Rural Dean of Hingham

Mandate to the rural dean of Hingham, recording that when the pope imposed limits on the receipt of procurations, whereby parish churches held by exempt and non-exempt religious and by secular persone *are to be exempt from visitation by and the payment of procurations to archbishops, the proctors of the province of Canterbury, considering the welfare of churches to be threatened, especially since if the archbishop had obtained procurations from parish churches bishops would in future demand for themselves the same, granted to the pope, in the name of the clergy of the province, six thousand marks. The bishop has divided the sum levied upon him proportionately among all churches, according to the taxations returned to him, and he orders the dean to collect the appropriate sum, compelling objectors by ecclesiastical censure, and to deliver it to the bishop's clerks specially deputed in this matter at Norwich on Monday 24 March.*   London, 3 February 1253

B = BL ms. Cotton Nero D i (Liber additamentorum of Matthew Paris) fo. 110v. s. xiii med. Pd in *Chron. Maj.* vi 232–3.

Walterus Dei gratia Norwicensis episcopus dilecto filio decano de Hengam salutem. Cum dominus papa nuper in procurationibus recipiendis, que quandoque absque modo et supra modum requirebantur, certum modum imposuerit, ut ecclesias parrochiales exemptorum et non exemptorum et secularium personarum a visitatione et procuratione archiepiscoporum perpetuis temporibus relevaverit, procuratores provincie Cantuariensis, attendentes ecclesiarum commodum in hac parte non modicum versari, et maxime quia si dominus Cantuariensis ab ecclesiis parrochialibus procurationes optinuisset, episcopi per se futuris temporibus procurationes consimiles cogerent, domino pape sex milia marcarum nomine cleri Cantuariensis provincie concesserunt et dederunt. Et quoniam portionem nobis impositam per omnes ecclesias secundum taxationes nobis transmissas proportionaliter fecimus imponi, vobis mandamus quatinus dictam summam fideliter colligatis, contradictores per censuram ecclesiasticam compellentes; proviso quod dictam pecuniam die Lune proxima ante mediam Quadragesimam apud Norwicum promptam habeatis et paratam clericis nostris ad hoc specialiter deputatis persolvendam. Datum Londoniis tertio nonas Februarii pontificatus nostri anno octavo.

> As resentment grew in 1251 against archbp Boniface's receipt of the annates of vacant benefices in his province and against his vigorous exercise of metropolitical visitation, it was decided first to send to the *curia* a large delegation of two proctors from each diocese; but this was rescinded, and eventually at Winchcombe on 6 November the bps jointly appointed master John of Cheam to represent their case (*C. & S.* II i 447–8). He obtained the issue by pope Innocent IV of a decretal which defined more precisely than hithero the level of archiepiscopal procurations and completely exempted parish churches from visitation by and payment of procurations to the archbp *sede plena* (*Ann. mon.* i 300–3). In return he consented to the payment by the clergy of the province of Canterbury to the pope of a subsidy; on 5 June 1252 Innocent IV authorised the bps of Lincoln, London and Worcester (all of whom had been at the *curia* in 1250) to apportion a levy of 6000 marks (2000 marks for the expenses of master John of Cheam, 4000 marks as a gift to the pope) among all the non-exempt churches of the province. The bps of London and Worcester ordered the other bps to ascertain the value of each church and prebend and of the temporalities of non-exempt religious houses and to forward their lists to the collectors at St Paul's, London, by 13 December 1252. The rate was probably a twentieth of these 1252 valuations, themselves based on the 'ancient valuation' of 1217; see Lunt, *Financial Relations* 225–7.

69. Holme, St Benet's Abbey

Grant to the monks in proprios usus of the church of Horning at their gate, in the parish of which they were founded, to take effect when it falls vacant. All the fruits of the church shall be distributed by the almoner to the poor at the abbey gate, except for five marks to be given by the almoner to the infirmarer for the use of the frail and the sick. All who may divert the revenues to other uses shall incur excommunication. The bishop reserves to himself the power to make other arrangements in the future, with the advice of the abbot and convent, should it appear expedient so to do. Thorpe, 1 October 1248

> B = BL ms. Cotton Galba E ii (St Benet cartulary) fo. 49r (20r). s. xiii ex. C = Bodl. ms. Norfolk roll 82 (St Benet roll) k. s. xiv in. D = ibid., 1 (*inspeximus* by prior Simon and convent of Norwich). E = BL ms. Cotton roll iv 57 (St Benet roll) 10. s. xiv.

Omnibus Cristi fidelibus ad quos presens scriptum pervenerit Walterus Dei gratia Norwicensis episcopus salutem in Domino sempiternam. Addicti militie regulari, sicut[a] Cristi bonus odor celesti conversatione redolentes, dignis[b] caritatis operibus dant operam incessanter, ita digne[c] sunt amplioribus beneficiis honorandi, ut et[d] onus levius ferant ex honore et ad sue liberalitatis imitationem[e] ceteros avidius animent et invitent; inter quos dilectos filios abbatem et conventum sancti Benedicti de Hulmo tanto specialius benigno favore prosequi debemus quanto multipliciter maiorem nostre dilectionis meruerint prerogativam. Optantes igitur ipsis ex nostri debito officii tamquam dignis[f] et bene meritis benefacere, ecclesiam de Horningge[g] ad portam eorundem, in qua siquidem parochia fundati noscuntur, eisdem et ecclesie sue in proprios usus cum vacaverit concedimus, ita scilicet quod omnes ecclesie ipsius proventus per manus elemosinarii eiusdem domus ad portam ipsius abbatie pauperibus distribuantur, exceptis quinque marcis per manum ipsius elemosinarii infirmario domus annuatim solvendis et in usum debilium et infirmorum fideliter expendendis. Omnes autem qui ipsius proventus in alios usus converterint sententia excommunicationis innodamus, reservata tamen nobis[h] potestate alio modo ordinandi cum consilio abbatis et conventus si viderimus futuris temporibus expedire. In huius rei testimonium presenti scripto sigillum nostrum fecimus apponi. Hiis testibus: magistro R. archidiacono Colecestrie,[j] magistro W. archidiacono Suff', domino W. de Pakeham, [k-]Thoma de Walcote,[l] Willelmo de Wichingham[m] clericis, domino Iohanne de Holkham capellano, Willelmo de Acle clerico et aliis.[-k] Dat' apud Thorp' kalendas Octobris anno Domini millesimo CC° XL° octavo.

[a] sicud C   [b] dingnis C, E   [c] dingne C, D, E   [d] et *interl.* C, *om.* D   [e] ymitationem C, D   [f] tanquam dingnis C, D, E   [g] Horningg' D; Hornyngg' E   [h] nobis tamen C, E   [j] Colecestr' B, E   [k-k] *om.* B, *substitutes* etc.   [l] Walkote C, E   [m] Wichyngham E

For a grant by bp William Turbe of the church of Horning, for the support of the poor and the construction of outbuildings, *c.* 1150 × 1153, see *EEA* 6 no. 98, which from its terms, and since the vill of Horning with its appurtenances was part of the abbey's original endowment, might be assumed to be an early act of appropriation, although the term *in proprios usus* is not used. In 1254, however, before bp Suffield's appropriation had taken effect, the church was valued at £6 13s 4d and the abbot's portion at only 10s (*VN* 414); in 1291 the church, appropriated to the abbey, was valued at £10, apart from a vicarage not liable to the tenth (*Taxatio* 86b). There was also a hospital at Horning under the supervision of the almoner (*MRH* 365).

70. Holme, St Benet's Abbey

Grant to the monks in proprios usus *of the church of [Wood]bastwick, which is of their advowson, in compensation for the enormous damage and expense suffered by them through the loss, while the bishop was abroad, of the church of Scottow, which for many years past they had held* in proprios usus.

Eccles, 30 December 1249

A = Norfolk RO, ms. Tanner I, insert at p. 148. No endorsement visible; approx. 180 × 62 mm., cut off at base; single slit, tag and seal missing.
B = BL ms. Cotton Galba E ii (St Benet cartulary) fo. 49r (20r). s. xiii ex.

Omnibus Cristi fidelibus presens scriptum visuris vel audituris Walterus Dei gratia Norwicensis episcopus salutem in Domino sempiternam. Cum iuxta officii nostri debitum bona religiosorum fovere, tueri pariter et protegere teneamur eorumque adversitati et miserie condolere, maxime quorum probitatis merita crescere novimus in misericordie et caritatis fervorem, dilectorum filiorum abbatis et conventus sancti Benedicti de Hulmo iacture compatientes, qui nobis agentibus in remotis ecclesiam suam de Scothowe, quam a multis retro temporibus habuerunt in proprios usus conversam, amittendo enorme dispendium incurrerunt, ad[a] sublevandam eorum aliquatenus iacturam divina moti pietate, ecclesiam de Bastwik, que de eorum est patronatu, in proprios usus illis caritative duximus concedendam, hac nostre concessionis gratia perpetuis valitura temporibus. Et ne hoc a quoquam in posterum possit revocari in dubium, presens scriptum sigilli nostri fecimus impressione roborari. Dat' apud Eccles tertio kalendas Ianuarii pontificatus nostri anno quinto et anno Domini M° CC° X°L nono.

^aad *om.* B

The church of Scottow was appropriated to the monks by bp Thomas Blundeville in 1232 , to take effect on the death or resignation of two named rectors (*EEA* 21 no. 66). This dual rectory, in a church where there is no twelfth-century evidence of a division into medieties, may itself be an indication of disputed patronage in the early thirteenth century. *Oxenedes* (297) notes that in the time of abbot Robert (of Torksey), 1237–51, the monks were deprived, through the perjury of false men who wished them ill, of the patronage of the churches of Lammas and Scottow, the latter of which they held *in proprios usus*. On 15 May 1248 pope Innocent IV issued a mandate to bp Suffield instructing him not to allow the monks to be molested with regard to Scottow church, granted to them by the last (*sic*) bp, of which Stephen of Reedham, knight, asserts he is patron, as determined by the king's justices, and has presented William of Bath to the bp's official for institution; the verdict in a secular court and subsequent acts were declared null by the pope (*Reg. Inn. IV* no. 4516; *CPL* i 255). It is perhaps significant that the inquisition in 1248 into the rightful patronage of the church was taken before Henry of Bath, royal justice (*Cl. R. 1247–51* 218). The church was eventually, a century later, restored to he monks *in proprios usus* by bp William Bateman in 1348; in 1338 they had, in a petition to bp Bek for the appropriation of North Walsham, stated that they had recently by action of the lay power irrevocably lost the church of Scottow, of which the patron was now Sir Hugh Peverel (*Reg. Bateman* nos 13–15).

The appropriation of Woodbastwick had originally been authorised by bp William Turbe, 1154 × 1161, but had not been put into effect (*EEA* 6 no. 99).

Scottow was valued at £25 6s 8d in 1254 (*VN* 366); Woodbastwick at £6 13s 4d in 1254, and at £8, including the vicarage, in 1291 (*VN* 365; *Taxatio* 78b).

71. Holme, St Benet's Abbey

Notification that when there was a dispute because the monks had presented Giles of Stalham to the church of Potter Heigham, while master Berard de Nimpha, papal writer, had by apostolic authority collated the same church to Peter Lena, clerk, son of Bartholomew Alex[i]us, citizen of Rome, and the parties eventually swore to submit to and observe the bishop's ordinance, he ordained that Giles should hold the church at the monks' presentation and that Peter should each year receive five marks from the monks' camera, until they should provide him with an ecclesiastical benefice, according to the obligation which they had entered into with him. Since it is just that he should bear the burden who receives the profit, he decrees that the abbot and convent should receive these five marks from the goods of the church by the hand of Giles or whomsoever should be rector, but that after Peter has died or has secured from them an ecclesiastical benefice, the monks may not demand this sum from the rector or his successors.   Hevingham, 12 July 1253

B = BL ms. Cotton Galba E ii (St Benet cartulary) fo. 49r–v (20r–v). s. xiii ex.

Omnibus Cristi fidelibus has litteras visuris vel audituris Walterus miseratione divina Norwicensis episcopus salutem in Domino. Cum dilecti filii abbas et conventus sancti Benedicti de Hulmo Egidium de Stalham clericum ad ecclesiam de Potterehecham nobis presentassent et magister Berardus de Nimpha scriptor domini pape Petro Lene clerico nato nobilis viri Bartholomei Alexi civis Romani eandem ecclesiam auctoritate apostolica contulisset, ac super hoc inter predictum Petrum ex una parte et dictos abbatem et conventum ac Egidium ex altera questio verteretur, tandem partes nostre ordinationi se totaliter subiecerunt, prestito sacramento corporali quod nostram ordinationem fideliter observarent. Nos igitur nobiscum habita deliberatione taliter duximus ordinandum, partium etiam subse-[fo. 49v]cuto consensu, quod dictus Egidius habeat et possideat memoratam ecclesiam ad presentationem abbatis et conventus predictorum, et predictus Petrus de camera eorundem abbatis et conventus quinque marcas percipiat annuatim, donec ei in beneficio ecclesiastico secundum formam obligationis ei facte provisum fuerit per eosdem. Et quoniam de iuris equitate ipsius debet esse onus cuius est emolumentum, volumus et ordinamus quod predicti abbas et conventus dictas quinque marcas percipiant de bonis ecclesie memorate eis per manus dicti Egidii vel rectoris qui pro tempore fuerit fideliter solvendas, ita tamen quod post decessum dicti Petri vel postquam beneficium ecclesiasticum assecutus fuerit ab eisdem, non competat eis ius petendi vel exigendi predictam summam pecunie a rectore memorato vel suo successore, sed quod ad eorum exonerationem eis concessum est ipsis liberationem consecutis cessare volumus omnino. In cuius rei testimonium presenti scripto sigillum nostrum unacum sigillo dicti rectoris est appensum. Dat' apud Hevingham quarto idus Iulii pontificatus nostri anno nono.

> Berard of Nimpha, papal scribe living in England, was appointed in October 1246 as one of two papal collectors in England; Matthew Paris accused him of dishonest practices, although implying that he was only following papal instructions; he was still active in claiming arrears and unpaid legacies for the crusade in 1257; he died the following year (Lunt, *Financial Relations* 433–4, 613–4, 616). Peter, son of Bartholomew de Alexio, a Roman citizen, rector of Sutton-on-Trent (Nt.), on 11 March 1254 received an indult from pope Innocent IV to hold an additional benefice in the province of Canterbury (*Reg. Inn. IV* no. 6425; *CPL* i 284). Five years earlier the same pope had instructed papal agents in England to make provision of a prebendal or other church to Angelo, scholar, son of Bartholomew Alexius of Rome, presumably Peter's brother *Reg. Inn. IV* no. 4513; *CPL* i 256).

72. Holme, St Benet's Abbey

Reiteration for the monks of the grant in proprios usus *by his predecessors of the church of Neatishead, in consideration of the dangers and misfortunes by which they are at this time affected and the very great loss which they have incurred with regard to this church. A suitable vicarage will be taxed by the bishop, to which when it is vacant the monks shall present a suitable* persona.

Norwich, 2 September 1256

B = BL ms. Cotton Galba E ii (St Benet cartulary) fo. 49v (20v). s. xiii ex. C = ibid., fo. 51v (22v) (*inspeximus* by prior Simon and convent of Norwich, 16 September 1256).

Universis Cristi fidelibus Walterus miseratione divina episcopus Norwicensis salutem in Domino sempiternam. Oculo pietatis considerantes ius quod dilecti filii abbas et conventus sancti Benedicti de Hulmo ex largitione predecessorum nostrorum et nostra in ecclesia de Neteshirde nostre diocesis habere noscuntur, ac etiam qualiter ecclesia sancti Benedicti hiis temporibus periculis et infortuniis variis et diversis multipliciter fuerit collisa, ipsique maximam propter eandem ecclesiam de Neteshirde sustinuerunt iacturam,[a] et ob hoc volentes eisdem benefacere ut saltem de periculis et dampnis habitis in aliquo releventur, ecclesiam ipsam eis in proprios usus prius concessam, que de ipsorum est patronatu, auctoritate episcopali concedimus eisdem in proprios usus perpetuis temporibus possidendam, salva vicaria competenti in eadem per nos taxanda, ad quam cum vacaverit ipsi nobis personam ydoneam presentabunt. In cuius rei testimonium huic scripto sigillum nostrum duximus apponendum. Dat' Norwic' quarto nonas Septembris pontificatus nostri anno duodecimo et anno Domini M° CC° L° sexto.

[a] C *ends here with* etc.

The church was originally appropriated to the monks by bp William Turbe, 1154 × 61, but this obviously was not put into effect (*EEA* 6 no. 99). At the end of the twelfth century the abbey was in receipt only of a pension of one mark (ibid. no. 245); in 1204 a vicar was presented to the perpetual vicarage by the rector, with the consent of the monks as patrons, who now received an annual pension of two marks (ibid. no. 356). Bp William Raleigh, 1239 × 43, confirmed the original appropriation by bp Turbe (*EEA* 21 no. 136). *Oxenedes* (297) attributes the appropriation of Neatishead, and also of the churches of Felmingham and Woodbastwick, to the efforts of abbot Adam of Neatishead (May 1256–August 1268). In 1254 Neatishead was valued at £13 6s 8d or £16 13s 4d, in different mss, with no note of any vicarage (*VN* 414). In 1291 the church was assessed at £18 13s 4d, apart from a vicarage not subject to the tenth (*Taxatio* 86b).

73. William Ingelond

Grant, with the consent of the chapter of Norwich, to William, the bishop's sergeant, and the legitimate heirs of his body, for their homage and service, of all the land at Thorpe which was held by William the cobbler, with messuage and buildings thereon with all appurtenances, but excepting that part, with meadow and heath, held thereof by William Talebot, to be held for an annual rent of twenty-one pence. Should anything of this tenement be sold or otherwise alienated, or should William die without legitimate heirs of his body, the tenement shall revert in whole to the bishop or his successors.

[19 February 1245 × 19 May 1257]

A = Norfolk RO, DCN43/47. Endorsed: Pokethorp (s. xiv); approx. 75 × 137 + (?) mm., damaged at lower edge; seals missing, parchment tag on (remaining) right-hand slit.

Omnibus Cristi fidelibus presens scriptum visuris vel audituris Walterus Dei gratia Norwicensis episcopus salutem in Domino sempiternam. Noverit universitas vestra nos de consensu et voluntate capituli nostri Norwicensis concessisse, dedisse et presenti carta confirmasse Willelmo Ingelond' servienti nostro, pro homagio et servitio suo, totam terram cum mesuagio, edificiis et omnibus pertinentiis ad dictam terram spectantibus, que fuit Willelmi sutoris in villa de Thorp', excepta illa parte cum prato et bruario quam Willelmus Talebot inde tenet, habendam et tenendam predicto Willelmo et heredibus suis de se legitime procreatis de nobis et successoribus nostris libere, quiete, in pace et hereditarie, reddendo inde annuatim nobis et successoribus nostris viginti et unum denarios, scilicet ad festum sancti Andree sex denarios, ad festum Annunciationis beate Marie sex denarios, ad festum sancti Iohannis Baptiste tres denarios et ad festum sancti Michaelis sex denarios, pro omni servitio, consuetudine et exactione, ita tamen quod nec ipse nec heredes sui de se legitime procreati aliquid de dicta terra possint vendere, dare vel aliquo modo alienare; quod si fecerint, liceat nobis vel successoribus nostris predictam terram ingredi et sine contradictione aliqua vel clamio predicti Willelmi vel heredum suorum in perpetuum retinere. Quod si contingat predictum Willelmum sine herede de se legitime procreato in fata decedere, tota predicta cum suis supradictis pertinentiis totaliter et integre et sine diminutione aliqua ad nos et successores nostros quieta et soluta revertetur. In cuius rei testimonium huic scripto sigillum nostrum unacum sigillo predicti capituli nostri fecimus apponi. Hiis testibus: Willelmo de Gernemuta, Ricardo de Walkot', Reginaldo de Hemelingtun', Michaele de Lingwde, Galfrido de Hemelintune, Iohanne del Gap, Willelmo de le Heythe, Iohanne filio suo, Iohanne filio Iohannis de Thorp', Ricardo le Franceys, Roberto Dosseth', Willelmo de Grimmere, Willelmo Dosset et aliis.

William Ingelond is almost certainly the same William de Inlande who was a fairly frequent witness of mid thirteenth-century charters relating to Sedgeford, North Elmham, Gately and Newton and Trowse (*Norwich Cathedral Charters* ii index, *s.v* Inlande).

74. Kersey Priory

Notification that, since in the vacancy of the priory the bishop has for reasons of justice quashed the election made by the canons and has in accordance with the [Fourth Lateran] Council [c. 23] appointed a prior by his ordinary authority, he has issued these letters patent lest in future any prejudice should accrue to the canons in the matter of election or to the patron regarding presentation.

Blythburgh, 7 April 1245

A = TNA, E42/362. Endorsed: Keres' (s. xiii); approx. 156 × 62 + 11 mm.; parchment tag, fragment of seal, natural wax varnished light brown, counterseal.
B = Cambridge, King's College archives KER/638 (Kersey charter roll) m. 3r. s. xiv in.

Omnibus Cristi fidelibus ad quos presens scriptum pervenerit Walterus Dei gratia Norwicensis episcopus salutem eternam in Domino. Universitati vestre notum facimus quod cum vacante prioratu ecclesie de Kerseih' nos electionem canonicorum dicte ecclesie iustitia mediante cassaverimus et secundum formam concilii priorem ibidem auctoritate ordinaria prefecerimus, ne hec nostra collatio canonicis et patrono dicte ecclesie aliquod inposterum possit preiudicium[a] generare quominus alia vice salva sit eisdem canonicis sua electio et patrono sua presentatio has litteras nostras patentes fecimus eisdem. Dat' apud Bliburg' .vii. Idus Aprilis pontificatus nostri anno primo.

   [a] aliquid in posterum possit in preiudicium B

   A prior Henry occurs from 1218 × 1219 until 1245; his successor William first occurs on 22 July 1245 (*HRH* ii 399).

75. Lewes Priory

Notification that when a composition was agreed between the monks on one side and John Malet, rector of Sculthorpe, on the other concerning the great and lesser tithes of the demesne of Sculthorpe and also of the lands brought into cultivation after the tithes were granted to Lewes, the names of which are included in the composition, and the parties urgently requested the bishop to examine, if necessary amend, and confirm it, he approved and confirmed this composition, but changed the times of payment and modified the penalty to be applied in this way: that where it was written that if John Malet or any of his successors were to fail to pay 63s 4d to the monks at the Easter synod or to their sergeant of Heacham within fifteen days, and similarly at the other term, he and his successors should lose in perpetuity the right to receive the tithes, the bishop has modified the terms so that if John or his successors were to fail to pay this sum to he monks at the Easter synod or the feast of the nativity of St John the Baptist or to their sergeant at Heacham within a month, then the monks may on their own authority take possession of the said tithes without contradiction by the rector, and may receive and peaceably possess them until full satisfaction is made to them for the money due. If the rector or his successors should default for a whole year, then he shall in perpetuity forfeit possession of and right to the tithes, with no reservation of such right to him or his successors.

Gaywood, 10 December 1246

   A = TNA, E40/14072. Endorsed: Carta Walteri episcopi Norwic' inter priorem de Lewes et Iohannem Malet super decimis de Sculphord' (s. xiii); Norw' dioc' ix (s. xv); approx. 172 × 118 + 13 mm.; parchment tag, seal, natural wax varnished green, counterseal.
   B = TNA, E40/14066 (single sheet transcript of various Sculthorpe documents). s. xiv in. C = ibid. E40/14065 (i) (single sheet transcript). s. xiv in.

Universis Cristi fidelibus presentes litteras inspecturis Walterus Dei gratia Norwicensis episcopus salutem in Domino. Noverit universitas vestra quod cum inter priorem et conventum de Lewes ex una parte et Iohannem Maleth rectorem ecclesie de Sculthorp ex altera iniretur compositio super decimis tam maioribus quam minutis de dominicis de Sculthorp necnon et de terris extractis postquam decime Lewensibus erant concesse, quarum nomina in dicta compositione continentur, ac partes in nostra presentia constitute dictam compositionem a nobis examinari, corrigi vel modificari si videremus expedire ac sic confirmari peterent instanter, nos dictam compositionem ratam habentes et confirmantes sic terminos solutionis mutavimus et penam in compositione adiectam modificamus, videlicet ubi scriptum fuerit quod si Iohannes Maleth vel aliquis successorum suorum non solverit sexaginta et tres solidos et quatuor denarios in sinodo Paschali priori et conventui Lewensibus vel servienti eorum de Hecham infra quindenam post, et tantumdem in alio termino in compositione contento, dictus I. et successores sui caderent a iure et possessione percipiendi dictas decimas inperpetuum, sic duximus moderandum, quod si dictus I. vel aliquis successorum suorum non solverit .lxᵃ. tres solidos et quatuor denarios priori et conventui Lewensibus in sinodo Paschali vel servienti eorum de Hecham infra mensem post, et tantundem in forma consimili in festo nativitatis sancti Iohannis Baptiste eisdem vel servienti eorundem de Hecham infra mensem post, licebit dictis priori et conventui propria auctoritate possessionem dictarum decimarum libere ingredi sine contradictione rectoris ecclesie de Sculthorp ac eas recipere et pacifice possidere quousque de pecunia eisdem debita plenarie fuerit satisfactum; quod si dictus rector vel aliquis successorum suorum in solutione dicte pecunie cessaverit per annum, ex tunc cadat a possessione et iure dictarum decimarum inperpetuum, nulla questione vel iure aliquo sibi vel successoribus suis super dictis decimis reservato, dictis Lewensibus veris effectis possessoribus et proprietariis dictarum decimarum. In cuius rei testimonium presentibus litteris sigillum nostrum apposuimus. Dat' apud Geywde quarto idus Decembris pontificatus nostri anno secundo.

The tithes of Sculthorpe, a manor held by the Pavelli family of the honour of Warenne, were a matter of intermittent dispute for over 150 years. At some time after summer 1203 papal judges delegate, acting by authority of a general mandate of pope Innocent III to adjudicate in cases brought by the monks against, amongst others who were allegedly damaging their interests, those in Norwich diocese who detained tithes due to Lewes, in a case relating to Sculthorpe ordered the restitution of the disputed tithes to the monks by the rector, William de Pavelli, who issued a notification that he had received all the tithes of the lordship from the monks for an annual payment of £1 8s in two instalments (*Letters of Innocent III* no. 500; *Lewes Cartulary, Norfolk Portion* nos. 112, 135–6).

On 18 September 1219 pope Honorius III issued a mandate to the prior, archdn and dean of Huntingdon to investigate the monks' complaint against Theophania de Pavelli, the patron, and N. and G., clerks, over the tithes of Sculthorpe; on 30 October Nicholas, *persona*, admitted the monks' right thereto, and their proctor granted him the tithes at farm for his lifetime for £2 13s 4d *p.a.*; the judges, however, reserved judgement and ratification of this agreement until enquiry had been made as to what lands had been brought into cultivation since the tithes had been conferred on the monks by the earls of Warenne when they themselves held the manor; this enquiry they delegated to the rural deans of Burnham and Walsingham (*Lewes Cartulary: Norfolk Portion* nos. 112–3). Although it was intended that the court should reconvene in Whitsun week 1220, the same judges did not apparently deliver judgement until Whitsun 1225 (although there may be a mistake in dating in the cartulary), when they awarded the tithes of these assarted lands too to the monks; a schedule of these was included in the award, and they amounted to approximately 320 acres (ibid. no. 138). It appears that the dispute was renewed with the appointment of a new rector, Henry of Dunton. Judges delegate were appointed by an undated mandate of pope Honorius III (after Whitsun 1225, when Nicholas was still rector, and before the pope's death on 18 March 1227). Dunton agreed to receive the demesne tithes at farm from mr Alexander of Walpole, the monks' proctor, for £3 p.a.; when he died, or should he resign, the tithes were to revert to mr Alexander, were he still alive and a secular, and otherwise to the monks themselves (ibid. nos 140–1). In 1235 another new rector, Martin de Crowele, entered into an agreement to lease the tithes of the demesne and of all the free land in the vill for five years for £12 p.a. (ibid. no. 146). In 1240 and 1241 the lease was renewed for a year for a farm of £4 (ibid. nos 147–8). In October 1242 prior Albert and the convent leased the tithes to the same rector for his lifetime by an agreement which was to be renewed every five years, in which fifth year the monks should have the tithes collected by their own agents in token of their right thereto, although they were to be handed over immediately to the rector (ibid. no. 145). By March 1243, however, Crowele had either died or resigned, and the prior entered into an agreement with the new rector, John Malet, whereby he leased the tithes to him and his successors in perpetuity for an annual farm of 9½ marks, but with the same clause regarding the quinquennial collection by the prior's sergeants; two pairs of documents were drawn up, sealed alternately by the parties, but in one pair there should be no mention of this quinquennial clause, and this pair should be deposited in the treasury of Coxford priory until the bp and chapter of Norwich should confirm this agreement, which confirmation both parties promised to endeavour to obtain; thereafter the deeds stored at Coxford should replace those kept in the interim in the hands of the parties (ibid. no. 114). The two copies of the deed lacking the quinquennial clause were drawn up on 23 November 1243 (during the controversy over bp Raleigh's translation from Norwich to Winchester), with the agreement of the lady Eustachia de Pavelli, the patron. It was this composition which bp Suffield now confirmed (above). The terms of the agreement were, however, subsequently adapted by the bp himself, for after John Malet, the rector, had breached its terms, Suffield in October 1252 penalised him by increasing the annual farm from £6 6s 8d to £7 6s 8d (no. 76).

It is probable that the rector again reneged on the agreement thirteen years later, for in April 1265 bp Walton signified Malet to Chancery as an obdurate excommunicate (178). By 1269 he had been replaced as rector by Richard son of John, with whom on 19 October prior Miles and the convent reached an agreement, with the consent of John earl Warenne (who at that time held the advowson), by which the rector and his successors should in perpetuity lease all the tithes of Sculthorpe for £6 p.a. (*Lewes Cartulary: Norfolk Portion* no. 142). There was further litigation in October 1304 in the court of the bp of Norwich, when the decision was given for the monks, the plaintiffs, to whom the tithes were restored and damages and costs of £40 awarded against Ralph, then rector (ibid. no. 115). The final reference in the cartulary is to an agreement of 1360, presumably after further litigation, by which the rector was bound to the prior in the sum of £144 10s, being arrears of the annual farm of £6 6s 8d plus damages, which suggests that the farm may not have been rendered for about twenty years; this sum was reduced to £40, to be paid over six years, but in the event of non-payment the prior might distrain for the full sum due (ibid. no. 116).

76. Lewes Priory

Notification that, whereas once a composition was made between prior Albert and the convent on the one part and John Malet, rector of Sculthorpe, on the other concerning tithes detailed therein, and sealed by the parties and by the lady Eustachia de Pavelli, then patron of the church, according to the terms of which the bishop had modified the penalty and changed the times of payment, and since that penalty was imposed on John Malet because he did not observe the composition, whereby the bishop might by rights punish him for perjury, he has however, because of the intercession of good and praiseworthy men dealt mercifully with him, and sent him to his penitentiary to receive penance for that perjury, ordering, with John's own consent expressed on oath, that whereas he was bound to the payment of nine and a half marks at the terms stipulated in the composition as modified by the bishop, henceforth he and his successors in perpetuity should pay eleven marks a year to the monks or their sergeant of Heacham by Hunstanton, in two instalments at the Easter synod at Norwich and at the feast of the Nativity of St John the Baptist or within a month of these terms. If he or any of his successors should default, then the monks may freely, by their own authority, enter into possession of these tithes without contradiction by the rector, and may receive and possess them in perpetuity, the rector and his successors being permanently deprived thereof; and if any rector should resist such restoration of the tithes to the monks, he shall be deprived of the church, and the bishop for the time being shall admit to the church at the presentation of the patron. John Malet shall use his full endeavours to procure the appending to this document of the seals of the lady Eustachia, patron of the church, and of the noble John de Warenne, as well as his own. Stratford,[1] 19 October 1252

B = TNA, E40/14065 (ii) (single sheet transcript). s. xiv in.

Omnibus Cristi fidelibus ad quos presens scriptum pervenerit Walterus Dei gratia Norwicensis episcopus salutem in Domino. Noverit universitas vestra quod cum olim quedam interveniret compositio inter Albertum priorem Lewensem et eiusdem loci conventum ex una parte et Iohannem Malet rectorem ecclesie de Sculthorp ex altera super decimis in eadem compositione contentis[a] secundum formam et dispositionem eiusdem compositionis signate signis utriusque partis et signo domine Eustachie de Pavily tunc temporis patrone dicte ecclesie, sub modificatione pene et mutatione terminorum quam eidem compositioni litteris nostris patentibus adiecimus, prout ex tenore dicte compositionis et litterarum nostrarum inspectione liquere[b] poterit evidenter, cum ex parte dicti Iohannis Malet pena in dicta compositione contenta commissa fuisset quia dictam compositionem non observaret, licet iuramento suo firmata fuisset, unde ipsum merito de periurio punire possemus, ad instantiam tamen proborum virorum et laudabilium misericorditer agentes cum ipso, ad penitentiarium nostrum ipsum pro penitentia de periurio recipienda transmisimus, statuentes et precipientes, de consensu ipsius Iohannis expresso et religione iuramenti sui firmato, quod ubi novem marcas et dimidiam ad terminos in predicta compositione contentos ex nostra miseratione modificatos solvere tenebatur, decetero annuas undecim marcas priori et conventui Lewensibus vel servienti eorum de Hecham iuxta Hunstanestun' persolvat ipse et successores sui inperpetuum, videlicet ad synodum Paschalem Norwyc' vel infra mensem post quinque marcas et dimidiam, et tantundem in forma consimili in festo nativitatis sancti Iohannis

Baptiste vel infra mensem post dictum festum; quod si ipse vel aliquis successorum suorum non fecerit, licebit dictis priori et conventui propria auctoritate possessionem dictarum decimarum libere ingredi sine contradictione ipsius vel rectoris ecclesie de Sculthorp qui pro tempore fuerit, ac eas recipere et pacifice possidere inperpetuum, predicto rectore et successoribus suis possessione et iure dictarum decimarum privatis inperpetuum, nulla questione vel iure aliquo sibi vel successoribus suis super dictis decimis reservato, dictis Lewensibus vero remanentibus possessoribus et proprietariis dictarum decimarum. Et si ipse vel aliquis successorum suorum impedimentum dictis religiosis prestiterit quominus, ut predictum est, possessionem dictarum decimarum ingredi possunt et eandem detinere, ex tunc proprietate et possessione predicte ecclesie sit ipso iure privatus, et episcopus qui pro tempore fuerit ad presentationem patroni ad eandem ecclesiam libere admitterit presentatum. Procurabit etiam dictus Iohannes Maleth, quatenus in ipso est fideliter, signum dicte Eustachie patrone predicte ecclesie et signum nobilis viri Iohannis de Warrennia una cum suo sigillo suo proprio huic scripto apponi. In cuius rei testimonium presentibus litteris sigillum nostrum fecimus apponi. Dat' apud Stratford' anno Domini millesimo CC° quinquagesimo secundo .xiiii°. kalendas Novembris.

[1] Possibly Stratford-atte-Bowe; the prelates met in London on 13 October 1252 (*HBC* 538); Suffield may have stayed at the convent on his way back to his diocese.

[a] contentas B   [b] linquere B

See no. 75.

77. Lewes Priory

Grant to the monks in proprios usus, *because of the bishop's devotion to the Cluniac order, in the merits of which the priory shares, of the church of Toftrees, vacant by the death of Ranulf Brito, lately rector, reserving to himself the taxation of a vicarage.*   Lynn, 13 December 1246

> A = TNA, E40/14927. Endorsed: Walteri episcopi Norwicensis de ecclesia de Thoftes (s. xiii), iuxta Fakenham, appropriatio, ix (s. xv); notarial sign; approx. 188 × 118 + 16 mm.; parchment tag, fragment of seal, green wax.

Universis Cristi fidelibus hoc presens scriptum visuris vel audituris Walterus Dei gratia Norwicensis ecclesie minister humilis salutem eternam in Domino. Cum sublimis ordo Cluniacensis, olim in disciplina funditus que morum est ordinata correctio, in suo proposito sic proficiat quod in observantiis regularibus non deficiat, sic odore sue conversationis bone omnes reficiat quod nonnullos sui exemplo ad meliora invitet prout a puplica mundi lingua predicatur, unde plenitudinem favoris et gratie erga omnes promerunt, equum est inter benefactores suos qui eum possessionibus ditarunt et extulerunt honoribus nos, quos a prima persone nostre notitia semper inter viscera caritatis specialiter gesserit, sibi non inveniat indevotos. Hinc est quod venerande religionis domum Lewensem, meritis sue conversationis Deo et hominibus dilectam, nobilis Cluniacensis filiam et a matre morum venustate et regulari observantia non degenerem, pro favore prosequentes, priori ipsius et conventui, quorum conversatio sublimis eos omni honore reddit dignos, gratiam nostram volentes non deesse, ipsis ecclesiam de Thoftes iuxta Fakenham in Norfolk, vacantem per mortem Ranulfi Britonis quondam rectoris eiusdem, que de eorundem est advocatione, in proprios usus concessimus possidendam, reservata nobis facultate taxandi vicariam in eadem cum voluerimus. Et ut hec nostra concessio perpetuam habeat firmitatem, huic scripto sigillum nostrum apponi fecimus. Hiis testibus: magistro Willemo de Horham officiali Norwic', Iohanne de Holcham et Thoma de Teye capellanis, Alexandro rectore ecclesie de Koleby, Willelmo de Wytewell', Hugone de Corbrigg' et Willelmo de Sidsterne clericis. Dat' apud Lennam idus Decembris anno gratie millesimo ducentesimo quadragesimo sexto.

The deceased incumbent is probably the same Ranulf Brito who was canon of St Paul's and prebendary of Caddington Major, who died between 29 September and 8 December 1246 (*Fasti* i 33). In 1254 the church was valued at £16 13s 4d; in 1291 the church at £18 13s 4d and the vicarage at £5 6s 8d; the monks of Binham had separated tithes valued at £1 (*VN* 377; *Taxatio* 81).

78. Lewes Priory

Notification that the bishop, having received from the apostolic see a command that he should cause Henry de Monticello, nephew of [William] cardinal bishop of Sabina, to be provided to an ecclesiastical benefice of a stipulated value, wished to obey this mandate and to provide him to a portion of the church of Walpole, of the monks' patronage; but since he was ignorant of the true value of that benefice and that the monks were burdened by a similar provision, as they were prepared to prove, eventually, having heard the proposals of both the monks and of the clerk and having concluded that it was doubtful that provision should be made to this benefice, he strove to bring the parties to some agreement, and with their consent ordained that on this occasion the provision should not be implemented to this benefice, but that some provision should be made for the clerk who sought this grace until provision might be made according to the papal mandate; so that, in the meantime, he should receive each year from the rector for the time being fifteen marks in cash, to be paid at the feast of the Assumption at the New Temple in London. If at any term the rector should fail in this payment, he shall render £5 to the clerk and ten marks to the bishop for every term when he defaults. The bishop reserves to himself the power of compelling observance by the parties. The monks agreed that provision should be made for this clerk as quickly as possible to a benefice in their patronage in

*the diocese of Norwich, unless before this suitable provision had otherwise been
made for him by apostolic authority.*   Stoke by Clare, 15 November 1249

A = TNA, E40/14114. Endorsed: Walteri episcopi Norwic' de Walpol' (s. xiii), Norwic' dioc',
ix (s. xv); approx. 162 × 84 + 15 mm.; four parchment tags, fragment of one unidentifiable
seal, black wax.

Omnibus Cristi fidelibus presentes litteras inspecturis Walterus miseratione
divina Norwicensis episcopus salutem in Domino sempiternam. Cum nobis esset
a sede apostolica demandatum quod Henrico Montichello, nepoti venerabilis
patris Dei gratia Sabinensis episcopi sancte Romane ecclesie cardinalis, in
beneficio ecclesiastico certe estimationis faceremus auctoritate apostolica
provideri, nos cupientes mandatum apostolicum quod reverenter recepimus
adimplere, in portione ecclesie de Walepol nostre diocesis, que ad patronatum
[W.]ᵃ prioris et capituli de Lewes noscitur pertinere, ei volumus secundum
formam nobis traditam providere, ignari tamen vere estimationis beneficii
memorati et quod iidem . .ᵃ prior et capitulum alias ad mandatum apostolicum, ut
dixerunt probare parati, erant consimili provisione gravati. Nos tandem, auditis
que memorati . .ᵃ prior et capitulum pro se et clericus exadverso super dicta
provisione in nostra presentia proponebant, cum nobis videntur merito a
sapientibus dubitandum utrum provisio in beneficio prefato locum habere
deberet, partes ad viam concordie inducere nitebamur, de quarum consensu
taliter duximus ordinandum: quod in prefato beneficio hac vice provisio non
procedat, verum ut eidem clerico qui gratiam prosequitur in aliquo prospiciatur
donec ei fuerit provisum iuxta traditam nobis formam, quod ipse interim singulis
annis a rectore apud Novum Templum London' in festo Assumptionis virginis
gloriose de bonis dicte ecclesie, quicumque eam possideat, quindecim marcas
argenti in pecunia percipiat numerata. Et si forte aliquo termino in solutione
cessaverit rector qui pro tempore fuerit, centum solidos clerico et nobis decem
marcas solvat nomine pene pro quolibet termino non servato, potestate nobis
reservata ad compellendum partes ad observationem omnium premissorum, et
pena soluta obligatione nichilominus durature. Consenserunt etiam expresse ipsi
. .ᵃ prior et conventus quod in beneficio ad eorum patronatum spectante in nostra
diocesi, quam cito facultas se offeret, possit dicto clerico libere provideri,
secundum quod in directo nobis mandato apostolico continetur, eorum
oppositione cessante, nisi prius ei fuerit alibi auctoritate apostolica competenter
provisum. In cuius rei testimonium et signum consensus expressi prefati . .ᵃ prior
et conventus et clericus unacum sigillo nostro sigillis suis presentes litteras
muniverunt. Dat' apud Stok' monachorum .xvii. kalendas Decembris anno
Domini millesimo CCᵒ XLᵒ nono.

ᵃ *gap for initial* B

For earlier references to the church of Walpole, see *EEA* 6 nos. 111, 113; *EEA* 21 no. 73. The
advowson, as in the case of West Walton, with which it was frequently paired in documents,
was divided between the monks of Lewes and the bp. In 1254 the monk's portion was valued at
£40 and the bp's at £33 6s 8d; the monks themselves also received a pension (also called *portio*)

of £5 (*VN* 382). In 1291 the two parts of the church were descibed as 'of John of Evreux conferred by the prior of Lewes' and 'of John Langton' valued respectively at £42 13s 4d and £30 13s 4d, with the monks still receiving their portion of £5 (*Taxatio* 80). The monks also held substantial temporalities in the parish, valued at £20 in 1254 and £34 3s 3d in 1291 (*VN* 385; *Taxatio* 97).

Henry de Monticello was before 25 September 1250 collated by the bp on papal authority to the church of Bramford, normally in the gift of Battle abbey (*Reg. Inn. IV* no. 5355; *CPL* i 272), valued in 1254 at 50 marks (£33 6s 8d) (*VN* 458).

The cardinal bp of Sabina (1244–51) was William, formerly bp of Modena (Mas Latrie, *Tresor de Chronologie* (Paris, 1889) cols 1160, 1192). The prior of Lewes was William de Russelun (*HRH* ii 233).

79. Lewes Priory

Notification that, since the monks have on this occasion surrendered the church of Walpole, which is vacant, to the bishop's disposition, and he knows they will be burdened by many payments and that the annual pension of eighty marks which they are bound to render each year to John Spata, papal chaplain, would be extremely onerous for them, so that indebtedness will diminish their hospitality, he has ordained that the monks shall receive forty marks a year in exoneration of the said pension for as long as Spata lives, to be paid by the rector of the church from its goods each year at the feast of the Ascension at Walpole once he has the fruits of the church, that is, after the year's revenue paid towards the subsidy of Boniface, archbishop of Canterbury. If any rector should default in payment of these forty marks beyond the octaves of the Ascension, he shall be deprived of his right in and possession of the church, and the monks may freely present a suitable persona *to that church, vacant both in law and in fact. This is enacted saving to the monks their ancient pension due from the church, and to Henry de Monticello fifteen marks a year from the fruits of the church, until he be provided with an ecclesiastical benefice, as detailed more fully in the bishop's ordinance on this matter [78]. On the death of John Spata and the provision of Henry de Monticello the church shall revert in full to the clerk presented to and admitted by the bishop, saving to the monks their ancient pension. The monks have accepted and sworn to observe this ordinance in all particulars.*   Ipswich, 20 January 1250

A = TNA, E40/14118. Endorsed: Walteri episcopi Norwicensis de Walepol' (s. xiii), Norw' dioc', ix (s. xv); approx. 224 × 108 + 26 mm.; parchment tag, seal missing.

Omnibus Cristi fidelibus presentes litteras visuris vel audituris Walterus Dei gratia Norwicensis episcopus salutem in Domino sempiternam. Et si iuxta officii nostri debitum singulis in beneficiorum largitione simus debitores,[1] eis tamen precipue subvenire tenemur qui cum Maria ad pedes Domini decubantes assidue pro totius populi salute subnixis precibus altissimum flagitare non cessant. Cum igitur dilecti filii prior et conventus Lewenses ecclesiam de Walepol vacantem, ad ipsorum patronatum spectantem, nostre dispositioni et voluntati hac[a] vice commisissent omnino, nos plenius cognoscentes ipsos pluribus annuis prestationibus fore gravatos, ac annuam pensionem quater viginti marcarum quam singulis annis domino Iohanni Spade domini pape capellano solvere tenentur eisdem nimis fore honerosam, attendentes insuper ipsam ecclesiam sic debitis fore obligatam quod nisi citius subveniretur eisdem, hospitalitatis nomen que tanquam in sede propria regnare consuevit ibidem sedebit in margina, nos siquidem, visis circumstantiis et ponderatis gravaminibus ipsius ecclesie universis, sic de ipsa ecclesia duximus ordinandum: quod de bonis ipsius ecclesie quadraginta marcas in exonerationem pensionis predicti magistri Iohannis Spade quamdiu idem Iohannes vixerit per manus eiusdem rectoris ecclesie de bonis ipsius ecclesie prefati prior et conventus percipient annuatim in festo Assensionis Domini apud Walepol, postquam idem rector fructus ipsius ecclesie habuerit, videlicet transacto anno subventionis domini B. Cantuariensis archiepiscopi; videlicet quod si quicumque rector in solutione prestationis predictarum quadraginta marcarum suo termino cessaverit vel ad ultimum infra octabas non satisfecerit, eo ipso a iure et possessione ipsius ecclesie cadat privatus, et absolute predictis priori et conventui de Lewes ad ipsam ecclesiam tamquam de iure et de facto vacantem libere personam idoneam liceat presentare. Hanc siquidem ordinationem fecimus salva prefatis priori et conventui pensione antiqua ab ipsa ecclesia eisdem debita, et salvis Henrico de Monticello quindecim marcis de bonis ipsius ecclesie secundum nostram ordinationem annuatim percipiendis, donec eidem fuerit provisum in beneficio ecclesiastico prout in nostra ordinatione continetur. Decedente vero magistro Iohanne Spade et proviso dicto Henrico de Monticello in beneficio ecclesiastico prout in nostra ordinatione continetur, ipsa ecclesia de Walepol clerico nobis presentato et a nobis admisso cum integritate remaneat, salva semper prefatis priori et conventui pensione sua debita antiqua. Hanc autem ordinationem nostram iidem prior et conventus per omnia acceptantes, se ipsam in omnibus et per omnia observaturos fideliter promiserunt. In cuius rei testimonium huic scripto sigillum nostrum apponi fecimus. Dat' apud Gipewicum .xiii. kalendas Februarii anno Domini millesimo CC° XL° nono et pontificatus nostri anno quinto.

[1]Cf. Rom. 8: 12. [2]Cf. Luke 10: 39
[a] ac A

See no. 78 above. For a convenient synopsis of the relationship with Lewes priory of John Spata, a prominent papal jurist, active from 1229 to after 1254, see *Letters of Guala* no. 67n. and refs. there given. In 1230 a mediety of the church of Melton Mowbray, normally of the monks' advowson, had been collated to him by Stephen of Anagni, papal tax collector (TNA, 40/14942; see also *EEA* 22 no. 153), and some time afterwards, after the death or resignation of William of Calabria, Spata received the other mediety. The whole church (and even a mediety) was an extremely well-endowed benefice, valued in 1291, after its appropriation to the monks, at £110 in total (*Taxatio* 65b). In 1245, following complaints from Lewes, Spata resigned all his rights in Melton Mowbray to mr Jordan Pironti, a fellow jurist at the papal curia, and in return was promised an annual pension to be paid by the monks of Lewes pending his appointment at their presentation to another benefice in their gift. On 9 March 1246 pope Innocent IV acknowledged the appropriation of Melton Mowbray to Lewes, which the monks had previously claimed on a basis of a dubious charter. Spata's pension was apparently not paid, since *c.* 1257 pope Alexander IV wrote to Henry III and the bp of Lincoln demanding the sequestration of the revenues of Melton Mowbray church and all the monks' revenues in the parish in order that Spata might be compensated for non-payment and for damages which he had sustained in litigation; so heated was the dispute that Spata alleged that the prior had murdered his proctor.

Before 25 September 1250 Henry de Monticello was rector of the church of Bramford, normally in the gift of the monks of Battle (*Reg. Inn. IV* no. 5355; *CPL* i 272).

80. Lewes Priory

Admission, at the presentation of the monks, of William of Pakenham, clerk, to an annual pension of two shillings from the church of St Peter, [South] Lynn, on the surrender of John of Ingoldisthorpe, who was rector, and reserving to John all the residue of the church's revenues. William swore on the Gospels, in the bishop's presence, that he would not during John's lifetime seek to have the pension increased, nor trouble John over the residue or any part of it, nor over taking orders, maintaining residence or any matter beyond the pension itself. The bishop conceded, with the consent of the monks as patrons, that on the death or resignation of William, the whole church should be left to John as rector, but on the resignation or death of John the vicarage should be consolidated in its entirety with the personatus. Eccles, 6 March 1256

A = TNA, E40/14924. Endorsed: Norwic' de ecclesia de Lenn' (s. xiii), dioc' (added under Norwic'), ix (s. xv); approx. 192 × 94 + 14 mm., parchment tag, large fragment of seal, brown wax.

Omnibus Cristi fidelibus presentes litteras visuris etiam audituris Walterus miseratione divina episcopus Norwicensis salutem in Domino sempiternam. Universitati vestre volumus esse notum quod cum nos ad presentationem dilectorum nobis in Cristo prioris et conventus Lewensium et ad resignationem domini Iohannis de Ingaldestorp de ecclesia sancti Petri Lenn', cuius erat rector, factam, dilectum filium Willelmum de Pakeham clericum ad pensionem duorum solidorum de dicta ecclesia sancti Petri annuatim nomine personatus recipiendorum, salvo toto residuo illius ecclesie integritaliter dicto Iohanni, admisimus. Idem W. in nostra presentia constitutus iuravit tactis sacrosanctis ewangeliis quod pensionem illam in vita dicti I. augmentari nullatenus procurabit vel ipsum super residuo vel aliqua eius parte vel etiam super ordinum susceptione, residentia facienda vel aliis quibuscumque per que ultra pensionem memoratam gravari valeat, molestabit vel molestari aliquatenus procurabit. Nos etiam, de consensu et instantia dictorum prioris et conventus patronorum dicte ecclesie, concedimus et tenore presentium ordinamus quod, cedente vel decedente dicto Willelmo, tota ecclesia integritaliter dicto Iohanni remaneat ut rector; cedente vero vel decedente dicto Iohanne, vicaria ipsa personatui consolideretur et absque diminutione accrescat. In cuius rei securitatem et memoriam dicto Willelmo has litteras nostras patentes fieri fecimus sigilli nostri munimine roboratas. Dat' apud Eccles .ii. nonas Martii anno Domini M CC L quinto et pontificatus nostri anno duodecimo.

> William of Pakenham attests several acta of bp Walter, and represented him in the *curia regis*. On 25 July 1268 bp Roger Scarning notified William, as rector, that in view of the poverty of the rectory, and considering him suitable for the governance of the entire church, he was consolidating the vicarage created by the ordinance of bp Walter with the rectory, with the stipulation that the church should not be deprived of the divine office and that the canonical dues should be rendered to the diocesan (TNA, E40/14923). Soon afterwards William acquired a new site for the church after severe flood damage, and on 1 April 1271 issued a notification that he had transferred there the entire edifice, which move in no way affected the rights of patronage of prior Miles and the convent of Lewes, to whom he quitclaimed all right therein (TNA, E40/14112; cf. *Lewes Cartulary: Norfolk Portion* nos. 173–4). In both 1254 and 1291 the church was assessed at £8 (*VN* 382; *Taxatio* 80).

*81. London, St Paul's Cathedral

Indulgence granted to those who visit the tomb of bishop Roger Niger, or who make a donation to the fabric.   [19 February × 24 March 1245]

> Mention of indulgence, issued in 1244 and the first year of his pontificate, in W.Dugdale, *History of St Paul's Cathedral in London,* 2nd edn, ed. H. Ellis, London 1818, 9.

> This indulgence is not now in the file of episcopal indulgences for the cathedral (see no. 81A below). Roger Niger was bp of London from 10 June 1229 – 29 September 1241; for reported miracles at his tomb, see Matthew Paris, *Historia Minor* ii 493.

81A. London, St Paul's Cathedral

Remission of thirty days enjoined penance granted to those of his diocese, and to others whose diocesans ratify this indulgence, who, being contrite and confessed, give alms to the fabric of the cathedral, and to those who visit it to pray on the anniversary of its dedication.   London, 7 October 1250

> A = London, Guildhall Library, ms. 25124/26. No medieval endorsement; approx. 172 × 76 + 18 mm.; parchment tag, fragment of seal, natural wax varnished brown, counterseal.

Omnibus Cristi fidelibus ad quos presens scriptum pervenerit Walterus miseratione divina Norwicensis ecclesie minister humilis salutem in Domino sempiternam. Cum inter cetera caritatis opera sacra sanctorum limina visitare in conspectu altissimi non immerito[a] sit acceptum, nos de Dei misericordia, gloriose Dei genetricis Marie, beati doctoris gentium apostoli Pauli et omnium sanctorum meritis confidentes, omnibus de nostra diocesi, vel aliis quorum diocesani hanc nostram indulgentiam ratam habuerint, qui ad fabricam ecclesie beati Pauli London', cum sit magna et magnos sumptus exigat, pias elemosinas de bonis sibi a Deo collatis pie duxerint conferendas, quique eandem ecclesiam in anniversario dedicationis orandi gratia humiliter adierint et devote, si de peccatis suis vere contriti fuerint et confessi, triginta dies de iniuncta sibi penitentia misericorditer relaxamus. Dat' London' nonis Octobris anno Domini millesimo ducentesimo quinquagesimo.

ª inmerito A

82. London, St Paul's Cathedral

A. Mandate [as executor of the business of the cross appointed by the apostolic see] to the dean and [named] members of the chapter, ordering them to provide a written assessment of their annual revenue.   [Summer – Autumn 1254]
B. Second mandate relating to the same matter.
                                                    [Autumn 1254 × 10 February 1255]

> Mention of mandates (*mandatorum*) in the return made by W[alter de Salerne], dean, P[eter of Newport], archdeacon of London, and Hugh of St Edmunds and William la Feite, canons, of the revenues of the cathedral church, made after Ash Wednesday (10 February) 1255. Pd in *VN* 492–3.
>
> The new collectors, including bp Suffield, published their commission at London on 4 July 1254, and the work of collection had begun by 11 July (Lunt, *Financial Relations* 262), but the mandate to provide a written assessment was not despatched to Canons Ashby priory until 11 November (16). The St Paul's return was made *post compotum cinerum*, presumably after a second admonitory mandate.

83. Longueville Priory

Confirmation for the monks of the grant to them in proprios usus *by bishop William Raleigh of the church of St Mary, [Little] Witchingham, saving a vicarage which shall consist of the altarage and all the free land of the church. At any vacancy, the monks shall present to the bishop whomsoever he may nominate to them, and if they fail so to do within the time allowed, he may collate the church as he wishes. The vicar shall discharge all customary obligations of the church to bishop and archdeacon. The monks' proctor shall each year on Ash Wednesday distribute two seams of peas to the poor of the parish.*   Thorpe, 2 April 1251

> B = New College, Oxford, archives no. 9744 (Liber Niger) fo. 25r–v (*inspeximus* by prior Simon and the convent of Norwich, 4 July 1251). s.xvi in.
> Pd from B in *Newington Longville Charters* no. 118.

Omnibus Cristi fidelibus presentes litteras [fo. 25v] visuris vel audituris Walterus Dei gratia Norwicensis episcopus salutem in Domino sempiternam. Cum venerabilis pater dominus W. de Ralegh' predecessor noster dilectis filiis priori et conventui de Longavill' ecclesiam sancte Marie de Wychingham in usus proprios concesserit conferendam, nos, ipsius concessionem ratam habentes et acceptam, memoratam ecclesiam dictis priori et conventui in usus proprios conferimus, concedimus et auctoritate episcopali confirmamus, salva vicaria que consistit in alteragio prefate ecclesie et totali libera terra ipsius ecclesie; ad quam vicariam quotienscumque ipsam vacare contigerit dicti prior et conventus quemcumque per nos vel successores nostros duximus nominandum ad eandem vicariam nobis et successoribus nostris presentabunt; quod si infra tempus legittimum dicti prior et conventus personam a nobis vel successoribus nominandam ad dictam vicariam presentare distulerint, nos et successores nostri ipsam vicariam, irrequisito dictorum prioris et conventus assensu et consensu, cuicumque voluerimus conferemus. Vicarius vero qui pro tempore fuerit sustinebit omnia onera episcopalia et archidiaconalia debita et consueta. Ordinamus etiam quod procurator dicti prioris qui pro tempore fuerit distribuet singulis annis duas summas pisarum pauperibus parochie de Wychingham in capite ieiunii prout melius viderit expedire, salvis in omnibus episcopalibus consuetudinibus et nostre Norwicensis ecclesie dignitate. In cuius rei testimonium huic scripto sigillum nostrum apponi fecimus. Hiis testibus: magistro Willelmo de Suffeud archidiacono Norwic', magistro W. de Horham archidiacono Suthfolch', magistro R. de Insula archidiacono Colecestr', dominis Iohanne de Holcham et Thoma de Theye capellanis, Willelmo de Whitewell', Thoma de Walecot, Willelmo de Lutham clericis, Egidio de Whitewell' capellano et aliis. Dat' apud Thorp .iiii°. nonas Aprilis anno Domini millesimo CC° quinquagesimo primo et pontificatus nostri anno vii°.

The church was one of the gifts of earl Walter Giffard (*EEA* 6 no. 116). In 1254 the vicarage was valued at £3 6s 8d (*VN* 369), and in 1291 the church at £26 13s 4d and tne vicarage at £4 6s 8d (*Taxatio* 82b). Episcopal nomination to the vicarage continued after the possessions of the priory passed to New College, Oxford (*Newington Longville Charters* no. 120).

84. Luke, Archbishop of Dublin, Master Lawrence of Somercotes and John de Frosinone

Notification, with J[ohn Climping], bishop of Chichester, and R[ichard de Crokesle], abbot of Westminster, that having been commanded by the pope that they, with other suitable persons commissioned by them, should execute the business of the cross and the collection of a tenth of ecclesiastical goods in the kingdom of England and other lands subject to its king, they have committed to the recipients, as their deputies, their powers in the kingdom of Ireland with regard to the business of the cross, the granting of protection and justice to crusaders, the collection of a tenth of ecclesiastical goods, both greater and lesser, and the execution of all else without which the business may not proceed; and the commissioners will confirm and enforce the sentences of their deputies against rebels. They, as deputies, should place the money in safe places until they receive further instructions from the king or from the commissioners. If not all of them can attend to this business, one or two of them shall nevertheless execute it, providing that in the receipt and deposit of this money nothing at all shall be done without the presence of master Lawrence, whom by the king's advice they have set in charge of this matter, or of one specially deputed by him. If any doubt should arise as to the execution of this business, special powers of interpretation are granted to master Lawrence, who knows fully their intent. They have provided him with transcripts of the papal letters, of which some are sealed by the king and the papal commissioners, some by the commissioners only and some by the bishop of Chichester alone. [Shortly after 28 May 1254]

B = TNA, C54/67 (Close Rolls 38 Henry III) m. 5d. s. xiii med.
Pd in *Cl. R. 1253–54* 145–6; *EEA* 23 no. 210.

The collection of a tenth of ecclesiastical revenues for three years, originally granted on 11 April 1250 by pope Innocent IV to king Henry III for his projected crusade, was considerably delayed (Lunt, *Financial Relations* 255–6). A papal commission of 12 September 1253 appointed the bps of Chichester and Norwich and the abbot of Westminster as assessors and collectors (*Reg. Inn. IV* no. 6989; *CPL* i 290; cf. *Chron. Maj.* vi 296–8; *CPR 1247–58* 164). Bp Richard Wich of Chichester had originally been appointed as one of the collectors in October 1250, and in November 1252 had been placed in charge of preaching the crusade throughout England, but had died at Dover, while on a preaching tour, on 2/3 April 1253 (*EEA* 22 xxxix). John Climping received royal assent to his election on 23 May, but was not consecrated until 11 January 1254 (ibid. xl). He was thus bp-elect when the papal commission was issued, but bp when the collectors in the spring of 1254 planned their work, with the approval of the royal council (Prynne, *Records* ii 814; *CPR 1247–58* 370). The papal grant extended to the king's dominions beyond England: Ireland, Gascony and the Channel Islands, and this delegation of the collectors' powers in Ireland was issued five weeks before they published their commission in England, on 4 July 1254 (*Chron. Maj.* vi 296). On 28 May 1254 the king had instructed the chief commissioners to choose a clerk in whom they had confidence to work with the archbp of Dublin and John de Frosinone, papal collector in Ireland, and the reference to the appointment of master Lawrence is contained in a royal notification on 5 August to the archbp of the despatch to Ireland of master Laurence of Somercotes (*Cl. R. 1253–54* 92–3); see also no. 125 below.

    Luke, archbp of Dublin, had been a clerk of Hubert de Burgh and was subsequently controller of the king's wardrobe from January 1224 to April 1227 and dean of the college of St Martin le Grand, London; he had been the king's candidate for Durham in 1226–27 and had been elected to Dublin before 13 December 1228 (*Fasti* i 70; Powicke, *Henry III and the Lord Edward* 267–8). For mr Lawrence of Somercotes see above, intro. p. xlviii.

    Mr John of Frosinone, papal chaplain, was already acting as papal nuncio in Ireland in 1249, when on 16 March pope Innocent IV ordered that he should be inducted as a canon of Dublin cathedral, and simultaneously ordered the archbp and archdn of Dublin to revoke the sentences of suspension and excommunication imposed on him by the bps of Achonry and Killala on the pretext of papal letters obtained by the bp of Limerick; the pope also granted Frosinone an indult that while he was in the papal service no person should issue any spiritual sentence against him (*Reg. Inn. IV* nos. 447–9; *CPL* i 253). On 7 February 1252 the archbp of Tuam and bp of Annaghdown were ordered by the pope not to proceed with an enquiry into Frosinone's finances, with regard to 3000 marks from the 40,000 marks raised by him for the redemption of vows, legacies and other contributions to the Holy Land, which together with jewels and his annual procurations he was alleged to have appropriated to himself and deposited in various religious houses (*Reg. Inn. IV* no. 5788; *CPL* i 277). In early 1254, however, he was acting as papal collector in Scotland (Sayers, *Original Papal Documents* no. 459). On 26 September 1261 he was ordered by pope Urban IV to assemble all the money belonging to the Roman church in Ireland and England and to transfer it to cameral merchants (*Reg. Urban IV* no.10; *CPL* i 380); but on 24 November 1263 the archbp of Armagh was ordered, as well as forwarding the revenues of the Roman church from his province to the *curia*, to make enquiry into the money and goods which Frosinone, formerly papal nuncio, was said to have received; two days later the pope ordered the archbp and the bp of Meath to extend this enquiry to the whole of Ireland, to extract the money from the various depositories and to render a full account (*Reg. Urban IV* nos. 475–6; *CPL* i 392–3). This commission to the two prelates was renewed on 23 May 1266 by pope Clement IV, who noted that Frosinone did not appear to have rendered any account (*Reg. Clem. IV* no. 763; *CPL* i 423). It must remain ambiguous whether he was corrupt, or was the subject of a campaign of vilification by the Irish bps.

85. Marham Abbey

Notification that, with the consent of the prior and convent of Westacre and of Nicholas, vicar of the churches of Holy Trinity and St Andrew of Marham, he has conceded to the nuns in perpetuity free burial of their sisters and lay-sisters, with a chantry for them in the church or chapel so that masses and other divine offices may be celebrated by their own priest or priests. No parishioner of Marham may be buried there, nor may be admitted to the sacraments of the church, but if an outsider should choose burial there, he or she may be there buried, saving the canonical rights of their parish church.

North Elmham, 9 September 1251

B = Norfolk R.O., Hare ms 1/232 X (Marham cartulary) fo. 20r–v. s. xiv in. C = ibid. fo. 20v (*inspeximus* by prior Simon and the convent of Norwich, 16 September 1251).

Universis Cristi fidelibus presentes litteras inspecturis Walterus permissione divina episcopus Norwycensis salutem in Domino sempiternam. Ad omnium notitiam volumus pervenire nos, de consensu prioris et conventus de Westacra et Nicholai vicarii ecclesiarum sancte Trinitatis et sancti Andree de Marham, concessimus pontificali auctoritate qua fungimur monialibus Cysterciensis ordinis in dicta parochia Domino servientibus et earum successoribus in perpetuum Domino servituris sororum et conversarum suarum liberam sepulturam et in earum ecclesia vel capella per sacerdotem vel sacerdotes proprios cantariam, ut sibi faciant missa et alia divina officia celebrari, ita tamen quod nullum de parochianis dicte ecclesie ibidem faciant sepeliri nec ad ecclesiasticum sacramentum admitti; set si extraneus ibi elegerit sepulturam, salva canonica iustitia parochialis ecclesie, ad sepeliendum ibi libere admittatur. Dat' apud Norhelmham .v. idus Septembris[a] pontificatus nostri anno septimo.

[a] Sentendris B, C

The abbey of St Mary, St Barbara and St Edmund was founded by Isabelle, widow of Hugh d'Albini, earl of Arundel, and was consecrated in June 1249 or 1250 by Richard Wich, bp of Chichester; it was incorporated with the abbey of Waverley in 1252. It was one of only two abbeys of Cistercian nuns in England, but its endowment was smaller than that of many priories (*MRH* 272, 275). *Oxenedes* (184) notes under the year 1251 that the countess established there first nuns from overseas. In 1254 the portion of the prior of Westacre in Marham church was valued at £10 and the vicarage at £4, while separated tithes held by the prior of Castle Acre and Ralph le Waleis were listed at £4 and £2 respectively (*VN* 409). In 1291 the two churches of Marham, appropriated to Westacre, apart from a vicarage not subject to the tenth and from portions, of which one was not subject to the tenth, were listed at £10 13s and the portion of Castle Acre at £2 6s 8d (*Taxatio* 88b).

86. Marham Abbey

*Ordinance of the bishop concerning the agreement between Isabelle countess of
Arundel and the nuns on the one part and the canons of Westacre and the vicar
of the churches of Holy Trinity and St Andrew, Marham, on the other,
concerning the matters detailed in no. 85.*   North Elmham, 9 September 1251

B = Norfolk R.O., Hare ms 1/232 X (Marham cartulary) fo. 1r. s. xiv in.

Hec est ordinatio Walteri Norwicensis episcopi inter nobilem mulierem
Isabellam comitissam Arundel' et moniales de Marham ordinis Cisterciensis ex
parte una et priorem et canonicos de Westhacr' rectores ecclesiarum sancte
Trinitatis et sancti Andree de Marham et vicarium[a] earundem ex altera, videlicet
quod predicte moniales in parochia memorata in loco quo habitant libere et
quiete absque cuiusquam contradictione habeant perpetuis temporibus cantariam,
ac per suos capellanos divina sacramenta largiantur eisdem. Habebunt quoque
dicte moniales sibi suisque sororibus et conversis liberam ibidem sepulturam,
parochianis ipsarum ecclesiarum dumtaxat exceptis, qui nec etiam ad aliquid
aliud sacramentum ecclesiasticum admittantur ibidem. Extranei siquidem eligere
sibi poterint ibidem salvo iure matricis sue ecclesie, sepulturam. Hanc igitur
ordinationem auctoritate pontificali sic factam partes acceptaverunt, et ad
maiorem securitatem nostram et prefate comitisse et prioris et conventus de
Westacra, unacum signo vicarii supradicti, presentibus scriptis ad modum
cirographi factis sunt appensa. Dat' apud Northelmham .v. idus Septembris
pontificatus nostri anno septimo.

[a] vicarii B

In return for this concession, Countess Isabelle granted an annual rent of half a mark to the
canons of Westacre (fos. 1v–2r of B).

87. Marham Abbey

Grant to the nuns in proprios usus *and in perpetuity, by the will and with the
assent of Isabelle, countess of Arundel, their patron, of all the greater and lesser
tithes of the demesne and of the* curia *of the manor of Marham, which hitherto
secular clerks have received by grant of the lords of Marham. Any future
infringement of the nuns' rights therein is prohibited.*   Norwich, 20 June 1254

B = Norfolk R.O., Hare ms 1/232 X (Marham cartulary) fo. 1r. s. xiv in.C = ibid. fo. 20r. D =
ibid. fo. 20r (*inspeximus* by prior Roger and convent of Norwich, 18 May 1260).

Omnibus in Cristo fidelibus presentes litteras visuris vel audituris Walterus Dei
gratia Norwicensis episcopus salutem in Domino sempiternam. Universitati
vestre tenore presentium innotescat quod nos, de voluntate et assensu nobilis
mulieris domine Isabelle comitisse Arundelle patrone domus de Marham,
concessimus et assignavimus dilectis in Cristo filiabus abbatisse et monialibus de

Marham nostre diocesis in proprios usus omnes decimas maiores et minores de dominico et de curia manerii de Marham provenientes, quas clerici seculares ex donatione dominorum manerii de Marham hactenus percipere consueverunt, volentes et concedentes quod predicte moniales dictas decimas perpetuis temporibus libere percipiant et in usus proprios, sublato cuiuslibet conditionis obstaculo, sine diminutione convertant, sub attestatione divini nominis districtius inhibentes ne quis ipsas in posterum super iure seu possessione dictarum decimarum iniuste gravare vel molestiam eis inferre presumat; salvis in omnibus episcopalibus consuetudinibus et nostre Norwicensis ecclesie dignitate. In cuius rei testimonium presenti scripto sigillum nostrum apponi fecimus. Hiis testibus: magistro Roberto de Insula archidiacono Colecestr', Willelmo de Whitewell, magistro Hugone de Corbrig', Thoma de Walkote, Egidio de Whitewell capellano, Willelmo de Wichingham, Nicholao de Surlyngham, Willelmo de Bungeya clericis, et multis aliis. Dat' apud Norwicum .xii. kalendas Iulii anno Domini millesimo quinquagesimo quarto et pontificatus nostri anno decimo.

88. Norwich Cathedral Priory

Confirmation for the monks, for the use of the cellar, of various demesne tithes of the bishop at Thornage, Langham and Homersfield; and of others [named] at Postwick, Wroxham, Swanton [Morley], Buxton, 'Kinestorp' [in Buxton], Hockering, Deopham, Shotesham, Intwood, Sparham, Whitlingham, Barford, Irmingland, [North] Elmham, Threxton, Scarning, Witchingham, Cockthorpe, Fring, Thornham, 'Osegateshag' in Cressingham and Bircham Newton.

[North] Elmham, 29 April 1245

> A = Norfolk R.O., DCN 43/44. Endorsed: Confirmatio domini Walteri episcopi omnium decimarum pertinentium ad celerariam tempore Nicholai de Brater … tunc celerarii; decima (s. xiii); pressmark; Hugh of Mursley's notarial sign; approx. 228 × 102 + 16 mm.; tag and seal missing.
> B = Norfolk R.O., DCN 40/1 (general cartulary) fo. 228v (219v) (*inspeximus* by bp John Salmon, 9 March 1302). s. xiv in. C = ibid., DCN 40/4 (episcopal charters) pp. 113–15). s. xv in. D = ibid., pp. 297–8. E = ibid., pp. 218–20 (as B).
> Pd from A in *Norwich Cathedral Charters* i no. 212.

Omnibus Cristi fidelibus ad quos presens scriptum pervenerit Walterus Dei gratia episcopus Norwicensis salutem in Domino sempiternam. Noverit universitas vestra nos concessisse et hac carta nostra confirmasse dilectis in Cristo priori et monachis Norwicensibus ad opus celerarie sue omnes decimas infrascriptas, videlicet: duas partes decimarum omnium de dominico nostro de Tornedys et dimidiam partem decimarum omnium de dominico nostro in Langham, tertiam etiam partem decimarum omnium de dominico nostro de Humeresfeld', et duas partes decimarum omnium tam maiorum quam minorum de dominico quondam Margarete de Cressy in villis de Poswic et de Wroxham, duas etiam partes decimarum omnium tam maiorum quam minorum de dominicis Huberti quondam de Rya in villis de Swaneton', Bucston', Kinestorp, Hokering', Depham, et duas partes decimarum de dominico Oliveri de Vallibus in Sotesham, et duas partes decimarum de dominico Radulfi de Tyvill' in Intewde, duas etiam partes decimarum omnium de dominico quondam Willelmi de Sparham in eadem villa, et duas partes decimarum de dominico Rogeri filii Oseberti in Wytlingham, duas etiam partes decimarum de dominico Iohannis de Bereford in eadem villa, et de dominico Radulfi filii Simonis in Hyrminglond, et duas partes decimarum de dominico Simonis de Nuers in Helmham, et de dominico quondam domini Wygani Britonis in Trekeston', duas insuper partes decimarum de dominico Rogeri Gulafre in villa de Skerninges, et de dominico Galfridi de Lyuns in villa de Wychingham, duas etiam partes decimarum de dominico Warini de Thorp in Kokestorp, omnes etiam decimas tam maiores quam minores provenientes de dominico Willelmi de Freng' in eadem villa, et de dominico Thurstini quondam diaconi in Thornham, et de feodo dominici de Cressingham quod vocatur Osegateshag' in eadem villa, duas etiam partes decimarum tam maiorum quam minorum de dominico quondam domini Willelmi de Kerdeston' in villis de Brecham et de Neuton'. Memoratas igitur decimas ad opus celerarie sue dictis monachis confirmantes presens scriptum in testimonium sigillo nostro duximus muniendum. Hiis testibus: magistro Willelmo de Suffeld', Herveo de Fakeham, Willelmo de Horham, Adam de Bromholm, Thoma Bigot, Ricardo de Rybofi, Henrico de Bodekesham, Thoma de Walecote clericis nostris. Dat' apud Helmham .iii. kalendas Maii pontificatus nostri anno primo.

For a general confirmation by pope Innocent IV, dated 23 July 1249, while bp Suffield was at the *curia*, of the possessions of the cathedral priory, see *Norwich Cathedral Charters* i no. 302.

89. Norwich Cathedral Priory

Inspeximus *and confirmation of the confirmation for the monks by bishop Thomas [Blundeville] of various tithes for the use of the cellar [EEA 21 no. 78]. Confirmation also, for the same use, of two parts of the great and lesser tithes of the late lord William of Kerdiston in the vill of Bircham Newton.*

North Elmham, 29 April 1245

B = Canterbury D. & C., Ch. Ant. CA/N1 (*inspeximus* by prior Nicholas and convent of Christ Church, 1249). s. xiii med. C = Norfolk R.O., DCN 40/7 (general cartulary) fos. 32v–33r. s. xiii ex. D = ibid., DCN 40/5 (cellarer's cartulary) fos. 11v–12r. s. xiii ex. E = ibid., DCN 40/4 (episcopal charters) pp. 115–18. s. xv in. F = ibid., pp. 298–300.
Pd in *Norwich Cathedral Charters* i no. 213.

Omnibus Cristi fidelibus ad quos presens scriptum pervenerit Walterus ªDei gratia⁻ª Norwicensis episcopus salutem in Domino.ᵇ Cartam bone memorie Thome quondam Norwicensis episcopi inspeximus in hec verba: [*EEA* 21 no. 78]. Nos igitur predictam concessionem et confirmationem ratam habentes et acceptam, eam presenti scripto et sigilli nostri impressione corroboramus.

Confirmamus insuper auctoritate pontificali et presentis scripti tenore monachis supradictis ad opus dicte celerarie duas partes decimarum tam maiorum quam minorum de dominico quondam domini Willelmi de Kerdeston' in villis^c de Brecham et de Neuton'. Hiis testibus: ^{d}magistro Willelmo de Sutfeld', Herveo^e de Fakeham, Willelmo de Horham, Adam de Bromholm'^{f} et Thoma le Bigot, Thoma de Eccles, Ricardo de Ribof,^{g} Henrico de Bodekesham^h clericis nostris.$^{-d}$ Data apud Elmham^i .iii. kalendas Maii pontificatus nostri anno primo.

$^{a-a}$ miseratione divina D ^{b} D *adds* sempiternam ^{c} vill' B; villa D $^{d-d}$ *om.* D, *which has* etc.
^{e} Henrico B, D, E, F ^{f} Bromholme C ^{g} Ribost' C, D, E, F ^{h} Bodekesh' C, D, E, F
^{i} Emham D, F

For Hervey of Fakenham as witness of the bp's acta, see index, *s. n.*; there is no occurrence elsewhere of a Henry of Fakenham.

90. Norwich Cathedral Priory

Notification that, when the prior and convent claimed the exemption from episcopal jurisdiction in their manors to which they had been accustomed under his predecessors, the bishop, unwilling to extend his jurisdiction to their detriment, of his special grace granted that they might present to him some suitable man, beneficed and resident in the diocese, as dean, to hold custody of the spirituality of these manors. Having received from him an oath of canonical obedience, the bishop will without any difficulty admit this man to the custody, reserving to himself jurisdiction in cases of matrimony and crime. With the monks' consent he has reserved the right of visitation, correction and the exercise of episcopal jurisdiction to himself and his officials, whenever they may wish to exercise it. The dean presented by the monks shall have the same rights as other deans in the bishopric. If cases initiated in these manors before the bishop or his officials cannot conveniently be concluded therein, he reserves the right to bring them to a conclusion elsewhere and to summon litigants outside the manors. If any men of these manors should elect to be examined by the bishop or his officials in any manner of case, then the bishop and his official may hear such cases, notwithstanding any objection by the dean. No increase of jurisdiction is to accrue to archdeacons or deans in the said manors because of this concession.   Blofield, 4 February 1246

B = Norfolk R.O., DCN 40/7 (general cartulary) fo. 25r–v. s. xiii ex.
Pd in *Norwich Cathedral Charters* i no. 210.

Omnibus Cristi fidelibus ad quos presens scriptum pervenerit Walterus Dei gratia episcopus Norwycensis salutem in Domino. Noverit universitas vestra quod cum dilecti in Cristo filii prior et conventus sacrosancte Norwycensis ecclesie nostris temporibus in suis maneriis episcopalis iurisdictionis exemptionem vendicassent quam, ut dicebant, predecessorum nostrorum habere temporibus consueverant, nos in^a eorundem iniuriam nostram iurisdictionem dilatare nolentes, eisdem de gratia concessimus speciali quod ad custodiam spiritualitatis maneriorum aliquem virum idoneum in episcopatu Norwycensi beneficiatum et residentem tamquam decanum nobis possint presentare, et nos ab eodem presentato obedientia recepta canonica, ipsum ad memoratam custodiam sine omni difficultate admittemus, matrimonialium et criminalium causarum cognitionibus in eisdem maneriis nobis specialiter reservatis. De eorundem etiam assensu et voluntate visitandi et corrigendi potestatem et exercendi iurisdictionem nostram pleno iure in prefatis maneriis cum nos vel officiales nostri ad eadem personaliter voluerimus declinare nobis et officialibus expresse reservavimus, conce[fo. 25v]dentes eisdem quod presentatum ad ipsis in iure quod alii decani in nostro episcopatu optinent plenarie conservabimus. Si vero in prefatis maneriis coram nobis vel officialibus nostris incepte cause comode in eisdem nequiverint terminari, extra dicta maneria ipsas causas evocandi et litigantibus diem prefigendi nobis et officialibus nostris potestatem pariter reservavimus. Volumus etiam quod si dictorum maneriorum homines in aliquibus causis movendis nostrum examen vel officialis nostri duxerint eligendum, ut tunc nobis vel eidem officiali easdem causas libere audire liceat, dicti decani contradictione non obstante. Nolumus siquidem quod per hanc concessionem nostram archidiaconis seu decanis in prefatis maneriis ullum iurisdictionis tribuatur[b] incrementum. In huius rei testimonium presenti scripto sigillum nostrum duximus apponendum. Data apud Blafeld .ii. nonas Februarii pontificatus nostri anno primo.

^a ordin *marked for deletion* B   ^b tribuant B

This concession repeats almost verbatim that of bp William Raleigh in 1241 (*EEA* 21 no. 141), except that here bp Suffield does not reserve to the bp testamentary jurisdiction in these manors. On 23 February 1256 pope Alexander IV confirmed the jurisdiction of the dean appointed by the prior and convent in their manors (*Norwich Cathedral Charters* i no. 305).

91. Norwich Cathedral Priory

Notification that the bishop has, with the consent of the prior and convent, who hold the church of Martham in proprios usus, taxed therein a vicarage, to which whenever it is vacant they should present a suitable clerk to the bishop and his successors. The vicarage should consist of the manse and all oblations and lesser tithes of the church, except for half of the tithe of turves and of hay, which he has reserved to the monks. On this occasion, at their presentation he has admitted to the vicarage his beloved son master Walter Picard, to whom he has committed the cure of souls. Whoever is vicar shall discharge all customary obligations to bishop and archdeacon. Norwich, 21 February 1246

B = Norfolk R.O., DCN 40/7 (general cartulary) fo. 35r. s. xiii ex. C = ibid., DCN 40/5 (cellarer's cartulary) fos. 38v–39r. s. xiii ex. D = ibid., DCN 40/1 (general cartulary) fo. 42r–v (28r–v, 31r–v). s. xiv in. E = ibid., fo. 231v (222v) (*inspeximus* by bp John Salmon, 9 March 1302). F = ibid., DCN 40/2/2 (general cartulary) fo. 29r. s. xiv in. G = ibid., DCN

40/4 (episcopal charters) pp. 104–5. s. xv in. H = ibid., pp. 290–1. J = ibid., pp. 192–3 (as
E).
Pd in *Norwich Cathedral Charters* i no. 205; from D in *First Register* 130–2.

Omnibus Cristi fidelibus has litteras visuris vel audituris Walterus miseratione
divina Norwicensis episcopus eternam in Domino salutem. Noveritis nos, de
consensu dilectorum filiorum prioris et conventus Norwicensium, vicariam in
ecclesia de Martham, quam dicti prior et conventus habent in proprios usus,
taxasse, ad quam quotienscumque eam vacare contigerit dicti prior et conventus
clericum idoneum nobis et successoribus nostris presentabunt. Consistit autem
dicta vicaria per nos taxata in quodam manso et in omnibus oblationibus et
minutis[a] decimis ad dictam ecclesiam pertinentibus, excepta medietate
decimarum turbe et feni, quam medietatem dictis priori et conventui
reservavimus. Ad dictam siquidem vicariam hac vice dilectum filium magistrum
Thomam Picardum ad presentationem dictorum prioris et conventus admisimus
eique curam animarum commisimus, salvis in omnibus episcopalibus
consuetudinibus et nostre Norwicensis ecclesie dignitate. Sustinebit autem
vicarius dicte ecclesie qui pro tempore fuerit omnia onera episcopalia,
archidiaconialia, debita et consueta. In cuius rei testimonium presenti scripto
sigillum nostrum duximus apponendum. Hiis testibus: magistro[b] Willelmo de
Suffeud,[c] Adam de Bromholm, Adam de Wrstede,[d] Alexandro de Audeberg',[e]
domino Iohanne de Holcham,[f] capellano, Willelmo de Pakeham,[g] Thoma de
Walcote,[h] Hugone de Corbrig',[j] et aliis. Dat'[k] apud Norwicum .ix°. kalendas
Martii pontificatus nostri anno secundo.

[a] minimis D, F   [b] magistris B   [c] Sufeud D, F   [d] Wordstede D, F; Wrdeste G; Wrdestede H
[e] Audebergh' H   [f] Melcham G   [g] Pagenham D; Pakenham F; Pakham G, H   [h] Walecote D, F
[j] Cornbrigg' D, F   [k] Data G

For an earlier dispute between bp and monks, in the late 1190s, concerning the advowson, see
EEA 6 no. 268 and Appx 1. 72–3. The church was granted to the monks *in proprios usus* by bp
Gray (ibid., nos. 400, 406). In 1226–27 the monks were still receiving an annual pension of £5
from the church, but later in bp Blundeville's episcopate they were inducted into corporal
possession (*EEA* 21 nos. 76, 90; Appx 2. 22). In 1254 the church was valued at £20 and the
vicarage at one mark; in 1291 at £20, including the vicarage (*VN* 379; *Taxatio* 79).

92. Norwich Cathedral Priory

*Notification that, when a dispute arose between the monks, who claimed to be
patrons of the church of Ashby in Lothingland and that the church had been
granted to them* in proprios usus *by the bishop's predecessors, and John son of
Geoffrey of Ashby, who claimed to be the true patron, after much argument the
parties submitted to the bishop's ordinance. He decreed that the advowson and
the right of free presentation at every vacancy should reside in perpetuity with
John and his heirs, but that the monks should receive from the rector for the time
being two marks a year, to be paid in equal instalments at the two Norwich*

synods, to be put to the use of the almonry. The parties swore to observe the terms of this composition. Happisburgh, 19 April 1246

B = Norfolk R.O., DCN 40/2/i (almoner's cartulary) fo. 77v (87v).
Pd in *Norwich Cathedral Charters* i no. 216.

Omnibus Cristi fidelibus has litteras visuris vel audituris Walterus Dei gratia Norwicensis episcopus eternam in Domino salutem. Cum inter dilectos filios priorem et conventum Norwic' asserentes se patronos ecclesie de Askebi in Ludinglond et eam a predecessoribus nostris eis in proprios usus fuisse concessam[a] ac Iohannem filium Galfridi de Askebi asserentem se eiusdem ecclesie verum esse patronum questio verteretur, tandem post multas altercationes partes se commiserunt ordinationi nostre. Nos igitur, divina gratia inspirante, inter eos duximus ordinare, videlicet quod patronatus dicte ecclesie et liberum ius presentandi ad eandem, quotiens eam vacare contigerit, penes dictum Iohannem et heredes suos perpetuo remanebit. Dicti autem prior et conventus a rectore prenominate ecclesie qui pro tempore fuerit duas marcas argenti in duabus sinodis Norwicensibus equis portionibus solvendas ad opus elemosinarie sue de bonis dicte ecclesie annuatim percipient. Ad hanc igitur compositionem fideliter observandam partes coram nobis corporali sacramento se astrinxerunt. In cuius rei testimonium presenti scripto sigillum una cum sigillo capituli nostri duximus apponendum. Sigillum etiam ipsius patroni est appensum. Dat' apud Hapesburg' .xiii. kalendas Maii pontificatus nostri anno secundo.

[a] concessum B

No *actum* by a previous bp granting the church *in proprios usus* is apparently extant. The church was valued at £5 in 1254 (*VN* 465); in 1291 the church was assessed at £6, excluding the almoner's portion of £1 6s 8d (*Taxatio* 116b).

93. Norwich Cathedral Priory

Notification that, when a dispute arose between the prior and convent on the one part and the rector and vicar of Marsham on the other concerning two parts of the tithes of the episcopal demesne there, and the parties eventually submitted to the bishop's ordinance, although it was clear to him from the acta *of his predecessors that these tithes had formerly been assigned to the monks in* proprios usus *and that the rector and vicar had no right thereto, except that the vicar's predecessors had held them at farm from the monks, to whom they rendered five shillings a year, considering nevertheless that the present vicar was worthy of special grace and honour, with the consent of the parties the bishop has ordained that the present vicar should for his lifetime hold these tithes at farm, rendering five shillings a year to the monks, but that on his death or resignation the monks may choose to lease the tithes at farm or to dispose of them, as they are appropriated to them, as seems best to them.*

Norwich, 25 February 1247

B = BL ms. Cotton roll ii 19 (*inspeximus* by bp John Salmon of charters of St Paul's hospital, 17 March 1302) no. 16. s. xiv in. C = Norfolk R.O., DCN 40/1 (general cartulary) fo. 241v (232v) (as B). s. xiv in.
Pd from B in *Norwich Cathedral Charters* i no. 259 (16).

Omnibus Cristi fidelibus has litteras visuris vel audituris Walterus Dei gratia Norwicensis[a] episcopus salutem in Domino sempiternam. Orta dissensione inter dilectos filios priorem et conventum Norwic'[b] ex parte una [et] rectorem et vicarium ecclesie de Marsham ex altera super duabus partibus decimarum de dominio nostro ibidem provenientium, partibusque post aliqua intermedia nostre ordinationi omnino suppositis, quamquam per instrumenta predecessorum nostrorum nobis constiterit evidenter dictas decimas dictis priori et conventui in proprios usus dudum fuisse assignatas dictosque rectorem et vicarium in eisdem nichil iure obtinere nisi quod predecessores vicarii memorati eas nomine firme possiderant, predictis priori et conventui quinque solidos annuatim persolvendo; pensatis tamen meritis vicarii prelibati specialiori gratia et honore non indigni, sic duximus providendum, partium interveniente consensu, quod dictas decimas obtineat suo perpetuo tanquam firmarius, reddendo annuatim quinque solidos priori et conventui memoratis, quo decedente vel recedente[c] in ipsorum sit electione dictas decimas ad firmam dimittere vel de eis tanquam de sibi appropriatis[d] disponere prout melius viderint expedire. In cuius rei testimonium presenti scripto sigillum nostrum duximus apponendum. Datum apud Norwicum[e] .v. kalendas Martii pontificatus nostri anno tertio.

[a] Norwycensis C   [b] Norwyc' C   [c] vel recedente *om.* C   [d] apropriatas B   [e] Norwycum C

These tithes had been granted by the monks to St Paul's hospital in the early twelfth century (*Norwich Cathedral Charters* i no. 259 (1)), and confirmed to the hospital by bps John of Oxford and Thomas Blundeville (ibid. no. 257, 259 (11); *EEA* 6 no. 269; *EEA* 21 no. 95). The church was in the bp's collation (*EEA* 6 no. 391).

94. Norwich Cathedral Priory

Notification that, because of the daily increase in the religious observance of the monks, the bishop has granted to them in proprios usus, for the prior's mensa, the church of Hemblington, of which he holds the advowson, and which is in future to be served by a suitable chaplain. Sentence of excommunication is promulgated against any who may controvert this grant.

Norwich, 6 October 1248

B = Norfolk R.O., DCN 40/5 (cellarer's cartulary) fo. 26r. s. xiii ex. C = ibid., DCN 40/1 (general cartulary) fo. 42v (28v, 31v). s. xiv in. D = ibid., fo. 232r (223r) (*inspeximus* by bp John Salmon, 9 March 1302). E = ibid., DCN 40/2/2 (general cartulary) fo. 29r. s. xiv in. F = ibid., DCN 40/4 (episcopal charters) pp. 105–6. s. xv in. G = ibid. pp. 291–2. H = ibid. pp. 193–4 (as D).
Pd in *Norwich Cathedral Charters* i no. 206; from C in *First Register* 132.

Omnibus Cristi fidelibus presens scriptum visuris vel audituris Walterus Dei gratia Norwicensis episcopus salutem in Domino sempiternam. Cum dilectorum filiorum prioris et conventus Norwicensium sancta religio de die in diem magis ac magis amplificetur et amplius ac perfectius nomen Domini nostri magnificetur in ipsis, volentes ipsos quod specialiter diligimus speciali dilectione confovere, ecclesiam de Hemelyngton',[a] que de nostro patronatu est, in proprios usus concedimus eisdem, ipsam mense dicti domini prioris perpetuis temporibus assignantes, et auctoritate pontificali ecclesie Norwicensis confirmantes eandem, et volentes quod dicte ecclesie futuris temporibus per capellanum ydoneum inperpetuum deserviatur, excommunicationisque sententia omnes illos involventes qui contra nostram huiusmodi donationem, collationem et concessionem aliquid fraudis vel doli presumpserint attemptare vel eidem contraire. In cuius rei testimonium presentibus sigillum nostrum apponi fecimus. Hiis testibus: magistro R.[b] archidiacono Colcestr', magistro A. de Bromholm', magistro I. de Saham,[c] domino W. de Witewell', domino W. de Pakenham,[d] domino I. capellano, domino Thoma capellano, Thoma de Walecote,[e] Willelmo de Sidersterne, Willelmo de Acle,[f] clericis. Dat' apud Norwicum die sancte Fidis anno Domini millesimo CC° XL° octavo et pontificatus nostri anno quarto.

[a] Hemlington' F [b] D., F [c] Seham F [d] Pankesham B [e] Walkote B [f] Ade C, E

The church of Hemblington was valued at £5 in 1254, and at the same figure, including the vicarage, in 1291 (*VN* 366, 502; *Taxatio* 79). The circumstances of this grant are explained in *First Register* 140–2. Litigation arose between the monks and Walter of Mautby, who had held the lease at fee farm of the manors of Hemsby and Martham from the cathedral priory; the farm being two years in arrears, the monks has reseised the disputed land. The bp brokered a solution, whereby Walter of Mautby on 3 November 1248 quitclaimed this estate (described in the final concord as a messuage and three carucates) to the prior, who in return granted him all the land held by the cathedral priory at Beckham (*Norwich Cathedral Charters* i no. 333). The bp, however, granted the monks the church of Hemblington in recompense for any loss.

95. Norwich Cathedral Priory

Confirmation for the monks of the churches of All Saints, Wicklewood, and Hempstead, granted to them in proprios usus by the bishop's predecessors, saving vicarages to be taxed by him or his successors, which should not be burdensome to the convent. [25 March 1249 × 18 February 1250]

A = Norfolk R.O., DCN 43/45. Endorsed: de ecclesiis omnium sanctorum de Wiclewde et de Hemstede; in decanatu de Hengham (s. xiii); pressmark; Hugh of Mursley's notarial sign; approx. 232 × 118 + 19 mm.; fragment of parchment tag; seal missing.

B = Norfolk R.O., DCN 40/5 (cellarer's cartulary) fo. 36r. s. xiii ex. C = ibid., DCN 40/1 (general cartulary) fos. 42v–43r (28v–29r, 31v–32r). s. xiv in. D = ibid., fo. 232r (223r) (*inspeximus* by bp John Salmon, 9 March 1302). s. xiv in. E = ibid., DCN 40/2/2 (general cartulary) fo. 29r–v (20r–v, 102r–v). s. xiv in. F = ibid., DCN 40/4 (episcopal charters) pp. 107–8. s. xv in. G = ibid., p. 292. H = ibid., pp. 194–5 (as D).

Pd from A in *Norwich Cathedral Charters* i no. 207; from C in *First Register* 132–4.

Omnibus Cristi fidelibus ad quos presens scriptum pervenerit Walterus Dei gratia Norwicensis episcopus salutem eternam in Domino. Addicti militie regulari sicut Cristi bonus odor celesti conversatione redolentes dignis caritatis operibus dant operam incessanter, ita digne sunt amplioribus beneficiis honorandi, ut onus levius ferant ex honore et ad sue liberalitatis imitationem ceteros avidius animent et invitent. Licet igitur singulorum religiosorum cura nobis sit commissa, dilectorum tamen filiorum prioris et conventus Norwicensium curam tenemur gerere specialem et eos amplioribus prosequi beneficiis quos dilectionis amplectimur prerogativa. Hinc est quod dictorum prioris et conventus paci, securitati ac indempnitati providere cupientes, concedimus et presenti carta nostra confirmamus eisdem in proprios usus beneficia ecclesiastica inferius annotata a predecessoribus nostris eisdem collata, videlicet ecclesiam omnium sanctorum de Wiclewde et ecclesiam de Hemstede, quas ecclesias cum pertinentiis dictis priori et conventui in proprios usus perpetuo concedimus possidendas, salvis vicariis competentibus nostro conventui quidem non onerosis per nos et successores nostros taxandis, salvis etiam in omnibus iure episcopali et consuetudinibus. Dat' anno Domini M° CC° XLIX°, pontificatus nostri anno quinto.

One mediety of All Saints, Wicklewood, had been granted to the monks by Agnes de Reflei and confirmed by Pandulph as bp-elect (*EEA* 21 no. 20); they initially received an annual pension of 4s, but in 1227 bp Blundeville granted this mediety *in proprios usus* to the almonry (ibid., nos. 76, 89). The other mediety, the gift of Nigel of Happisburgh, chaplain, was similarly appropriated to the use of the almonry in 1235 (ibid. no. 94). The church was valued at £5 in 1254 and, with the vicarage, at £5 6s 8d in 1291 (*VN* 398, 504; *Taxatio* 85b).

By a final concord in the *curia regis* on 2 July 1183 Simon of Hempstead and Hamo his son, the claimants, quitclaimed the advowson of Hempstead to Henry de Marisco, who had been granted by the monks, in fee and heredity, all their land there (*Norwich Cathedral Charters* i no. 318; *EEA* 6 no. 260). In 1240 prior Simon sued the wives of Richer and Stephen of Cawston (perhaps co-heiresses of Henry de Marisco) through their husbands for the advowson of the church; the defendants quitclaimed the advowson to the prior, and in return they and their heirs were to hold all the lands in Hempstead, Plumstead and Baconthorpe, for which they had formerly paid £3 10s a year to the monks, for £3 in future (*Norwich Cathedral Charters* i no. 356). In 1303 William of Ormesby and Agnes his wife unsuccessfully sued the prior for the advowson, which they quitclaimed in the *curia regis* on 28 April; a declaration was made after inquest that the prior and his predecessors had held this advowson long before the Statute of Mortmain (ibid. no. 371). In 1254 the church was valued at £10 and the vicarage at 6s 8d (*VN* 371, 502); in 1291 the church, apart from the vicarage and the portion of the monks of Beadlow, was assessed at £10 (*Taxatio* 81b).

96. Norwich Cathedral Priory

Restitution to the monks of four marks from the church of [Great] Cressingham, of which he has found them to have been deprived. Cressingham, 26 July 1251

B = Norfolk RO, DCN 40/5 (cellarer's cartulary) fo. 10r (9r). s.xiii ex.

Omnibus Cristi fidelibus presentes litteras visuris vel audituris Walterus Dei gratia Norwicensis episcopus salutem in Domino sempiternam. Cum ecclesiam Norwicensem super annua perceptione quatuor marcarum de ecclesia de Cressingham percipiendarum invenerimus spoliatam, nos dicte ecclesie Norwicensis indempnitati providere volentes, eam ad dictam perceptionem annuam quatuor marcarum duximus restituendam. In cuius rei testimonium huic scripto sigillum nostrum apponi fecimus. Dat' apud Cressingham .vii. kalendas Augusti anno Domini M CC L primo.

> The church had been granted in the time of bp Herbert Losinga by Godwin the deacon, together with whatever he held there of the bp's fee (*Norwich Cathedral Charters* i no. 106). It was confirmed to them by bp William Turbe, 1170 × 1174 (*EEA* 6 no. 132); but in the settlement of 1205, bp John de Gray confirmed to the monks whatever they held at Cressingham, except the fishpond and the advowson of the church (ibid. nos 380, 383). A pension of four marks was confirmed by bp Thomas Blundeville (*EEA* 21 no. 76). In 1267 bp Roger Scarning, stating that he was confirming similar grants by his predecessors, granted the church when next vacant to the monks *in proprios usus*; at this time the rector was mr Walter of Calthorpe, a nephew of bp Suffield (*Norwich Cathedral Charters* i no. 222). In 1297, however there was still a secular rector who was in dispute with the monks over this pension, as well as over jurisdictional rights in the parish (ibid. no. 235).

97. Norwich Cathedral Priory

Confirmation for the monks in proprios usus of all the churches and benefices granted to them by his predecessors, as listed in their charters, except for those churches the patronage of which now pertains to the bishop. Confirmation also in full of the annual dues customarily received from the priors, instituted by the bishop in chapter to exercise the cure of souls, of Lynn, Yarmouth and Aldeby, saving to the priors the residue of the revenues of these priories for the sustenance of the monks therein and the maintenance of Christ's poor. All these churches he has confirmed saving vicarages to be conferred in the customary manner, and saving also all episcopal rights and customs.

Norwich, 28 July 1253

B = Norfolk R.O., DCN 40/7 (general cartulary) fo. 33r–v. s. xiii ex. C = ibid. DCN 40/4 (episcopal charters) pp. 121–2. s. xiv in. D = ibid. pp. 302–3.
Pd in *Norwich Cathedral Charters* i no. 215.

Omnibus Cristi fidelibus presentes litteras visuris vel audituris Walterus Dei gratia Norwicensis[a] episcopus salutem in Domino sempiternam. Licet singulorum religiosorum cura nobis sit commissa, dilectorum tamen filiorum prioris et conventus Norwicensium[b] curam tenemur gerere specialem et eos amplioribus prosequi beneficiis, quos dilectionis amplectitur[c] prerogativa. Hinc est quod dictorum prioris et conventus paci, securitati et indempnitati[d] providere cupientes, concedimus et presenti carta nostra confirmamus eisdem in proprios usus omnes ecclesias et beneficia a predecessoribus nostris eis collata,[e] prout in cartis[f] eorundem continetur, exceptis ecclesiis quarum ius patronatus ad nos in presenti spectare dinoscitur; et insuper annuum redditum quem percipiunt et percipere consueverunt cum omni integritate et absque diminutione de prioratibus de Lenna, de Gernemuta et de Audeby[g] percipiendum perpetuis temporibus per manus priorum ibidem commorantium, qui per nos et successores nostros in capitulo Norwicensi[h] priores instituuntur et curam animarum in ipsis ecclesiis gerendam recipiunt, salvo residuo omnium proventuum prioribus antedictis ipsarum ecclesiarum de Lenna, de Gernemuta et de Audeby[g] ad eorundem priorum et monachorum ibidem commorantium sustentationem et pauperum Ihesu Cristi refectionem. Omnes autem easdem ecclesias cum pertinentiis dictis priori et conventui in proprios usus perpetuo concedimus[j] possidendas, salvis vicariis more solito conferendis, salvis etiam in omnibus iure episcopali et consuetudine. In huius rei testimonium huic scripto sigillum nostrum apponi fecimus. Dat' apud Norwicum[k] quinto kalendas Augusti anno Domini millesimo ducentesimo quinquagesimo tertio.

[a] Norwycensis B　　[b] Norwycensium B　　[c] ampliatur C　　[d] indempnitate C　　[e] collecta B　　[f] cantis, n *marked for deletion*, r *superscript* B　　[g] Audebi B　　[h] Norwycensi B　　[j] concedimus *om*. C　　[k] Norwycum B

For comprehensive agreements made in 1205 between bp John de Gray and the chapter concerning the patronage of parish churches, see *EEA* 6 nos. 390–1, and for confirmation of the latter in 1211, no. 409. From a period when accounts are extant, in the fourteenth century, the payments made by the priors of cells to the mother house were: from Lynn, to the prior £3 6s 8d, to the cellarer £13 6s 8d, to the precentor and the chamberlain, 13s 4d each; from Yarmouth, to the prior £3 6s 8d, to the cellarer £26 13s 4d; from Aldeby, to the cellarer £5 (Saunders, *Introduction to Obedientiary Rolls* 146–7). Although the priors of dependant cells were appointed by the bp in chapter, a bull of Innocent III of 1200 forbade him to remove perfectly suitable priors in order to replace them by monks less suitable (*Letters of Innocent III* nos. 205–6).

98. Norwich Cathedral Priory

Grant to the monks in proprios usus, *for the prior's* mensa, *in consideration of the increasing burdens which fall upon them, of the church of Worstead, with all its free land, meadows and other appurtenances and with all the land, meadows and appurtenances pertaining to the chapel of St Andrew, excepting an acre of land adjacent to the chapel, which the bishop has assigned to the vicar's manse; saving a vicarage to which the monks shall present to the bishop a suitable* persona *who shall at his institution swear to observe the bishop's ordinance and to reside in person. The vicarage shall consist of the foresaid acre for the manse and of everything pertaining to the altarage of the church, that is, the tithes of flax, hemp and all lesser tithes and revenues, excluding the tithe of the mill and of any other mill or mills of the monks, if they should have such in that vill, and excluding [the tithe of] fruits of the earth, with whatever sort of grain or seed it may be sown, saving to the vicar flax and hemp as stated. The vicarage shall consist also of the assised rents of the chapel of St Andrew, and its oblations and revenues, unless through the devotion of the faithful such revenue shall in future exceed five marks, when the excess thereover shall be rendered by the vicar to the monks, according to his oath; the rents, however, are not to be included in this calculation. The vicar shall discharge all the burdens of the church and shall also maintain the fabric and ornaments of the chapel, and cause it to be served in perpetuity by a suitable chaplain, under penalty if he fails so to do of twenty shillings payable to the almoner of the cathedral. Because previously the bishop had assigned a mediety of this church to the cellar and has now granted it in its entirety to the prior's* mensa, *he has assigned to the* cellar *in proprios usus the church of Hemblington.* Norwich, 1 April 1256

A = Norfolk R.O., DCN 43/46. Endorsed: de Wrhested' (s. xiii); pressmark; Hugh of Mursley's notarial sign; approx. 254 × 137 + 19 mm.; tag and seal missing.

B = Norfolk R.O., DCN 40/5 (cellarer's cartulary) fo. 21r–v (20r–v). s. xiii ex. C = ibid., DCN 40/1 (general cartulary) fos. 43v–44r (29v–30r, 32v–33r). s. xiv in. D = ibid., DCN 40/2/2 (almoner's cartulary) fos. 29v–30r (20v–21r, 102v–103r). s. xiv in. E = ibid., DCN 40/4 (episcopal charters) pp. 118–21. s. xv in. F = ibid., pp. 300–2.

Pd from A in *Norwich Cathedral Charters* i no. 214; from C in *First Register* 136–8.

Omnibus Cristi fidelibus Walterus miseratione divina episcopus Norwicensis salutem in Domino sempiternam. Cum ex debito officii nostri omnibus graciosi esse et benefacere teneamur, precipue tamen dilectos filios priorem et conventum nostrum Norwicensem, qui quasi membra capitis nostri specialiter nobis adherent, favore benivolo et gratia tenemur prosequi ampliori. Hinc est quod, onera eisdem incumbentia et quin de die in diem in immensum excrescentia diligentius intuentes et ob hoc ut tenemur eisdem prospicere cupientes, ecclesiam de Wurdested' nostre diocesis cum tota terra libera eiusdem ecclesie, pratis et aliis pertinentiis eiusdem, insuper cum tota terra ad capellam sancti Andree eiusdem ville pertinente, pratis etiam et aliis eiusdem pertinentiis, excepta una acra terre iuxta predictam capellam existente quam ad mansum vicarii qui pro tempore fuerit assignavimus, eisdem perpetuis temporibus in proprios usus duximus concedendam, mense videlicet prioris qui pro tempore fuerit assignandam, salva vicaria per nos in eadem ut inferius patet taxata ad quam dicti prior et conventus nobis et successoribus nostris personam idoneam presentabunt, qui in sua institutione iurabit se fideliter nostram in hac parte ordinationem observare et personaliter in eadem ecclesia residere. Consistit autem vicaria in predicta acra terre ad mansum vicarii faciendum, et in omnibus ad alteragium dicte ecclesie spectantibus, videlicet lino, canabo et omnibus aliis minutis decimis et proventibus universis, exceptis decimis molendini vel etiam molendinorum propriorum ipsorum prioris et conventus, si contigerit ipsos molendinum vel molendina plura habere in eadem villa, exceptis etiam fructibus terrarum quocumque genere bladi vel seminis seminatarum, salvis tamen vicario lino et canabo, ut est prenotatum. Insuper consistit vicaria ipsa in redditibus assisis ad dictam capellam sancti Andree spectantibus, ac etiam oblationibus eiusdem capelle et proventibus universis, tamen si ob devotionem fidelium futuris temporibus quinque marcas argenti excedant oblationes et proventus capelle predicte, tunc quicquid ultra fuerit dictis priori et conventui a vicario qui pro tempore fuerit in virtute iuramenti prestiti fideliter persolvetur; redditibus tamen predictis inter hec nullatenus computatis. Ac vicarius dicte ecclesie quicumque fuerit sustinebit omnia onera dictam ecclesiam contingentia, debita videlicet et consueta; sustinebit etiam dictam capellam tam in reparationibus capelle debitis quam in ornamentis eiusdem, ac per capellanum idoneum eidem perpetuis temporibus in divinis honeste et reverenter faciet deserviri; qui si non fecerit ac monitus per priorem et conventum predictos infra competentem terminum defectus tam reparationis capelle quam ornamentorum et servitii non suppleverit, nomine pene dictis priori et conventui in viginti solidis argenti tenebitur eiusdem domus elemosinario persolvendis, ad quos ac etiam ad alios defectus capelle quoscumque absque cause cognitione per episcopum loci qui pro tempore fuerit efficaciter compellatur. Et quia aliquando celerarie dicte domus medietatem prefate ecclesie cum suis pertinentiis assignaverimus, quam nunc totaliter mense prioris eiusdem domus qui pro tempore fuerit deputavimus imperpetuum, volentes dicte celerarie prospicere ut valemus, ecclesiam de Hemelington' nostre diocesis cum omnibus suis pertinentiis absque ullo retenemento et in proprios usus eidem celerarie duximus perpetuis temporibus assignandam. Hec siquidem acta sunt de consensu et voluntate dictorum prioris et conventus qui hoc in pleno capitulo suo totaliter acceptaverunt. Acta Norwic' kalendis Aprilis anno Domini M CC L sexto.

> Worstead church was granted to the monks by Robert son of Richard of Worstead, and confirmed by Pandulph as bp-elect in 1219 (*EEA* 21 no. 19). It was appropriated to them in 1227 by bp Blundeville, who in 1235 authorised their corporal induction (ibid. nos. 86, 93). On 17 January 1236 pope Gregory IX confirmed their possession (*Norwich Cathedral Charters* i no. 296). In 1254, however, the church was valued at £10 and the monks' portion at £2, with *bona* in the parish assessed at £1 0s 6d, which *bona* are described in a Norwich ms. as rents and lay fees, now the vicar's (*VN* 415, 503). In 1291 the church was valued at £16 13s 4d, excluding the untaxed portion, and the vicarage separately at £5 (*Taxatio* 87).

99. Norwich Cathedral Priory

Institution, at the presentation of the monks, of Warin of Testerton, chaplain, to the vicarage of the church of Worstead, the endowment of which is detailed as in no. 98.   Norwich, 25 July 1256

> B = Norfolk R.O., DCN 40/5 (cellarer's cartulary) fos. 21v–22r. s. xiii ex. C = ibid., DCN 40/1 (general cartulary) fo. 43r–v (29r–v, 32r–v). s. xiv in. D = ibid., fo. 232r–v (223r–v) (*inspeximus* by bp John Salmon, 9 March 1302). E = ibid., DCN 40/2/2 (general cartulary)

fo. 29v (20v, 102v). s. xiv in. F = ibid., DCN 40/4 (episcopal charters) pp. 108–10. s. xv in. G = ibid., pp. 292–4. H = ibid., pp. 195–8 (as D).
Pd in *Norwich Cathedral Charters* i no. 208; from C, in *First Register* 134–6.

Universis Cristi fidelibus Walterus miseratione divina episcopus Norwicensis[a] salutem in Domino sempiternam. Universitati vestre volumus esse notum nos ad presentationem dilectorum in Cristo[b] filiorum prioris et conventus Norwicensium dilectum filium Warinum de Thesterton'[c] capellanum ad vicariam ecclesie de Wrstede[d] nostre dyocesis admisisse ipsumque[e] vicarium in eadem canonice instituisse, salvis in omnibus episcopalibus iuribus et consuetudinibus et sancte Norwicensis ecclesie[f] dignitate. Consistit autem vicaria ipsa in uno manso iuxta capellam sancti Andree in eadem villa continente in se unam acram terre, et in omnibus ad alteragium dicte ecclesie spectantibus, videlicet lino, canabo et omnibus aliis minutis decimis et proventibus universis, exceptis decimis molendini vel etiam[g] molendinorum propriorum ipsorum prioris et conventus, si contigerit ipsos molendinum vel molendina plura habere in eadem villa, exceptis etiam fructibus terrarum, quocumque genere bladi vel seminis seminatarum; salvis tamen vicario lino et canabo ut est prenotatum. Insuper consistit vicaria ipsa in redditibus assisis ad dictam capellam sancti Andree spectantibus, ac etiam oblationibus eiusdem[h] capelle et proventibus universis. Tamen[j] si ob devotionem fidelium futuris temporibus quinque marcas argenti excedant oblationes et proventus capelle predicte, tunc quicquid ultra fuerit dictis priori et conventui a vicario qui pro tempore fuerit in virtute iuramenti prestiti fideliter persolventur,[k] [l-]redditibus tamen[m] predictis inter hec nullatenus computatis;[-l] ac vicarius dicte ecclesie quicumque fuerit sustinebit omnia onera[n] dictam ecclesiam contingentia,[o] debita videlicet et consueta. Sustinebit[p] etiam dictam capellam tam in reparationibus capelle debitis quam in ornamentis eiusdem, ac per capellanum idoneum eidem perpetuis temporibus in divinis honeste et reverenter faciet deserviri; que si non fecerit, ac monitus per priorem et conventum predictos infra competentem terminum defectus tam reparationis capelle quam ornamentorum et servitii non suppleverit, nomine pene dictis priori et conventui in viginti solidis argenti tenebitur eiusdem domus elemosinario persolvendis, ad quos ac etiam ad alios defectus capelle quoscumque absque cause cognitione per episcopum loci qui pro tempore fuerit efficaciter compellatur. In cuius rei testimonium huic scripto sigillum nostrum duximus apponendum. Dat' Norwic' octavo kalendas Augusti pontificatus nostri anno duodecimo et anno Domini millesimo CC° quinquagesimo sexto.[q]

[a] Norwicensis episcopus C, D, E   [b] in Cristo *om.* B   [c] Testretone C, D, E; Thesneton' F; Threstreton H   [d] Wurstede C, E; Wrthestede D, F   [e] et ipsum B   [f] ecclesie Norwicensis C, D, E   [g] etiam *om.* B, D   [h] dicte C, E   [j] Tandem C, E   [k] persolventur F   [l-l] *om.* B   [m] tamen *om.* C, E   [n] onera *added* F   [o] contingenda B   [p] sustinebunt F   [q] F, G *add* Duplicatur.

100. Norwich Cathedral Priory

Notification that, in view of his special obligation to the monks, the bishop has caused them, for their greater security, to exhibit before him all documents relating to their churches and other ecclesiastical possessions, which he has found to be authentic. He therefore confirms to them all the oblations of the cathedral church in proprios usus, *and burial dues, and also all their dependent cells and their parish churches (listed), including those of the hospital of St Paul. In addition, he grants and confirms to them in* proprios usus *the churches of Denham, Hempstead, Attlebridge, and a mediety of Barford.*

Norwich, 25 July 1256

B = Norfolk R.O., DCN 40/1 (general cartulary) fo. 44r–v (30r–v, 33r–v). s. xiv in. C = ibid., fo. 233r–v (224r–v) (*inspeximus* by bp John Salmon, 9 March 1302). D = ibid., fos. 234v–35r (as C). E = ibid., DCN 40/2/2 (general cartulary) fo. 30v. s. xiv in. F = ibid., DCN 40/4 (episcopal charters) pp. 111–13. s. xv in. G = ibid., pp. 295–7. H = ibid., pp. 201–3 (as C). J = ibid., pp. 230–2 (as C).
Pd in *Norwich Cathedral Charters* i no. 211; from B in *First Register* 138–40.

Omnibus Cristi fidelibus ad quos presens scriptum pervenerit Walterus Dei gratia Norwicensis episcopus salutem eternam in Domino. Addicti militie regulari sicut Cristi bonus odor celesti conversatione redolentes, dignis caritatis operibus dant operam incessanter, ita digne sunt amplioribus beneficiis honorandi, ut etiam onus levius[a] ferant ex honore et ad sue libertatis imitationem ceteros avidius animent et invitent. Licet igitur singulorum religiosorum cura nobis sit commissa, dilectorum tamen filiorum prioris et conventus Norwicensium curam tenemur gerere specialem et eos amplioribus prosequi beneficiis quos dilectionis amplectimur[b] prerogativa. Hinc est quod dictorum prioris et conventus paci, securitati ac indempnitati providere cupientes, omnia instrumenta que super ecclesiis suis et aliis bonis ecclesiasticis optinent coram nobis presentari fecimus et exhiberi. Quibus inspectis et diligenter examinatis invenimus eos super eisdem sufficienter munitos et eadem omnia iuste et canonice adeptos ac diutius pacifice possedisse, videlicet omnes oblationes que fiunt in ecclesia Norwicensi[c] cathedrali in usus proprios, et sepulturas ab omni exactione liberas et quietas; cellulas suas de Gernemuta, de Lenna,[d] de Audeby, de Hoxa, sancti Leonardi iuxta Norwicum, hospitale sancti Pauli in Norwico; ecclesiam de Lenna[d] cum capellis et ecclesiis dependentibus ab eadem; ecclesiam de Mintlingge,[e] ecclesiam de Gernemuta, ecclesias sancte Marie, sancti Martini, sancti Stephani, sancti Petri, sancti Iohannis, sancti Egidii, sancti Iacobi, sancti Vedasti, sancte Crucis, sancti Sepulcri, sancti Salvatoris, omnium sanctorum, sancte Margarete in Norwico; ecclesiam sancti Nicholai in Brakendele, ecclesias de Audebi, sancti Leonardi, sancti Willelmi in bosco; ecclesias de Northelmham, de Seccheford,[f] de Hemesbi, de Martham, de Hindringham, de Hindolveston',[g] de Trouse,[h] de Wichtone, de Wrthstede,[j] de Becham, de Wigenhale, de Cruchestoke, de Lakenham, de Ameringhale, de Cattone,[k] de Etone,[l] de Scrouteby,[m] de Babourgh,[n] de Henleye,[o] de Hopetone, de Plumstede, de Wiclewode; capellam sancti Edmundi de Hoxne, capellam de Ringeshale; ecclesias sancti Pauli in Norwico, et de Ormesbi hospitali sancti Pauli assignatas, in nostra diocesi constitutas. Hec autem omnia et singula cum ceteris bonis, possessionibus et beneficiis eorumdem ecclesiasticis omnimodis ad eos vel ad memoratas cellulas suas seu ad dictum hospitale sancti Pauli spectantibus, sibi et successoribus suis per predecessores nostris collata, concessa vel confirmata ex certa scientia tenore presentium eisdem concedimus et confirmamus. Insuper damus, concedimus et confirmamus eisdem monachis nostris Norwicensibus ecclesias de Denham, de Hempstede,[p] de Hemelingtone, de Attlebrigge,[q] et medietatem ecclesie de Bereforde,[r] habendas in proprios usus perpetuo[s] possidendas, salvis in omnibus nobis et successoribus nostris iure et dignitate episcopali et pontificali. Dat' Norwic' octavo kalendas Augusti anno Domini millesimo ducentesimo quinquagesimo sexto et pontificatus nostri anno duodecimo.

[a] levius om. B, E   [b] ampliamur F   [c] Norwici F   [d] Linna B, E   [e] Myntlynge B; Mintlinge C [f] Schecheford C; Secheford D, F, H, J   [g] Hindolvestone C, H, J; Hyndolvestone G   [h] Treusse B, E   [j] Wrthestede D; Wurthstede E; Worthestede G, H; Wurthested J   [k] Catton' D, E   [l] Eton' E   [m] Scrowtebi D, F; Scroutebi H   [n] Bauueberg C; Bauueburg D; Babourth' E; Baubrug' F; Bauburg' G, J   [o] Henleya B   [p] Hemstede E, G; Hemestede F; Hempsted J   [q] Atlebrig' B, E; Attelbrig' C, J; Attelbrigg' D   [r] Berforde C; Bereford D, E; Berford' F, H, J   [s] perpetuo om. F

The church of Denham, near Scole, in Hoxne hundred, was valued in 1254 at £8, and in 1291, appropriated to the cathedal priory, at £8 13s 4d (VN 451; Taxatio 116). Hempstead, in Holt hundred, was assessed at £10, and the portion of the monks of Battle at £1, at both dates; in 1254 the vicarage was listed at 6s 8d, and in 1291 as not liable to the tenth (VN 371; Taxatio 81b). Attlebridge was assessed at £3 6s 8d in 1254 and, appropriated, at £4 in 1291 (VN 363; Taxatio 78b). The whole church of Barford was listed in 1254 at £6 13s 4d, from which a tenth of 13s 4d was due but only 6s 8d paid; in 1291 the monks' mediety was valued at £4, and the other mediety was not subject to the tenth (VN 398; Taxatio 85b).

101. Norwich Cathedral Priory

Inspeximus *and confirmation for the monks of the grant by bishop Herbert [de Losinga] of the church under construction at Lynn dedicated to St Mary Magdalen, St Margaret and all holy virgins, of the churches of Yarmouth, Aldeby, [North] Elmham and Hemsby, and of the grant to benefactors of the church at Lynn of forty days remission of penance [EEA 6 no. 16].*

Norwich, 25 July 1256

B = Norfolk R.O., DCN 40/1 (general cartulary) fo. 233r (224r) (*inspeximus* by bp John Salmon, 9 March 1302). s. xiv in. C = ibid., DCN 40/4 (episcopal charters) pp. 110–11. s. xv in. D = ibid., pp. 294–5. E = ibid., pp. 199–201 (as B).
Pd in *Norwich Cathedral Charters* i no. 209.

Universis Cristi fidelibus presens scriptum visuris vel audituris Walterus Dei gratia episcopus Norwicensis salutem in Domino sempiternam. Pateat[a] universitati vestre nos inspexisse cartam bone memorie Herberti episcopi[b]

quondam predecessoris nostri in hec verba: Herbertus episcopus filiis suis circa Lennam[c] salutem. Rogatu vestro incepi edificare ecclesiam apud Lennam[c] in honore sancte Marie Magdalene, sancte Margarete et omnium sanctarum virginum. Unde precor vos ut adiuvetis ad perficiendum ipsum opus. Et notum facio omnibus de Norfolc[d] et Suffolc[e] quod dedi ipsam ecclesiam Deo et monachis sancte Trinitatis de Norwico. Dono etiam eis ecclesias de Gernemuta,[f] de Aldeby, de Elmham et de Hemesby[g] cum omnibus terris et aliis pertinentiis ad dictas ecclesias quietas et liberas ab omni servitio et secularitate. Quicumque in dicta ecclesia de Len' fecerit elemosinam suam habeat perdonationem quadraginta dierum de penitentia sua. Huius donationis testes sunt Walterus archidiaconus, Sampson, Guido[h] dapifer, Herveus pincerna, Alanus constabularius, Turgidius de Eggemere.[j] Et ut hec mea donatio firma sit, confirmo eam signo sancte crucis et astipulatione sigilli mei. Signum Herberti episcopi. + Nos vero[k] presciptas donationes ratas et firmas habentes, easdem[l] Deo et monachis sancte Trinitatis de Norwico tenore presentium pro nobis et successoribus nostris concedimus inperpetuum et confirmamus. Dat'[m] apud Norwicum octavo kalendas Augusti anno Domini millesimo ducentesimo[n] quinquagesimo sexto et pontificatus nostri anno duodecimo.

[a] Place C   [b] episcopi om. C, D   [c] Linnam E   [d] Norfolk E   [e] Suff' C, D   [f] Gernernemuta B
[g] Hemesbi C   [h] Gwido C; Guydo E   [j] Egmere C   [k] vero om. B   [l] eiusdam D   [m] Data C, E
[n] M° CC° B

On 23 February 1256 pope Alexander IV issued for the monks a confirmation of the their possession of the dependent cells (*Norwich Cathedral Charters* i no. 304).

102. Diocese Of Norwich

Synodal statute, recorded in the form of letters patent, concerning the last testaments of incumbents. The bishop remembers that, when he held a lesser office, it was commonly held that any rector or vicar of the diocese who was still alive on Easter day might freely dispose in his last testament of all the fruits of his church or vicarage which might accrue to the following Michaelmas. Contrary to this, however, it has been legitimately maintained that, from the time of the foundation of the church of Norwich, the practice has been that the fruits and goods of churches vacant from Easter day to the Easter synod should not fall to the disposition of the deceased incumbent who has made a legitimate testament, but should pertain to the discretion and disposition of the diocesan; whereby the estate of the deceased is seriously diminished and the will of testators is frequently not put into effect. In order, therefore, that the estate of all men of the church should be restored, and that freedom and proper custom should be reestablished, the bishop, presiding in the Michaelmas synod at Norwich, with the consent of his chapter and by his authority as diocesan and that of the synod, by the agreement of all those attending, has decreed and granted that, in accordance with ancient custom which he now reaffirms, all rectors and vicars still alive on Easter day, but dying at any time from then until the Michaelmas synod, may dispose freely in their testaments, according to ancient custom, of the fruits and obventions of their benefices, reserving to the bishop's disposition the fruits of churches vacant before Easter, in which no rector has been instituted by then. The bishop for the time being should not wittingly, through dishonest greed, defer admission of those presented until after Easter day. Those who infringe or amend this constitution shall incur sentence of excommunication. Norwich, 4 October 1255

A = Original now lost, formerly in the archive of the hospital of St Giles, Norwich.
B[1] = Cambridge UL ms. Ii. 3. 7 (Norwich cathedral ms.) fo. 143v. s. xiv in. C = Cambridge, Trinity College ms. O. 4. 14 (1245), fo. 147v. s. xiv in. D = Ipswich Central library, pd. edition of Lyndwood's *Provinciale* (Paris, 1506) (from Butley priory), ms. addition after colophon. s. xvi in. E = Dublin, Trinity College ms. E. 2. 22, p. 124. s. xiv ex. F = Norwich, D. & C. Library, *Liber sextus* (formerly Phillips ms. 3623), fo. 468v. s. xv. G = Lincoln Cathedral Chapter Library, ms. C. 2. 9 (among additions to glossed *Decretales* and *Liber sextus*), fo. 304r. s. xv med. H = Cambridge, Corpus Christi College, EP. R. 2 (as D) fo. 189v. s. xvi in. K = Cambridge, Gonville and Caius College, ms. 36, fo. vi[v]. s. xv ex. L = TNA, E164/30 0 (register of archdnry of Norwich), fo. 24v (margin). s. xiv med.
Pd (from ms. now lost) in Spelman, *Concilia* ii 301, whence Wilkins, *Concilia* i 708; (from all mss.) in *C. & S.* II i 499–501.

Walterus Dei gratia Norwycensis episcopus dilectis in Cristo filiis universis abbatibus, prioribus, archidiaconis, officialibus,[a] decanis ecclesiarum,[b] rectoribus, vicariis et omnibus Cristi[c] fidelibus per diocesim Norwycensem[d] constitutis salutem, gratiam et benedictionem. Ad officium pastorale licet indingni assumpti[e] et loco eminenti inmerito constituti, summo et pio desiderio affectamus, nunc bene operando, nunc malum extirpando, dingnos Deo fructus ex nostro inpendere officio. Sane recolimus,[f] dum adhuc in minori essemus officio constituti, wlgariter esse dictum et optentum[2] quod quilibet rector sive vicarius nostre dyocesis qui vivus die Pasce expectaret, de omnibus fructibus nomine ecclesie sive vicarie sue usque ad synodum sancti Michaelis proximo sequentem percipiendis libere ut vellet suum conderet testamentum. Set contra hanc consuetudinem a fundatione ecclesie Norwycensis, prout novimus et legittime constat optentam, a quibusdam voluntarie extitit introductum et servatum quod fructus et bona ecclesiarium vacantium a die Pasce usque ad synodum Pasce non in usus decedentium et condentium legittime testamenta cederent ut premisimus, set voluntati et dispositioni loci diocesani[g] relinquerentur omnino; propter quod status decedentium graviter ledebatur[h] et testantium frequenter non processit voluntas.[e] Ut igitur status ecclesie[j] singulorum reparetur, ac ad[k] libertatem et consuetudinem[l] debitam et consuetam[m] singuli[n] revocentur, nos Walterus de Suffeld'[o] episcopus Norwycensis in synodo sancti Michaelis Norwic'[p] presidentes, de consensu capituli nostri, diocesana et presentis synodi autoritate, omnibus existentibus in synodo sancta consentientibus, diffinimus, statuimus et precipimus et concedimus ut, iuxta antiquam consuetudinem quam renovamus, reintegramus, approbamus et confirmamus, omnes rectores et^q vicarii viventes die Pasce et ex tunc quandocunque^r morientes usque ad synodum sancti Michaelis de fructibus et obventionibus beneficiorum suorum libere sua secundum consuetudinem antiquam^s condant testamenta, salvis nobis^t et successoribus nostris fructibus ecclesiarum vacantium ante diem Pasce et^u in quibus rector die Pasce non reperitur institutus. Et caveat sibi episcopus qui preest et qui pro tempore fuerit ne causa lucri inhonesti absque causa rationabili canonice presentatos usque post diem Pasce voluntarie differat admittere. Omnes autem illi^v qui hanc nostram constitutionem, concessionem et libertatem infringere, immutare sive perturbare presumpserint excommunicationis sententiam nostram^w et presentis sancrosancte synodi auctoritate incurrent.^{x} In cuius rei testimonium^y presentibus sigillum nostrum et sigillum capituli nostri sunt appensa, testibus^z archidiaconis Norwycensis eccleie, abbatibus, prioribus, decanis, rectoribus, vicariis et omni clero et^{-z} populo sinodi. $^{aa-}$Actum^{bb} die synodi, scilicet die lune proximo post festum sancti Michaelis^{cc} in ecclesia sancte Trinitatis Norwyci^{-aa} anno Domini millesimo CC$^{o\ dd}$ LV° et pontificatus^{ee} nostre anno^{ff} xi^o.^{gg}

[1]To avoid unnecessary confusion, the sigla (from B-L) used in *C. & S.* II i 498 have been retained here, although they are not in chronological order.
[2]Cf. the mandate of bp William Raleigh, dated 16 September 1243 (*C. & S.* II i 342).

[a] archidiaconis *om.* G; officialibus *om.* BFGK   [b]ecclesiarum *om.* BFG   [c]Cristi *om.* BG   [d] nostram for Norwycensem CDH   [c-c]*om.* CH, *replaced by* etc.   [f]recolamus B   [g] ordinarii D   [h]ledatur B   [j]CDH *add* et   [k]For ac ad, CH *substitute* et in; D in; L ac ac   [l]consuetudinem et libertatem CDHL   [m]et consuetam *om.* CDH   [n]singula CH   [o]Southfeld' CG; Sowthfeld DFH; Suttefelde E; Suthfeld L   [p]Norwic' *om.* BGH; Norwici E   [q]*om.* B   [r]quandoque F   [s]CDEFHKL *substitute* Deum for consuetudinem antiquam   [t]B adds tamen   [u]et *om.* BG   [v]illos CDFL; F *omits remainder of statute and adds*: Clausula ponenda in testamento rectoris vel vicarii decedentis...Item lego...salutem anime mee.   [w]nostram *om.* BG; D *ends here*   [x]incurrunt BEGL   [y]Test' CEHL; C *om.* until anno; Datum etc BG, *which end here*; G *adds*: Originale huius statuti consingnatum residet in hospitali sancti Egidii Norwyc' etc.   [z-z]E,L; *om.* CDFHK   [aa-aa]E,K,L; *om.* DH   [bb]Actum *om.* K   [cc]K *adds* archangeli   [dd]CCC°E, *in error*   [ee]pontificatus E   [ff]anno *om.* CHK   [gg]E *adds*: Tempus limitatum per Walterum de Suttefeld' Norwic' episcopum infra quod clerici libere valeant condere testamenta sua et disponere de fructibus ecclesiarum suarum patet in littera suprascripta; L *om.* et consecrationis nostre anno xi°.

For a full discussion of the mss., see *C. & S.* II i 498–9. This decree is not included among the collected synodal statutes of the bps of Norwich (ibid. 342–64). In one ms. (G) it is precedes a similar statement of custom by bp William Raleigh (ibid. 342). Suffield's statute is elucidated in an answer by bp William Bateman (1344–55) to a vicar of Mildenhall, newly instituted, known as the Declaration, which in five mss. follows Suffield's statute (ibid. 501). The vicar asked whether the executors of his predecessor, who had died after the Easter synod, should receive the fruits and obventions of the vicarage from the time after his own induction. Bp Bateman replied that oblations, mortuaries and other revenues accruing to the altar should pertain to the current vicar, who was bound to continuous residence, but that the great tithe and such *extrinseca* which by composition pertain to the vicarage should pertain to the deceased vicar and to his executors, so long as he made specific mention of them in his testament; if, however, he had left a testament but made no specific mention of the said tithes and obventions, then they should pertain to the current vicar rather than to his predecessor's executors. Suffield's statute was cited in the wills of incumbents until the Reformation; cf. *Reg. Morton* iii nos. 94, 121, 125, 180, for instances in 1499. On 27 June 1260 pope Alexander IV confirmed to the bp of Norwich the first fruits of churches vacant at Easter (*Norwich Cathedral Charters* i no. 306).

103. Norwich, Hospital Of St Giles

First foundation charter and statutes. [*c.* 1249 × 24 July 1251]

A = Norfolk RO, NCR 24b/1. Endorsed: Regula fundatoris; column of main headings of statutes on right-hand quarter (s. xiii); exhibita apud Northelmam .ix. kal' Aprilis [1281]; Hugh of Mursley's notarial sign (s. xiii ex); approx. 470 × 340 + 25 mm.; two tags and seals missing (double slits).
B = Norfolk RO, NCR 24b/4 (*inspeximus* by bp Simon Walton, 21 June 1265, no. 188 below).
C = ibid., DCN 40/7 (general cartulary of Norwich cathedral priory) fos 76r–78r. s. xiii ex.
Pd (translation) in Rawcliffe, *Medicine for the Soul* 242–48.

Ave Maria gratia plena Dominus tecum. In nomine Patris et Filii et Spiritus Sancti Amen. Nos Walterus Norwicensis ecclesie episcopus licet indigni, omisso cuiuslibet provocationis sive prefationis tenore, votum cui desudavimus et propositum quod in mente gessimus et desiderium quod omnem affectum cordis nostri exsuperat presentibus duximus exprimendum, ordinandum, statuendum et diffiniendum, et quod id perpetuis temporibus observetur. Fundamus siquidem hospitale quod dicitur beati Egidii in honore sancte Trinitatis, gloriose virginis Marie, beate Anne et beati Egidii omniumque sanctorum in villa Norwic' in fundo nostro et terra nostra ac feudo ecclesie nostre, et abutat capud ipsius hospitalis super vicum qui est ex opposito ecclesie sancte Elene sub muro curie prioris et conventus Norwic', et se extendit in latitudine usque ad aquam currentem per eandem villam versus aquilonem; in longitudine vero se extendit versus pontem episcopi usque ad fossatum quod est inter feudum nostrum et feudum domine Ysabelle de Cressi. In hoc hospitali volumus et ordinamus quod perpetuis temporibus sit magister qui curam hospitalis sollicite gerat in remissione peccatorum, et habebit secum quatuor capellanos honestos in divino officio instructos qui divinum cultum pariter sectantes primo et principaliter obsequio vacabunt divino. Vacabunt siquidem sic: omnes in mane et aurora consurgent, pulsata maiori campana, simul locum dormitorii egredientur et ecclesiam simul intrabunt in suppellitiis et capis clausis, matutinas et horas cum cantu et tractu moderato perpsallent et missam de die cum cantu statim psallent; nec antequam hec compleantes quis eorum per domos vel curiam discurrat, nisi magister solus qui ex causa necessaria poterit tunc exire, sive iusta exigente comoditate aliis poterit licentiam honeste impendere. Tres autem misse in hospitali diebus singulis celebrabuntur, una de die, alia de beata virgine, tertia pro defunctis. Una tamen die semper in ebdomada fiat plenum servitium de sancto Egidio, tempore quadragesimali excepto vel alias sollempnitas continua hoc impediat. Dormiet magister et eius capellani in una domo, de uno pane et potu reficientur. Post prandium vero magister cum capellanis suis et fratribus, post gratiarum actiones, non sumpto potu, capellam hospitalis pulsata campana maiori ingredientur, psalmodizantes psalmum 'Miserere mei Deus', et dicta oratione in capella cum devota inclinatione, poterit magister, assumptis secum quos voluerit, ad hospites redire, non quidem potationis immoderate sive sessionis longioris causa, sed hospitum gratia et recreationis debite honestate. Simul cubabunt dicto completorio nisi per hospites, laborem sive aliam causam honestam oporteat magistrum morari, vel alium de suo speciali precepto. Hoc siquidem hospitale, cum fundo in quo situm est cum omnibus suis pertinentiis, perpetue damus libertati, et omnia que in clauso sunt ipsius hospitalis eidem hospitali, magistro et fratribus eiusdem domus ad eorum et pauperum sustentationem in puram, liberam et perpetuam damus et concedimus elemosinam, absque omni seculari servitio, exactione, secta curie et demanda quacumque, salvis nobis et successoribus nostris iure patronatus eiusdem hospitalis et in spiritualibus omnium ibidem commorantium correctione et reformatione. In hoc hospitali sic fundato reficientur singulis diebus per annum in ipsa domo hospitalis ad ignem in yeme ante caminum hospitalis tresdecim pauperes, et habebunt panem sufficientem et bonum et ferculum carnis vel piscis, et quandocumque ovorum et casei, et potum competenter. Septem pauperes scolares dociles eligendi in fide ipsius magistri de scolis Norwic' de fideli consilio magistri scolarium singulis diebus dum scole durant unum habebunt ibidem pastum, et nutribuntur isti cum in gramatica fuerint convenienter edocti, et alii assumentur secundum modum antedictum. Et sic fiat perpetuis temporibus in hoc hospitali. Erunt siquidem in predicto hospitali triginta lecti, vel plures secundum facultatem domus, ubi pauperes infirmi volentes ibi decubare recipientur in culcitris, lintheamentibus choopertoriis,[a] et donec restituti fuerint sanitati, honeste et congrue procurabuntur, unusquisque iuxta suam infirmitatem, mutabunturque eorum superlectilia quotiens opus fuerit. Tres siquidem vel quatuor ad minus erunt in domo sorores, mulieres quidem honeste et vite per annos plurimos approbate, quinquaginta annos vel parum minus habentes, et iste infirmorum et aliorum decubantium curam gerent et sollicitudinem. Nec erunt ibi plures mulieres, sed omnia fiant per homines, in bracino et omnibus aliis officinis. In isto hospitali omnes pauperes capellani Norwicensis diocesis qui senio confracti vel continuo morbo sic laborantes quod divina celebrare non valeant nec alias habeant unde sustententur, quoad vixerint recipientur et iuxta facultates domus in ipso hospitali in loco honesto morabuntur et decubant et victualia congrue habebunt. Hoc hospitale archa erit Domini, de qua pauperes transeuntes singulis diebus iuxta facultates domus elemosinas recipient. A die vero Annunciationis beate Marie usque ad Assumptionem eiusdem virginis gloriose qualibet die sabbati communi hora diei, pulsata ante maiori campana, omnibus venientibus panis fiat distributio. Et erit panis quantitas ut egeriorum famem possit depellere illa vice. Hoc siquidem hospitale propria erit domus Dei et episcoporum Norwicensium ecclesie, et quotienscumque episcopus transiens per ipsam descenderit et infirmis decubantibus in eodem hospitali et commorantibus ibidem benedictionem largitus fuerit, tresdecim pauperes pro ipso et salute omnium vivorum et defunctorum in ipso hospitali pascentur, et in crastino pro eodem missa de sancto spiritu celebrabitur. Ad ministerium huius hospitalis quatuor in domo erunt fratres laici qui secundum voluntatem et preceptum magistri hiis qui intra et foris sunt vacabunt. Omnes quotquot sunt in domo, fratres, sorores, sacerdotes et clerici, districtioni et cohercioni magistri subiacebunt; et qualibet die dominica capitulum tenebit magister, et alias quotiens opus fuerit, et singulorum delicta et excessus corriget et delinquentes puniet iuxta delicti qualitatem. In ieiuniis et cibariis ac refectionibus modum illorum servabunt qui servant regulam beati Augustini, habitum tamen eorum non habebunt. In capella tamen magister et sacerdotes subpelliciis et capis nigris et rotundis in divino obsequio utentur. Singuli siquidem panno honesto et colore non prohibito vestientur. Magister redditus quoscumque in seculo habere poterit et retinere, sed postquam fuerit factus magister, que adquisierit ipsius erunt hospitalis; et hoc se facturum et curaturum corporali prestito sacramento promittet. Fratres et sorores nullum habebunt proprium; continentiam vovebunt et bonum obedientie promittent. Fratres albis tunicis et grisis scapulariis vestientur, sorores albis tunicis, grisis mantelis et nigris velis, et in omnibus de domo per manum et distributionem magistri necessaria recipient. Magister siquidem domus, sacerdotes, fratres et sorores in villa non comedent neque bibent nisi in domibus religiosorum. Sorores per se comedent et decubabunt, nec aliquis domum earum ingrediatur nisi causa necessaria, obtenta prius licentia a magistro domus memorate. Decedente vero vel recedente domino Hamone de Caletorp nunc magistro eiusdem hospitalis ac in posterum quandocumque vacante, dum vacat hospitale domus sub cura erit episcopi, et uni de discretioribus capellanis domus custodiam committet, nec de bonis ipsius hospitalis episcopus aliquid in ipsa vacatione recipiet, sed omnia ad opus ipsius hospitalis et pauperum Cristi conservabuntur. Vacatio autem domus, corpore magistri tradito sepulture, priori Norwicensi per duos fratres nuntiabitur, et ipse prior archidiaconos Norwic' et Norf' vocabit ut certo die apud Norwicum in ipso hospitali secum conveniant de magistri in ipso hospitali creatione secundum Deum tractaturi. Et continebit hec vacatio spatium trium septimanarum, et isti tres simul congregati, Deum habentes pre oculis, facta inquisitione per fratres ipsius domus iuratos super idoneitate capellanorum ibidem commorantium, in personam intus vel extra, secundum suam conscientiam, idoneam et congruam ad regimen domus eiusdem convenient et consentient et ipsum per litteras suas patentes episcopo, vel eius officiali si extra regnum fuerit, presentabunt, qui eundem absque difficultate admittet, et statim postquam fuerit admissus, residentiam iurabit et quod bona hospitalis in debito statu conservabit et presentem ordinationem observabit.[b] Quod si dicti archidiaconi non convenerint ad diem assignatum, expectabuntur per duos dies, quod si nec tunc venerint, prior Norwic' absque ulteriori dilatione, associatis sibi officiali consistorii Norwic' et decano Norwic', procedet in negotio memorato illa vice sicut procedere deberet cum duobus archidiaconis. Et si contingat archidiaconatum illo tempore vacare, unum de supradictis quem voluerit sibi associabit prior memoratus, et eundem modum observabunt archidiaconi si prior convenire noluerit cum eisdem vel tunc temporis prioratum vacare contigerit. Quod si infra quinque septimanas postquam traditum fuerit corpus sepulture persone supradicte in personam certam ut premittitur non consenserunt, episcopus illa vice de persona idonea secundum formam prenominatam hospitali provideat memorato, hoc semper observato, quod quicumque preficiatur sit sacerdos et iuret residentiam. Poterit tamen si beneficium habeat proprium ecclesiasticum, ibidem divertere, sed ultra octo dies morari nulla vice debebit. Magister hospitalis nullum secum habebit equitantem nisi fuerit unus de capellanis vel fratribus seu clericis eiusdem domus. Nec erunt in domo scutiferi vel pueri lascivi. Magister duobus vel tribus equitaturis maneat contentus. Nulla mulier admittetur ad perendinandum ibidem, et quotiens admittatur ipsorum capella sit a divinis suspensa. Commune sigillum domus sub duabus clavibus erit, magistri scilicet et fratris senioris. Omnibus autem hanc ordinationem nostram observantibus et ad eius observationem laborantibus Dei omnipotentis largimur benedictionem, et singulis annis perpetuo in festo beati Egidii quadraginta dies misericorditer relaxamus. Omnes autem illos qui ad huius nostre ordinationis subversionem laborabunt sive procurabunt vel fraudem in hac parte fuerint machinati, auctoritate Dei patris et filii et spiritus sancti excommunicamus. Et ne in posterum pro defectu necessariorum hec pia nostra provisio valeat impediri, omnes supradictas possessiones, bona et redditus, cum aliis omnibus que in presenti possident vel futuris temporibus poterunt adipisci, necnon et terram de Hayle cum omnibus suis pertinentiis, prefato hospitali, magistro et fratribus ad sustentationem pauperum concedimus et presenti carta confirmamus. Insuper ecclesias de Calethorp', de Costeseya, de Cringelford, de Hardele, sancte Marie de Walsam et de Senges in proprios usus concedimus, appropriamus et confirmamus eisdem, salvis dilectis filiis priori et conventui Norwic' decem marcis de ecclesia de Senges cum vacaverit annuatim in duabus synodis Norwic' per manum dicti magistri percipiendis. Insuper concedimus eisdem quod ecclesias sancte Marie de Walsam et de Senges cum vacaverint licite ingredi valeant et retinere presentis concessionis et confirmationis auctoritate. In hoc siquidem hospitali nec magister nec aliquis capellanorum erit negotiator nec turpilucro dabit intentionem. Insuper concedimus prefatis magistro et fratribus in sua capella, quam dedicavimus, et aliis suis oratoriis perpetuam et liberam cantariam et liberam sepulturam ad opus ipsorum et omnium decedentium ibidem necnon volentium ibidem sepeliri, salvo iure parochialium ecclesiarum. Et ut omnia supradicta imperpetuum firma sint et cum stabilitate roborata, presenti scripto sigillum nostrum unacum sigillo capituli nostri, de cuius consensu omnia supradicta concedimus, damus, ordinamus et confirmamus, fecimus apponi. Actum[c] in capitulo Norwic', presentibus Simone priore eiusdem domus et conventu memorato.

[a] coopertiris C   [b] observabunt B, C   [c] Dat' C

For a translation of the first and second statutes of the hospital, clearly indicating additions and modifications, see Rawcliffe, *Medicine for the Soul* 241–48, and for discussion, ibid. 29–33, where the models provided both by the Augustinian canons and by continental hospitals are emphasised. The traditional date of foundation is 1249, and it is perhaps significant that in the winter of 1247–48 Suffield had been on pigrimage to St Gilles en Provence, and that for a long period from some date after Michaelmas 1248 until autumn 1249 he had been at the papal *curia*, where he may have discussed his plans. These first statutes were probably at latest issued before 24 July 1251, when pope Innocent IV confirmed for the bp his foundation of a hospital for the support of aged and infirm priests, and a week later took the master and brethren under papal protection and confirmed their land and possessions, strictly forbidding that any endowments which the founder had assigned to the poor should be diverted to other uses (Sayers, *Original Papal Documents* nos. 400–1). The appropriation of Cringleford church was confirmed in no. 104, dated 28 June 1251, and that of Calthorpe, Costessy and South Walsham on 1 October 1251 (105), but that of Seething not until 20 October 1253 (106); these acta can hardly be used to date securely either these or the later statutes (107). Rawcliffe (p. 27) suggests the influence of mr Lawrence of Somercotes in the drafting of these, and possibly also of the revised statutes (107). He attested early acta of bp Suffield (9, 20, 109) and acted as his deputy for collection of the tenth in Ireland (84, 125). He became an expert on the subject of elections, producing in 1253–4 a Tractatus seu summa de electionibus episcoporum (ed. A. von Wretscke (1907); cf. J.C. Russell, *Dictionary of Writers of Thirteenth-Century England* (1936) 81–2).

104. Norwich, Hospital Of St Giles

Grant to the master in proprios usus, *for the maintenance of sick priests incapable of celebrating mass who are resident in the hospital, of the church of Cringleford, which is of the bishop's advowson.*   28 June 1251

A = BL ms. Add ch. 19278. Endorsed: Cringleford confirmatio fundatoris (s. xiii); approx. 164 × 51 + 15 mm.; fragment of seal on parchment tag, brown wax, counterseal.

Omnibus Cristi fidelibus presentes litteras visuris vel audituris Walterus Dei gratia Norwicensis episcopus salutem in Domino sempiternam. Noveritis nos ecclesiam de Cringelford, que de nostro est patronatu, magistro hospitalis sancti Egidii de Norwico et successoribus suis, ad sustentationem debilium sacerdotum divina celebrandi inpotentium et in prefato hospitali commorantium, in proprios usus caritatis intuitu contulisse et auctoritate pontificali confirmasse. In cuius rei testimonium huic presenti scripto sigillum nostrum apponi fecimus. Dat' in vigilia apostolorum Petri et Pauli anno Domini millesimo ducentesimo quinquagesimo primo.

The advowson was purchased by the bp from Alexander de Vaux (Rawcliffe, *Medicine for the Soul* 77 and n. 71). In May 1252 William of Cringleford, the plaintiff, quitclaimed to Hamo, master of the hospital, all right to the advowson, in return for payment of two marks (TNA, CP25/1/157/81/1185). In 1254 the church was assessed at £3 6s 8d, with separated tithes valued at 5s held by the sacrist of the cathedral priory (*VN* 417). The church was subsequently served by brethren or conducts of the hospital (Rawcliffe 73).

105. Norwich, Hospital of St Giles

Grant and confirmation to the master and brethren of the hospital, which he has founded, of all the lands and possessions, with buildings thereon, which he has acquired in Norwich from Henry de la Salle and Robert of Stamford, together with the churches of Calthorpe, Costessy, Cringleford and St Mary, [South] Walsham and all right which the bishop has in these churches and their advowsons, which with the consent of his [cathedral] chapter he has granted to them in proprios usus, *for the maintenance of four chaplains who shall in perpetuity celebrate in the chapel; of sick and impoverished chaplains of the diocese who have no other means of support; and of thirteen poor persons who shall be fed there once every day. This is given free from all service except the render on behalf of the bishop and his heirs of all services due to the capital lords of the fees, and saving to the bishop and his successors the patronage of the hospital. Warranty is granted.*   Norwich, 1 October 1251

B = Norfolk R.O., NCR 24b/3 (*inspeximus* by the prior and convent of Bromholm). s. xiii med.

Sciant presentes et futuri quod nos Walterus de Suthfeud Dei miseratione Norwycensis ecclesie minister indignus concessimus, dedimus et hac presenti carta nostra confirmavimus Deo, beate Marie, beate Anne, beato Egidio, omnibus sanctis et hospitali quod in honore eorundem fundavimus in Norwyco et magistro et fratribus in dicto hospitali servientibus omnes terras, possessiones et mesuagia cum omnibus edificiis que adquisivimus in villa de Norwyco de Henrico de la Sale et Roberto de Stamford, cum omnibus suis libertatibus et pertinentiis, unacum ecclesiis de Calethorp', Costeseya, Cringelford et ecclesia sancte Marie de Walesham, et totum ius quod habuimus in ecclesiis et in advocationibus earundem, quas quidem ecclesias de consensu nostri capituli eidem hospitali, magistro et fratribus in proprios usus perpetuo concessimus concedendas sine retenemento, ad sustentationem quatuor capellanorum qui in capella dicti hospitalis in perpetuum divina celebrabunt, et ad sustentationem capellanorum in diocesi Norwycensi debilitatorum et depauperatorum qui aliunde non habent unde possunt sustentari, et ad sustentationem tresdecim pauperum cotidie ibidem recipiendorum et hospitandorum, qui semel in die refectionem percipient ibidem, habenda et tenenda magistro et fratribus dicti hospitalis, eorundem successoribus et hospitali predicto libere, quiete, bene et in pace in perpetuum, reddendo et faciendo annuatim pro nobis et heredibus nostris pro predictis terris, possessionibus et mesuagiis capitalibus dominis feodorum servitia que ad predictas[a] terras, possessiones et mesuagia pertinent, salvo nobis et successoribus nostris iure patronatus in hospitali memorato. Et nos et heredes nostri warantizabimus, acquietabimus et defendemus predictis fratribus et successoribus eorundem et hospitali predicto omnia predictas[a] terras, possessiones et mesuagia cum omnibus edificiis et libertatibus et pertinentiis suis sicut predictum est, unacum ecclesiis de Calethorp, Costeseya, Cringelford et ecclesia sancte Marie de Walesham et ius quod in eisdem habuimus. In cuius rei testimonium presenti scripto sigillum nostrum unacum sigillo capituli nostri fecimus apponi. Hiis testibus: magistro Nicholao archidiacono Eliensi, magistro Roberto archidiacono Colecestr', Iohanne Knot, Hugone clerico, Gerardo Knot, Henrico Payn et Radulfo Gust burgensibus Nowyc'. Dat' Norwyc' kalendas Octobris pontificatus nostri anno septimo.

^a predicta B

Bp Suffield acquired the site of the hospital from Henry de la Salle (*de Aula*) and Roger of Stamford (Rawcliffe, *Medicine for the Soul* 46–7). The advowson of Calthorpe was acquired by the bp from his kinsman Peter of Hautbois (*de Alto Bosco*), 1246 × 48 (ibid. 72); it was valued in 1254 at £8 (*VN* 367). Costessey was valued in 1254 at only £1 13s 4d, the Cistercian abbey of Bon Repos (Côtes-du-Nord) having a portion of £3 6s 8d and Rumburgh priory separated tithes also valued at £3 6s 8d (VN 399; Rawcliffe 76). For Cringleford, see no. 104 above. Archdn William Suffield was involved in the acquisition of the advowson of St Mary's, South Walsham, which he confirmed to the hospital on the death of his brother, the bp (Rawcliffe 82–3); in 1254 the *personatus* was valued at £16 13s 4d and the vicarage at £5 (*VN* 365). These churches are not listed in the *Taxatio* of 1291, as pertaining to a 'poor' hospital.

106. Norwich, Hospital of St Giles

Notification that, since of the advowson of the church of Seething half pertains to the bishop and half to the prior and convent of Norwich, and the monks have committed all their right therein to the bishop, he has eventually ordained that the master and brethren of the hospital shall have the church with its appurtenances in proprios usus *after the death or resignation of master Richard, the present rector, saving a vicarage to be taxed by the bishop to which they shall at each vacancy present to him a suitable* persona. *The hospital shall annually pay from the revenues of the church to the almoner of the cathedral priory ten marks, that is, half a mark at least for the increase of alms on every Sunday from the Assumption of the Blessed Virgin Mary to the Annunciation of the Lord; and since it is said that ten marks will not suffice for such an increase in alms, the bishop has conceded and assigned five marks a year from elsewhere, as contained in his letter on this subject. The master and brethren shall each year on the bishop's anniversary sing* Placebo *and* Dirige *in their church, and each chaplain shall celebrate a mass for his soul, and adequate food and drink shall be distributed to a hundred poor persons. Three copies of this document have been made, to be retained by the bishop, the cathedral priory and the hospital.* Lambourne, 20 October 1253

A = Arundel Castle, duke of Norfolk's muniments, Seething ch. 280. Endorsed: Ecclesia de Senges et anniversarium Walteri episcopi celebrandum (s. xiii); approx. 167 × 118 + 19 mm.; three slits, tags and seals missing.
B = Norfolk R.O., NCR 24b/3 (*inspeximus* by prior and convent of Bromholm) s. xiii ex.
Pd (calendar) from A in *HMC Various Collections* vii 219.

Omnibus Cristi fidelibus has litteras inspecturis Walterus Dei gratia Norwicensis episcopus salutem in Domino sempiternam. Cum ius patronatus ecclesie de

Senges ad nos pro una medietate et ad dilectos in Cristo priorem et conventum
Norwicensem pro alia medietate pertineret, ac iidem prior et conventus totum ius
suum nostre ordinationi totaliter et absolute committerent, nos tandem taliter
duximus ordinandum, quod dilecti in Cristo filii magister et fratres hospitalis
sancti Egidii Norwic' predictam ecclesiam de Senges cum omnibus pertinentiis
suis, post decessum vel recessum dilecti in Cristo filii magistri Ricardi nunc
rectoris eiusdem, in proprios usus perpetuis temporibus possidebunt, et ipsam eis
ad presens quantum in nobis est concedimus et assignamus, salva vicaria ibidem
per nos taxanda ad quam quotiens ipsam vacare contigerit predicti magister et
fratres personam idoneam nobis et successoribus nostris libere presentabunt.
Magister siquidem et fratres antedicti dilecto in Cristo filio elemosinario
Norwicensi singulis annis decem marcas de bonis ecclesie memorate persolvent
ad elemosinam singulis diebus Sabbati a festo Assumptionis beate virginis Marie
usque ad festum Annunciationis Domini in dimidia marca ad minus perpetuis
temporibus augendam. Et quoniam predicte decem marce ad elemosinam toto
tempore prescripto, ut dictum est, augmentandam non sufficiunt, idcirco quinque
marcas annuas dicto elemosinario aliunde concessimus et assignavimus, prout in
littera nostra super hoc confecta plenius continetur. Dicti quoque magister et
fratres singulis annis die anniversarii nostri Placebo et Dirige in ecclesia sua
sollempniter cantabunt et singuli capellani unam missam pro anima nostra
specialiter celebrabunt, et centum pauperibus in cibo et potu victui necessaria
sufficienter ministrabunt. In cuius rei testimonium sigillum nostrum unacum
sigillis capituli Norwicensis et magistri hospitalis antedicti presentibus est
appensum, et facta sunt super hoc tria instrumenta eiusdem tenoris, quorum
unum residet penes nos, aliud penes prefatos priorem et conventum et tertium
penes magistrum et fratres supradictos. Dat' apud Lamburne .xiii. kalendas
Novembris anno Domini M° CC° L° tertio.

> The confirmation charter for the hospital of Roger Bigod, earl of Norfolk, relating to a tenement
> in Seething with the advowson, held of his fee, reveals that the bp had acquired his mediety of
> the advowson from the Premonstratensian canons of Langley, who had themselves obtained it
> from *dominus* Walter of Seething; the monks of Norwich had acquired their mediety from
> *dominus* William of Seething (BL ms Topham ch. 44). These grants were ratified by final
> concords in the *curia regis* in 1249 (Rye, *Norfolk Fines* 76 no. 1001, for Langley) and 1250
> (*Norwich Cathedral Charters* i no. 360). In 1254 the church was valued at £16 13s 4d (VN
> 405). The master and brethren were inducted into corporal possession in October 1264, on the
> resignation of Richard, the rector (187). See Rawcliffe, *Medicine for the Soul* 81.

107. Norwich, Hospital of St Giles

*Second 'foundation' charter and revised statutes for the hospital, with grant of
an indulgence of forty days at the feast of St Giles.*

                                                   Norwich, *c.* 1251 × 19 May 1257

B = Norfolk R.O., DCN 43/48 (*inspeximus* and confirmation by pope Alexander IV, 15 October
1257, ex archive of cathedral priory). s. xiii med. C = ibid., NCR 17b (Norwich

corporation Book of Pleas) fos. 48r–50r (*inspeximus* by bp Roger Scarning of pope Alexander IV's confirmation, as B, August 1272). s. xv med.
Pd (translation) in Rawcliffe, *Medicine for the Soul* 242–8.

Ave Maria gratia plena Dominus tecum. In nomine ᵃˉsancte et individue Trinitatisˉᵃ patris et filii et spiritus sancti Amen. Nos Walterus Dei miseratione episcopus Norwicensis, tenore cuiuslibet verbosi comentarii et etiam prefationis omisso, votum et propositum queᵇ diu in mente gessimus ac desiderium quod omnem affectum cordis nostri exstirpat et excedit presentibus duximusᶜ exprimendum, ordinantes, diffinentes et etiam statuentes ut ea que in presenti continentur scriptura perpetuis temporibus irrefragabiliter observentur. In primis fundavimus hospitale quod dicitur beati Egidii in civitate Norwicensi in honore sancte et individue Trinitatis, gloriose virginis Marie, beate Anne matris eiusdem virginis gloriose, beati Egidii et omnium sanctorum in fundo nostro et terra nostra que est de feodo nostre ecclesie Norwicensis a libere tenentibus ea nostra industria perquisitis. Huius hospitalis capud unum extendit se ad vicum qui est ex opposito ecclesie sancte Elene sub muro curie prioris et conventus Norwicensium; in latitudine autem extenditᵈ se versus aquilonem usque ad magnam ripam fluentem iuxta civitatem predictam; in longitudine vero extendit se versus pontem qui dicitur episcopi usque ad fossatum, id est inter feodum nostrum et feodum nobilis matrone domine Ysabelle de Cressy. Volumus insuper et etiam ordinamus quod in hoc hospitali perpetuis temporibus sit magister, qui curam hospitalis eiusdem gerat solicite tam in temporalibus quam in spiritualibus, sicut inferius exprimemus, et hoc ei in remissione iniungimus peccatorum. Quatuor etiam fratres laici perpetuo sint ibidem, negotia ipsius hospitalis secundum dispositionem magistri tam in ipso hospitali quam extra diligenter et fideliter vacaturi. Tres quoque vel quatuor ibidem erunt sorores bone vite et conversationis honeste per annos plurimos approbate, quinquaginta videlicet annos vel parum minus habentes, qui omnium infirmorum et aliorum languidorum ibi iacentium solicite curam gerant, lintheamina et alia vestimenta lectorum quotiens opus fuerit mutabunt, et eis humiliter in necessariis pro viribus ministrabunt; et ne plures sint ibi mulieres firmiter inhibemus, set omnia fiant per masculos tam in bracino quam in aliis officinis. Habebit etiam secum quatuor presbiteros bone fame et conversationis honeste et in officio divino competenter instructos,ᵉ item duos clericos, diaconum videlicet et subdiaconum qui, divino cultui et obsequio principaliter intendentes, preter ea que dominus nosterᶠ Ihesus Cristus singulis inspiraverit, hanc formam specialiter observabunt: omnes in aurora diei, pulsata videlicet maiori campana, consurgent et dormitorium simul exibunt et ecclesiam simul intrabunt, induti superpelliciis etᵍ cappis clausis, nigris scilicet et rotundis, et matutinas ac horas alias cum cantu debito et tractu moderato psallentʰ et statim missam de die solempniter celebrabunt, ibique fratres et sorores intersint et divina audiant reverenter; nec priusquam omnia ista completaʲ fuerint quisquam eorum ecclesiam exire aut per domos aut perᵏ curiam discurrereˡ seu vagari presumat, solo magistro excepto, qui ex causa necessaria exire poterit et aliis pro utilitate domus exeundi licentiam impertiri. In hiis siquidem ecclesie officiis divinis consuetudinem ecclesie Sar'[m] volumus observari. Tres quoque missas in hospitali singulis diebus volumus et statuimus celebrari, unam de die, aliam de beata et gloriosa virgine Maria et tertiam pro defunctis, ita tamen quod una die cuiuslibet septimane fiat plenum servitium de beato Egidio, nisi hoc propter quadragesimalis temporis aut aliorum festorum solempnium contingat forsitan impediri. Post peracta vero[n] divinorum officia presbiteri ipsi et clerici non per civitatem vel placeas vagabundi discurrant, sed in lectionibus, orationibus, visitationibus infirmorum et aliis operibus caritatis diem expendant, nisi de precepto[o] et licentia magistri ipsos ad alia negotia utilia et honesta se transferre contingat;[p] idem in fratribus et sororibus volumus observari. Et in huiusmodi licentiis dandis, sicut in correctionibus et aliis factis, sit magister providus et discretus. In hoc vero[q] hospitali erunt triginta lecti, vel plures secundum facultates ipsius, cum culcitris,[r] lintheamentibus et etiam coopertoriis ad opus pauperum infirmorum, ita quod cum aliquis pauper infirmitate laborans[s] illuc accesserit, recipietur benigne et donec sanitati restitutus fuerit[t] iuxta qualitatem sue infirmitatis congrue procurabitur et honeste. Cum vero sanus factus fuerit, omnibus que secum portavit sibi fideliter restitutis, libere cum eisdem recedat. Porro in ipso hospitali omnes pauperes presbiteri diocesis Norwicensis qui senio sunt confracti vel continuo morbo detenti, ita quod divina celebrare non possunt, si alias non habeant[u] unde valeant sustentari, recipientur ibidem quoad vixerint moraturi et sustentabuntur congrue de bonis hospitalis iuxta facultates eiusdem. Sane septem pauperes scolares in gramatica docibiles de scolis Norwic', in fide ipsius magistri per fidele consilium magistri scolarum fideliter eligendi, habebunt singulis diebus anni[v] dum scole durant unum pastum in hospitali predicto, et cum isti fuerint in gramatica edocti competenter,[w] loco ipsorum assumantur septem alii successive eligendi secundum formam superius recitatam, et hoc volumus perpetuis temporibus observari. Ad hec, reficientur in hoc hospitali singulis diebus anni, in ipsa videlicet domo hospitalis, tresdecim pauperes qui sedebunt in hyeme[x] iuxta ignem ante caminium, in estate similiter ibidem, et habebunt bonum panem et potum ac unum ferculum carnis vel piscis, quandocumque autem casie et ovorum. Hoc quidem[y] hospitale erit archa Domini, de qua pauperes transeuntes singulis diebus iuxta facultates ipsius elemosinas recipient et grata subsidia caritatis. A die vero Annuntiationis beate Marie usque ad Assumptionem eiusdem virginis gloriose qualibet die sabbati certa hora diei, pulsata vero[z] prius maiori campana, singulis pauperibus tunc presentibus distributio fiat[aa] panis, cuius panis quantitas recipientis famem repellere valeat illa vice. Et quia hoc[bb] hospitale erit propria domus Dei et episcoporum Norwicensium, volumus et etiam[cc] ut quotienscumque episcopus Norwicensis[dd] transitum faciens per ipsum hospitale ipsum[ee] intraverit, et infirmis ac languidis in ipso hospitali iacentibus benedictionem dederit, tresdecim pauperes pro ipsius et omnium vivorum ac etiam defunctorum salute eodem[ff] die pascantur ibidem, et in crastino celebretur missa de sancto spiritu[gg] pro eodem et omnibus defunctis.[hh] Magister quoque, presbiteri et fratres communiter in una domo et uno cibo et potu vescantur. Post prandium vero omnes simul Deo omnipotenti gratias referentes[jj] post versiculam, non sumpto potu, pulsata maiore campana, ingrediuntur ecclesiam hospitalis sancti Egidii predicti,[kk] dicentes psalmum 'Miserere mei Deus'. Quibus ex more peractis, poterit[ll] magister, assumptis secum quos voluerit, ad hospites non potationis set recreationis et honestatis causa redire.[mm] Absente vero magistro, presbiter senior suppleat vices eius. In ieiuniis siquidem, refectionibus et cibariis magister, presbiteri, fratres et sorores modum illorum qui tenent regulam beati Augustini tenebunt et etiam servabunt,[nn] eorum tamen habitum non portabunt. Magister vero[oo] et presbiteri panno honesto et non[pp] vetito sive indecenti pro sua voluntate utentur, proviso quod in ecclesia habeant superpelicia et nigras cappas rotundas, sicut superius est expressum. Fratres vero[qq] albis tunicis et grisis scapularibus vestientur, sorores vero albis tunicis et grisis mantellis erunt indute nigrasque velas portabunt. Porro magister et presbiteri sub uno tecto dormiant et quiescant; fratres vero[rr] similiter per se in uno domo iacebunt; [ss-]sorores vero per se in una domo simul commedant et iacebunt, nec aliquis ingredi domum audeat earundem,[-ss] nisi ex causa necessaria, petita et optenta prius licentia a magistro. Dicto vero completorio, omnes ad dormitorium simul accedant, nisi magistrum vel alium de suo speciali mandato vel licentia propter hospites vel propter[tt] aliam honestam causam seu necessariam opporteat remanere. Magister siquidem hospitalis predicti, presbiteri, fratres et sorores in civitate Norwici extra domum suam, nisi in domibus religiosis, non commedant neque bibunt, [uu-]et ut sint negotiatores vel dent operam turpo lucri firmiter inhibemus. Magister libere fratres et sorores recipiet et admittet, nec eos episcopo presentare debebit; omnesque in dicto hospitali commorantes, presbiteri videlicet, fratres, sorores, clerici et ministri discretioni ipsius magistri et cohercioni canonice subiacebunt. [-uu] Fratres autem et sorores continentiam vovebunt. Proprium non habebunt, sed per manum et discretionem magistri de domo necessaria recipient universa. Promittent quoque sicut et[vv] presbiteri magistro obedientiam et servabunt. Volumus etiam quod magister qualibet die dominica, et alias quotiens fuerit opportunum, capitulum teneat et singulorum excessus et delicta corrigat et emendet,[ww] ac delinquentes iuxta delicti qualitatem puniet et castiget. Magister siquidem hospitalis ipsius neminem secum habeat equitantem[xx] nisi fuerit unus de presbiteris, fratribus seu clericis hospitalis eiusdem, ita quod trium evectionum numerum nunquam[yy] excedat. Nolumus etiam quod in dicto hospitali scutiferi vel pueri sint lacivi. Ceterum nolumus quod[zz] aliqua mulier recipiatur ad perendinandum[a] vel morandum in hospitali predicto, et quotiens contra statutum[b] factum fuerit, volumus et etiam ordinamus quod capella ipsius hospitalis dum mulier ibi steterit ipso facto a divinis officiis sit suspensa; una tamen missa propter infirmos ad altare deprope submissa voce tantummodo celebretur.[c] [d-]Magister etiam hospitalis unum beneficium ecclesiasticum, etiam curam habens animarum annexam, ac alias possessiones que antequam magister ibidem factus fuerit canonice extitit, assecutus magistratum illo habere poterit et tenere. Omnia tamen que adquisierit postquam magister effectus fuerit erunt hospitalis eiusdem et omnia in ipsius hospitalis dominio conservabuntur ac penes ipsum hospitalem perpetuis temporibus remanebunt; et hoc se facturum et efficaciter curaturum corporali prestito sacramento in sua confirmatione promittet.[d] Commune siquidem sigillum domus sub duabus clavibus erit, magistri videlicet et fratris senioris[e] eiusdem, nec aliquid nisi in capitulo et in presentia fratrum tunc domi existentium sigillabitur de eadem. Decedente vero vel recedente[f] dilecto in Cristo Hamone de Calthorp nunc magistro hospitalis eiusdem, circa electionem hanc formam volumus perpetuis temporibus observari. Defuncto magistro et eius corpore tradito sepulture, vel etiam alias eo cedente, vacatio hospitalis per duos fratres nuntiabitur priori Norwicensi,[g] et ipse archidiaconos Norwic' et Norff' huius nostre ordinationis auctoritate protinus evocabit ut certo die infra tres septimanas numerandas a morte magistri vel cessionis ipsius apud Norwicum in ipso hospitali conveniant de futuri magistri creatione unanimiter tractaturi; et hii tres, facta prius inquisitione diligenti per fratres eiusdem hospitalis iuratos super ydoneitate presbiterorum in eodem hospitali commorantium, de ipsis presbiteris aut etiam aliis forensibus, prout eis secundum Deum et suas conscientias visum fuerit expedire, ad regimen dicti hospitalis personam congruam et honestam eligent et assument, quam episcopo Norwicensi infra octo dierum spatium post electionem celebratam per suas literas patentes presentabunt; et[h] si episcopus Norwicensis tunc[j] fuerit extra regnum, persona electa presentabitur officiali Norwicensi, qui ipsam sicut episcopus sine obstaculo cuiuslibet contradictionis admittet. Si autem dicti archidiaconi ad diem assignatum[k] non convenerint, ipsos per duos dies proximo[l] sequentes volumus expectari,[m] et si non venerint taliter expectati,[n] dictus prior, associatis sibi officiali consistorii Norwici et decano Norwic', procedet in dicto negotio illa vice, sicut procedere deberet cum archidiaconis antedictis; et eandem formam volumus observari si dictos archidiaconatus tunc vacare contingat. Si autem unus archidiaconatuum vacans fuerit vel unum archidiaconum tamen abesse contigerit, tunc dictus prior cum archidiacono presente, associato sibi dicto officiali consistorii vel decano, in negotio procedat[o] secundum formam superius recitatam; et eandem formam ab ipsis archidiaconis volumus observari si prior convenire noluerit cum eisdem vel prioratum tunc vacare[p] contingat. Volumus eciam[q] quod si vacante prioratu Norwici magistrum hospitalis cedere contingat vel decedere, vacatio eiusdem hospitalis dictis archidiaconis protinus nuntietur, ut ipsi ad eligendum magistrum in forma prescripta conveniant et accedant. Quod si prior et alii superius numerati infra quinque septimanas postquam corpus magistri dicti hospitalis traditum fuerit sepulture vel post cessionem eiusdem in personam certam ut provisimus non consenserint, episcopus Norwicensis illa vice de persona ydonea hospitali provideat memorato; hoc firmiter observato, quod quicumque prefici debeat sit sacerdos et iuret continuam residentiam se facturum, [r]ita tamen quod si habeat beneficium ecclesiasticum ad illud quandocumque valeat declinare, proviso quod ibidem ultra octo dies vice aliqua non[s] moretur.[r] Iurabit insuper dictus magister in creatione sua quod ipsum hospitale et omnia ad ipsum pertinentia bene et fideliter quantum in ipso est custodiet et tractabit, quod etiam immobilia[t] eiusdem non alienabit et quod mobilia in usus ipsius domus et pauperum ibi Cristi fideliter secundum nostram ordinationem expendet et expendi efficaciter procurabit. Dictum autem hospitalem cum omnibus suis pertinentiis dum vacans fuerit erit sub custodia et cura Norwicensis episcopi sub hac forma, quod episcopo in ipsa vacatione nichil omnino de bonis eiusdem recipiet hospitalis, sed statim et absque difficultate aliqua uni de discretioribus prebiteris dicti hospitalis interim custodiam ipsam committet, qui omnia ad opus pauperum et infirmorum per sacramentum suum fideliter et absque fraude conservet et magistro qui ibidem creabitur de omnibus interim perceptis et expensis reddat fideliter rationem. Hec siquidem statuta nostra et alia quoad correctionem, reformationem, honestatem et utilitatem dicti hospitalis et ibidem commorantium a nobis in posterum statuenda volumus et precipimus similiter observari. Hoc siquidem hospitale sic fundatum cum omnibus suis pertinentiis damus perpetue libertati, et omnia que sunt infra septa eiusdem hospitalis eidem hospitali, magistro et fratribus, ad eorum ac pauperum sustentationem, in liberam, puram et perpetuam elemosinam concedimus atque damus absque omni servitio seculari, exactione, sectis curiarum et demanda, salvis nobis et successoribus nostris iure patronatus hospitalis eiusdem, correctione etiam et reformatione in spiritualibus omnium in dicto hospitali commorantium nobis et successoribus nostris specialiter reservata. Et ne hec nostra provisio et ordinatio pro defectu necessariorum futuris temporibus valeat impediri, possessiones supradictas et terram de Hethell[u] cum suis pertinentiis prefato hospitali, magistro et fratribus ad sustentationem pauperum et infirmorum concedimus, et omnia predicta unacum aliis bonis que in presenti possident vel futuris temporibus adipisci poterint carte presentis munimine confirmamus, ecclesias insuper de Calthorp', de Costesey,[v] de Kringelford,[w] sancte Marie de Walsham, de Hardele et de Senges eis in proprios usus concedimus et etiam confirmamus, salvis dilectis in Cristo filiis priori et conventui Norwicensis ecclesie decem marcis de bonis ecclesie de Senges cum vacaverit, eisdem in duabus synodis Norwicensibus per manum magistri eiusdem hospitalis annuatim solvendis, postquam dicte ecclesie possessionem pacificam fuerit assecutus. Concedimus etiam eisdem quod possessionem ecclesiarum sancte Marie de Walsham et de Sengis cum vacaverint licite ingredi valeant et tenere auctoritate huius nostre confirmationis et collationis, alterius consensu vel assensu minime requisito. Concedimus insuper eis perpetuam et liberam cantariam in capella dicti hospitalis quam consecravimus, necnon et[x] aliis suis oratoriis, unacum sepultura ad opus omnium ibidem decedentium necnon aliorum omnium ibidem volentium et eligentium sepelliri, ecclesiarum parochialium iure salvo. Omnibus autem hanc nostram ordinationem observantibus et ad eius conservationem consilio et auxilio laborantibus, benedictionem inperpetuum Dei omnipotentis et Domini Ihesu Cristi, et singulis annis in festo sancti Egidii quadraginta dies de iniuncta sibi penitentia misericorditer relaxamus. Illos autem qui ad huius nostre ordinationis subversionem laborabunt seu aliquid procurabunt quo minus nostra ordinatio futuris temporibus sortiatur effectum vel quicquid contra ipsam maliciose fuerint machinati, auctoritate Dei omnipotentis, patris et filii et spiritus sancti, excommunicationis vinculo innodamus. Et ut omnia supradicta in perpetuum firma et stabilia et rata consistant, presenti scripto sigillum nostrum unacum sigillo capituli nostri Norwicensis, de cuius expresso consensu ac assensu omnia supradicta concedimus, ordinamus et confirmamus, est appensum. Dat' in capitulo Norwicensi, presentibus dilectis in Cristo filiis Symone priore Norwicensi et suo conventu.

[a-a] *om.* B [b] que in C [c] duximus *om.* B [d] extendit *om.* B [e] distinctos C [f] noster *om.* B [g] et in B [h] perpsallent C [j] completa *om.* B [k] per *om.* B [l] discurre B [m] Sarr' B; Sarre C [n] vero *om.* C [o] preceptu B [p] contingant B [q] hoc vero *repeated* B; hoc quoque C [r] culcitis C [s] laborans *om.* B [t] sanitati fuerat restitutus B [u] si habeant non alias C [v] anni *om.* B [w] competenter edocti C [x] in hyeme *om.* B [y] equidem C [z] vero *om.* C [aa] fiet B [bb] hoc *om.* B [cc] etiam *om.* B [dd] Norwici C [ee] ipsumque C [ff] eo B [gg] spiritu sancto C [hh] et omnibus defunctis *interl.* B, *om.* C [jj] rifferentes B [kk] sancti Egidii predicti *om.* C, *substitutes* predictam [ll] predictus B [mm] rediret B [nn] observabunt C [oo] etenim C [pp] non *om.* C [qq] vero *om.* B [rr] etiam C [ss-ss] *om.* B [tt] propter *om.* B [uu-uu] *om.* B [vv] et sicut C [ww] emendat B [xx] nullum habeat equitantem secum B [yy] nusquam C [zz] quoque B [a] perhendinandum C [b] statutum *om.* B [c] deprope ad altare eis tantummodo celebretur B [d-d] *om.* B [e] senioris fratris B [f] cedente vero vel decedente B [g] ecclesie Norwici C [h] quod C [j] tunc *om.* B [k] assingnatum B [l] proximo *om.* C [m] exspectari C [n] exspectati C [o] procedant B [p] vacare tunc B [q] autem B [r-r] *om.* C [s] non *interl.* B [t] mobilia B [u] Hethelle C [v] Costeshey C [w] Cryngelford C [x] et *om.* B

The translation in Rawcliffe, *Medicine for the Soul*, clearly indicates additions to and adaptations from the first statutes (103). It is impossible (despite nos. 105–6) to date precisely this second version, which was specifically confirmed by pope Alexander IV on 15 October 1257, five months after Suffield's death, probably because of the desire of the master and brethren for greater security (Norfolk RO, NCR 17b, fos. 48r–50r). They were presumably revised some time after the composition of the first version, in the light of experience. It is tempting to associate them with a third visit to the *curia* by Suffield; he departed from Dover under royal protection in October 1253 (*Cl. R. 1251–53* 510) and may have had discussions about the hospital at the papal court. Pope Innocent IV died on 7 December 1254, but on 10 March 1255 his successor, Alexander IV, in a bull addressed to the bp, confirmed the foundation (*Reg. Alex. IV* no. 254; *CPL* i 312).

108. Norwich, St Paul's Hospital

Inspeximus *and confirmation of the general confirmation for the hospital by bishop Thomas [Blundeville] of its churches and tithes [EEA 21 no. 95], and grant also of a third part of all tithes of assarts, made or to be made, in the episcopal manor of Thorpe.* [North] Elmham, 29 April 1245

B = Canterbury D. & C., Ch. Ant. CA/N1 (*inspeximus* by prior Nicholas and convent of Christ Church, 1249). s. xiii med. C = BL ms. Cotton roll ii 19 (*inspeximus* by bp John Salmon, 17 March 1302) no. 14. s. xiv in. D = Norfolk R.O., DCN 40/1 (general cartulary) fo. 241r (232r) (as C). s. xiv in.

Pd from C in *Norwich Cathedral Charters* i no. 259 (14).

Omnibus Cristi fidelibus hoc[a] presens scriptum[b] visuris vel audituris Walterus
Dei gratia Norwicensis[c] episcopus salutem in Domino. Cartam bone memorie
Thome Dei gratia Norwicensis[c] episcopi inspeximus in hec verba: [*EEA* 21 no.
95]. Nos igitur predictam donationem et confirmationem ratam habentes et
acceptam, eam presenti scripto et sigilli nostri inpressione corroboramus. Insuper
autem concedimus et huius scripti tenore confirmamus eidem hospitali ad opus
dictorum pauperum tertiam partem omnium decimarum provenientium [d-]de
omnibus nunc assartis nostris de Thorp' et de assartis in posterum in eadem villa
faciendis perpetuo[e] possidendam et percipiendam.[-d] Hiis testibus: magistro
Willelmo de Sutfeld,[f] Herveo de Fakenham,[g] Willelmo de Horham, Ada[h] de
Bromholm' et Thoma le Bigot,[j] [k-]Thoma de Eccles, Ricardo de Ribof,[-k] Henrico
persona de Beston'[l] clericis nostris, et aliis. Dat' apud Elmham .iii. kalendas
Maii pontificatus nostri anno primo.

[a] hoc *om.* B   [b] pervenerint *struck through* C   [c] Norwycensis D   [d-d] de omnibus assartis
nostris de Torp' in perpetuo possidendam C, D   [e] in perpetuo B, D   [f] Sutfelde C; Suthfelde D
[g] Fakeham B, C   [h] Adam C, D   [j] le *om.* D   [k-k] *om.* C, D   [l] Best' C, D

109. Norwich, St Paul's Hospital

*Confirmation, for the support of hospitality, of a third part of the tithe of the
bishop's assarts at Thorpe, as granted to them by bishop William Raleigh; and
grant also to them of the same third part of tithes of assarts to be made there in
future.*   Norwich, 24 February 1247

> B = BL ms. Cotton roll ii 19 (*inspeximus* by bp John Salmon, 17 March 1302) no. 17. s. xiv in.
> C = ibid. no. 18 (*inspeximus* by bp Roger Scarning, 1275–6). D = Norfolk R.O., DCN
> 40/1 (general cartulary) fo. 241v (232v) (as B). s. xiv in. E = ibid. fos. 241v–242r (232v–
> 233r) (as C).
> Pd from B in *Norwich Cathedral Charters* i no. 259 (17).

Omnibus Cristi fidelibus has litteras visuris vel audituris Walterus Dei gratia
Norwicensis[a] episcopus salutem in Domino. Quoniam iuxta verbum Domini
quod minimo de membris Cristi factum est et[b] Cristo factum esse intelligitur, eos
benigno favore prosequi oportet qui iugiter hospitalitati vacantes singulis
hospitalitatis gratiam largiuntur. Cum igitur dilecti filii prior et conventus
Norwycenses in hospitali sancti Pauli Norwic'[c] ibidem commorantibus se causa
Dei reddant hospitales pariter et gratiosos, nos optantes tanti meriti fieri
participes et oneris coadiutores, ut cum honore onus ferant levius, ipsis et prefato
hospitali tertiam partem decimarum assartorum nostrorum de Torp' eisdem per
venerabilem patrem W. de Ralege predecessorem nostrum concessam
concedimus et confirmamus. Et ne nos qui uberrimam gratiam tenemur
impendere in beneficiis eisdem largiendis retrogradi videamur, quod de
presentibus assartis eisdem est concessum et de assartis inposterum in eadem
villa faciendis hoc idem ipsis concedimus et presenti carta confirmamus. In cuius
rei testimonium presenti scripto sigillum nostrum duximus apponendum. Hiis

testibus: magistris Willelmo de Horham,[d] Laurentio de Sumercote,[e] dominis
Iohanne de Holcham, Thomas de Colecest' capellanis, Willelmo de Withewell,[f]
Willelmo de Pakeham, Willelmo de Sidersterne, Thoma de Walecot'[g] clericis.
Dat' apud Norwicum[h] .vi. kalendas Martii pontificatus nostri anno tertio.

[a] Norwycensis D, E   [b] et *om.* B   [c] Norwyc' D, E   [d] Eiham B, D   [e] Sumertone D   [f]
Wythewell' C   [g] Walekot' C, E; Walcott D   [h] Norwycum D, E

A third part of the bp's demesne tithe at Thorpe had been confirmed by bps John of Oxford and
Thomas Blundeville (*Norwich Cathedral Charters* i nos. 259 (11), 257; *EEA* 6 no. 269; *EEA* 21
no. 95). Suffield himself granted a third part of the tithe of assarts there in 1245, without
mention of any grant by bp Raleigh (108).

110. Nuneaton Priory

*Notification that, when the nuns submitted the church of St Gregory with the
chapel of St Peter [Sudbury], which is of their advowson, to his disposition, the
bishop, considering their poverty and especially the deficiency of their vestments,
has with the consent of his chapter granted them a perpetual benefice of ten
marks in the church, to be rendered by the rector at the feast of the Purification
[2 February]. If the rector should default in payment within eight days, he shall
lose the church. The bishop reserves to himself power to make further provision
for the nuns in this church, or elsewhere wheresoever he wishes and of
exonerating this church. On the death or resignation of master Adam of
Bromholm, the present rector whom he has admitted at the nuns' presentation,
he will nominate to them another suitable* persona *according to his will, whom
within a month of notification they shall present to the church; and if they fail so
to do at any vacancy, the bishop may proceed by collation.*

Norwich, 22 March 1245

A = BL ms. Add. ch. 47959. Endorsed: Sudbur', non irrotulatur, sed tamen mensio sit (s. xiii);
approx. 176 × 140 + 14 mm.; parchment tag; seal, dark green wax, counterseal.

Omnibus sancte matris ecclesie filiis presens scriptum visuris vel audituris
Walterus miseratione divina Norwicensis episcopus salutem eternam in Domino.
Inter ceteras Ierusalem filias circumquaque diffusas, illas nos decet studiosius et
sollicitius honorare que in honore gloriose virginis Marie sunt constricte. Cum
igitur dilecte in Cristo filie priorissa et moniales de Eton' ecclesiam sancti
Gregorii cum capella sancti Petri ad eam pertinente, que de ipsarum est
advocatione, nostre omnino subiacerint voluntati, nos paupertatem ipsarum
attendentes, et precipue defectum quem in vestimentis patiuntur, decem marcas
annuas de bonis dicte ecclesie nomine perpetui beneficii de consensu capituli
nostri dictis monialibus caritative concessimus, a rectore eiusdem ecclesie qui
pro tempore fuerit ad festum Purificationis beate Marie apud Subir' integre
percipiendas, ita quod si rector cessaverit aliquotiens in solutione dicte pecunie
post prefatum terminum, ipso iure cadit a possessione ecclesie memorate;

reservata nobis potestate uberius providendi dictis monialibus in eadem ecclesia vel in alia ubicumque voluerimus, et eandem ecclesiam liberandi. Decedente vero vel cedente magistro Adam de Bromholm nunc rectore eiusdem ecclesie, quem ad presentationem dictarum monialium ad eam admisimus, nominabimus predictis monialibus aliam personam ydoneam quam voluerimus, quam ipse nobis infra mensem postquam de nominatione nostra eis constiterit per litteras suas patentes ad eandem ecclesiam presentabunt; quod si facere noluerint, nos nichilominus supradictam ecclesiam illa vice cui voluerimus conferremus, et illud in qualibet vacatione eiusdem ecclesie tam erga nos quam successores nostros inperpetuum observabitur. In cuius rei testimonium huic scripto sigillum nostrum apponi fecimus. Hiis testibus: magistro Herveo de Fakeham, magistro Willelmo de Horham, magistro Ada de Bromholm, magistro Willelmo de Bec, Thoma de Walcot' clerico et aliis. Dat' apud Norwicum .xi. kalendas Aprilis anno Domini M° CC° XLIIII.

> For earlier documents relating to this church, see *EEA* 6 nos 136, 269A-B, 412A; Appx 1. 78. In 1254 the rector's portion of the church of St Gregory with the chapel of St Peter was £13 6s 8d and the nuns' portion £6 13s 4d (10 marks) (*VN* 438); by 1291 the rector's portion was listed at £16 13s 4d (*Taxatio* 122b). St Gregory's, which had been an important church, probably of secular canons, before the Conquest, again became a collegiate foundation of Simon of Sudbury, bp of London and future archbp of Canterbury, in February 1375 (*MRH* 440).

111. Nuneaton Priory

Grant to the nuns, in the same general terms as no. 110, of a perpetual annual benefice of ten marks in the church of St Gregory with the chapel of St Peter, Sudbury, to be paid in pennies and halfpennies within the octave of Easter; reserving to the bishop the right of making further provision for the nuns in this church or elsewhere. They shall, after the death or resignation of master Joceus de Monstrato, present a persona *at the bishop's nomination, or otherwise he will after a month collate the church. Payment to the nuns shall be made by whomsoever receives the tithes of the church. Excommunication is pronounced against any who may infringe this ordinance.*   Hevingham, 25 June 1252

> A = BL ms. Add. ch. 47960. Endorsed: Sudbir', confirmatio episcopi Norwyc' super pensione ibidem, iiiᵃ, extra (s. xiii); approx. 197 × 130 + 20 mm; two parchment tags, on the left fawn cloth seal-bag.
> B = BL ms. Add. ch. 47963 (*inspeximus* by bp Roger Longespee of Coventry and Lichfield, 21 July 1266).

Omnibus sancte matris ecclesie filiis presens scriptum visuris vel audituris Walterus miseratione divina Norwicensis episcopus salutem eternam in Domino. Inter ceteras Ierusalem filias circumquaque diffusas, illas nos decet studiosius et sollicitius honorare que in honore gloriose virginis Marie sunt constricte. Cum igitur dilecte in Cristo filie priorissa et moniales de Eton ecclesiam sancti Gregorii de Subir' cum capella sancti Petri ad eam pertinente, que de ipsarum est advocatione, nostre omnino subiecerint voluntati, nos paupertatem ipsarum attendentes et precipue defectum quem in vestimentis patiuntur, decem marcas annuas de bona et legali moneta, videlicet in denariis et obolis, de bonis dicte ecclesie nomine perpetui beneficii de consensu capituli nostri dictis monialibus caritative concessimus, a rectore eiusdem ecclesie qui pro tempore fuerit in octabe Pasche apud Subir' integre percipiendas, ita quod si rector cessaverit aliquotiens in solutione dicte pecunie per octo dies post prefatum terminum, ipso iure cadat a possessione ecclesie memorate; reservata nobis potestate uberius providendi dictis monialibus in eadem ecclesia vel in alia ubicumque voluerimus et eandem ecclesiam liberandi. Decedente vero vel cedente magistro Iocio de Monstrato nunc rectore eiusdem ecclesie, quem ad presentationem dictarum monialium ad eam admisimus, nominabimus dictis monialibus aliam personam idoneam quam voluerimus, quem ipse nobis infra mensam postquam de nominatione nostra eis constiterit per litteras suas patentes ad eandem ecclesiam presentabunt; quod si facere noluerint, nos nichilominus supradictam ecclesiam illa vice cui voluerimus conferemus, et illud in qualibet vacatione eiusdem ecclesie tam erga nos quam successores nostros inperpetuum observabitur. Et est sciendum quod solutio prefate prestationis sequetur perceptionem decimarum ante perceptarum, unde quicumque fructus habuerit de decem marcis in octabe Pasche post perceptionem fructuum satisfaciet. Quicumque contra hanc nostram ordinationem venerit, et excommunicationem et Dei maledictionem incurrat. In cuius rei testimonium huic scripto sigillum nostrum unacum sigillo capituli nostri apponi fecimus. Hiis testibus: magistro R. de Insula archidiacono Colecestr', Thoma de Theye capellano, Willelmo de Pakeham, Willelmo de Whitewell', Thoma de Walkot', Willelmo de Ludham et aliis. Dat' apud Hevingham .vii. kalendas Iulii anno gratie millesimo ducentesimo quinquagesimo secundo.

112. Amauri de Pecche

Concession, with the consent of the canons of [Great] Bricett, to Amauri de Pecche and his wife, the daughter of the late Ralph [fitz] Brien, of the right to have a chantry in the chapel at their house at Bricett. The chaplain who is to minister there, on the day of his arrival, shall in the presence of the prior or his proctor swear on the holy gospels that he will render in full to the mother church all manner of oblations and obventions, on the day he might receive them or the day following, and that he will not admit any parishioner of the mother church to confession or to any other sacrament, unless death is imminent. The chapel shall be subject to the mother church, in token whereof Amauri, his wife and his heirs shall, if resident, go with their household to pray at the mother church at Christmas, Easter, Pentecost, the Assumption of the Blessed Virgin Mary and the feast of St Leonard, and shall offer the customary oblations at high mass.

Sentence of excommunication is promulgated against any who may seek to undermine or evade the terms of this concession. Hoxne, 21 July 1250

A = King's College, Cambridge, GBR 37. Endorsed: Almar' Pech' (s. xv); approx. 185 × 78 + 18 mm.; parchment tag, fragment of seal, red wax, counterseal.

Pd in *Mon. Angl.* vi 175, no. 6.

Omnibus Cristi fidelibus presentes literas visuris vel audituris Walterus Dei gratia Norwicensis episcopus salutem in Domino sempiternam. Noveritis nos, voluntate et assensu prioris et conventus de Brisete, dilecto filio Almarico Peche et uxori sue, filie et heredi quondam Radulfi Brien, et eorum heredibus cantariam in capella infra septa curie eorum de Brisete constructa concessisse sub hac forma: videlicet quod capellanus in eadem ministraturus in primo suo adventu, presente priore vel suo procuratore, iurabit inspectis sacrosanctis ewangeliis quod omnes oblationes et obventiones undecumque eidem capelle obvenientes matrici ecclesie, eadem die qua percipiuntur vel proxime sequenti, integre et absque diminutione restituet, et quod nullum parochianum matricis ecclesie ad confessionem vel aliquod alium ecclesiasticum sacramentum admittet, nisi periculum mortis immineret. Erit siquidem prefata capella matrici ecclesie subiecta, et in signum subiectionis prefatus Almaricus, uxor eius et eorum heredes, una cum eorum familia, ad matricem ecclesiam diebus infrascriptis, scilicet die Natalis Domini, die Pasche, die Pentecostes, die Assumptionis gloriose virginis et die sancti Leonardi, cum debitis et consuetis oblationibus ad magnam missam, si ibidem fuerint, prefatam ecclesiam veneraturi [sunt]. Nos autem omnes illos qui aliquid in huiusmodi nostre concessionis preiudicium sive fraudem machinaverint sive fieri procuraverint sententia excommunicationis innodamus. In cuius rei testimonium huic scripto sigillum nostrum apponi fecimus. Dat' apud Hoxum .xii. kalendas Augusti pontificatus nostri anno sexto.

Amauri de Pecche was an adherent of the king throughout the troubles of the 1250s and 1260s. On 30 August 1247 he was granted an escheat in the king's hands at Honing (Nf.) to maintain himself in the king's service (*Cl R 1242–47* 533). On 8 May 1254 he was amongst those granted letters of protection on going with the king and queen to Gascony (*CPR 1247–58* 376). On 1 November 1254 he and Herbert his brother were knighted with the lord Edward by king Alphonso of Castile (*Cl R 1253–54* 271). In October 1255 he was granted the marriage of Cecily, widow of Richard of Wortham (*CPR 1247–58* 428). In September 1265 he was appointed as one of two commissioners in Cambridgeshire and Huntingdonshire to take the lands of the rebels into the king's hands (*CPR 1258–65* 490); as sheriff of those counties, he was initially impeded from the collection of royal dues by the activities of the rebels entrenched in the Isle of Ely *(Cl. R. 1268–72* 19–20).

113. Pentney Priory

Concession to the canons, made with the consent of the patron and rector of Ashwicken church, that they may have an oratory in their house at 'Wlveleye' where divine service may be celebrated when they come there, or others by chance come. All oblations and offerings made by any person shall within three

*days be rendered to the mother church, to which the oratory shall be subject in
all things; no sacrament shall be administered there to any person, nor shall it
have any characteristic of a mother church. Servants staying there shall on
feastdays go to the mother church and just like other parishioners pay their
oblations and offerings, except on days when the prior or other members of the
convent happen to be there, when oblations and offerings made by the servants
or others shall be rendered within three days to the mother church; and even
then on such days as parishioners customarily go with their oblations to the
mother church, then they too should go there in person with the others.*

Gaywood, 11 March 1247

A = Dublin, Trinity College ms. 1208/374 (= 108 dated 1 bis). Endorsed: de capella Wlveleie
(s. xiii); approx. 161 × 80 + 13 mm.; parchment tag, seal, white wax, counterseal.

Omnibus Cristi fidelibus presens scriptum visuris vel audituris Walterus Dei
gratia Norwicensis episcopus salutem in Domino sempiternam. Noverit
universitas vestra nos de consensu patroni et rectoris ecclesie de Wicune
concessisse priori et conventui de Panten' oratorium in curia sua de Wlveleye, in
quo eis licebit cum ibidem accesserint sibi et aliis casu venientibus divina
celebrare, ita tamen quod omnes oblationes et obventiones a quibuscumque [qui]
ibidem pervenerint matrici ecclesie infra triduum persolvantur; quod quidem
oratorium dicte matrici ecclesie in omnibus erit subiectum, nec in eo
ecclesiasticum aliquod cuiquam ministrabitur sacramentum, nec ullum habebit
idem oratorium matricis ecclesie insignium. Servientes vero ibidem moram
facientes ad matricem diebus festivis accedent sicut et alii parochiani oblationes
et obventiones debitas et consuetas ibidem oblaturi, exceptis diebus quibus
continget priorem vel aliquem de conventu ibidem interesse, et tunc oblationes
seu obventiones a dictis servientibus vel ab aliis ibidem oblate dicte matrici
ecclesie infra triduum similiter persolvantur, nisi illi dies tales fuerint quibus ex
debito vel consuetudine parochiani ad ipsam matricem ecclesiam cum
oblationibus teneantur accedere, et tunc ipsi unacum aliis ad matricem ecclesiam
personaliter accedant. In cuius rei testimonium presenti scripto sigillum nostrum
duximus apponendum. Dat' apud Geywode quinto Idus Martii pontificatus nostri
anno tertio.

This actum is among a small group of Pentney charters at Trinity College, Dublin,
supplementing the larger collection at TNA.

The *Taxatio* (96b) shows Pentney to hold rents and customs valued at 18s 11d at 'Wyken'
in Lynn deanery. *VN* (384) shows this to be Ashwicken, ESE of Lynn.

114. Pontigny Abbey

Inspeximus *with R[ichard Wich], bishop of Chichester, of a grant of fifty marks
a year from Romney church to Pontigny made by Stephen [Langton], archbishop
of Canterbury, in 1222; of a confirmation of this by prior John and the convent*

of Christ Church, Canterbury, 1222; of an augmentation of this pension by a further ten marks made by Edmund [of Abingdon], archbishop of Canterbury, in 1238; and of an inspeximus *of this last by prior N[icholas of Sandwich] and the convent of Christ Church, dated September 1245.*

[September 1245 × 3 April 1253]

A = Musée de Sens, Sens cathedral, Trésor muniments H. 26. No endorsement; 433 × 285 + 25 mm.; bp of Chichester's seal missing; parchment tag, bp of Norwich's seal, brown (natural) wax, counterseal.

Pd in *EEA* 22 no. 167; (calendar) *St Edmund of Abingdon*, 322; *St Richard of Chichester* 43.

The charters confirmed are printed in *Thesaurus NA* iii 1246–7; *Acta Stephani Langton* no. 55; and *Le Premier Cartulaire de l'Abbaye Cistercienne de Pontigny (xiie-xiiie siècles)*, ed. M. Garrigues (Paris, 1981), nos. 241–3.

Bp Richard of Chichester died on 2 or 3 April 1253 (*EEA* 22 xxxix).

115. Ramsey Abbey

Licence granted to the abbot that he may construct an oratory in his manor of Burwell, where he or his monks may celebrate divine office when they come there; given with the consent of the rector of Burwell and saving the right and indemnity of the parish church.   South Elmham, 29 September 1246

B = TNA, E164/28 (Ramsey cartulary) fo. 166v. s. xiv med.
Pd in *Ramsey Cartulary* ii no. 317.

Omnibus Cristi fidelibus has literas visuris vel audituris Walterus Dei gratia Norwicensis episcopus salutem in Domino. Attendentes religiosos, precipue cum divina debeant interesse officiis, a strepitu laicali penitus fore segregandos, quibus in ecclesiis parochialibus, populari multitudine multotiens concurrente, non minus tediose quam periculose intenderent, volentes singulorum honestati prospicere in quantum possumus, viro venerabili et discreto abbati de Rameseia construendi oratorium in manerio suo de Burewelle, nostre diocesis, in quo liceat sibi vel monacho suo cum ibidem venerint, ad opus suum et familie sue divina celebrare, rectoris ecclesie de Burewelle interveniente consensu, iure et indemnitate ecclesie prelibate salvis in omnibus, ex gratia speciali liberam concedimus facultatem. In cuius rei testimonium sigillum nostrum duximus apponendum. Dat' apud Suthelmgham tertio kalendas Octobris pontificatus nostri anno secundo.

Ramsey had a large estate at Burwell, valued in 1291 at £52 13s 4d (*Taxatio* 130). The rector is of St Mary's, a substantial benefice valued at £53 6s 8d, plus Ramsey's portion of £2, whereas the church of St Andrew was appropriated to Fordham priory (ibid. 121). In *EEA* 6, index p. 388, for Burwell, church (of St Andrew), read (of St Mary).

116. Rattlesden Church

Inspeximus *and confirmation of a charter of Hugh [of Northwold], bishop of Ely, confirming the agreement whereby Matthew de Louvain, knight, quitclaimed to Henry of Hilgay, rector of Rattlesden, eighteen acres of arable land there which Henry claimed for his church, and by a composition between them granted in perpetuity to Henry and his successors three acres of arable land for four acres of arable in the field called 'Rodescroft', and also seven acres of arable with appurtenances in Rattlesden for five acres of woodland, all free from secular service and suit of court, with warranty being granted. The bishop of Ely, as patron, has approved this agreement as being to the utility of the church. The bishop of Norwich confirms as diocesan.* Bacton, 20 May 1251

A = Ipswich, Suffolk R.O., HD1538/324/2, no. 184. Approx. 150 × 98 + 12 mm.; parchment tag, seal, natural wax varnished light brown, counterseal.

Universis Cristi fidelibus presentes litteras inspecturis Walterus Dei gratia Norwycensis episcopus salutem in Domino sempiternam. Inspeximus litteras venerabilis patris Hugonis Dei gratia Elyensis episcopi sub hac forma: Universis Cristi fidelibus presentes litteras inspecturis Hugo Dei gratia Elyensis episcopus salutem in Domino sempiternam. Cum dominus Matheus de Luvein miles pro se et heredibus suis quietas clamaverit Henrico de Helegeya rectori ecclesie de Ratlesden' decem et octo acras terre arabilis cum pertinentiis in Ratlesden' quas dictus Henricus vendicabat esse ius ecclesie sue predicte, et per compositionem quandam inter eos initam concesserit et dederit eidem Henrico et successoribus suis in dicta ecclesia tres acras terre arabilis pro quatuor acras terre arabilis iacentibus in campo qui vocatur Rodescroft, quas dictus Henricus a dicto Matheo petebat, necnon concesserit ac dederit in escambium eidem Henrico et successoribus suis et ecclesie prefate septem acras terre arabilis cum pertinentiis in Ratlesden pro quinque acris bosci quas dictus Henricus vendicabat esse ius ipsius ecclesie, ita quod tota terra predicta inperpetuum remaneat sibi et successoribus suis et ecclesie antedicte quieta et soluta ab omni seculari exactione et ab omni secta curie et demanda, et dictus dominus Matheus et heredes sui warantizabunt et defendent dictas tres acras terre pro quatuor antedictis acris per tactam compositionem datas et dictas septem acras pro quinque acris bosci concessas predicto Henrico et successoribus suis et ecclesie sue predicte contra omnes gentes inperpetuum, sicut in scripto inter eos confecto continetur. Nos, attendentes illud factum esse in utilitate sepedicte ecclesie, quod factum est in hac parte approbamus, ratum habemus et quantum ad patronum pertinet tenore presentium confirmamus. In cuius rei testimonium huic scripto sigillum nostrum fecimus apponi. Nos igitur, estimantes in hoc facto utilitatem predicte ecclesie esse procuratam, factum prescriptum quantum ad diocesanum pertinet approbamus et pontificali auctoritate qua fungimur confirmamus. Dat' apud Baketon' anno Domini M° CC° LI°, .xiii. kalendas Iunii.

Rattlesden, in Thedwestrey hundred, lay within the liberty of St Edmund, but the church of Ely held six carucates there from before 1066 (*DB* ii 381b), and the bp of Ely held very substantial liberties within the manor, and also the advowson (*Kalenda*r 5, 16). The Domesday endowment of the church was twenty-four acres (*DB* ii 381b), so the grant recorded above was a very substantial increase; in 1254 the church was valued at £16 13s 4d (*VN* 426). Matthew I de Louvain (d. 1261) was lord of Little Easton, Ess. (*English Baronies* 130), and presumably descendant of one of the six Domesday tenants of St Etheldreda in Rattlesden.

*117. Reading Abbey

Remission of twenty days enjoined penance to [visitors to or benefactors of] the abbey [at various feasts] throughout the year.

[19 February 1245 × 19 May 1257]

Mention of indulgence in a list of episcopal indulgences from the mid-twelfth to mid- thirteenth centuries (*Reading Abbey Cartularies* i no. 217 (p.178)).

The final section of this list, in which this indulgence is included, is headed *per totum annum*.

118. Repps Church

Inspeximus *and confirmation of the charter of William of Sparham whereby he granted to master William [Suffield], the rector, and his successors, two parcels of his land in the vill of Repps, in exchange for two parcels of the free land of the church there. Because this exchange was to the advantage of the church, he has confirmed it and, with the consent of the foresaid William and of Roger of Suffield, knights, patrons of the church, and of the rector, has also confirmed to that church two pence annual rent from Nicholas Dune and his heirs and two pence from Alexander de Aula and his heirs for two parcels of the free land of the church, to be paid at Michaelmas.* Terling, 24 October 1248

A = Norfolk R.O., ms. Phillips 290. No endorsement; approx. 173 × 110 + 14 mm.; tag and seal missing.

[Universis]ᵃ Cristi fidelibus ad quos presens scriptum pervenerit Walterus Dei gratia Norwicensis episcopus salutem in Domino sempiternam. Noverit universitas vestra nos cartam domini Willelmi de Sparham plenius inspexisse, qua dedit, concessit et confirmavit duas pecias terre sue in villa de Repps magistro Willelmo rectori eiusdem suisque successoribus, in excambium pro duabus peciis terre libere ecclesie memorate. Et quia perpendimus predictum excambium ad utilitatem ecclesie predicte fuisse factum, ratum habentes et gratum, illud de consensu predicti Willelmi et domini Rogeri de Sutfeld militum, prefate ecclesie patronorum, auctoritate pontificali duximus confirmandum, duos denarios annui redditus de Nicollao Dune et heredibus suis pro una pecia libere terre et duos denarios annui redditus ab Alexandro de Aula et heredibus suis pro una pecia libere terre ecclesie annuatim in festo sancti Michaelis solvendos de consensu dictorum rectoris et patronorum simili confirmatione ratificantes. In cuius rei testimonium presens scriptum sigillo nostro duximus muniendum. Hiis testibus: R. de Insula archidiacono Collecest', W. de Horham archidiacono Suffol', domino Ade de Wrhsted, Willelmo de Pakeham, Willelmo de Qwytewell, Thoma de Thya capellano, Willelmo de Ludham, Willelmo de Hakel' et Willelmo de Hindringham clericis, et aliis. Datum apud Therling' nono kalendas Novembris pontificatus nostri anno quarto.

ᵃ *corner torn away* A

In November 1247 there had been litigation, probably collusive, before the justices in eyre at Huntingdon between Roger Suffield (represented by William of Pakenham, the bp's clerk) and William Suffield, plaintiffs, and William of Sparham, defendant concerning 80 acres of land at Ashby, Oby, Bastwick and Repps, and a *placitum conventionis* was concluded by a final concord by which William of Sparham recognised the land to be the right of the Suffields by his gift (TNA, CP25/1/157/71/936). William Suffield, the bp's brother and archdn of Norwich, was the rector, who after the bp's death, as *patronus et persona*, granted the advowson to St Giles's hospital, to which the church was subsequently appropriated (186). The above transaction was part of a series which appear to have been designed to consolidate the revenues of Repps church before its projected transfer to the hospital.

119. St Albans Abbey

Notification to the abbot and convent that the bishop has received a mandate of pope Innocent [IV] addressed to himself and the bishop of Winchester, reminding them that he had previously written to them and to the bishops of Lincoln, Worcester, London and Coventry to the effect that, whereas recently before their return to England he had arranged with them that the subsidy of six thousand marks from the English church to the apostolic see should be apportioned between the bishoprics according to their determination, they should as soon as possible inform him by letters, to be entrusted to the bearer, of their actions in this matter, notifying him of the date and place of payment. If all of them could not be present for the execution of this business, then two or three at least should proceed. Now, because no report has reached him, he warns and commands them, on receipt of these letters, to order the other bishops by apostolic authority to meet with them on the twentieth day thereafter and to finalise the allocation. If none of them come, the two addressees shall themselves cause the forestated sum to be paid, within a month and at a place of their choosing, to themselves or their agents, according to the assessment formerly made by master Martin, clerk of the papal camera, which the pope now sends to them. They shall compel all contrariants by ecclesiastical censure without recourse to appeal, notwithstanding any indult or privilege or the constitution de duabus diebus issued in the general council. They shall without delay inform the pope of their actions by a transcript to be sent by Linasius, papal writer and bearer of these letters. If one of them cannot be present to execute this business, the other shall nevertheless proceed. By authority of this mandate, the bishop orders them by apostolic authority that they should pay their allocation of this subsidy, which is eighty marks, at the New Temple in London three weeks after Easter, showing such diligence that he may justifiably commend their devotion to the pope. He alone has written, since the bishop of Winchester has excused himself for a time. London, 24 March 1246

B = Corpus Christi College, Cambridge, ms. 16 (Matthew Paris's autograph), fo. 203v.
Pd from B in *Chron. Maj.* iv 555–7.

Walterus Dei gratia Norwicensis episcopus viris venerabilibus abbati et conventui sancti Albani salutem sempiternam. Mandatum domini pape in hec verba suscepimus: Innocentius episcopus, servus servorum Dei, venerabilibus fratribus Wintoniensi et Norwicensi episcopis salutem et apostolicam benedictionem. Olim, sicut bene meminimus, vobis et venerabilibus fratribus nostris Lincolniensi, Wigornensi, Londoniensi et Coventrensi episcopis scripsimus sub hac forma: cum nuper, priusquam a presentia nostra in Angliam rediretis, una vobiscum duxerimus ordinandum ut sex milium marcarum subsidium, quod ab ecclesiis Anglicanis pro apostolica sede fuerat postulatum, inter episcopatus Anglie dividere curaretis pro vestre arbitrio voluntatis, fraternitati vestre per apostolica scripta quatinus quicquid inde feceritis, vel iam forte fecistis, nobis per literas vestras latori presentium assignandas, exprimendo tempus solutionis et locum, studeatis quam citius intimare. Quod si non omnes hic exequendis poteritis interesse, saltem tres vel duo vestrum ea nichilominus exequantur. Quia hic nichil est postmodum nostris auribus intimatum, fraternitatem vestram, de qua fiduciam gerimus specialem, monemus attente ac per apostolica vobis scripta firmiter precipiendo mandamus quatinus episcopos memoratos, qui presentes fuerint in partibus Anglicanis, receptis istis literis, admonentes et eisdem auctoritate nostra mandantes ut vicesimo die post susceptionem presentium in certo loco, quem vos duxeritis eligendum, vobiscum pro divisione conveniant prelibata, cum illis episcopis quod eodem die ibidem contigerit convenire, distributionem huiusmodi priusquam ab illo loco recesseritis facere procuretis. Si vero ipsis aut nullo convenientibus eorum non fuerit super negotio prenominato processum, ex tunc infra unius mensis spatium prescriptam subsidii quantitatem faciatis vobis vel nuntiis vestris ad opus apostolice sedis in loco quem elegeritis assignari, iuxta ordinationem per dilectum filium nostrum magistrum Martinum, camere nostre clericum, auctoritate nostra in illis partibus quondam factam, quam ad presens sub bulla nostra vobis duximus destinandam; contradictores per censuram ecclesiasticam appellatione postposita compescendo, indulgentia quacumque vel privilegio quolibet aut constitutione de duabus diebus in generali concilio edita non obstante;[1] quicquid hactenus factum est vel fuerit in hac parte nobis absque more dispendio per dilectum filium Linasium scriptorem nostrum, latorem presentium, rescripturi; proviso quod super premissis illam sollicitudinem habeatis quod non possitis exinde de negligentia reprehendi, sed potius de diligentia commendari. Quod si non ambo his exequendis poteritis interesse, alter vestrum ea nichilominus exequatur. Huius igitur auctoritate mandati vestram in Domino monemus et exhortamur fraternitatem, vobis in virtute obedientie qua sedi apostolice tenemini firmiter iniungentes, quatinus de portione prefati domini pape subsidii vobis assignata nuntiis nostris literas nostras patentes super solutione eiusdem deferentibus apud Novum Templum Londoniarum a die Pasche in tres septimanas satisfaciatis, talem in facto presenti adhibentes diligentiam ut devotionem vestram summo pontifici merito debeamus commendare. Est autem portio vestra octaginta marcarum esterlingorum. Valete semper in Domino. Datum Londoniis nono kalendas Aprilis anno Domini M° CC° XL° V. Nos soli scribimus, quia venerabilis frater Wintoniensis episcopus, collega noster, ad tempus se excusavit.

[1]IV Lateran c. 37.

For other mss of the *Chronica Maiora*, see *Chron. Maj.* i pp. xi-xiii, and R. Vaughan, *Matthew Paris* (Cambridge 1958) 30–1, 50–9.

    Mr Martin, clerk of the papal camera, had arrived in England at Easter 1244, to act as papal collector and with instructions to seek a new subsidy from the English church. This matter he first broached at a great council in November. The prelates there postponed an answer until 23 February 1245, when they again declined to respond to the demand. Meeting again during Lent, they were forbidden by the king to grant any subsidy to pope or archbp until they had agreed to the request for a subsidy to the crown. Probably also during Lent a protest against papal exactions was drawn up, to be delivered by the royal delegation to the forthcoming general council at Lyons, summoned for 24 June 1245. Before the envoys' departure in early June, the king prohibited payment of any subsidy until their return, and in July mr Martin left England. Pope Innocent IV placed pressure on the English bishops at the council, and the group of six named above agreed to undertake assessment and collection of a subsidy. The king, however, was displeased by the pope's failure to respond to the complaints of the English delegation, and in Lent 1246 consulted the great council. A new statement of grievances was formulated and despatched to the *curia*, and the collection of the proposed papal subsidy was again deferred. In the meantime pope Innocent had sent the above unregistered letter (which in Matthew Paris's copy, and presumably in bp Suffield's letter, is undated). The bishops began to put the papal instructions into operation just as the great council was deliberating, and the king forbade the clergy to pay the subsidy or the bishops to collect it, which led to a protest by bp Grosseteste of Lincoln. The royal envoys returned from the *curia* and reported to a parliament on 7 July, and the king once more ordered that no subsidy should be paid. Some prelates, spurred by a subsequent papal mandate that the subsidy must be paid by 15 August, remonstrated with the king who, faced by the threat of interdict on the kingdom, finally relaxed his prohibition, so that the subsidy first sought in 1244 was eventually levied late in 1246. The bps apparently used the apportionment of taxation determined by mr Martin in 1244, and the 6000 marks probably represents one twentieth based on the valuation of 1217 or of 1229 (*VN* 31–6; Lunt, *Financial Relations* 206–19, esp. 217–9; *C & S* II i 388–9).

120. St Neots Priory

Notification that, when there was conflict between the monks and master Adam of Bromholm, the rector, over an annual payment, known as a perpetual benefice, of three and a half marks from the church of Heveningham, alleged by the monks to have been conceded by bishop Thomas [Blundeville] and confirmed by his chapter, but claimed by the rector to have been recently imposed contrary of the decrees of the general council [III Lateran c. 7], after much dispute the parties submitted the matter to the bishop's ordinance. He, having examined the evidence and taken advice from learned men, decreed that this payment should cease, but the monks should have twelve acres of the free fee of the church of Heveningham, free from all exaction and payment of tithe, and these twelve acres should in perpetuity be the free fee of the church of Ubbeston, to which church tithes should be rendered. The monks should still receive the annual pension of twenty shillings long due to them from Heveningham church. The twelve acres, in thirteen parcels, are listed and described. This settlement was agreed by the monks, master Adam of Bromholm, then rector, and Robert of Weston, the present rector, who together with the bishop and his chapter appended their seals. [19 February 1245 × 19 May 1257]

B = BL ms Cotton Faust. A iv (St Neot's cartulary) fos 127r–128r. s. xiii med.

Omnibus sancte matris ecclesie filiis ad quos presentes litere pervenerint Walterus Dei gratia Norwicensis episcopus salutem in Domino. Noveritis quod cum contentio esset inter priorem et conventum de sancto Neoto ex una parte et magistrum Adam de Bromholm rectorem ecclesie de Hevenigham ex altera super annua prestatione nomine perpetui beneficii trium marcarum et dimidie ab ecclesia de Hevenigham per manum rectoris eiusdem ecclesie priori et conventui solvenda, sibi ut dicebant a bone memorie predecessore nostro Thoma de Blonvill' Norwicensi episcopo collata et consensu capituli eiusdem confirmata, dicto magistro A. dictam annuam prestationem contra generalis statuta concilii de novo impositam asserente, et post multas altercationes dicte partes dictam contentionem ordinationi nostre realiter et perpetuo valiture, impetratis et impetrandis specialiter renuntiando, totaliter et se absolute submiserunt. Nos vero, auditis huiusmodi propositis tam instrumentis dicti Thome predecessoris nostri quam capituli eiusdem inspectis, necnon rationibus alterius [fo . 127v] partis intellectis, de permissione divina realiter et perpetuo sciti de prudentium consilio, duximus ordinandum, videlicet quod, cessante prestatione dictarum trium [marcarum] et dimidie, perpetuo supradicti prior et conventus habebunt duodecim acras terre de libero feodo ecclesie de Hevenigham ab omni exactione quietas et a solutione decimarum solutas, et a rectore qui pro tempore fuerit contra omnes warantizandas; quas duodecim acras terre ecclesie de Hubeston' liberum feodum perpetuo esse et iure parochiali ipsas decimas eidem ecclesie solvi deberi decernimus, salva nichilominus eisdem priori et conventui in eadem ecclesia de Heveningham annua prestatione viginti solidorum ab antiquo eis debita. Et iacent dicte duodecim acre terre in parochia de Hevenigham in tredecim peciis, quarum una pecia iacet inter terram Rogeri Dune ex una parte et terram Roberti filii Iohannis ex altera, et abutat unum capud super terram eiusdem Roberti et aliud capud super terram comitis; alia pecia iacet in eodem campo inter terras hospitalis sancti Iohannis de Dunewic', et abutat unum capud super terram prioris de Snapes et aliud capud super terram comitis; tertia pecia

iacet in eodem campo inter terram Rogeri Scarlet et terram Iohannis Regin', et
abutat unum capud super Stanstret' et aliud capud super terram dicti hospitalis;
quarta pecia iacet prope ecclesiam de Hevenigham inter terram Willelmi Malffe
et terram Willelmi fabri, et abutat unum capud super viam ecclesie et aliud capud
super terram Hugonis Hackesalt; quinta pecia iacet in eodem campo inter terram
Hugonis Hackesalt et viam, et abutat unum capud super viam ecclesie et aliud
capud super mesuagium Roberti clerici; sexta pecia iacet in eodem campo inter
terras Thome Garvoyse, et abutat unum capud super dictam viam et aliud capud
super terram Willelmi fabri; septima pecia est roda que iacet iuxta rodam prioris
de sancto Neoto, quarum utramque habet uxor quondam Roberti Prinne; octava
pecia iacet prope illam rodam inter terram Hugonis Hackesalt et Thome
Gargveyse, et abutat unum capud super viam ecclesie et aliud capud super
limitem parochie de Hevenigham et de Hubeston; nona pecia iacet in declivum
versus pratum inter terram vicarii de Ubeston' et terram Willelmi fabri, et abutat
unum capud super pratum et aliud capud super terram Hugonis Hackesalt;
decima pecia iacet iuxta molendinum de Hevenigham inter terram Willelmi Berr
et terram Hugonis famuli, et abutat unum capud super terram Eudonis de Vall' et
aliud capud super terram Willelmi Dick; undecima pecia iacet in eodem campo
inter terram Ricardi Umfrei et viam regiam, et abutat unum capud super aliam
viam et aliud capud super terram Walteri Chel; duodecima pecia iacet in Torper'
inter terram Willelmi fabri et Willelmi Chede, et abutat unum capud super
Carmedwe et aliud super terram Willelmi Berd; tredecima pecia iacet in Torper'
superius inter terram Willelmi Blanchard et terram abbatis et conventus de
Sibeton', et abutat unum capud super torrentem et aliud capud super terram
dictorum abbatis et conventus; de quibus tredecim se clamant pacatos prior et
conventus predicti pro duodecim acris terre. Et ut hec nostra ordinatio realiter et
perpetuo inter predictos priorem et conventum et dictum Adam tunc temporis
dicte ecclesie [fo. 128r] rectorem ac Robertum de Weston' eiusdem ecclesie
nunc rectorem, qui similiter in omnibus premissis huic nostre ordinationi se
sponte supposuit, necnon et quoslibet futuris temporibus predicte ecclesie
rectores, robur firmitatis optineat, huic scripto ordinationis nostre sigillum
nostrum unacum sigillo capituli nostri huic ordinationi prebentis assensum ac
sigillis predictorum Ade et Roberti nunc eiusdem ecclesie rectoris fecimus
apponi. Hiis testibus etc.

For the grant of a perpetual benefice by bp Blundeville, see *EEA* 21 no. 104. The ancient
pension of 20s from Heveningham is recorded in 1254 and 1291 (*VN* 445; *Taxatio* 118b).

121. Simon of Shouldham

*Concession to the lord Simon of Shouldham and his heirs that he may have a free
chantry in his chapel at Marham, with the consent of the prior and convent of
West Acre, patrons and rectors of the churches of Marham, and of the vicar. The*

*chaplain who is to minister there, on the day of his arrival, shall in the presence
of the cellarer of West Acre or his proctor swear on the holy gospels that he will
render in full to the mother church all manner of oblations and obventions, on
the day he might receive them or the day following, and that he will not wittingly
admit any parishioner of the mother church to confession or to any other
sacrament, unless death is imminent. The chapel shall be subject to the mother
church, in token of which Simon and his heirs shall, unless prevented by
infirmity, go with their household to pray at the mother church at Christmas,
Easter, the Assumption of the Blessed Virgin Mary and the dedication of the
church, and shall offer the customary oblations at high mass. Simon has also
granted to the canons of West Acre twelve pence a year, to be received from
Walter son of Huelina and Richard his brother.*   Shouldham, 27 August 1252

> B = Norfolk R.O., Reg. 5/10 (register of bp Brouns) fo. 93r (confirmation by bp Thomas
> Brouns, 24 August 1442, of *inspeximus* and confirmation by bp Anthony Bek, 2
> December 1338). s. xv med.

Omnibus Cristi fidelibus presentes litteras visuris vel audituris Walterus Dei
gratia Norwicensis episcopus salutem in Domino sempiternam. Noverit
universitas vestra nos, de consensu prioris et conventus de Westacra patronorum
et rectorum ecclesiarum de Marham et vicarii earundem, domino Simoni de
Shouldham et heredibus suis, ad opus suum et familie sue, liberam cantariam in
capella sua de Marham concessisse sub hac formula, videlicet quod capellanus in
eadem ministraturus in primo suo adventu, in presentia celerarii de Westacre vel
alicuius ex parte sua deputati, inspectis sacris ewangeliis iurabit quod omnes
oblationes et obventiones undecumque obvenientes matrici ecclesie eadem die
qua percipiuntur vel proxima sequenti integre et absque diminutione restituet, et
quod nullum parochianum predicte matricis ecclesie ad confessionem seu
aliquod alium sacramentum ecclesiasticum scienter admittat, nisi periculum
mortis immineret.ᵃ Erit siquidem prefata capella matrici ecclesie subiecta, et in
signum subiectionis predictus Simon et heredes sui cum familia sua ad matricem
ecclesiam accedent diebus infrascriptis, nisi corporalis infirmitas, impotentia vel
debilitas ipsos reddiderint excusatos, videlicet die Natalis Domini, die Pasche,
die Assumptionis beate Marie et festivitatis ecclesie, cum debitis et consuetis
oblationibus ad magnam missam prefatam ecclesiam veneraturi. Insuper
predictus Simon concessit predictis priori et conventui duodecim denarios
annuatim redditus percipiendos de Waltero filio Huline et Ricardo fratre suo de
Marham. In cuius rei testimonium huic scripto sigillum nostrum apponi fecimus.
Dat' apud Schouldham .viᵒ. kalendas Septembris pontificatus nostri anno octavo.

ᵃ minieret B

For Shouldham's manor, about a mile SE of Shouldham and straddling the boundary with
Marham, see Blomefield, *Norfolk* 7 416–7. Two-thirds of the demesne tithe was held by Castle
Acre priory.

*122. Sibton Abbey

Appropriation to the monks of the church of Rendham and establishment of their revenues therefrom, valued at £13 6s 8d. The monks shall have all the tithe of grain, beans and peas, all the hay from the demesne of the church without payment of tithe, half the hay of the whole parish, the messuage at the site of the church and half its free land, free from all episcopal and archidiaconal dues. They shall present a suitable persona to the church.

[19 February 1245 × 19 May 1257]

Mention of actum in BL Add. ms. 34560 (extent of the abbey's estates). fo. 19r. s. xiv in.

Abbas de Sybton tenet ecclesiam de Rendham ex appropriatione dominorum Walteri et Simonis episcoporum Norwic', taxatam 13 1. 6s 8d; et taxata est talis, videlicet quod iidem abbas et conventus habebunt omnem decimam bladi eiusdem ville, fabarum et pisarum, totum fenum de dominico ipsius ecclesie absque decimatione, et medietatem feni totius parochie cum mesuagio in fundo ecclesie et cum medietate libere terre spectantis ecclesie, libera absque omni onere tam episcopali quam archidiaconali; et ad hanc vicariam predicti abbas et conventus personam idoneam presentabunt.

In 1211–12 Elias of Rendham won seisin of the advowson against Matilda, his niece, but in November 1239 Tristram, Elias's son, quitclaimed the *ius patronatus* to Herbert de Alençon, who shortly afterwards granted it to Sibton for the spiritual welfare of himself, his wife and Elias, specifically for the lodging of guests and the maintenance of the hospital and gate (*Sibton Charters* i, 29, 88, 136; ii, no. 29 (i) f). The appropriation by bp Walter, and subsequently by bp Simon (192) is noted in an early fourteenth-century extent of the abbey's lands. The appropriation was confirmed on 28 May 1268 by the papal legate Ottobuono (*Sibton Charters* iv 55–6, no. 1005 (vi)). In 1254 and 1291 the church was valued at £10 13s 4d, and in the former valuation a vicarage assessed at 15s (*VN* 443; *Taxatio* 119b). Written evidence of the appropriation was produced at episcopal visitations from the mid fourteenth to early fifteenth centuries (*Sibton Charters* iv 101–2, nos. 1168–72).

123. Sibton Abbey

Notification that when controversy arose between the monks and Robert of Darnford because of the violence done to the abbot and the damage to lands and possessions inflicted by Robert, the bishop eventually made peace between them on these terms: that Robert quitclaimed and confirmed by charter all disputed lands and possessions, and also all tenements which the monks hold of his fee and all grants made to them by his ancestors, as more fully detailed in their charters and Robert's own confirmation charter. Robert submitted himself and his heirs to the bishop for the time being and his official, by whom they might be coerced by sentence of interdict and excommunication into observance of this agreement and confirmation, and if he or his heirs should henceforth disturb or molest the monks in contravention of this agreement, they may be punished by any legitimate penalty which their misconduct may merit.

South Elmham, 31 March 1245

B = BL ms. Arundel 221 (Sibton abbey cartulary) fos. 87v–88r. s. xiii ex.
Pd in *Sibton Charters* ii no. 258.

[O]mnibus Cristi fidelibus presens scriptum visuris vel audituris Walterus Dei gratia Norwicensis episcopus salutem et benedictionem. Noverit universitas vestra quod cum inter abbatem et conventum de Sybetun' et Robertum de Derneford' super violentia eidem abbati necnon et super iniuriis et dampnis tam in terris quam possessionibus et rebus aliis prefatis abbati et conventui a dicto Roberto illatis esset suborta contentio, nos qui universorum pacem et quietam desideramus Dei interveniente adiutorio eos ad pacem sub hac forma reduximus et concordiam, videlicet quod dictus Robertus omnes terras et possessiones de quibus inter eos erat contentio predictis abbati et conventui quietas clamavit et per cartam suam confirmavit, [fo. 88r] et insuper omnia tenementa que ipsi monachi tenent de feodo suo et omnes concessiones et donationes ab antecessoribus suis ipsis monachis factas, secundum quod plenius tam in cartis antecessorum quas idem monachi habent quam in carta confirmationis eiusdem Roberti ipsis facte continetur. Ad hec autem subiecit se et heredes suos sepedictus Robertus potestati nostre et episcopi Norwicensis qui pro tempore fuerit et eius officialis, et per presentem scripturam obligavit ut possit ipsum et heredes suos de plano ad dicte conventionis et confirmationis observationem per interdicti et excommunicationis sententias compellere. Si contigerit ipsum Robertum vel heredes suos in aliquo sepedictos abbatem et conventum contra conventionis et confirmationis sue tenorem de cetero inquietare, molestare vel gravare, nichilominus aliqua pena legitima, si protervitate[a] delinquerit, quod absit, meruerit mulctari. In cuius rei testimonium presens scriptum sigillum nostrum est appensum. Dat' apud Suthelmam .ii. kalendas Aprilis pontificatus nostri anno primo.

[a] protervitas B

For the Darnford family of Foxhall, where they were tenants of the Pecche family, see *Sibton Charters* i 47; for Robert's confirmation charter, ibid ii nos. 255–6.

124. Sibton Abbey

Inspeximus of the charters of the bishop's predecessors William [Turbe], John [of Oxford] and Thomas concerning the church of St Peter, Sibton, and the chapel of St Michael, Peasenhall [EEA 6 nos. 139, 282; EEA 21 nos. 105–6], by which it is evident that the church and chapel were granted and confirmed to the monks in proprios usus for hospitality and the support of the poor. These he confirms, saving the perpetual vicarage taxed by bishop Thomas. The vicar shall receive all the tithes and oblations of the church and chapel, with the exception of the tithes of sheaves and vegetables, which he has confirmed to the monks.

Hoxne, 26 August 1246

B = Ipswich, Suffolk R.O., ms. HD 1538/345, no. 12 of original documents in bound volume
(*inspeximus* by the official of bp of Norwich, 3 November 1434). s. xv med.
Pd in *Sibton Charters* iv no. 1005 (v).

Omnibus Cristi fidelibus ad quos presens scriptum pervenerit Walterus Dei gratia
Norwicensis episcopus salutem in Domino. Inspeximus bone memorie Willelmi,
Iohannis et Thome predecessorum nostrorum Norwicensium episcoporum cartas
dilectis filiis nostris monachis de Sibetun Cisterciensis ordinis super parochiali
ecclesia sancti Petri de Sibetun et capella beati Michaelis de Pesehal' indultas,
per quas nobis constat dictam ecclesiam cum capella predictis monachis ad
hospitalitatem et sustentationem pauperum Cristi ibidem confluentium in
proprios usus fuisse concessam et confirmatam. Nos autem, pie religionis affectu
circa memoratos monachos favorem propensius exequentes ac predecessorum
nostrorum concessiones et confirmationes ratas habentes et acceptas,
suprascriptam ecclesiam sancti Petri cum capella beati Michaelis et cum omnibus
ad eam pertinentibus sepedictis monachis confirmavimus, salva perpetua vicaria
in eadem ecclesia cum capella per bone memorie Thomam predecessorem
nostrum taxata, cuius estimationem et taxationem presentibus literis duximus
inserendam, videlicet ut vicarius qui pro tempore fuerit omnes decimas et
obventiones prefate ecclesie et capelle nomine vicarie percipiet, preter decimas
garbarum et leguminum,[a] quas predictis monachis in usus proprios ut dictum est
auctoritate pontificali confirmavimus. In cuius rei testimonium presentes literas
fieri fecimus et sigillo nostro muniri. Dat' apud Hoxon' .vii. kalendas Septembris
anno Domini millesimo ducentesimo quadragesimo sexto pontificatus nostri
anno secundo.

[a] ac silvarum *added as interlineation in slightly later hand, but interlineation is not noted in the
notary's eschatocol.*

In 1254 the church was valued at £2 13s 4d, and in 1291 at £4; the portions of Horsham St Faith
and Rumburgh were assessed at £1 and £1 6s 8d in 1254, £1 4s and 13s 4d in 1291; Peasenhall
was separately valued at £4, and later at £4 13s 4d (*VN* 445–6; *Taxatio* 118b).

125. Master Lawrence of Somercotes

*Notification, with J[ohn Climping], bishop of Chichester, and R[ichard de
Crokesle], abbot of Westminster, that with the consent of R[ichard], earl of
Cornwall, and other royal councillors they have agreed with master Lawrence,
whom they are sending to Ireland for the furtherance of the business of the Cross
and for the collection of a tenth of ecclesiastical revenues, that he should from
the feast of St Mary Magdalene [22 July] 1254 receive £100 per annum from the
proceeds for the expenses of himself, his clerks and his* familia, *to be paid to him
by his colleagues in the same business, or if one of them dies, by the survivor. He
shall receive this allowance for as long as he is engaged on this business, or
until the commission which they have issued to him is revoked. If he should
himself die, a due proportion of the allowance should be paid to his executors for*

the time up to his death. He has taken an oath to fulfil diligently this task and to render a true account.   [*c.* 22 July 1254]

B = TNA, C54/67 (Close Rolls 38 Henry III) m. 5d. s. xiii med.
Pd in *Cl. R. 1253–54* 146; *EEA* 23 no. 226.

For discussion, see no. 84. For royal ratification of the appointment and allowance, see *Cl. R. 1253–54* 92–3.

126. Stafford, Deanery of Christianity

Mandate, issued as executor of the business of the cross appointed by the apostolic see, to the dean of Christianity and those of the chapter under oath, that whereas he had recently received a sworn undertaking from the dean and other trustworthy men of his deanery who had been summoned that they would faithfully investigate the true value of all ecclesiastical benefices, they should now, in obedience to the apostolic see and being aware of the penalties for perjury, make a full enquiry, employing their own knowledge and that of the rectors, vicars and other appropriate persons, as to a realistic estimate of all greater and lesser ecclesiastical revenues within the deanery, by whomsoever they are held, exempt or non-exempt, including an estimate of separated tithes, that is, of tithes, pensions and other revenues held within parishes by special right. These estimates should be despatched in the form of sealed letters patent to the bishop. The goods of religious, however, which do not pertain to their appropriated churches nor are separated tithes, will be assessed by the religious themselves, if their house lies within the deanery; but if the house lies beyond the deanery, then its goods should be assessed by the dean and his associates, but should be clearly distinguished in their return. They are given power to compel all within the deanery to swear to the truth of the information given and to compel those who refuse by sentence of interdict or excommunication. They should themselves be diligent and truthful, notwithstanding any previous assessments, and should be mindful of their salvation and careful that they should not subsequently be found to have merited the sentence of excommunication promulgated against those who wittingly commit fraud in this matter or who refuse to pay. Anyone whose church is farmed should answer for the tenth according to the farm which he receives, as long as this seems just to the assessors. This task is imposed upon them for the remission of their sins, and by apostolic authority they shall be participants in the relaxation of penance granted to all those giving aid to the Holy Land. Their estimates shall be sent under seal to the bishop or his proctor at Lichfield.   [Summer – Autumn 1254]

B = BL ms. Cotton Vesp. E iii (Burton chronicle) fo. 46v. s. xiii ex.
Pd from B in *Ann. mon.* i 325–6.

Walterus permissione divina Norwicensis episcopus, negotii crucis executor a sede apostolica deputatus, discretis viris decano Cristianitatis de Stafford et

iuratis de capitulo salutem in Domino. Cum nuper, convocatis vobis et aliis de
decanatu vestro viris fidedignis, sacramentum a vobis receperimus quod, prout
vobis inferius iniungetur, iustas estimationes omnium ecclesiasticorum
beneficiorum fideliter inquiretis, vobis in virtute obedientie qua sedi apostolice
tenemini et sub religione sacramenti ac pena periurii iniungimus quatenus, tam a
vestris conscientiis propriis quam rectoribus, vicariis et aliis quibuscumque
personis magis videritis expedire, plenius inquiratis veritatem que sit iusta
estimatio omnium proventuum ecclesiasticorum, tam maiorum quam minorum,
cuiuscumque sint, exemptorum vel non exemptorum, in decanatu vestro
existentium, et que estimatio decimarum separatarum, videlicet si quas decimas,
pensiones vel alios proventus percipiant et habeant in parochiis ecclesiarum iure
speciali, sive aliquis nomine eorum eas teneat. Predictas siquidem iustas
estimationes in scriptis fideliter sub pena antedicta redigatis et per literam
patentem signis vestris signatam nobis habere faciatis ad terminum et locum
vobis infra prefigendos. Bona autem religiosorum que non pertinent ad ecclesias
eis appropriatas nec sunt decime separate per ipsos religiosos taxabuntur, si
abbatia vel cella seu prioratus ad quos huiusmodi bona pertinent in vestro fuerint
decanatu. Si vero in vestro decanatu non existant, bona ipsorum per vos
taxabuntur, et eorum taxationem nobis dilucide et aperte in scriptis habere
faciatis. Damus siquidem vobis omnibus et singulis plenam potestatem
compellendi ad iurandum omnes et singulos de decanatu vestro pro veritate vobis
in hac parte manifestanda, prout melius videritis expedire; contradictores et
rebelles, si quos in officio vestro inveneritis, per interdicti aut
excommunicationis sententias, nostra freti auctoritate, compescendo. Consulimus
insuper ad vestram salutem et communem liberationem quod in taxationibus
faciendis sic diligentes [et] veraces sollicitudine et facto vos habeatis, non
obstantibus aliquibus taxationibus prehabitis, ne ex post facto alii facta vestra et
dicta scrutantes vos inveniant a via veritatis manifeste declinasse et in sententiam
excommunicationis incidisse, que per sedem apostolicam in omnes illos qui
scienter in dicta decima subtrahenda vel non solvenda fraudem commiserint
promulgari demandatur. Volumus etiam, si iustum vobis visum fueri, quod
unusquisque cuius ecclesia tenetur ad firmam iuxta quantitatem firme quam
recepit respondeat de decima, dum sua voluntate et communi pactione ipsa firma
durabit. Hoc siquidem officium vobis in remissione peccatorum iniungimus,
concedentes vobis auctoritate sedis apostolice ut relaxationis indulte omnibus
terre sancte subvenientibus participes efficiamini in Domino. Predictas autem
estimationes in scriptis fideliter redactas nobis vel certo nuntio nostro sigillis
vestris signatas tali die apud Lichefeld habere faciatis.

The collectors published their commission in London on 4 July 1254 (63A), and the king had
hoped for collection of the first year's tenth by Michaelmas (29 September); but the mandate to
Canons Ashby priory (16) was not delivered until 11 November 1254. For other similar letters
see nos. 8, 34, 126. See also intro. p. lviii.

127. Stoke by Clare Priory

Ordination for the monks, in consideration of their merciful works in the provision of hospitality and aid for the poor flocking to their house, and upon the resignation of the pension of ten shillings in the church of Rede granted by his predecessors, of a perpetual benefice therein of fifty shillings, to be rendered annually by the rector at the two Ipswich synods. When the present rector dies or resigns, they shall have the church in proprios usus, *saving a vicarage to be taxed by the bishop or his successors.*   Sibton, 11 April 1245

> B = BL ms. Cotton Appx. xxi (Stoke by Clare cartulary) fo. 45r–v. s. xiii ex. C = ibid. fo. 45v
> (*inspeximus* by prior Simon of Elmham (1235–57) and the convent of Norwich).
> Pd from B and C in *Stoke by Clare Cartulary* i no. 93.

Omnibus Cristi fidelibus ad quos presens scriptum pervenerit Walterus Dei gratia Norwicensis episcopus salutem eternam in Domino. Etsi omnium religiosorum episcopali pululemus dilectione, illos tamen maiori tenemur prosequi beneficio qui in nostra diocesi constituti hospitalitatis causa se ipsos eviscerant et depauperant. Cum igitur dilecti filii prior et conventus de Stok' operibus misericordie intendentes hospitalitatis gratia cunctis se insignes reddent et pauperibus undique ad eos confluentibus congrua subsidia administrent, nos, illis decem solidos annuos quos nomine pencionis ex collatione predecessorum nostrorum in ecclesia de Rede optinebant in manus nostras resignantibus et se super eandem ecclesiam in omnibus voluntati nostre committentibus, volentes eis gratiam facere specialem, quinquaginta solidos in eadem ecclesia nomine perpetui beneficii annuatim concessimus ad duos synodos de Gypiswic'[a] a rectore eiusdem per-[fo. 45v]cipiendos, ita quod decedente vel recedente nunc rectore eiusdem ecclesie, ipsa ecclesia cedat eis in proprios usus, salva vicaria per nos vel successores nostros taxanda. Datum apud Sybeton'[b] .iii. Idus Aprilis pontificatus nostri anno primo.

> [a] Gyppiswic' C   [b] Sybetun' C

> The pension of 10s from the church had been granted by bp John of Oxford (*EEA* 6 nos. 285, 290). For the history of the church, see *Stoke by Clare Cartulary* iii 27. In 1254 it was valued at £10 (*VN* 434), and in 1291, presumably without the vicarage, at £6 13s 4d (*Taxatio* 120b).

128. Stoke by Clare Priory

Notification that, having found by inquisition that a vicarage had not hitherto been taxed in the church of Crimplesham, although some persons have certain pensions therein, he has taxed one thus: the vicarage shall consist of all the altarage, half the tithe of hay and one acre of the free land of the church, and the vicar shall pay the synodals and the cost of books and ornaments for the church; the monks shall have the tithe of corn and half the tithe of hay, and they shall

maintain the chancel and pay the archdeacon's procuration. When the vicarage
falls vacant, they shall present to the bishop a suitable persona.

Hevingham, 12 March 1253

B = BL ms. Cotton Appx. xxi (Stoke by Clare cartulary) fo. 44v. s. xiii ex. C = ibid. fos. 44v–
    45r (*inspeximus* by prior Simon of Elmham and the convent of Norwich, 13 March 1253).
Pd from B and C in *Stoke by Clare Cartulary* i no. 91.

Universis Cristi fidelibus presentes literas audituris vel visuris Walterus Dei
gratia episcopus Norwicensis[a] salutem in Domino sempiternam. Quoniam per
inquisitionem invenimus vicariam in ecclesia de Cremplisham[b] actenus non
fuisse taxatam, licet aliqui in eadem certas habuerint portiones, ne de taxatione
vicarie predicte futuris temporibus hesitetur,[c] eam duximus sic taxandam.
Consistit vicaria in toto alteragio ecclesie memorate et medietate [decime] feni et
in una acra libere terre ecclesie antedicte, et vicarius sustinebit sinodalia et
expensas librorum et aliorum ornamentorum ecclesie sepedicte, salvis priori et
monachis de Stokes omnibus decimis bladi et medietate decime feni, et dicti
monachi reficient cancellum et solvent procurationem archidiaconi; et cum
vacaverit vicaria prefata presentabunt nobis vel successoribus nostris dicti
monachi personam ydoneam ad eandem. In cuius rei testimonium sigillum
nostrum presentibus duximus apponendum. Datum apud Hevingham die sancti
Gregorii anno Domini mcclii.

    [a] Norwicencis B   [b] Cremplesham C   [c] hestitetur B; essitetur C

    In the time of bp John of Oxford (1175–1200) the monks were receiving seven marks *p.a.* from
    Crimplesham church (*EEA* 6 nos. 285, 290). There is mention of a vicar in 1229, acting in a
    legal case concerning land in concert with the prior as rector; but since the vicar was mr
    Thomas of Huntingdon, who acted as bp's attorney in the *curia regis*, it is very likely that he
    was not a vicar in the proper canonical sense, but rather paid this pension to the priory (*CPR
    1225–32* 290; *EEA* 21 Appx 2. 41A). That there was some dispute concerning the church is
    implied by the specific mention of Crimplesham in an otherwise general confirmation by pope
    Gregory IX in 1234 (*Stoke by Clare Cartulary* i no. 138). In 1254 the church was valued at £13
    6s 8d (*VN* 410), and in 1291 at £14 13s 4d, with a vicarage not subject to the tenth (*Taxatio*
    88b). For the history of the church, see *Stoke by Clare Cartulary* i 19.

129. Stoke by Clare Priory

Grant to the monks in proprios usus *of the church of Cavenham. They shall*
receive all the great tithe of the whole parish and shall hold the manse with the
church buildings. All other tithes and revenues shall be retained by the rector,
who shall be presented by the monks at the nomination of the bishop and his
successors.   Ipswich, 17 December 1254

B = BL ms. Cotton Appx. xxi (Stoke by Clare cartulary) fo. 40v. s. xiii ex. C = ibid. fos. 40v–
    41r (*inspeximus* by prior Simon of Elmham and the convent of Norwich, 13 January
    1255).
Pd from B and C in *Stoke by Clare Cartulary* i no. 75.

Omnibus Cristi fidelibus presentes literas inspecturis Walterus miseratione divina Norwicensis episcopus salutem in Domino sempiternam. Ut religiosi viri domus sancti Iohannis Baptiste de Stok' nostre diocesis quietius et devotius Domino famulentur et hospitalitatis gratia habundantius caritative petentibus impendatur, nos ecclesiam de Caveham nobis lege diocesana subiectam, in qua ipsi optinent patronatum, taliter eorum propriis usibus duximus concedendam quod iidem perpetuo percipiant omnes decimas garbarum totius dicte parochie[a] et mansum habeant cum edificiis ecclesie memorate, omnibus aliis decimis et proventibus rectori qui ecclesiam predictam pro tempore gubernabit retentis, qui per nos et nostros successores ibidem ordinabitur successive, ita tamen quod prefati viri religiosi ipsum a nobis et successoribus nostris nominatum presentabunt. Rector vero omnia onera dicte ecclesie debita et consueta sustinebit. In cuius rei testimonium presentibus literis sigillum nostrum fecimus apponi. Datum apud Gypeswycum[b] sextodecimo kalendas Ianuarii anno gratie MCC quinquagesimo quarto.

[a] parochie dicte B   [b] Gippiswic' C

Bp John of Oxford had granted that the monks should have the church *in proprios usus* at the next vacancy, with provision for a vicar, 1190 × 1200 (*EEA* 6 no. 293). The appropriation was confirmed by pope Innocent III (*Stoke by Clare Cartulary* i no. 74) and by bp John de Gray (*EEA* 6 no. 417), but the monks did not apparently obtain possession until now. Earlier in this year their portion in the church was valued at £1 16s (*VN* 433). In 1291 the value of the appropriated church was assessed at £13 6s 8d, and there was no mention of the rector's portion (*Taxatio* 121).

*130. Thornham, Anchorite Of

The bishop, in his last testament, leaves to him all contained in the deed given to him.   [19 February 1245 × 19 June 1256]

Mentioned in the bp's last testament (138).

131. Walden Abbey

Taxation of a vicarage in the church of Chippenham, held in proprios usus *by the monks. The vicar shall have all the altarage and lesser tithes, and all the tithes of the Hospital there and of the nuns of Chicksands, and also the tithe of five other virgates of land [described]; he shall also have a third part of all the free land of the church, and the messuage which Thomas the vicar, lately deceased, acquired of the abbot's fee, free of all service. The monks shall have the messuage which was previously assigned to the vicarage, and in recompense for the vicar's messuage they shall have an annual rent of eighteeen pence from Thomas of Badlingham, merchant, which the vicar used to receive. The vicar shall discharge all customary obligations to bishop and archdeacon, and bear the cost of candles and lamps, previously paid by the monks. When the vicarage is vacant the monks shall present a suitable* persona *to the bishop.*

Hadham, [1 or 2] January 1248

B = BL ms. Harley 3697 (Walden cartulary) fo. 50r (35r). s. xiv ex. C = ibid. fo. 50r–v (35r–v) (*inspeximus* by prior Simon and convent of Norwich, 8 June 1250).

Omnibus Cristi fidelibus presens scriptum visuris vel audituris Walterus miseratione divina Norwicensis episcopus salutem in Domino sempiternam. Universitati vestre tenore presentium notum fiat nos in ecclesia de Chippenham nostre diocesis, in proprios usus dilectorum nobis in Cristo abbatis et conventus de Waleden' concessa, vicariam pontificali auctoritate taliter taxavisse, quod vicarius institutus in eadem et instituendus pro tempore habebit integritaliter alteragium totum ecclesie memorate et omnes minutas ac maiores decimas hospitalis et monialium de Chikessaund, cum omnibus decimis quinque virgatarum terre in eadem parochia existentis, videlicet unius virgate et dimidie de terra Walteri de Chippenham, trium virgatarum terre Ricardi filii Galfridi et dimidie virgate de terra Roberti filii Ricardi. Habebit etiam tertiam partem[a] totius libere terre ad dictam ecclesiam pertinentis, mesuagium quoque quod Thomas nuper vicarius iam defunctus adquisierat de feodo memorati abbatis liberum absque omni servitio et onere universo. Ad hoc idem abbas et conventus habebunt mesuagium quod prelibate vicarie antiquitus fuit assignatum, et in recompensationem dicti mesuagii dicte vicarie assignati percipient memorati abbas et conventus decem et octo denarios annui redditus a Thoma mercatore de Badlingham reddendos, quod quondam vicarius percipere consuevit.Onera autem universa episcopalia et archidiaconalia debita et consueta vicarius sustinebit, unacum onere cereorum et lampadarum quod prius ad abbatem et conventum spectabat. Abbas vero et conventus ad vicariam cum pro tempore vacaverit nobis vel successoribus nostris[b] quem[c] voluerint personam idoneam presentabunt. In cuius rei testimonium huic presenti scripto signum nostrum apponi fecimus. Dat' apud Hadham quinto[d] nonas Ianuarii anno Domini millesimo CC^mo XL° septimo.[e]

[a] partem tertiam C   [b] nostris successoribus C   [c] si *for* quem B, C   [d] .v. C. *This date represents the kalends, and is possibly in error for* quarto   [e] B, C *conclude:* Exhibit' fuit .viii.

Chippenham church was part of Walden's original endowment, given by the founder Geoffrey II de Mandeville (fo. 18r of B). For a summary of the history of the church, see *Foundation of Walden* 194, and for comital charters ibid. 169, 173, 175, 177, 188. For episcopal confirmation, see *EEA* 6 nos 154, 301; for the initial grant *in proprios usus* by bp John of Oxford, see ibid. no. 302, and for institution to the vicarage in June 1223 by bp Pandulph, *EEA* 21 no. 24. Pandulph on 10 November 1224 also inspected and confirmed bp John's appropriation (ibid. no. 25); this is one of his last recorded *acta* issued in England before his final return to the papal *curia*, and the taxation of the vicarage was presumably undertaken by his official. The note concerning exhibition refers to documents to be produced at episcopal or archiepiscopal visitations.

The Hospitaller house at Chippenham, founded by William de Mandeville in 1184, was used to house sick brethren of the order, and had a cemetery attached (*EEA* 6 no. 303). The nuns of Chicksands had a grange there, valued in 1254 at £2, as was the grange of Sibton abbey; Hurley priory held a portion of the church assessed at £5; the church itself was then valued at £30 13s 4d and the vicarage at £5 (*VN* 432); in 1291 the valuations were £33 6s 8d and £8 13s 4d respectively (*Taxatio* 121). In November 1311 bp John Salmon, when ordering the official of the archdn of Sudbury to investigate the circumstances of the vacancy of the vicarage, specifically instructed him to enquire whether collation or nomination pertained to the bp, and received the reply that this had never been so (fos. 50v–51r of B). There is obvious ambiguity in bp Suffield's *acta* relating to presentation at future vacancies. In no. 131 the clause *si voluerint* is strange, and reminiscent of the familiar *quam nos et successores nostri voluerint*, signifying from the time of bp Pandulph onwards the episcopal right of nomination of a vicar who should then be presented to him by the normal patrons (*EEA* 21 pp. lviii–lix). It is possible that the provision is here garbled, or even deliberately adapted and falsified; similarly in no.132 the addendum after the dating clause is strange, and may represent the monks' own addition. In an institution of a vicar in 1349 there was no mention of episcopal nomination (*Reg. Bateman* no. 1180).

132. Walden Abbey

Notification that the bishop has found that the vicarage of the church of Chippenham, granted to the monks in proprios usus *by a previous bishop, was taxed not by the bishop but by the official of Norwich. Considering that the taxation of vicarages and portions in churches pertains to the bishop, whose function it is to make divisions and unions therein, he has caused this vicarage to be taxed anew by episcopal authority [in terms almost identical to no. 131].*

Hadham, [1 or 2] January 1248

B = BL ms.Harley 3697 (Walden cartulary) fo. 50v (35v) (*inspeximus* by bp Roger Scarning, 18 May 1275). s. xiv ex.

Omnibus Cristi fidelibus hoc scriptum visuris vel audituris Walterus Dei gratia Norwicensis episcopus salutem in Domino sempiternam. Noverit universitas vestra nos in ecclesia de Chippenham, dilecto nobis in Cristo abbati et conventui de Waleden' per episcopum appropriata, invenisse vicariam non per episcopum set per officialem Norwic' fuisse taxatam. Nos igitur, attendentes ad episcopum solum taxationes vicariarum et portionum in ecclesiis pertinere, cuius est sectiones et uniones facere in eisdem, dictam vicariam de novo pontificali duximus auctoritate taxandam, ita videlicet quod vicarius in eadem instituendus habebit totum alteragium cum omnibus ad illud pertinentibus, et omnes minutas decimas, et decimas de terra hospitalis et monialium de Chikessand, et omnes decimas quinque virgatarum terre, scilicet de una virgata terre et dimidia de terra Walteri de Chippenham, item de tribus virgatis terre Ricardi filii Galfridi et de dimidia virgata terre Roberti filii Ricardi. Habebit etiam tertiam partem totius libere terre ad dictam ecclesiam pertinentis. Habebit etiam vicarius qui pro tempore fuerit mesuagium quod vicarius nuper defunctus adquisierat de feodo memorati abbatis [et] conventus absque omni servitio imperpetuum, et dicti abbas et conventus habebunt mesuagium quod per predictum officialem prelibate vicarie antiquitus fuerat assignatum, et in recompensationem dicti mesuagii vicarie assignati habebunt memorati abbas et conventus decem et octo denarios annui redditus de Thoma mercatore de Badlingham percipiendos, quod vicarius nuper defunctus percipere solebat. Item vicarius sustinebit omnia onera episcopalia et archidiaconalia debita et consueta; item onus cereorum et lampadarum quod memorati abbas et conventus sustinere in eadem ecclesia consueverunt. Et ne hanc nostram taxationem possit inposterum quisquam minuere vel infirmare, eam auctoritate pontificali confirmamus. In cuius rei testimonium presens scriptum sigillo nostro fecimus muniri. Dat' apud Hadham quinto nonas Ianuarii anno Domini millesimo CC° quadragesimo septimo. Volumus etiam quod cum dictam vicariam vacare contigerit, predicti abbas et conventus personam ydoneam nobis et successoribus nostris perpetuis presentent temporibus.

See no.131 above.

*133. Waltham Abbey

*Mandate (*preceptum*) [as executor of the business of the cross appointed by the apostolic see] to the canons, ordering them to provide a written assessment of their annual revenues.*   [probably Summer - Autumn 1254]

Mention in the return made by Humphrey of Dereham and Richard de la Lade, canons. Pd in *VN* 520–4.

The Waltham return was tardy, mentioning the arrival (about Michaelmas 1255) of mr Rostand, who on 22 May 1255 was commissioned with archbp Boniface to replace the previous collectors (*VN* 84). Bp Suffield's mandate was, however, probably sent within months of the publication of his commission, with others, on 4 July 1254 (63A).

134. West Dereham Abbey

Concession to the canons, with the consent of his [cathedral] chapter, that they may serve the parish church of St Andrew, in which they were founded and which they hold in proprios usus, *by suitable chaplains to be appointed by them at their own responsibility and to be removed at their will, so that they may draw the full revenues from the church and no occasion may be given for the reduction of their renowned hospitality.*   [19 February 1245 × February 1253]

B = BL ms. Add. 46353 (West Dereham cartulary) fo. 13r (6r). s. xiv in.

Omnibus Cristi fidelibus presens scriptum visuris vel audituris Walterus Dei gratia Norwycensis episcopus salutem in Domino sempiternam. Dilectorum filiorum abbatis et conventus de Derham pie religionis attendentes fervorem, necnon elemosinas et beneficia que omnibus et singulis ad domum suam confluentibus incessanter inpendunt, ut ecclesia parochiali sancti Andree, in qua fundatur, quam etiam in proprios usus habent, libera integritate fruantur, ne ferventi eorum caritati aliquo perturbante refrigescendi prebeatur occasio, de consensu capituli nostri, invocata spiritus sancti gratia, eis[a] duximus concedendum ut per capellanos ydoneos periculo suo eligendos et pro voluntate sua amovendos memoratam ecclesiam faciant deserviri, ita quod cura animarum in eadem solicite[b] geratur nobisque et successoribus nostris competenter in aliis respondeatur. In cuius rei testimonium presenti scripto signum nostrum fecimus apponi. Hiis testibus: Radulfo de Insula archidiacono Colecestr' et multis aliis.

[a] eiis B   [b] scilicite B

For Ralph de Insula, probably vice-archdeacon to mr Robert de Insula, see *Fasti* i 19–20; mr Hugh of St Edmunds, the next archdn of Colchester, had been succeeded as archdn of Essex by February 1253 (ibid. 20).

The two churches of St Andrew and St Peter stood in the same churchyard. St Peter's had been appropriated to the canons by bp John of Oxford (*EEA* 6 no. 312), St Andrew's by bp Thomas Blundeville, with provision for a vicarage (*EEA* 21 no. 117). In 1254 the two churches were assessed together at £13 6s 8d, and in 1291 at £14 (*VN* 408; *Taxatio* 88b). In 1401 the canons obtained a papal indult authorising the union of the parishes and releasing the parishioners from the obligation to keep St Peter's in repair (*CPL 1396–1404* 415–6). See Colvin, *White Canons* 133–4.

135. Wymondham Priory

Institution, at the presentation of the monks, of Nicholas of Burgh, chaplain, to the vicarage of Wymondham, vacant by the death of William of Buckenham. So that vicars may the better take up residence there, they shall, with the assent of the monks, receive in addition to what the late William had as his vicarage, and while they maintain residence, a monk's corrody. With this they shall be content, and for all time shall demand nothing more from the monks. When the vicarage is vacant, a new vicar shall be admitted by the bishop and his successors without hindrance to this portion and corrody. Cressingham, 26 July 1251

B = BL ms. Cotton Titus C viii (Wymondham cartulary) fo. 71v. s. xiii med.

Omnibus Cristi fidelibus presentes litteras visuris vel audituris Walterus Dei gratia Norwicensis episcopus salutem in Domino sempiternam. Cum per mortem Willelmi de Bukeham vicaria de Wymundham[a] vacasset, nos ad presentationem dilectorum filiorum prioris et conventus loci eiusdem dilectum filium Nicholaum de Burgo capellanum ad dictam vicariam admisimus. Ut autem vicarii qui pro tempore fuerint melius ibidem possint facere residentiam, preter ea que dictus Willelmus defunctus nomine vicarie in prefata ecclesia percipere consuevit, de assensu dictorum prioris et conventus unum corredium monachi de prefatis priore et conventu dum fecerint residentiam perciperent, quibus contenti de ceteris a predictis priore et conventu nomine vicarie nichil exigant inperpetuum. Et cum dictam vicariam vacare contigerit, vicarius substituendus ad dictam portionem cum corredio memorato sine difficultate a nobis et successoribus nostris admittatur. In cuius rei testimonium huic scripto sigillum nostrum apponi fecimus. Act' apud Cressingham .vii. kalendas Augusti anno Domini M° CC° quinquagesimo primo.

^a de Wymundham *added in margin, with mark for insertion*

This *actum* is followed by a note that it was confirmed by the prior and convent of Norwich, and then by a memorandum that the vicarage of Wymondham consists of half the oblations of the parish church, except at Christmas, Easter and the Purification and Nativity of the Blessed Virgin Mary, when the monks should receive all the offerings; the vicar should also receive all the grain called 'loscorn' and all the wax-scot, and half the tithes of hemp, wool, cheese, milk, lambs, calves, chickens, geese, piglets, sheep and gardens (fo. 71v of B). As part of the agreement of 1228 between bp Blundeville and the priors of Binham and Wymondham concerning jurisdiction over the monks' churches, it was stipulated that a vicarage in Wymondham church should be assessed either at one sixth of the valuation of 1215, or else an eighth part of a new valuation to be made in the ruridecanal chapter (*EEA* 21 Appx 2. 27). In 1254 the church with the manor was valued at £84 6s 8d, the vicarage at £6 13s 4d (*VN* 399); in 1291 the church was estimated at £80 and the vicarage at £8 13s 4d (*Taxatio* 85b).

136. York, St Mary's Abbey

Grant to the monks, with the consent of his own chapter, of a perpetual annual benefice of eight marks in the church of Banham, that is, six marks for the monks and two marks for their cell of Rumburgh, to be received from the rector for the time being at the two Norwich synods.   Norwich, 30 March 1245

> B = Northamptonshire RO, Finch-Hatton ms. FH453 (charter roll of St Mary's abbey) no. 8. s. xiv in. C = ibid. (*inspeximus* by prior Simon and the convent of Norwich).

Omnibus Cristi fidelibus ad quos presens scriptum pervenerit Walterus miseratione divina Norwicensis episcopus salutem eternam in Domino. Inter ceteras Ierusalem filias circumquaque diffusas illas nos decet studiosius ac sollicitius honorare que in honore gloriose virginis Marie sunt constructe. Quocirca dilectis in Cristo filiis abbati et conventui sancte Marie Ebor' octo marcas annuas nomine perpetui beneficii in ecclesia de Banham nostre diocesis de consensu capituli nostri caritative concessimus, videlicet sex marcas annuas ad opus ipsorum abbatis et conventus et duas marcas annuas ad opus celle sue de Romburg' a rectore eiusdem ecclesie qui pro tempore fuerit ad duas sinodos Norwicenses percipiendas. In cuius rei testimonium has litteras nostras patentes fieri fecimus eisdem. Hiis testibus: magistro Herveio de Kakeham, domino Ada de Wrdestede, magistro Willelmo de Horham, magistro Ada de Bromholm, domino Iohanne Malet, domino Thoma Bigot, Thoma de Walcot' clerico et aliis. Dat' apud Norwicum .iii. kalendas Aprilis anno Domini M°CC°XL° quinto^a pontificatus nostri anno primo.

^a quarto B, C

If Suffield had been elected before 30 March 1244 (which is very unlikely, since papal rejection of the royal appeal against the translation of bp William Raleigh from Norwich to Winchester was announced only on 28 February 1244, and royal confirmation of Suffield's election came on 9 July 1244), and if he dated his pontifical years from his election, he would here be described as *electus*, since he was not consecrated until February 1245. It is virtually certain that *quarto* here is in error for *quinto*, either by the scribe of the original or by the copyist of B and C.

Bp William Turbe had granted the church to St Mary's York *in proprios usus*, ordering that provision should be made for a vicarage, 1161 × 1173 (*EEA* 6 no.160). This appropriation had apparently never taken effect. Earlier thirteenth-century documents refer to a pension of 8 marks, rather than to a perpetual benefice. Mr Lambert of Beverley acknowledged his liability to pay this in two instalments at York, and in addition 2 marks p.a. to the monks of Rumburgh. He should also receive the abbot honourably in his house once a year when he came to Norfolk, and should provide necessities for any monks of St Mary's who might come, and for their horses; he would also, out of charity, give the monks twenty sesters of wine at York at the feast of the Assumption (15 August); and he would discharge all obligations of the church to the bp and other burdens upon it (BL ms. Campbell ch. ix 9, no. 8). John de Longo Campo, rector, acknowledged his obligation to payment of a pension of 8 marks to St Mary's, with no mention of Rumburgh, and would receive any monks with their horses; should he not be resident, his proctor would discharge these obligations for him (ibid. no. 9).

137. York, St Mary's Abbey

Institution, at the presentation of the monks, of master William of Horham to the church of Banham, saving to the monks an annual benefice of eight marks, that is, six marks for their use and two marks for the use of the cell of Rumburgh.

Norwich, 30 March 1245

B = Northamptonshire R.O., Finch-Hatton ms. FH453 (charter roll of St Mary's abbey) no. 7. s. xiv in.

Omnibus Cristi fidelibus ad quos presens scriptum pervenerit Walterus permissione divina Norwicensis episcopus salutem eternam in Domino. Noveritis nos ad presentationem dilectorum filiorum abbatis et conventus sancte Marie Ebor' dilectum filium magistrum Willelmum de Horham ad ecclesiam de Banham admisisse ipsumque in eadem canonice rectorem instituisse, salvis dictis abbati et conventui octo marcis annuis nomine perpetui beneficii, videlicet sex marcis ad opus eorundem abbatis et conventus et duabus marcis ad opus celle sue de Romburg', salvis etiam in omnibus episcopalibus consuetudinibus et nostre Norwicensis ecclesie dignitate. Datum apud Norwic' .iii. kalendas Aprilis pontificatus nostri anno primo.

On the following day mr William made written acknowledgement of his obligation to render this benefice in two annual instalments at the Easter and Michaelmas synods at Norwich (BL ms. Campbell ch. ix 9, no. 10).

138. Last testament of the bishop

Will of bishop Walter   Hoxne, 19 June 1256

A = Norwich RO, NCR 24b/2. Endorsed: + Hoc testamentum ego Walterus de Sutfeld
Norwicensis episcopus conpos et sanus mente condidi, et volo quod hoc meum sit
testamentum et suprema mea voluntas. In cuius rei testimonium presentem manu propria
feci annotationem die Lune proxima ante festum sancti Iohannis Baptiste anno Domini
millesimo CC° quinquagesimo sexto, pontificatus nostri anno duodecimo; approx. 400 ×
440 + 15 mm.; on left, episcopal seal, dark brown wax, counterseal; seven smaller seals,
three vessica-shaped, four round, all dark brown wax.
Pd (summary translation) in Blomefield, *Norfolk*, iii, 486–92.

+ In nomine patris et filii et spiritus sancti Amen. Ego Walterus de Suthfeld
Norwicensis episcopus sic meum condo, facio et ordino testamentum. In primis,
commendo Deo et beate Marie et beatis Anne et Egidio et omnibus sanctis
animam meam, et corpus meum sepeliendum coram altare beate Marie in nova
capella ecclesie Norwicensis, ubi inperpetuum erit monachus celebrans pro
anima mea ad altare eiusdem virginis, et scribetur nomen monachi in singulis
ebdomadis in tabula. Item, prior et conventus facient aniversarium meum
perpetuo; et die aniversarii habebit conventus viginti solidos ad pitanciam, et
elemosinarius viginti solidos ad distribuendum pauperibus; et pro beneficio hoc
michi gratis concesso, lego eidem conventui centum marcas, quas si non solvero
in vita mea solvantur per executores meos. Item, ad exequias meas faciendas
lego centum libras; et provideatur sollicite et fideliter quod per viam per quam
contigerit corpus meum deferri, larga fiat pauperibus distributio; et quod
ubicumque quiescat corpus usque ad completam sepulturam, assint pauperes
circa illud, nunc senes, nunc vidue, nunc pueri pauperes, et singulis in suo
decessu detur denarius argenteus; et frequenter de die et nocte mutentur.
Volumus etiam et precipimus quod omnia debita nostra integre et plenarie
solvantur. Item, viginti quinque capellani requirantur in mea diocesi, eiusdem
diocesis sed diligenter provideatur quod sint honesti, et illi uno eodemque anno,
si fieri potest, celebrent pro anima mea et pro animabus eorum quorum bona
recepi ex quacumque consuetudine Norwicensis ecclesie et pro animabus eorum
quorum fui executor sive quorum bona ab intestato vel aliunde devenerunt; et ad
ipsorum capellanorum sustentationem lego centum marcas. Item, in
recompensationem omnium eorum que recepi in mea diocesi quocumque titulo
sive quacumque causa ex qua possim et debeam habere conscientiam lesam, lego
centum marcas distribuendas pauperibus mee diocesis per manus executorum
meorum secundum quod melius viderint expedire. Item, lego ad distribuendum
per maneria nostra pauperibus de maneriis in pecunia et robis, per manus
Willelmi de Whitewell, Galfridi de Lodn' et Willelmi de Pakeham, centum
marcas. Item, ad relevandos oppressos in officialitate mee diocesis lego viginti
marcas distribuendos per manus Daniel de Beccles. Item, cathedrali ecclesie mee
Norwicensi lego magnam cuppam meam cum elevaturis ad corpus Cristi
reponendum et ad reliquias si voluerint. Item, ecclesie Norwicensi duos equos

qui portent corpus meum, et capellam meam sicut eam ab eisdem recepi, cum uno equo. Mitram siquidem non furratam que michi data fuit et baculum pontificale quem dedit michi dominus Wintoniensis lego abbatie sancti Egidii Provincie, unacum viginti marcis argenti. Item, pro honore et beneficiis michi a Norwicensi ecclesia collatis et pro expensis et laboribus diversis circa electionem meam factis, et ut aniversarii mei diem officiis divinis et elemosinis recolant ut premisimus, quieti eos et plenam presto liberationem a tempore mortis mee super annua prestatione sexdecim marcarum in quibus tenebantur Martino quondam rectori ecclesie de Denham, quem quidem redditum idem Martinus per cartam suam quamdiu viveret michi vel cuicumque dare vel assignare voluerimus dedit et concessit. Item, hospitali sancti Egidii de Norwico, quod in remissione omnium peccatorum meorum construxi, lego trecentas marcas; et volo et precipio quod convertantur in utilitate eiusdem hospitalis de consilio magistri domus et executorum meorum. Et precipio meis executoribus et fidei eorundem committo ut ipsi predictum hospitale foveant et eidem beneficiant in omnibus quibus poterunt de bonis meis; ex hoc tamen generali dicto nolo quod hospitale contra executores meos aliquam competat actionem vel eisdem aliqua moveatur questio. Item, eidem hospitali lego cuppam deauratam que fuit beati Edmundi; et semper volo quod predictum hospitale habeat predictas trecentas marcas. Item, firmam terre Willelmi Mauduyt quam habui in Therlinge usque ad terminum completum, cum duabus carucis, lego hospitali predicto, salvo michi blado in horreis existente. Item, ad distribuendum pauperibus Norwicensis diocesis pro anima Willelmi le Enveyse et ad satisfaciendum illis quibus tenebatur in eadem diocesi lego viginti marcas, et tradentur domino Rogero de Tremleye executori suo, et si mortuus fuerit distribuantur per manus executorum meorum. Item, eodem modo et consimilibus personis mee diocesis distribuantur triginta marce pro anima Dionisii de Cottun' per manus Willemi de Whitewell, et si mortuus fuerit idem Willelmus, distribuatur eadem pecunia per manus executorum meorum pauperibus mee diocesis et ubi natus fuit idem Dionisius. Item, lego viginti marcas distribuendas pauperibus parochianis de Hevingham pro anima eiusdem Dionisii. Item, monachis de sancta Fide unam marcam pro anima eiusdem. Item, lego pauperibus de Becles et Wyrlingwurth' et parentibus pauperibus Galfridi de Beccles viginti marcas distribuendas inter eosdem per manus domini Philippi sequestarii nostri et Daniel de Beccles. Item, lego viginti marcas ad distribuendum pauperibus pro animabus Th. de Brisewurth' militis et Thome de Acout per manus executorum meorum in partibus de Acolt et de Brisewurth' mee diocesis. Item, lego viginti marcas distribuendas pauperibus in mea diocesi pro anima Petri de Hautboys per manus domini Hamonis de Calethorp et executorum meorum, si idem H. moriatur. Item, lego viginti marcas distribuendas pro anima Thome de Cressingham in villa de Cressingham et pauperibus vicinis per manus executorum meorum et Willelmi de Cressingham. Item, domino regi lego unam cuppam et unum palefridum et motam canum meorum. Item, ad luminare altaris beate Virginis in nova capella Norwic' do et assigno decimas de dominicis de Thornham perpetuo, et viginti marcas ad redditum comparendum per executores meos. Item, unicuique domui fratrum predicatorum et minorum mee diocesis lego quinque marcas. Item, communitati fratrum predicatorum et minorum Anglie lego triginta marcas. Item, pauperibus scolaribus Oxon' centum solidos. Item, ad reparationem ecclesie de Suffeld viginti marcas. Item, pauperibus eiusdem parochie pro anima Ricardi rectoris eiusdem viginti marcas, et aliis pauperibus mee diocesis lego pro anima eiusdem Ricardi viginti marcas. Item, lego sexaginta marcas ad distribruendum pauperibus mee diocesis in maneriis eiusdem diocesis ubi dotata fuit Matildis comitissa Warann' pro anima eiusdem. Item, viginti marcas lego pauperibus mee diocesis distribuendas pro anima Ricardi de Wendovere socii mei per manus executorum meorum. Item, domine Ele sorori mee unum anulum pretii viginti solidorum. Item, Agneti de Therling' sorori mee unum anulum eiusdem pretii. Item, Ele nepti mee centum solidos ad providendum sibi de sustentatione victus in reclusorio. Item, pueris Iohannis de Baningham senioris qui redditum non habent, quinqe marcas, et eodem modo pueris Henrici de Ingewurth. Item, aliis pauperibus consanguineis meis, maxime ex parte matris, lego viginti marcas distribuendas eisdem in mea diocesi per manus executorum meorum et secundum ordinationem eorundem. Item, pauperibus parochianis meis de Wintertun' et de Sumerton' quatuor marcas. Item, pauperibus parochianis meis de Burgo in Fleg' quatuor marcas. Item, pauperibis parochianis meis de Burgo in Suffolch quatuor marcas, et ad capellam sancti Botulphi in eadem parochia quatuor marcas. Item, pauperibus parochianis de Cressingham tres marcas. Item, pauperibus parochianis de Naringes tres marcas. Item, pauperibus inclusis mee diocesis decem marcas. Item, monialibus de Carhoge quinque marcas, et monialibus de Campese quinque marcas. Item, monialibus de Blaberge duas marcas. Item, domui ubi moratur mater[a] fratris Iohannis de Stamford quadraginta solidos. Item, fratri Radulfo de Huntedon' parvam bibliam meam quam emi de eius consilio. Item, anchorite de Thornham lego quod in mea carta quam habet continetur. Item, pauperibus parochianis meis de Therlinge, de Hoxne et de Thornham quindecim libras, et distribuantur in victu et vestitu; anachorite de Suffeld' unam marcam, et anachoritis de Stratton' unam marcam; anachoritis de Massingham, scilicet nepte mee et socio eiusdem, viginti solidos. Item, hospitali sancti Iohannis Lenn' quinque marcas; hospitali sancti Egidii de Norwico firmam terre Willelmi Mauduyt in Therlinge usque ad terminum meum completum, cum duabus bonis carucis, cum toto blado in horreis ibidem invento et cum omni stauro vaccarum, bidentium et porcorum. Item, archidiacono Norwic' fratri meo anulum qui fuit domini Rogeri fratris mei et magnam cuppam meam de mazre de qua bibo in mensa. Item, Waltero nepoti meo unam cuppam, Decretum meum quod fuit magistri Iohannis de Offington', Summam Hugeci quam habet magister Iohannes de Atleberg' de presto nostro; item, omnes libros theologie quos emi de executoribus magistri Ade de Bromholm, item Decretales meas et libros filosophie eidem lego, et fidei eius committo ut ipse pro anima mea singulis annis quoad vixerit die Assumptionis beate virginis Marie pascat centum pauperes; item, tribus annis sequentibus mortem meam quolibet anno faciet celebrare unum annuale; item, quolibet die quoad vixerit et fuerit domo sua unum ante ipsum pro anima mea reficiat pauperem. Item, Willelmo fratri suo de Calethorp' totum ferrum meum, scilicet arma, unum ciphum pulcrum cum pede, unum anulum cum smaragdine; et quia multa bona feci eidem, fidei eius committo ut die Assumptionis beate Virginis singulis annis quoad vixerit pascat centum pauperes pro anima mea, item singulis diebus ante se unum pauperem reficiat in prandio, et quod qualibet septimana per capellanum suum in capella sua faciat celebrare unam missam pro anima mea. Item, Willelmo de Whitewell', fideli et caro meo, ymaginem beate Marie quem michi dedit magister Rogerus de Raveningham; item tabulam pictam de manu magistri Petri; item, duos libros sermonum; item, zonam meam magnam qua cingatur cum senuerit; item, ciphum meum de quo bibo cum patena. Item, Willelmo de Pakeham unum ciphum argenteum cum pede et psalterium meum; et quoniam nichil nisi mors nos separare potuit, anime mee benefacere studeat. Item, Galfrido de Lodnes maritagium heredis Rogeri de Wichingham, ciphum meum qui vocatur Godet; item, album ciphum de mazre; item viginti marcas argenti; fidelitas sua sufficienter rogabit ipsum benefacere anime mee. Item, hospitali sancti Egidii bibliam quam emi a magistro Symone Blundo; item, ciphum de quo pueri pauperes bibunt. Item, domino H. custodi dicti hospitalis sancti Egidii unum ciphum pulcrum cum pede, et missale quod ipsemet michi fieri fecit. Item, archidiacono Colecestr' unum anulum; magistro Herveo de Fakeham unum anulum; magistro Hugoni de Corbrig ciphum cum pede, et bibliam meam spissam, pulcram sed falsam. Item, Egidio capellano unum mazre, unam cappam bene furratam, missale quod michi dedit Rogerus de Granario, unum ciphum argenteum et quinque coclearia argentea. Item, Willelmo clerico capelle quadraginta solidos et librum canticorum qui fuit Iohannis Bygot. Item, Mattheo capellano quinque marcas et unam de melioribus robis meis. Item, Willelmo de Wychingham unum ciphum cum pede et centum solidos argenti; Hugoni de Camera totum lectum meum, exceptis culcitris de serico, quas unacum omnibus reliquiis meis lego hospitali sancti Egidii. Et volo quod si ita longe moriar a mea ecclesia quod corpus meus aperiatur, cor meum sepeliatur in capella hospitalis in concavitate facienda in muro iuxta altare. Item, H. de Caylli remitto totum quod michi debet, et unum anulum lego uxori eius. Item, Radulfo de Crakeford unum ciphum; Reginaldo de Refham quinque marcas. Item, Iohanni coco quinque marcas; Gilberto salsario unam liberationem, videlicet victum et vestitum sufficienter et congrue in dicto hospitali, et fiat ei super hoc carta; Ade palefridario centum solidos; Coleman quinque marcas; Hugoni le Buteler quinque marcas; Wakke quatuor marcas; Iohanni hostiario quinque marcas; Thoward centum solidos; Semanno de coquina quinque marcas. Item, Gille duas marcas; Galfrido de Lodn' quondam hostiario coquine duas marcas; Radulfo hostiario camere tres marcas; Galfrido pistori tres marcas. Item, Nicholao braciatori viginti solidos; Capun viginti solidos. Item, parvo Symoni triginta solidos; Iohanni carectario tres marcas et unam de secundis robis; Ricardo carectario tres marcas; Dusing triginta solidos; Hobbe carectario viginti solidos;

Rogero carectario, qui est apud Hoxn', tres marcas. Item, Symoni feratori tres marcas. Item, Galfrido vigili unam marcam. Item, Matildi lotrici viginti solidos. Item, Stephano nuntio duas marcas; Wyndelaboys decem solidos; Willelmo nuntio meo proprio centum solidos; Buleys decem solidos; Petro pistori viginti solidos, et sociis suis viginti solidos; Willelmo braciatori viginti solidos, et garcionibus suis unam marcam. Item, duobus pagis meis, Nicholao et Willelmo, tres marcas; Gase decem solidos. Item, Sandre decem solidos, Neve decem solidos. Item, Banigham, qui custodit sumarium lecti mei unam marcam; duobus aquatoribus coquine, cuilibet quindecim solidos; Martino de coquina unam marcam; Roberto ki dort unam marcam. Item, Galfrido hostiario coquine unam marcam; Godwino de coquina decem solidos. Item, Willelmo peletario, Henrico sutori et Ricardo sutori, unicuique quinque solidos. Item, Galfrido de Camera viginti solidos; Trot et Nicholao Syre et Gwyliot, unicuique quinque solidos, et tantumdem Warde de Hasingham, Ingeram, Scot nudo, Cruste et garcioni vigilis[b], unicuique tres solidos. Item, garcioni Willelmi de Wichingham et garcioni Hugonis de Camera, unicuique dimidiam marcam. Item, Willelmo de Foceston' clerico unum ciphum de argento; Danieli de Becles unum ciphum[c] cum pede, et viginti marcas pro bonis que habui de magistro W. de Horham, computatis michi omnibus expensis quas feci circa ecclesiam de Grundesburg'. Item, debeo Hugoni capellano de Dingineton' viginti marcas. Item, lego decem marcas distribuendas pauperibus de Burnedis per manus executorum meorum de consilio domini rectoris ecclesie de Dingineton'. Item, Willelmo de Pakeham iuniori quinque marcas; Osberto Trenchefolie duas marcas; Roberto de Ilsington duas marcas; Willelmo de Lega duas marcas. Item, magistro Nigello unum anulum. Item, hospitali sancti Iohannis Oxon' viginti solidos; hospitali Magdalene de Norwico viginti solidos. Item, priori et conventui de Bromholm remitto quicquid isti michi debent ac si michi remittant omnia que de eis habui. Item, leprosis mee diocesis per se vel communiter habitantibus centum solidos secundum ordinationem executorum meorum. Item, cuilibet leproso[d] venienti ad meas exequias, duos denarios. Item, cuilibet anachorite Norwic' die sepulture mee sex denarios, preter commune legatum. Item, Iohanni carpentario tres marcas; Iohanni cementario tres marcas. Item, cementario qui vivit apud Caham unam marcam; ad perficiendum opus quod fecimus inchoari in feretro beati Edmundi de Pontiniaco viginti marcas; fratri Ricardi cementarii scolari tres marcas; Iohanni capellano sancti Egidii, unum anulum; Roberto capellano de hospitale sancti Egidii, sustentationem in dicto hospitali, et fiet ei carta. Item, reparationi pontium per episcopatum duas marcas, et unam marcam ponti de Cattiwade. Item, domui de Weybrig' duas marcas; hospitali de Bek unam marcam; fratri Philippo de Flicham duas marcas. Item, Roberto vicario de Ludham ciphum cum pede; Thome de Bukeham ciphum argenteum; Iohanni de Northelmham ciphum argenteum; Ricardo de Branteston quinque marcas; Roberto de Crakeford quinque marcas; Willelmo de Hevingham quinque marcas; Willelmo de Harpele quinque marcas; Galfrido de Crakeford unum anulum; Roberto servienti de Baketon' quatuor marcas; servienti de Wykes viginti solidos; Willelmo de Anglia quatuor marcas; Scoto de Hoxn' quatuor marcas; Scoto de Therling' quinque marcas; Pruet apud Geywud tres marcas; Willelmo Sopere unam marcam; Shynnyng unam marcam; Hamoni de Fincham viginti solidos; Willelmo fabro meo viginti solidos; Iohanni Stuket tres marcas; Waltero de Grey, servienti Lond', viginti solidos. Item, Ade senescallo meo Lenn' centum solidos, et preter hoc assigno ei decem marcas quolibet anno quamdiu fuerit senescallus pro expensis suis. Item, Ricardo aurifabro meo Lenn' tres marcas. Item, pro animabus eorum qui michi servierunt et mortui sunt, per executores meos duo fiant annualia in mea diocesi. Item, viginti marce tradentur domino H. capellano, magistro hospitalis sancti Egidii, ad erogandum pro anima mea in mea diocesi locis et personis quibus viderit expedire; Iohanni clerico, scriptori curie nostre, viginti solidos; Ade de Wichingham viginti solidos; Gotte de Suthelmham tres marcas; Ade^e warnario de Eccles viginti solidos; et in communi omnibus warnariis meis tres marcas secundum ordinationem executorum meorum. Item, cuilibet garcioni qui habet per annum robam integram de me et cui non est specialiter aliquid legatum, lego dimidiam marcam. Item fratri^f meo qui post me reget ecclesiam Norwicensem lego cuppam meam antique fabrice, et Dominus disigna^g eum in via salutis eterne, et post Norwicensem ecclesiam specialiter ei commendo hospitale sancti Egidii et omnes nos servientes qui michi et ecclesie mee in omnibus fidelissime servierunt, et ob hoc do eis benedictionem Dei et meam; et si in aliquo deliquerunt, totum eis remitto et quantum possum a peccatorum nexibus absolvo. In nomine patris et filii et spiritus sancti. Filiis meis monachis de Norwico lego duas marcas ad unam pitanciam die sepulture mee et unum dolum de meliori vino meo; et post illum, unum hospitali; Galfrido de Lodn', Willelmo de Pakeham et Willelmo de Whitewell, cuilibet unum, et similiter cuilibet executori; conventui de Strafford, ad unam pitanciam, decem marcas. Item decem marce dentur magistro de Semplingham pro nigro palefrido quem nobis misit. Et ad hoc testamentum meum perficiendum, assigno et lego argentum et aurum, iocalia et equos, blada seminata et non seminata, wardas et firmas et omnia que michi pro eisdem debentur, et quecumque habeo in bonis mobilibus et immobilibus et hominibus, et quecumque mea sunt vel esse debent, quocumque nomine censeantur. Omnia tamen que michi debentur pro sequestris sive etiam ipsa sequestra tempore mortis mee^h ipsis ecclesiis et pauperibus parochianis integre lego et assigno. Huius autem testamenti executores constituo Walterum de Calethorp' nepotem meum, Galfridum de Lodn', Willelmum de Whitewell', Willelmum de Pakeham, dominum Hamonem magistrum hospitalis sancti Egidii, magistrum Hugonem de Corbrig' et Willelmum de Wichingham. Dat' apud Hoxn' et perfectum die Lune proximo ante festum sancti Iohannis Baptiste anno Domini millesimo ducentesimo quinquagesimo sexto et pontificatus mei anno duodecimo.

^a mater interl. A ^b vigili A ^c ciphum *interlined* A ^d leprosi A ^e Adam A ^f *reading uncertain, possibly* patri ^g disigat A ^h mea A

Royal licence had been granted to Suffield on 17 April 1251 to make his will of all his goods, pertaining to his barony and otherwise, without impediment, so that neither the king nor any other might lay hands upon them, saving any debts which he might owe to the crown (*CPR 1247–58* 92). On 30 May 1257 a mandate was directed to the royal custodians of the bishopric that, having taken sufficient security from the executors to pay any debts due, they should grant them free administration of the bp's lands and chattels for the execution of his testament (*Cl.R. 1256–59* 59).

SIMON WALTON

139. Profession

Profession of obedience made to Boniface [of Savoy], archbishop of Canterbury.
[Canterbury, 10 March 1258]

A = Canterbury D. & C., Ch. Ant. 115/133. Endorsed: Bonifac'. Ista professio facta fuit die
eadem qua prescripta professio Coventr' (s. xiii med.); approx. 222 × 107 mm.
B = Canterbury D. & C. register A (prior's register) fo. 268r. s. xiv med.
Pd in *Canterbury Professions* no. 197.

Ego Symon, ecclesie Norwicensis electus et a te, reverende pater Bonefaci,
sancte Cantuariensis ecclesie archiepiscope et totius Anglie primas,
consecrandus antistes, tibi et Cantuariensi ecclesie et successoribus tuis canonice
substituendis debitam et canonicam obedientiam et subiectionem me per omnia
exhibiturum profiteor et promitto secundum decreta Romanorum pontificum,
tuorumque et Cantuariensis ecclesie iurium adiutor ero ad defendendum et
retinendum, salvo ordine meo. Sic me Deus adiuvet. Et predicta omnia propria
manu subscribendo confirmo. +

The endorsement to this profession ties it to that of Roger Longespée, elect of Coventry, made
on 10 March 1258 at Christ Church Canterbury (*Canterbury Professions* no. 196). This is the
best evidence for the date of Walton's consecration; cf. *Fasti* ii 57.

140. Battle Abbey

*Delegation to the prior of Holy Trinity, Ipswich, and the official of the
archdeacon of Sudbury of the making of an ordinance in settlement of disputes
between master Roger of Leckhampstead, clerk, and Thomas, [rural] dean of
Loes, over the church of Bramford, the decision of which they have, with the
consent of the abbot and convent as patrons, submitted to the decision of the
bishop or his delegates.* Gaywood, [?2] May 1260

B = San Marino, Huntington Library, HEH/BA 29 (Battle cartulary) fo. 94r (83r). s. xiii ex.

Simon Dei gratia Norwicensis episcopus dilectis filiis priori sancte Trinitatis de
Gybewico et officiali archidiaconi Suff' salutem, gratiam et benedictionem. Cum
dilecti filii magister Rogerus de Lechamsted clericus et dominus Thomas
decanus de Lose super omnibus controversiis inter ipsos motis ratione ecclesie
de Bramford nostre diocesis se nostre ordinationi vel aliquorum quibus vices

nostras committere dignaremur, consensu patronorum abbatis et conventus de Bello ad hoc interveniente, submiserint, vobis de consensu eorundem ordinationem predictam committimus. Dat' apud Geywode .vi°.ᵃ nonas Maii pontificatus nostri anno septimo.

ᵃ .vii°. B; no such date should be possible, as it would be the kalends

141. Bury St Edmunds Abbey

Inspeximus *of an indult of pope Alexander [IV] that on the death or resignation of the rector of Pakenham the monks may, without licence of the diocesan, appropriate to their own use for hospitality and enter into corporal possession of that church, which is of the abbot's advowson and from the revenues of which, estimated by ancient valuation at thirty marks,the convent receives an annual pension. Decent provision shall be made for a perpetual vicar, who shall discharge the obligations of the church to the bishop and its other dues. In this the pope follows in the footsteps of his predecessor A[lexander] III, notwithstanding that after that pope's indult many secular clerks have been instituted by the diocesan at the abbot's presentation; the right of presentation of vicars is reserved to the abbot and his successors; dated at Anagni, 16 September 1256. The bishop, having investigated the value of the portions of the church, has caused the vicarage to be taxed thus: the vicar shall have the manse, all the free land and meadow of the church, with the tithes therefrom, all the altarage and the tithe of mills, hay, lambs, chickens, milk and wool, and all other lesser tithes, oblations and obventions. The prior and convent shall receive all the great tithe, except that of the free land of the church itself, assigned as above to the vicar. For the supplement of the vicar's portion, the prior and convent shall pay from their portion forty shillings a year in equal instalments at the two Ipswich synods. When the vicarage is vacant the abbot shall present a suitable clerk. The prior and convent have consented to this taxation and sworn to observe all contained therein.* Thornage, 28 March 1261

B = TNA, DL 42/5 (Bury cellarer's cartulary) fo. 54v (35v). s. xiii ex.

[U]niversis Cristi etc. Simon Dei gratia episcopus Norwicensis salutem. Abbati et conventui monasterii sancti Aedmundi [indultam] a domino papa concessam inspeximus in hec verba: Alexander episcopus servus servorum Dei dilectis filiis abbati et conventui monasterii sancti Aedmundi ad Romanam ecclesiam nullo medio pertinentis, ordinis sancti Benedicti, Norwicensis diocesis, salutem et apostolicam benedictionem. Religionis vestre meretur honestas ut vos favore benivolo prosequentes petitionibus vestris quam cum Deo possumus annuamus. Hinc est quod nos, vestris precibus inclinati ut ecclesiam de Pakeham, Norwicensis diocesis, in qua tu, fili abbas, ut asseritis ius optines patronatus, et de cuius proventibus, valorem .xxxᵃ. marcarum annis singulis secundum communem et antiquam estimationem patrie excedentibus, filii conventus annuam certe quantitatis pecunie percipitis pensionem, cedente vel decedente rectore ipsius in usus proprios et perpetuos filii conventus pro sustentatione hospitum ad vos declinantium convertere valeatis et ipsius possessionem corporalem ingredi auctoritate propria, diocesani loci assensu minime requisito, reservata de proventibus ipsis vicario in ecclesia perpetuo servituro congrua portione pro sustentatione sua et oneribus episcopalibus et aliis supportandis, vobis felicis recordationis A. pape .iii. predecessoris nostri vestigiis inherendo auctoritate presentium indulgemus, non obstante quod post huiusmodi predecessoris nostri indulgentiam vobis factam ad presentationem abbatis monasterii vestri per loci diocesanum plures clerici seculares rectores instituti fuerunt in eadem, representandi vicarium pro tempore in eadem instituendum ecclesia tibi, fili abbas, tuisque successoribus qui fuerint pro tempore iure salvo. Nulli ergo homini liceat hanc paginam nostre concessionis infringere vel ei ausu temerario contraire. Si quis autem hoc attemptare presumpserit, indignationem omnipotentis Dei et beatorum Petri et Pauli apostolorum eius se noverit incursurum. Dat' Anagn' .vii. kalendas Octobris pontificatus nostri anno secundo. Nos igitur, facta diligenti inquisitione super contingentibus statum dicte ecclesie de Pakeham ac super estimatione singularum portionum ad dictam ecclesiam pertinentium, consideratisque circumstantiis universis, vicariam dicte ecclesie taxavimus in hunc modum, videlicet quod vicarius qui pro tempore fuerit in eadem habeat mansum ecclesie et totam liberam terram et pratum dicte ecclesie cum decimis inde provenientibus, totumque alteragium cum decimis molendinorum, fenorum, agnorum, pullorum, lactis et lane et omnibus aliis minutis decimis, oblationibus et obventionibus undecumque provenientibus. Prior vero et conventus monasterii supradicti percipiant omnes decimas garbarum ad dictam ecclesiam spectantes, preterquam de libera terra dicte ecclesie assignata vicarie supradicte. Et in supplementum portionis vicarii qui pro tempore fuerit, solvent dicti prior et conventus vicario antedicto .xl. solidos annuos ad .ii. synodos Gipewic' pro equali portione percipiendos de bonis dicte ecclesie de Pakeham ad prefatos priorem et conventum pertinentibus, assensu domini abbatis sancti Aedmundi, ipsius ecclesie patroni, et eiusdem loci conventus in omnibus premissis mediante. Idem quoque vicarius sustinebit omnia onera episcopalia et archidiaconalia debita et consueta. Et cum dictam ecclesiam vacare contigerit, dominus abbas sancti Aedmundi et sui successores ad vicariam ipsam clericum idoneum libere presentabunt. Hanc siquidem taxationem prior et conventus sancti Aedmundi gratam habentes et acceptam, se eam servaturos quantum in eis est fideliter promiserunt. In cuius rei testimonium presenti scripto sigillum nostrum apponi petimus. Dat' apud Thorned' .v. kalendas Aprilis anno gratie M° CC° LX° primo.

No indult of pope Alexander III relating specifically to Pakenham church is apparently extant, although there is one relating in such terms to the abbey's parish churches in general (*PUE* iii no. 322; *Pinchbeck Register* 11–12). Pope Alexander's indult was enregistered (*Reg. Alex. IV* no. 1253; *CPL* i 337). For the common valuation of the church at 30 marks, see Jocelin 64. In

1254 the portion of the rector was valued at £28, that of the monks at £2 13s 4d; in the 1268 valuation of the income of St Edmunds the church was listed at £20, with portions of the sacrist and almoner of £1 and £1 6s 8d respectively; in 1276 the valuation of the church was £40 (*VN* 425, 541, 552). In 1291 the church, appropriated to the convent, was assessed at £21 6s 8d and the vicarage at £10 13s 4d (*Taxatio* 119b).

142. Caen, St Stephen's Abbey

Confirmation for the monks of two-thirds of the demesne tithes of Gilbert de Tany at Bures, which they have held from time immemorial.

Gaywood, 25 July 1265

B = Norfolk R.O., DCN 40/7 (general cartulary of cathedral priory) fo. 79v (*inspeximus* by prior Roger and the convent, 17 September 1265). s. xiii ex.

Universis Cristi fidelibus presentes literas inspecturis vel audituris Symon miseratione divina Norwycensis episcopus salutem in Domino sempiternam. Quia intelleximus quod abbas et conventus de Cadomo et eorum antecessores quasdam decimas, videlicet duas partes decimarum garbarum provenientium de dominico Gilberti de Tany in parochia de Bures a retroactis temporibus quorum non existit memoria consueverunt libere et pacifice possidere, nos easdem decimas quatenus predicti religiosi illas rite possiderunt sibi et eorum successoribus auctoritate dyocesana confirmamus. In cuius rei testimonium presentibus literis sigillum nostrum fecimus aponi. Dat' apud Geywde octo kalendas Augusti anno gratie M° CC° LX° quinto, pontificatus nostri anno octavo.

Bures straddles the Essex-Suffolk county boundary. For the confirmation of these tithes by king Henry II, see *CDF* 156, and by archbp Richard of Dover, *EEA* ii no. 64. Gilbert de Tany, who died in 1221, was the last of the direct line (*English Baronies* 4).

143. Castle Acre Priory

General confirmation for the monks of their possessions in the diocese of Norwich.

Gaywood, 31 July 1265

A = Bodl. Norfolk ch. (a. 1) 54. Endorsed: Concessio episcopi Norwic' de omnibus ecclesiis, appropriationibus, pensionibus et portionibus Acrensibus, exhibita in visitatione; Mussel exhibitis per Adam de Fak' quatuor instrumentis subsid' probationis appropriationem; Hugh of Mursley's notarial sign (s. xiv in); further illegible endorsement relating to visitation; approx. 360 × 265 + 34 mm.; seal missing, two diagonal slits, apparently for cords.

B = BL ms. Harley 2110 (Castle Acre cartulary) fos. 136r-37r (129r-30r). s. xiii ex.

Universis Cristi fidelibus ad quos presens scriptum pervenerit Symon Dei gratia Nortwicensis episcopus salutem in Domino sempiternam. Sacra scriptura testante cognovimus quod in elemosinarum largitione ab ipso fonte misericordie fidelibus peccatorum sunt indulta remedia, quorum devotio spe venie consequende pietatis usibus plura consuevit conferre beneficia. Cum igitur debitores simus[1] ut ea que religiosis devotio fidelium contulit pie sollicitudine tueamur, ad universitatis vestre notitiam volumus pervenire nos, predecessorum nostrorum vestigiis inherentes, pietatis intuitu et favore sacre religionis canonice concessisse et episcopali auctoritate presentibus confirmasse dilectis filiis nostris monachis de Castelacra ecclesias, pensiones et decimas subscriptas in proprios usus eorum et ecclesie sue imperpetuum convertendas; videlicet ecclesiam sancti Iacobi de Castelacra, ecclesiam de Newetun', ecclesiam de Kemestun', ecclesiam de Suthcreic, ecclesiam de Westbarsham, ecclesiam de Melewde et ecclesiam beate Marie Magdalene de Wigehale cum omnibus pertinentiis earundem, salvis vicariis debitis portionibus qui in eisdem ministrabunt; insuper antiquas pensiones subscriptas, videlicet .v^{que}. marċas annue pensionis de ecclesia de Haverhille, et tres marcas de ecclesia de Trunch, et .ii. solidos de ecclesia sancte Marie de Dunham, et .ii. solidos de ecclesia sancti Andree de Dunham, et .ii. solidos de ecclesia de Baggetorp, et .i^{am}. marcam de ecclesia de Westbrige, et .1^{am}. marcam de ecclesia de Trekestun', et .i^{am}. marcam de Wichingesete, et .xx. solidos de ecclesia de Estbarsham, et .xx. solidos de ecclesia sancti Andree de Tatersete, et dimidiam marcam de ecclesia omnium sanctorum de Tatersete, et .xl. solidos de ecclesia de Fulmodestun' et .x. marcas de eadem ad opus infirmorum monachorum de Castelacra, et .i^{am}. marcam de ecclesia sancti Michaelis de Fincham, et .i^{am}. marcam de ecclesiis apostolorum Petri et Pauli de Wesehamthorp', et dimidiam marcam de ecclesia de Estlechesham, et .xii. d. de ecclesia de Otringehithe, et .ii^{as}. marcas de ecclesia de Haspehalle; item decimas subscriptas: in Weseham, .ii^{as}. partes decimarum de dominicis Roberti de Stuteville, Alani filii Rogeri et Galfridi filii Iohannis Lambert; in Gressinghale, Ausing' et Welingham, .ii^{as}. partes omnium decimarum de dominico dicti Roberti de Stuteville; in Gressinghale et Skerninge, .ii^{as}. partes decimarum de dominicis Willelmi de Kirtling, Radulfi Crowar, Henrici quondam filii Ysabelle et Radulfi de Hyngringeshoe de tenemento quod fuit Petri Tupaz; in Witheresfeld et Eastlechesham, omnes decimas de dominico dicti Roberti de Stutevill'; in Grimestune, .ii^{as}. partes decimarum de dominico comitis Warrenn'; in Depedene, .ii^{as}. partes omnium decimarum de dominico Radulfi de Wanci et liberorum hominum suorum; in Waterdene, .ii^{as}. partes decimarum de dominicis Roberti de Barsham, Reginaldi de Sancto Martino,[a] et medietatem decimarum .xxx. acrarum de dominico Willelmi de Burnham; in Houtun', Rokelund et Northwolde, .ii^{as}. partes decimarum de dominicis Baldwini de Rosay, Hugonis filii Ricardi, Willelmi de Houtun', Roberti de Katestun', Rogeri de Paveli, Radulfi de Duntun et Gilberti de Waleham; in Winebotesham, decimas de terra quam Willelmus camerlencus tenuit; in Congham, .ii^{as}. partes decimarum de dominicis Augustini, Galfridi filii Radulfi, et totam decimam de dominicis Ricardi de Wighale et sanctimonialium de Blakeberwe; in Fincham, .ii^{as}. partes decimarum de dominicis Nigelli et Willelmi de Spinevill', Sampsonis Talebott, Ricardi de Meyners, Ricardi de Lacumbe et Iohannis de Litlewell'; in Blonorton,

.ii^{as}. partes [fo. 136v] omnium decimarum de dominico quondam Radulfi filii Gilberti domini de Telnetesham; in Gaitun, Hillingetun', Flicheam, .ii^{as}. partes omnium decimarum de feodo comitis Warren' et Ricardi de Merlay; in Gatele, totam decimam de sartis nemoris Willelmi de Lesewis et decimam de terra que vocatur Tobisnap'; in Rucham, .ii^{as}. partes decimarum de dominico quondam Hugonis de Fokintune et medietatem omnium decimarum de dominico quondam Iuliane filie Willelmi filii Ricardi de Wyrmelle quod nunc est Willelmi Buteler et quorundam hominum suorum; in Holkham et Claye, .ii^{as}. partes omnium decimarum de dominicis quondam Huberti de Montecanesii et Gilberti filii Ricardi; in Nortbarsham, .ii^{as}. partes decimarum de dominicis quondam Willelmi Braunche, Willelmi et Reginaldi et de terra quondam Hoeli de Waterdene; in Westwyniz, .ii^{as}. partes decimarum de dominico Ricardi filii Symonis; in Hersham, totam decimam de dominico Willelmi de Freney; in Westlechesham, decimam de terra que vocatur Ralniswde, de dominico Willelmi filii Ricardi de Lechesham, et in eadem .ii^{as}. partes decimarum de dominico quondam Rogeri de Cressy; in Lirlinge, .ii^{as}. partes decimarum de dominico quondam Osberti de Lirlinge; in Stanham, Crokefeldet et Hesse, .ii^{as}. partes decimarum de dominicis Galfridi filii Herlewine, Petri de Narford, Hugonis de Rikingehale et Walterii de Hethfeld; in Totleshale, .ii^{as}. partes decimarum de dominicis Roberti de Verli et Willelmi Capri; in Greinestun', .ii^{as}. partes decimarum quondam Rogeri de Greinestun'; in Wychingesete, .ii^{as}. partes decimarum de dominico quondam Petri Buzun; in Wechesham, .ii^{as}. partes decimarum de dominico quondam Gyrardi; in Fueldune, .ii^{as}. partes omnium decimarum de dominico quondam Roberti de Frivill'; in Fildedalling', .ii^{as}. partes omnium decimarum de dominicis quondam Rogeri Bachun et Ricardi Bachun; in Skerninge, .ii^{as}. partes de dominico Saeri de Frivill' et decimas de sartis de Heringeshae; in Taverham et Draytun, .ii^{as}. partes decime bladi de toto dominico Willelmi filii Baldrici; in Wirham et Buketun', tertiam partem decimarum de feodo Arnaldi de Moesy et Philippi Engleis; in Thomestun' et Thoftis, .ii^{as}. partes decimarum de dominicis eorundem monachorum; in Sypedeham et Rokelund, .ii^{as}. partes decimarum de dominico Iohannis de Kattestun'; in Narford, .ii^{as}. partes omnium decimarum de dominicis quondam Godwini, Galfridi et Bundon' filiorum Saulis; in Magna Massingham, .ii^{as}. partes decimarum de feodo quondam Roberti de Frivill' de toto feodo de Caylli; in Wendling, totas decimas de Magna et Parva Dichwud de dominico quondam Reginaldi filii Elwold, tam de feodo Giffardi quam Willelmi de Franchevill'; in Fransham et Skerninge, .ii^{as}. partes decimarum de dominico Gilberti militis; in Kerdestun' et Thymelthop, .ii^{as}. partes decimarum de dominico Godefridi de Bellomonte; in Tatersete, .ii^{as}. partes decimarum de dominico quondam Willelmi de Bellomonte; in Clypestun, .ii^{as}. partes decimarum de dominico Willelmi de Grantaut; in Snetesham, .ii. solidos de decimis de feodo comitis Warrenn' percipiendos per manus prioris de Wymundham; in Stanford, .ii^{as}. partes omnium decimarum de dominico Roberti de Mortemer; in Clopptun, .ii^{as}. partes decimarum de dominico Petri Giffard de feodo comitis Warren'; in Stiberde, .ii^{as}. partes decimarum de dominicis

Humfridi de Esthawe et participum suorum; in Estbarsham, totam [decimam] de dominicis quondam Willelmi de Beaumunt, Philippi de Snaring', Reginaldi de sancto Martino; in Burnham, .ii^{as}. partes decimarum de dominicis quondam Philippi de Burnham, Willelmi de Grancurt, Iohannis filii Radulfi, Hugonis de Polestede, Willelmi de Gymingham, Roberti Angre; et in Depedale, .ii^{as}. partes decimarum de dominico Willelmi filii Henrici; in Sidesterne, .ii^{as}. partes omnium decimarum de dominico quondam Alani filii Briani; in Dunham, totam decimam .xxx. acrarum de terra Atelund; in Alder-[fo. 137r]ford et Westorp', .ii^{as}. partes decimarum de dominicis quondam Willelmi de Bottun' et Ricardi filii Roberti de Westorp; in Santun', .ii^{as}. partes decimarum de dominico Ade de Hachebeche; in Feltewelle, .ii^{as}. partes decimarum de dominico quondam Willelmi de Spinevill'; in Sutacra, totam decimam de terra cementarii; in Ho, .ii^{as}. partes decimarum de dominico Iohannis militis; in Suldham, .ii^{as}. partes decimarum de dominicis Symonis filii Hugonis, Rogeri filii Galfridi, Rogeri Trussebut, Thome de Gruville, Willelmi filii Lambert, et de terra Theribaldi; in Marham, .ii^{as}. partes decimarum de dominico quondam Hermeri de Bechewell' et medietatem decimarum de toto feodo quondam Walterii de Marham; in Tyringetun', .ii^{as}. partes omnium decimarum de dominico Willelmi Herlewin' de feodo quod tenet de domino Willelmo Bardolf; in Clenwaretun', .ii^{as}. partes decimarum terre de la Hoe. Ut igitur hec nostra concessio et confirmatio perpetuam habeat firmitatem, eas scripto presenti et sigilli nostri appositione communimus; inhibentes firmiter sub pena anathematis ne quis sive ex malitia sive ex temeritate contra eas venire presumat vel illas infringere aliquatenus attemptet. Datum apud Geywud pridie kalendas Augusti anno Incarnationis .M^{o}. CC^{o}. L^{o}. XV°., pontificatus nostri anno octavo.

[1]Cf. Rom. 8: 12.

144. Creake Abbey

Grant to the canons in proprios usus, because of their recent foundation and poverty, of the church of Gateley, which is of their patronage, in accordance with papal letters authorising them to enter into full possession thereof on the death or resignation of John the rector, which authorisation, however, they feel might not be put into full effect without the consent of the diocesan. The rector has consented and has resigned the church into the bishop's hands, submitting to his ordinance. The abbot and convent shall receive annually as the personatus *twenty shillings in instalments at the two Norwich synods from John, who shall retain the residue; but on his death or resignation they may without further authorisation enter into full possession, saving to the vicar who shall minister therein a suitable portion of the revenues from which he may live and discharge the dues of the church to the bishop and others. The right to tax this vicarage is reserved to the bishop and his successors.*

North Elmham, shortly before 6 January [1259 × 1265], possibly 5 January 1259

B = Christ's College Cambridge, Creake Abbey muniments 7 (Creake abbey charter roll). s. xiii ex.

Universis Cristi fidelibus presentes litteras inspecturis Simon Dei gratia Norwycensis episcopus salutem in Domino sempiternam. Licet dilecti filii abbas et canonici ecclesie sancte Marie de Crek, ordinis sancti Augustini, nostre diocesis, litteras apostolicas de gratia sedis eiusdem speciali optinuissent quod, cedente vel decedente Iohanne rectore ecclesie de Gateleg', cuius veri patroni existunt, ecclesiam ipsam in proprios usus libere retinerent, iidem animadvertentes quod propositum suum super hoc sine consensu diocesani ad plenum consequi nequiverint, nobis humiliter supplicarunt ut sibi super hoc paterna solicitudine providere curaremus. Attendentes igitur quod quanto dictorum religiosorum cura propinquius ad nos spectare dinoscitur, tanto circa commodum propensius vigilare tenemur, et quod eorum ecclesia, pro eo maxime quod nova existit plantatio, adeo proventus habeat tenuos et exiles quod ex eis non possunt commode sustentari, ut liberius et quietius Deo famulentur in futurum, ecclesiam predictam de Gatele, de consensu et voluntate eiusdem rectoris qui eam in manibus nostris resignavit et ordinationi nostre simpliciter et absolute se submisit, dictis religiosis in proprios usus concessimus perpetuo possidendam, sub forma tamen et ordinatione subscripta, videlicet quod dicti abbas et canonici viginti solidos annue pensionis nomine personatus per manus dicti Iohannis percipiant annuatim pro rata portione ad duas sinodos Norwycenses. Residuum autem fructuum et proventuum eiusdem ecclesie integre et libere permaneat penes antedictum Iohannem. Cedente autem vel decedente dicto Iohanne, dicti religiosi dictam ecclesiam in proprios usus eisdem concessam libere ingrediantur cuiuscumque consensu irrequisito et eam integre possideant in futurum, salva vicario in eadem ecclesia perpetuo servituro de ipsius proventibus congrua portione de qua sustentare valeat, et tam episcopalia quam alia eius onera sustinere; quam vicariam taxandi nobis et successoribus nostris reservamus potestatem. In quorum testimonium nos litteras nostras patentes dictis religiosis dedimus sigilli nostri munimine roboratas. Dat' apud Northelmham die Dominica proxima ante epiphaniam Domini M° CC° L° [ ].ª Hiis testibus: magistro Stephano de Strumpeshale etc.

ª *om.* B

The date 1250 is obviously incorrect. Pope Alexander IV's indult, copied in this roll, is dated 28 March 1257. The first feast of Epiphany after Walton's consecration was 1259; he died on 2 Jan. 1266, when the Sunday before Epiphany was 3 Jan.

In 1254 Gateley was valued at £20, and the portion of Castle Acre at 6s 8d (*VN* 379); in 1291 the church, appropriated to the canons, was assessed at £17 6s 8d, apart from Castle Acre's portion and the vicarage, which was not subject to the tenth (*Taxatio* 79b).

144A. Reginald Deubeneye

Confirmation, with the consent of the chapter of Norwich, to Reginald, the bishop's squire, his heirs and assigns, of all the messuage with its appurtenances which he holds in North Elmham by purchase from Nicholas de la Bruer, and also of all the land which he purchased from Walter de la Bruer.

[10 March 1258 × 2 January 1266]

A = Norfolk R.O., ms. 1392, 4D7. Dorse not visible; approx. 218 × 120 + 19 mm.; slits for two seals, tags and seals missing.
Pd (calendar) *Norwich Cathedral Charters* ii, no. 120.

Omnibus Cristi fidelibus presens scriptum visuris vel audituris Symon divina miseratione Norwycensis episcopus salutem in Domino sempiternam. Noverit universitas vestra nos de unanimi assensu et voluntate capituli nostri Norwycensis concessisse et hac presenti carta nostra confirmasse Reginaldo Deubeneye valletto nostro totum mesuagium cum terris et tenementis et omnibus aliis pertinentiis que idem Reginaldus tenet in villa de Northelmham, que videlicet mesuagium et terre fuerunt de perquisitione Nicholai de la Bruer', et preterea totam terram cum omnibus suis pertinentiis quam predictus Reginaldus de Warino de la Bruer' perquisivit, habenda et tenenda sibi et heredibus suis vel suis assignatis libere, quiete, hereditarie, inperpetuum, faciendo inde domini feodi illius servitia inde debita et consueta. In cuius rei testimonium sigillum nostrum una cum sigillo capituli Norwycensis presenti scripto fecimus apponi.Hiis testibus: dominis Hamone Burth et Hamone de Pattesl', Hamone Chevre, Iohanne de Preston', Augustino de Brom', Rogero de la Gyrn', Iohanne Tebaud et aliis.

145 . Ely Cathedral Priory

Notification that when the bishop taxed the vicarage of Lakenheath at a true value of ten marks, he ordained that it should in perpetuity consist of half the land of the church with a suitable manse, with the oblations, obventions and other elements of the altarage pertaining to the vicarage; reserving to the monks, who hold the church in proprios usus *by papal concession, the tithe of wool, lambs and sheaves, and the other half of the land with the manse which was the rector's. The vicar shall discharge all ordinary obligations to bishop and archdeacon.*
Gaywood, 15 May 1264

B = CUL, EDR ms. G3/28 (Ely cartulary) pp. 207b-208a. s. xiii ex. C = ibid., p. 208a-b
(*inspeximus* by prior Roger and convent of Norwich, 28 September 1264).

Universis sancte matris ecclesie filiis ad quos presentes littere pervenerint Symon miseratione divina ecclesie Norwycensis humilis minister salutem in Domino. Ad notitiam vestram volumus pervenire quod cum vicariam ecclesie de Lakingh'ᵃ ad verum valorem .x. marcarum de consilio peritorum taxaverimus, eandem vicariam in rebus infrascriptis perpetuo consistere finaliter ordinamus, videlicet in medietate terre ad dictam ecclesiam de Lak' pertinentis cum manso convenienti et oblationibus, obventionibus et aliis utilitatibus omnibus ad alteragium predicte vicarie spectantibus, hoc salvo, quod prior et conventus Elyenses, qui dictam ecclesiam de Lak' ex concessione sedis apostolice in proprios usus habere dinoscuntur, decimam lane, agnorum, garbarum, et aliam dicte terre medietatem, cum manso qui fuit dicte ecclesie rectoris, inperpetuum habebunt. Et dictus vicarius qui pro tempore fuerit in ecclesia memorata omnia onera ordinaria tam episcopalia quam archidiaconalia sustinebit. In cuius rei testimonium huic scripto sigillum nostrum fecimus apponi. Dat' in manerio nostro de Geywode idibus Maii anno Domini M° CC° LX° IIII°.

ª Lak' C

As early as 1152 the monks complained to pope Eugenius III that Lakenheath church, assigned to the maintenance of the monks, was held against their will by Wlvard the clerk (*Liber Eliensis* 353–4; *PUE* ii no. 69). In 1254 the church was valued at £6 13s 4d, and the portion of the prior of Ely at £5; the prior also held the manor there, valued at £20 (*VN* 432). On 26 Aug. 1255 pope Alexander IV, acting in accordance with letters of pope Celestine [III], granted to the monks the churches of Stapleford (Ca.), Lakenheath and Winston (Sf.), valued at thirty marks, which the diocesans had wrongfully given to several secular clerks; these grants were to take effect on the death or resignation of the rectors, and perpetual vicars were to be appointed (*Reg. Alex. IV* no. 800; *CPL* i 322–3). In 1291 the church, appropriated to Ely, was valued at £14 13s 4d, with the vicarage not listed (*Taxatio* 121).

146. Eye Priory

Grant to the monks in proprios usus *of the church of Yaxley, of their advowson, saving a vicarage taxed by the bishop. The monks shall receive as the* personatus *half the tithe of sheaves; the vicar shall receive the other half, together with the altarage and the messuage, houses and free land of the church. The vicar shall discharge all customary obligations to bishop and archdeacon; the monks and the vicar shall discharge extraordinary burdens proportionately. Whenever the vicarage falls vacant, the monks shall freely present a suitable* persona.

5 January 1264

B = Chelmsford, Essex R.O., D/Dby. Q. 19 (Eye cartulary) fo. 53r–v. s. xiii ex.
Pd (calendar) in *Eye Cartulary* i no. 101.

Omnibus Cristi fidelibus presentes litteras inspecturis vel audituris Symon divina miseratione episcopus Norwycensis salutem in Domino sempiternam. Noveritis nos divine religionis intuitu dilectis in Cristo filiis priori et conventui de Eya ecclesiam de Iakeleye, in qua ius optinent patronatus, salva vicario qui pro tempore fuerit in eadem deservituro vicaria a nobis taxata, in proprios usus concessisse perpetuis temporibus possidendam, salvis nobis et successoribus nostris et nostre ecclesie Norwycensi in omnibus iure et dignitate. Et ut prioris et conventus predictorum separata sit portio et distincta ab ea quam vicarius optinebit, eas sic duximus distinguendas, ordinantes quod iidem prior et conventus medietatem decimarum garbarum ad dictam ecclesiam de Iakeleye spectantium percipiant nomine personatus; aliam vero medietatem cum alteragio, mesuagio, domibus et libera terra ad eandem ecclesiam pertinentibus habebit vicarius, qui omnia onera debita et consueta episcopalia et archidiaconalia sustinebit; onera vero extraordinaria dicti prior [fo. 53v] et conventus et vicarius pro rata suarum portionum inter se partientur. Et quotiens dictam vicariam vacare contigerit, prefati prior et conventus ydoneam personam nobis et successoribus nostris ad eandem libere presentabunt. Quam ordinationem pontificali confirmantes auctoritate, presenti scripto sigillum nostrum fecimus apponi. Hiis testibus: magistris Iohanne archidiacono Suff', Adam de Wautun' et Iohanne de Wygorn', Roberto de Wymecot', Iohanne de Norwyco, Iohanne Thebaud et aliis. Dat' nonas Ianuarii anno Domini millesimo ducentesimo sexagesimo tertio, pontificatus nostri anno sexto.

On 25 Jan. 1264 Martin Adelum of Mellis quitclaimed to the monks all right in the advowsons of the churches of Yaxley and Mellis (*Eye Cartulary* i no. 103). In 1254 Yaxley church was valued at £13 6s 8d and the prior's portion at 13s 4d (*VN* 430); in 1291 the church was listed at £12, with the vicarage untaxed (*Taxatio* 123b).

147. Eye Priory

Institution of Ralph of Eccleshall, clerk, to the vicarage of the church of Yaxley, at the presentation of the prior and monks.

Ipswich, [5 January × 24 March] 1264

B = Chelmsford, Essex R. O., D/Dby. Q. 19 (Eye cartulary) fo. 53v. s. xiii ex.
Pd (calendar) in *Eye Cartulary* i no. 102.

Omnibus Cristi fidelibus presentes litteras visuris vel audituris Simon divina miseratione episcopus Norwycensis salutem in Domino sempiternam. Noverit universitas vestra nos ad presentationem prioris et conventus de Eya Radulphum de Ecleshal clericum ad vicariam ecclesie de Iakele admisisse ipsumque in eadem cum suis pertinentiis perpetuum vicarium canonice instituisse, salvis nobis et ecclesie nostre Norwycensi in omnibus iure et dignitate. In cuius rei testimonium presentibus litteris sigillum nostrum apponi fecimus. Dat' apud Gypewyc' anno gratie M° CC° sexagesimo tertio.

At or shortly after the taxation of the vicarage (146).

*148. Field Dalling Priory

Confirmation for the monks of a portion of tithes. [*c.* 1265]

Noted in R.Taylor, *Index Monasticus* 13.

Taylor notes that Maud de Harscolye, or Harscove, *temp.* Henry II, gave to the abbey of Savigny a manor in Field Dalling, whereupon the monks established a cell or priory; *MRH* (129–30) indicates a date *c.* 1138 for the foundation of a priory, which seems to have been little more than a grange, which was sometimes treated as part of the grange of Long Bennington (Li.).. See also Tanner, *Notitia Monastica* 352; Blomefield, *Norfolk* 9 221. Several fines of the early thirteenth century record the settlement of disputes between the abbot of Savigny and various persons concerning land in Field Dalling (*Fines* ii nos. 52, 56–7, 264). In 1265 a portion of tithe was confirmed to that priory by the bp. In 1254 the church of Field Dalling was listed at £13 6s 8d, the tithes of Castle Acre at 10s, the portion of the Cistercian order at £1 and the lay fee of the Cistercian order at £10 13s 4d (*VN* 372). In 1291 the church was valued at £26 13s 4d, the portion of Castle Acre at 6s 8d and the *portio de Stitesterne sive abbatis de Saveneye* at £1; it is possible that Savigny had leased this portion to William of Syderstone, a member of bp Suffield's *familia*; the temporal goods of Savigny at Field Dalling were valued at £21 10s 3½d (*Taxatio* 82, 111).

149. Flixton Priory

Notification that, at the request of the lady Margery of Creake, who has granted the vill of Flixton for the foundation of a house of nuns, the bishop has dedicated a site there in honour of God, the Blessed Virgin and St Katherine, and has blessed a cemetery, where with God's will a monastery may be built; and he has bestowed upon certain women the habit and veil of religion, decreeing that they shall live under the Rule of St Augustine, with the addition of the following observances:

i) that they shall live enclosed, so that none of them shall leave their enclosure, save only for the prioress, with one or two others whom she may choose, when the necessities of the house so demand.

ii) that neither the prioress nor any nun may eat or drink with a man, lay or ordained, in their own house or elsewhere in the vill.

iii) because provision has been made by the lady Margery, the founder, for the nuns, at the house's inauguration seven in number, so that each shall have 50s annual rent for her sustenance, with suitable maintenance for two chaplains and for the necessary servants, it is decreed that no nun should be admitted beyond that number until the resources of the house have been increased to the extent that the sister newly admitted may have 50s for her maintenance from that increase. Any prioress who contravenes this ordinance shall be removed from office and another put in her place, and the admission shall be void.

iv) because idleness is the death and burial of the living, by the advice of religious men and with the consent of the founder it is ordained that the nuns, after they and the other women living within the enclosure have heard divine office, should work at all tasks befitting women and profitable to the house.

v) it is decreed that these ordinances shall be observed, along with the Rule, by the present nuns and their successors, for the remission of their sins and the salvation of their souls.

vi) wishing that the house may prosper, the bishop has confirmed to the nuns the alms and gifts reasonably granted and to be granted, that is, the lands and rents which they have in Flixton by the gift of the lady Margery of Creake, and all grants which she or anyone else may make to them in that vill or elsewhere in the diocese, and he confirms to them by diocesan authority the grants which they hold now or may by God's will acquire in future.   Colchester, 23 August 1259

B = BL ms. Stowe ch. 292 (*inspeximus* by prior Roger and convent of Norwich, 14 January 1260). s. xiii med.

Omnibus Cristi fidelibus ad quos presentes littere pervenerint Symon Dei gratia Norwicensis episcopus salutem in Domino sempiternam. Noverit universitas vestra nos ob favorem religionis et divini cultus augmentum, ad instantiam nobilis mulieris domine Margarie de Crek, que divinitus mota villam de Flixton' ad fundendum ibidem domum quandam monialium dedit et concessit, locum quendam in villa eadem in honore Dei, beate virginis Marie et sancte Katerine dedicasse cimiteriumque in eodem loco benedixisse, in quo ad opus monialium basilica Deo auctore construetur; in quo quidem loco mulieribus quibusdam vite approbate et honeste habitum monialium et velum imposuimus, statuentes ut que nunc sunt et que in futurum fuerint admittende secundum regulam beati Augustini vivant et eam profiteantur, adicientes ut eedem moniales observantias inferius annotandas, quas de bonorum consilio et consensu dicte domine duximus providendas, inviolabiliter observent, videlicet quod predicte moniales incluse vivant, ita ut nulla extra clausum earum egrediatur, nisi solummodo priorissa cum una vel duabus quas secum eligere voluerit, quibus tantummodo propter necessitatem domus licitum sit exire. Item, quod nec priorissa nec aliqua alia eiusdem domus monialis comedat seu bibat cum homine laico vel ordinato in curia propria seu alibi in villa de Flixton'. Et quia predictis monialibus, que in hac novitate septem sunt numero, provisum est in sustentatione competenti per dictam dominam Margeriam eiusdem domus fundatricem, videlicet quod quelibet domina ibidem velata usque ad numerum antedictum quinquaginta solidos sterlingorum annui redditus per annum habeat unde sustentetur, salva nichilominus duobus capellanis et servientibus predicte domui necessariis sustentatione competenti, volumus et in virtute obedientie firmiter precipimus quod nulla fiat in eadem domo monialis ultra numerum pretaxatum quousque bona dicte domus in tantum fuerint aucta quod illa de novo recepta ex novo incremento habere valeat quinquaginta solidos per annum ad sui sustentationem, statuentes ut priorissa que contra hoc preceptum nostrum aliquam admiserit ab administratione sua amoveatur et alia loco sui subrogetur, et admissio invalida censeatur. Item, quia otium mors est et vivi hominis sepultura, de consilio religiosorum et assensu predicte domine Margerie sic duximus statuendum, quod eiusdem domus moniales, postquam divina audierint et omnes alie mulieres que infra clausum fuerint permansure, laborent et operentur in omnibus operibus feminas[a] decentibus que predicte domui fuerint necessaria vel oportuna. Istas autem observantias prescriptas precipimus et iniungimus predictis monialibus ibidem existentibus et aliis post illas ibidem venturis ad tenendum et utendum una cum regula predicta, in remissione peccatorum et ad salutem animarum suarum. Attendentes igitur ut huius domus fundatio et dedicatio ad honorem Dei prosperos habeat successus et incrementa, universis notum esse volumus nos pietatis intuitu confirmasse monialibus loci predicti Deo, beate Marie virgini et sancte Katerine ibidem servientibus et servituris elemosinas et beneficia eis rationabiliter collata et conferenda, videlicet terras et redditus que habent in villa de Flixton' de dono domine Margerie de Crek, omnia insuper alia bona quecumque dicta Margeria vel aliquis alius in villa predicta vel alibi in nostra diocesi dictis monialibus iuste et rationabiliter intuitu caritatis contulerit vel conferet infuturum. Beneficia etiam que in presenti canonice possident vel futuris temporibus annuente Domino poterunt adipisci auctoritate diocesana confirmamus, sancte Norwicensis ecclesie iure, dignitate et honore et debitis consuetudinibus in omnibus et per omnia salvis. Ut autem omnia et singula in forma prescripta perpetuis temporibus robur optineant firmitatis, presenti scripto sigillum nostrum apposuimus. Dat' apud Colecestr' vigilia sancti Bartholomei pontificatus nostri anno secundo.

ᵃ feminis B

A small collection of the priory's charters is contained within the Campbell and Stowe charters in the BL.

In her 'foundation' charter, attested by bp Simon, Margery of Creake established the house for the souls of her parents and ancestors and of her late husband, Bartholomew of Creake. She granted the nuns the manor of Flixton with all appurtenances, including patronage of a mediety of the parish church. She renounced all rights of a patron during a vacancy, including any part in the election of a prioress (BL ms. Stowe ch. 291 ; *Monasticon* VI (i) 593–4). Licence had been granted by her overlord, Robert of Tattersall, for her to found a religious house on the fee held of him in Flixton (BL ms. Campbell ch. XII. 20). In 1280 Margery petitioned the king, and received royal licence, that after her death patronage of the house should pass to the bps of Norwich, and in the same year bp William Middleton issued for the nuns a version of the statutes in Anglo-Norman French (BL ms. Stowe ch. 336).

150. Flixton Priory

Revision of no. 149; with the addition of the grant of free right of burial in their cemetery, saving the rights of the mother church; omitting the section on enclosure and the prohibition of eating with men; with the addition that one of the two chaplains should in perpetuity celebrate especially for the souls of the lady Margery of Creake, her ancestors and heirs; with the addition that, to aid their work necessary for the welfare of the house, a shorter form of service should be provided for the nuns.   Norwich, 24 December 1261

B = BL ms Stowe ch. 293 (*inspeximus* by prior Roger and convent of Norwich, 27 December 1261). s. xiii med.

Noverit universitas vestra nos ob favorem religionis et divini cultus augmentum, ad instantiam nobilis mulieris domine Margerie de Crek, que divinitus mota villam de Flixton' ad fundandum ibidem domum quandam monialium dedit et concessit, locum quendam in villa eadem in honore Dei, beate Virginis Marie et sancte Katerine dedicasse cimiteriumque in eodem loco benedixisse ac ibidem sepulturam liberam concessisse, salva matricis ecclesie indempnitate, in quo quidem cimiterio ad opus monialium basilica Deo auctore construetur, ubi etiam mulieribus quibusdam vite approbate et honeste habitum monialium et velum imposuimus, statuentes ut que nunc sunt et que in futurum fuerint admittende secundum regulam beati Augustini vivant et eam profiteantur. Et quia predictis monialibus, que in hac novitate septem sunt numero, provisum est in sustentatione competenti per dictam dominam Margeriam eiusdem domus fundatricem, videlicet quod quelibet domina ibidem velata usque ad numerum antedictum quinquaginta solidos sterlingorum annui redditus per annum habeat ut simul unde sustententur, salva nichilominus duobus capellanis sustentatione competenti, quos dicta Margeria assignavit quod unus eorum pro anima sua specialiter et pro animabus antecessorum et heredum suorum perpetuis temporibus in dicta domo celebret, statuimus et in virtute obedientie firmiter precipimus quod nulla fiat in eadem domo monialis ultra numerum pretaxatum quousque bona dicte domus in tantum fuerint aucta quod illa de novo recepta ex novo incremento habere valeat quinquaginta solidos per annum ad sui sustentationem; statuentes ut priorissa que contra hoc preceptum nostrum aliquam admiserit ab administratione sua amoveatur et alia loco sui subrogetur, et admissio invalida censeatur. Item quia otium mors est et vivi hominis sepultura, de consilio religiosorum et assensu predicte domine Margerie sic duximus statuendum, quod eiusdem domus moniales, postquam divina audierint et omnes alie mulieres que infra curiam earum fuerint permansure, laborent et operentur in omnibus operibus feminas decentibus que predicte domui fuerint necessaria vel oportuna, qua de causa concedimus quod dictis monialibus brevius servitium provideatur. Istas autem observantias prescriptas precipimus et iniungimus predictis monialibus modo ibidem existentibus et aliis post illas ibidem venturis ad tenendum et utendum una cum regula predicta in remissione peccatorum et ad salutem animarum suarum. Affectantes igitur ut huius domus fundatio et dedicatio ad honorem Dei prosperos habeat successus et incrementa, universis notum esse volumus nos pietatis intuitu confirmasse monialibus loci predicti Deo, beate Marie virgini et sancte Katerine ibidem servientibus et servituris elemosinas et beneficia eis rationabiliter collata et conferenda, videlicet terras et redditus que habent in villa de Flixton' de dono domine Margerie de Crek, omnia insuper alia bona quecumque dicta Margeria vel aliquis alius in villa predicta vel alibi in nostra diocesi dictis monialibus iuste et rationabiliter intuitu caritatis contulerit vel conferet in futurum. Beneficia etiam que in presenti canonice possident vel futuris temporibus annuente Domino poterunt adipisci auctoritate diocesana confirmamus, sancte Norwicensis ecclesie iure, dignitate et honore et debitis consuetudinibus in omnibus et per omnia salvis. Ut autem omnia et singula in forma prescripta perpetuis temporibus robur optineant firmitatis, presenti scripto sigillum nostrum imposuimus. Dat' Norwic' vigilia Natalis Domini anno Domini M° CC° LX° primo.

151. Flixton Priory

Statutes supplementary to the Rule of St Augustine, promulgated for the nuns by the bishop, with the advice of men committed to the religious life, at the request of the lady Margery of Creake, the founder, and with the consent of the first prioress, Beatrice of Rattlesden, and the convent.

i) in order to avoid the poverty which so often vitiates the religious life of nuns, it is decreed that they should not admit sisters beyond the number determined by the founder, for each of whom she has made annual provision of 50s, from which provision they shall be maintained until the goods of the house increase to the extent that a nun newly received may also have annual provision of 50s. When a nun dies and her portion is vacant, another shall be received speedily, for the sake of the founder's soul.

ii) neither the present prioress nor any successor shall admit to any vacant portion anyone who is related to her more closely than in the third degree of consanguinity, nor anyone more distantly related unless the house's resources have grown by 50s a year; nor shall she allow any expenses or charges to her kin or the nuns' kin to the detriment of the monastery.

iii) the nuns shall not allow the alms which the lady Margery provided for them in perpetuity for distribution to be held back, but rather, from the grain grown on the demesne which they now hold or may acquire, after payment of tithe to the parish in which the demesne lies, they shall tithe again at the doors of their granges, and this tithe shall be given in full to men of religion who do not hold land or rents in demesne [? friars], and to other poor people, as seems to the prioress and convent most consonant with the will of God and the utility of their neighbours, without favouritism.

iv) if the nuns should acquire any church in proprios usus, *they should tithe all the grain which they may legitimately retain therefrom at the doors of their granges, and this second tithe should be distributed in full to the poor of that parish.*

v) if anyone should grant lands, rents or other goods in augmentation of these alms, it is forbidden for the nuns to expend these in any way other than in alms, in the foresaid manner.

vi) since these statutes are given so that the nuns may observe them without complaint for the perfecting of their souls, it is decreed that if the prioress should wilfully infringe any of them, or allow them to be infringed, in such a way that amends cannot be made, for that reason alone she may be removed from office and another substituted in her place.

vii) should any nun be an accomplice of the prioress in the infringement of any of these statutes, for that reason and on this occasion she should, after the removal of the prioress, be ineligible for that office.

viii) because these statutes are not contained within the Rule of St Augustine, to which with the statutes the nuns have made profession, the bishop has, with the consent of his chapter of Norwich, decreed that his chief confessor within that chapter shall, in the bishop's name, make an annual visitation of the nuns, with regard only to these statutes, informing the bishop of any infringement so that he may remedy it, but not without special episcopal licence usurping the right of visitation.

These statutes, confirmed by episcopal authority, shall be observed in perpetuity. A copy, sealed by bishop, founder and prioress, shall be retained in the archives of the prior and convent of Norwich. Ipswich, 23 March 1263

B = BL ms. Stowe ch. 294 (*inspeximus* by prior Roger and convent of Norwich). s. xiii med.

Omnibus Cristi fidelibus ad quos presentes litere pervenerint Symon Dei gratia Norwycensis episcopus salutem in Domino sempiternam. Noverit universitas vestra nos ob favorem religionis et divini cultus augmentum, ad instantiam nobilis mulieris domine Margerie de Crek fundatricis domus monialium de Flixton' et per propriam voluntatem Beatricis de Ratlesden' prime priorisse dicti loci et per assensum totius conventus sui, statuisse et firmiter iniunxisse, per gratiam Dei omnipotentis et per consilium virorum provectorum sancte religionis, ista statuta subscripta monialibus modo apud Flixton' existentibus et aliis post illas ibidem venturis, ad tenendum et utendum inperpetuum una cum regula beati Augustini in remissione peccatorum et ad salutem animarum suarum. Ut autem mala paupertas in dicta domo evitetur, qua religio mulierum sepe violatur, statuimus quod moniales dicte domus de Flixton' non recipiant aliquam mulierem ad velandum ultra numerum a dicta domina Margeria de Crek, dicte domus fundatrice, ibidem statutum, quibus per ipsam provisum est in sustentatione competenti, videlicet quod quelibet domina velata quam ibi posuit quinquaginta solidos sterlingorum annui redditus per annum habeat, ut inde simul sustententur quousque bona dicte domus in tantum fuerint aucta quod illa de novo recepta ex novo incremento habere valeat quinquaginta solidos per annum ad sui sustentationem, vel quod aliqua dictarum monialium mortua fuerit et eius portio vacua inveniatur, loco cuius alia festinanter pro anima dicte Margerie earum domus fundatricis caritative recipiatur; ita tamen quod priorissa dicte domus modo ibi existens neque aliqua alia post illam ibidem ventura non recipiet aliquam mulierem ad aliquam portionem vacuam in domo earum que sibi consanguinea fuerit proprius quam ad tertium gradum, neque aliquam mulierem que sibi predicte fuerit consanguinitatis recipiet ad velandum in dicta domo, nisi bona dicte domus ex novo creverint ad valorem quinquaginta solidorum per annum, neque etiam in parentibus suis seu monialium suarum aliquas expensas seu custamenta apponat unde domus illarum male possit gravari. Preterea statuimus quod dicte moniales elemosinam quam dicta domina

Margeria providit eis ad erogandum inperpetuum sustentari[a] non permittant, videlicet quod omnia blada que excolere poterunt in earum dominicis que modo habent vel que in futurum, annuente Domino, poterunt adipisci, post decimam debitam ecclesie in qua extant illa dominica, deciment ad hostia grangiarum suarum, et quod illa decima integre sine aliqua diminutione erogetur viris sancte religionis qui in dominicis nec tenent terras nec redditus, et aliis pauperibus, secundum quod priorissa dicte domus et eius conventus viderint quod magis sit ad voluntatem Dei et ad utilitatem proximorum suorum sine omni mala specialitate. Et si ita contingat quod dicte moniales aliquam ecclesiam in proprios usus poterunt adipisci, omnia blada que in dicta parochia ad opus earum iuste et rationabiliter poterunt retinere eodem modo debent decimare ad hostia grangiarum suarum, set quod illa secunda decima pauperibus in eadem parochia plenarie erogetur. Et si aliquis seu aliqua intuitu caritatis ad dicte elemosine augmentationem terras vel redditus vel aliqua alia bona dederit vel legaverit, prohibemus in virtute obedientie dictis monialibus quod illa bona divisa nec etiam decimam predictam non expendant nisi solummodo in elemosina modo quo predictum est. Et quia ista statuta predicta gratia Dei ita providimus quod moniales dicte domus ad perfectionem animarum suarum ea sine gravamine inviolabiliter possunt observare, statuimus quod si priorissa dicte domus aliquid dictorum statutorum sponte sua infrigerit vel etiam infringi permittat, ita quod ipsa illud emendare non possit, quod illa priorissa sola illa de causa ab administratione sua amoveatur et alia loco sui subrogetur. Si que etiam dicte domus monialis fuerit consentiens dicte priorisse ad aliquid dictorum statutorum infringendum, illa monialis post amotionem priorisse ea de causa vice illa ineligibilis permaneat. Et quia ista statuta prescripta non inveniuntur in regula beati Augustini, cui regule una cum dictis statutis moniales dicte domus suam fecerunt professionem, statuimus per assensum capituli nostri de Norwyco quod noster summus confessor dicti loci quolibet anno vice nostra semel visitet dictas moniales solummodo super statutis premissis, ita quod in aliis sibi non usurpet potestatem visitandi sine nostra licentia speciali; et si que invenerit contra aliquid predictorum statutorum ab aliqua seu ab aliquibus predictis monialibus temere attemptata,[b] nobis cum celeritate referat, ut in commissis salubre remedium apponamus. Ista autem statuta omnia et singula volumus inperpetuum observari et ea auctoritate pontificali confirmamus, salvis in omnibus nobis et successoribus nostris et ecclesie Norwycensis iure et dignitate. Et ut perpetua memoria presentium statutorum habeatur, providimus et ordinavimus quod ista omnia de verbo ad verbum sigillo nostro et sigillis dicte domine Margerie dicte domus fundatricis et dicte domine Beatricis prime priorisse dicti loci signata in custodia prioris et conventus nostri de Norwyco inperpetuum remaneant et observentur. Ut autem omnia et singula in forma prescripta perpetuis temporibus robur obtineant firmitatis, presenti scripto sigillum nostrum inposuimus. Dat' apud Gypewyc' die veneris proxima ante Annuntiationem beate virginis anno Domini M° CC° sexagesimo secundo.

ᵃ sustinare B   ᵇ attemptatum B

Although it is emphasised here that Beatrice of Rattlesen was the first prioress, a prioress Eleanor occurs in two final concords of January 1260 (TNA, CP25/1/214/26/86, 88).

152. Flixton Priory

Grant to the nuns in proprios usus *of the church of Dunston, with the consent of Margery of Creake, founder of the priory and patron of the church. Because of the poverty of this benefice, it is conceded that the nuns may have the church served by their own suitable chaplain.*   Hoxne, 4 January 1265

B = Norfolk R.O., DCN 40/7 (Norwich cathedral priory general cartulary) fos. 79v–80r (*inspeximus* by prior Nicholas and convent of Norwich, 12 May 1266). s. xiii ex.

Omnibus Cristi fidelibus presentes litteras inspecturis vel audituris Symon divina miseratione Norwycensis episcopus salutem in Domino [fo. 80r] sempiternam. Pie religionis fervorem quo dilecte in Cristo filie moniales de Flixton vigere dinoscuntur gratie nobis credite largitionem eisdem decernimus non dedisse. Nos igitur, de assensu et voluntate domine Margerie de Creke, fundatricis domus monialium de Flixton et patrone ecclesie de Dunston, eandem ecclesiam de Dunston prefatis monialibus in proprios usus concessimus perpetuis temporibus possidendam, salvis nobis et ecclesie nostre Norwycensi in omnibus iure et dignitate. Et propter exilitatem predicti beneficii, concedimus ut predicte moniales per capellanum proprium ydoneum eidem ecclesie competenter et honeste faciunt deserviri.ᵃ In cuius rei testimonium presentibus sigillum nostrum fecimus apponi. Dat' apud Hoxen' pridie nonas Ianuarii anno gratie Mº CCº LXº quarto et pontificatus nostri anno septimo.

ᵃ deservire B

Dunston church was valued at £3 6s 8d in 1254 (*VN* 416); it is not listed in the Taxatio of 1291.

153. Haveringland, Mountjoy Priory

Inspeximus *and confirmation of a charter of Peter of Narford whereby he granted in pure and perpetual alms to the canons two parts of all the tithes of his manor of Stansfield.*   Gaywood, 18 August 1265

A = TNA, E40/14060. Endorsed: Simonis episcopi Norwyc' confirmatio de decimis apud Stanesfeld (s. xiii); numeral IV struck through; approx. 188 × 122 + 16 mm.; green cord, fragment of seal, natural wax varnished dark brown.

Universis Cristi fidelibus presens scriptum visuris vel audituris Simon Dei gratia Norwycensis episcopus salutem in Domino. Noverit universitas vestra nos cartam Petri de Nereford inspexisse in hec verba: Omnibus Cristi fidelibus presens scriptum visuris vel audituris Petrus de Nereford salutem in Domino.

Sciatis me divine caritatis intuitu pro salute anime mee et animabus antecessorum meorum dedisse, concessisse et hac presenti carta mea confirmasse Deo et beate Marie et ecclesie sancti Laurentii de Heveriglond et canonicis ibidem Deo deservientibus et eorum successoribus in perpetuum, pro salute anime mee et pro animabus antecessorum meorum, in puram et perpetuam elemosinam duas partes omnium decimarum manerii mei de Stanesfeld, tam de grassis decimis quam de minutis, que quidem decime ad meam donationem spectare dinoscuntur, habendas et tenendas dictis canonicis ita libere et integre sicuti clerici antecessorum meorum eas liberius possiderunt. Et ut hec mea donatio et concessio et carte mee confirmatio rata et inconcussa permaneat in perpetuum, huic scripto sigillum meum apposui. Hiis testibus: domino Thoma de Pressenni, domino Roberto de Hulmo, Waltero vicario de Aysle, Iohanne de Nereford, Iohanne Launce, Willelmo de Crammavile, Henrico Frost. Cuius quidem donationem quantum in nobis est pontificali auctoritate confirmamus. In cuius rei testimonium presenti scripto sigillum nostrum fecimus apponi. Dat' apud Gaywode quintodecimo kalendas Septembris anno Domini millesimo ducentesimo sexagesimo quinto.

The chapel of St Lawrence had been founded during the reign of Richard I by William de Gisney, on his estate held of the honour of Clare at Haveringland, for two or three monks of Wymondham, but early in John's reign he transferred it to Augustinian canons; it became known as the priory of St Mary, St Michael and St Lawrence of Mountjoy, and perhaps housed five or six canons before the Black Death (*MRH* 71, 167). Peter of Narford occurs as a Bigod tenant in 1214 (*Bk Fees* 136), although the manor of Stansfield was held of the Clares.

There was litigation over these tithes in the early fourteenth century. In Sept. 1323 Elizabeth de Burgh, patron of Stansfield church, recorded that the rector had taken these tithes from the canons, and has made a composition with them with her assent. There was litigation before the official of Norwich in Nov. 1323. A composition was made on 6 Nov. 1332 whereby the canons should have for five years the tithes long received by the rector, and another composition, without any details, is noted in 1341 (abstract and copies from a lost cartulary by Peter le Neve, s. xvii, now Norfolk RO, ms. MC44/28–9, 500 X 1).

*154. Henry III, king of England

Letters patent of the bishop-elect notifying the king that when Nicholas of Coverham, clerk of Norwich diocese, was appealed before the king's justices on their last eyre in the county of Norfolk of the death of Girard of Humbleyard, and was afterwards claimed as a clerk before the justices by the official of the elect and was delivered to him, he purged himself as innocent before the official. by canonical purgation administered according to the custom of the church.

[13 October × 14 December 1257]

Mentioned in a royal writ to the sheriff of Norfolk, dated 14 Dec. 1257, ordering him to release to Nicholas his lands and chattels, which had been taken into the king's hands (*Cl. R. 1256–1259* 172).

Quod cum Nicholaus de Caverham, clericus Norwicensis diocesis, coram iusticiariis regis ultimo itinerantibus in comitatu Norf' appellatus est de morte Girardi de Humeleg', et postea ab officiali dicti electi a prefatis iusticiariis tanquam clericus requisitus et ei liberatus, idem Nicholaus canonica purgatione ei secundum morem ecclesie a dicto officiali indicta innocentiam suam super dicto crimine canonice et legitime purgavit coram officiali supradicto.

The royal justices were at Norwich 13 Oct.- 3 Nov. 1257 and at Yarmouth on 15 Nov. (Crook, *Records of the General Eyre* 126).

155. Henry III, king of England

Notification as bishop-elect addressed to Henry III asking that he bring secular authority to bear on Michael, rector of Brinton, who has remained excommunicate for more than forty days.   Hertford, 23 December 1257

A = TNA, C85/130/18. No endorsement; approx. 152 × 73 mm.; tongue torn away.

Excellentissimo domino suo H. Dei gratia illustri regi Angl', domino Hibern', duci Normann', comiti Andeg' et Aquit', devotus suus Symon miseratione divina Norwycensis electus salutem et debitam cum omni honore et ferventi dilectione reverentiam. Cum Michael rector ecclesie de Brinton' nostre diocesis in sententia excommunicationis, quam propter eius manifestam[a] offensam meruit innodari, per quadraginta dies et amplius iam steterit et adhuc in anime sue dispendium et aliorum cum eo communicantium, claves ecclesie contempnendo pertinaciter perseveret in eadem, excellentie vestre humiliter et devote supplicamus quatinus, cum ecclesia ultra quid faciat non habeat, iuxta regni vestri consuetudinem precipiatis de eo fieri iustitie complementum, ut quem Dei timor a malo non revocat secularis disciplina cohibeat a peccato. Valeat reverenda dominatio vestra per tempora longiora. Dat' apud Hortford' die dominica proxima ante natale Domini anno gratie M° CC° L° septimo.

[a] eius *repeated* A

*156. Henry III, king of England

Letters patent notifying the king that whereas Adam son of William of Hawkedon, clerk of Norwich diocese, was accused before the king's justices in eyre, when they were last at Cattishall, of the killing of Robert Darnel, and afterwards as a clerk was claimed by and delivered to the bishop, the said Adam successfully undertook canonical purgation according to ecclesiastical custom.
[10 × 27 March 1258]

Mentioned in a writ to the sheriff of Suffolk, dated 27 March 1258, ordering him to restore to Adam his lands and chattels, taken into the king's hands (*Cl. R. 1256–1259* 206).

Significavit regi Symon Norwicensis episcopus per litteras suas patentes quod cum Adam filius Willelmi de Huketon, clericus Norwicensis diocesis, coram iusticiariis regis ultimo itinerantibus apud Cateshull' diffimatus esset de morte Roberti Darnel, et postea a prefatis iusticiariis tanquam clericus ab eodem episcopo requisitus et ei liberatus, idem Adam canonica purgatione innocentiam suam super dicto crimine prefato episcopo canonice se legitime purgavit.

The justices were at Cattishall from 25 Nov.- 9 Dec. 1257 and on 14 Jan. 1258 (*Records of the General Eyre* 126). The bp was consecrated on 10 March.

157. Henry III, king of England

Notification addressed to Henry III asking that he bring secular authority to bear on Robert of Gedding, rector of Chelsworth, Robert le Quilter of Gedding, Hugh son of Walter of Stanton and Alice del Aker of Wyverstone, who have remained excommunicate for more than forty days.

Thetford, 22 November 1258

A = TNA, C85/130/19. No endorsement; approx. 170 × 59 mm.; tongue torn away.

Excellentissimo domino H. regi Angl', domino Hibernie, duci Normann', Aquit' et comiti Andeg', Simon miseratione divina Norwicensis ecclesie minister humilis salutem cum omni reverentia, obsequio et honore. Cum Robertus de Geddingh', rector ecclesie de Chelesworth', Robertus le Quilter de Gedding', Hugo filius Walteri de Stanton et Alicia del Aker de Wyvardeston' per quadraginta dies et amplius in excommunicatione iam steterint, in proprie salutis dispendium et aliorum cum eis communicantium, et adhuc in eadem perseverent, claves ecclesie pertinaciter contempnendo, excellentie vestre supplicamus quatinus, cum ecclesia Dei quid ultra faciat non habeat, iuxta regni vestri consuetudinem precipiatis de eisdem iustitie[a] fieri complementum, ut quod Dei timor a malo non revocat secularis saltem cohercio cohibeat a peccato. Valeat reverenda dominatio vestra per tempora longiora in Domino. Dat' apud Theford .x. kalendas Decembris anno gratie M° CC° L° octavo.

[a] iustie A

158. Henry III, king of England

Notification addressed to Henry III asking that he bring secular authority to bear on William Sturmi, Alexander of Barrow and John and Robert, his men, and Gilbert Russel, who have remained excommunicate for more than forty days.

Eccles, 4 December 1258

A = TNA, C85/130/20. No endorsement; approx. 174 × 57 mm.; tongue remains, tie torn away.

Excellentissimo domino H. Dei gratia illustri regi Angl', domino Hybernie, duci Norman', Aquit' et comiti Andeg', Simon miseratione divina Norwicensis ecclesie minister humilis salutem cum omni reverentia, obsequio et honore. Cum Willelmus Sturmi, Alexander de Barwe, Iohannes et Robertus homines ipsius Alexandri, et Gilebertus Russel per quadraginta dies et amplius in excommunicatione iam steterint, in salutis sue dispendium et aliorum cum eis communicantium, et adhuc in eadem perseverint, claves ecclesie pertinaciter contempnendo, excellentie vestre supplicamus quatinus, cum ecclesia Dei quid ultra faciat non habeat, iuxta regni vestri consuetudinem precipiatis de eisdem iustitie fieri complementum, ut quos Dei timor a malo non revocat secularis saltem cohercio cohibeat a peccato. Valeat reverenda dominatio vestra semper in Domino. Dat' apud Ecles pridie nonas Decembris anno gratie M° CC° L° VIII°.

*159. Henry III, king of England

Signification to the king of the excommunication of Eustace of Kimberley.
[Shortly before 15 September 1260]

> Mentioned in a royal writ to the bp, dated 15 Sept. 1260, ordering him that, whereas Eustace had complained that although he had frequently given undertakings to the bp that he would obey ecclesiastical mandates, the bp had refused to accept from him a legitimate *cautio*, that he should accept such a *cautio* and order his release from prison, and warning that should he fail to act, the sheriff of Norfolk should ensure that he did.
>
> Pd in *Cl. R. 1259–1261* 203.

quem per litteras vestras patentes secundum consuetudinem Anglie per corpus suum tanquam claves ecclesie contempnentem precimus iusticiari.

160. Henry III, king of England

Notification addressed to Henry III asking that he bring secular authority to bear, by the agency of the sheriff of Norfolk, on Gilbert of Beechamwell and Gilbert son of William of Caldecote, who have remained excommunicate for more than forty days. Norwich, 4 December 1260

A = TNA, C85/130/21. No endorsement; approx. 148 × 55 mm.; tongue and tie torn away.

Excellentissimo domino H. Dei gratia illustri regi Angl', duci Aquit', Simon miseratione divina Norwicensis ecclesie minister humilis salutem cum omni reverentia, obsequio et honore. Cum Gilebertus de Bichamwell et Gilebertus filius Willelmi de Caldekote in sententia excommunicationis iam steterint per quadraginta dies et amplius, claves ecclesie contempnendo, excellentie vestre supplicamus quatinus iuxta dingnitatem et regni vestri consuetudinem ipsos per vicecomitem Norff' capi et iustitiari, si placet, faciatis, donec beneficium absolutionis in forma iuris meruerint optinere. Valeat excellentia vestra per tempora longiora. Dat' Norwic' die sabbati proxima post festum sancti Andree apostoli anno Domini M° CC° sextodecimo.

Note the change in the royal title here. Henry III surrendered the titles of duke of Normandy and count of Anjou by the Treaty of Paris, 1259 (P. Chaplais, 'The Making of the Treaty of Paris and the Royal Style', *EHR* 67 (1952) 249–51.

161. Henry III, king of England

Notification addressed to Henry III asking that he bring secular authority to bear on Hugh of Blogate of Yaxley, clerk, who has remained excommunicate for more than forty days.   Hoxne, 20 March 1261

A = TNA, C85/130/22. No endorsement; approx. 152 × 56 mm.; tongue torn away.

Excellentissimo domino H. Dei gratia regi Angl', domino Hybernie et duci Aquit', Simon miseratione divina Norwycensis ecclesie minister humilis salutem cum omni reverentia, obsequio et honore. Cum Hugo de Blogate de Iachele clericus per quadraginta dies et amplius in excommunicatione iam steterit, in salutis sue dispendium et aliorum cum eo^a communicantium, et adhuc in eadem perseveret, claves ecclesie pertinaciter contempnendo, excellentie vestre supplicamus quatinus, cum ecclesia Dei quid ultra faciat non habeat, precipiatis de eodem iuxta regni vestri consuetudinem iustitie fieri complementum, ut quem Dei timor a malo non revocat secularis saltem cohercio cohibeat a peccato. Valeat reverenda dominatio vestra per tempora longiora in Domino. Dat' apud Hoxne die sancti Cuthberti anno gratie M° CC° sexagesimo.

ᵃ cum eo *interl.* A

162. Henry III, king of England

Notification addressed to Henry III asking that he bring secular authority to bear on Eustace of Paston, who has remained excommunicate for more than forty days.   London, 17 May 1261

A = TNA, C85/130/89. No endorsement; approx. 168 × 52 mm., damaged at top; tongue and tie torn away.

Excellentissimo [domino] H. Dei gratia illustri regi Angl', domino Hibern' et duci A[qu]it', Simon miseratione divina Norwycensis ecclesie minister humilis salutem cum omni reverentia, obsequio et honore. Cum Eustachius de Paston nostre diocesis in excommunicatione iam steterit per quadraginta dies et amplius, et adhuc in salutis sue dispendium et aliorum cum eo communicantium perseveret, claves ecclesie pertinaciter contempnendo, excellentie vestre supplicamus quatinus, cum ecclesia Dei non habeat quid ultra faciat, iuxta regni vestri consuetudinem precipiatis de eodem fieri iustitie complementum, ut quem Dei timor a malo non revocat secularis saltem cohercio cohibeat a peccato. Dat' London' .xvi. kalendas Iunii anno Domini M° CC° LX primo.

For a later signification of Eustace of Paston, see no. 166.

163. Henry III, king of England

Notification addressed to Henry III asking that he bring secular authority to bear on Hugh de Bruarr' of Thrandeston, who has remained excommunicate for more than forty days.   Norwich, 24 February 1262

A = TNA, C85/130/23. No endorsement; approx. 175 × 60 mm.; stub of tongue remains.

Excellentissimo domino H. Dei gratia illustri regi Angl', domino Hybern' et duci A', Simon miseratione divina ecclesie Norwicensis minister humilis salutem cum omni reverentia, obsequio et honore. Cum Hugo de Bruarr' de Randeleston nostre diocesis in excommunicatione iam steterit per quadraginta dies et amplius, et adhuc in salutis sue dispendium et aliorum cum eo communicantium perseveret in eadem, claves ecclesie pertinaciter contempnendo, excellentie vestre supplicamus quatinus, cum ecclesia Dei non habeat quid ultra faciat, iuxta regni vestri consuetudinem precipiatis de eodem fieri iustitie complementum, ut quem Dei timor a malo non revocat saltem secularis cohercio cohibeat a peccato. Dat' Norwic' .vi. kalendas Martii anno Domini M° CC° LX° primo.

164. Henry III, king of England

Notification addressed to Henry III asking that he bring secular authority to bear on Gilbert of Wells, William Wyphoscheved, Reginald Smelt, Raymund servant of Gilbert of Wells and Simon at Holand, who have remained excommunicate for more than forty days.   London, 9 May 1262

A = TNA, C85/130/24. No endorsement; approx. 155 x 60 mm., damaged at top; tongue torn away.

Excellentissimo domino H. Dei gratia regi Angl' illustri, [domino Hibern' et] duci Aquit', suus Simon miseratione divina Norwycensis ecclesie minister humilis salutem cum [omni reverentia, obsequio] et honore. Cum quidam Gilebertus de We[lle]s, Willelmus Wyphoscheved, Reginaldus Smelt, [Rai]mundus garcio Gileberti de Welles et Symon at Holand nostre diocesis in excommunicatione per quadraginta dies et amplius iam steterint, in sue salutis dispendium et aliorum cum eis communicantium, et adhuc in eadem perseverint, claves ecclesie pertinaciter contempnendo, excellentie vestre supplicamus quatinus, cum ecclesia Dei quid ultra faciat non habeat, iuxta regni vestri consuetudinem precipiatis de eisdem iustitie fieri complementum, ut quos Dei timor a malo non revocat secularis saltem cohercio cohibeat a peccato. Valeat reverenda dominatio vestra per tempora longiora. Dat' London' .vii. idus Maii anno gratie M° CC° sexagesimo secundo.

165. Henry III, king of England

Notification to Henry III that the bishop has examined the election of [Geoffrey, prior of the abbey of North Creake], to the abbacy of that house, has found it to be canonical and has therefore confirmed it.   [*c.* July – August] 1262

> A = TNA, SC1/63/1. No endorsement; fragment, approx. 105 × 53 mm.; tongue and tie torn away.

Excellentissimo domino H. Dei gratia regi Angl' illustri, domino Hybern' [et duci Aquit', Symon miseratione divi-]na Norwycensis ecclesie minister humilis salutem cum omni reverentia, o-[bsequio et honore. Vobis tenore pre-]sentium notum fecimus nos electionem in ecclesia beate Marie de Pratis de K[rec de Galfrido priore eiusdem cele-]bratam diligenter examinasse et eam canonicam invenisse, propt-[er..........] duximus confirmandam. Valeat dominatio vestra per tempora longa. Dat' apud [........M°].CC°. sexagesimo secundo.

> For Geoffrey, see *HRH* ii 435; the royal assent was given on 4 Aug. 1262 and the temporalities restored on 13 Aug. (*CPR 1258–66* 22b).

166. Henry III, king of England

Notification addressed to Henry III asking that he bring secular authority to bear on Eustace of Paston, who has remained excommunicate for more than forty days.   16 November 1262

> A = TNA, C85/130/25. No endorsement; approx. 158 × 50 mm.; tongue torn away.

Excellentissimo domino H. Dei gratia illustri regi Angl', domino Hybernie et duci Aquit', Simon miseratione divina Norwicensis ecclesie minister humilis salutem cum reverentia, obsequio et honore. Cum Eustachius de Pakeston nostre diocesis in excommunicatione steterit per quadraginta dies et amplius, et adhuc in salutis sue dispendium et aliorum cum eo communicantium perseveret in eadem, claves ecclesie pertinaciter contempnendo, excellentie vestre supplicamus quatinus, cum ecclesia Dei non habeat quid ultra faciat , iuxta regni vestri consuetudinem precipiatis de eodem iustitie fieri complementum, ut quem Dei timor a malo non revocat saltem secularis cohercio cohibeat a peccato. Valeat reverenda dominatio vestra in Cristo. Dat' .xvi. kalendas Decembris anno gratie M° CC° LX° secundo.

> For an earlier signification of Eustace of Paston, see no. 162.

167. Henry III, king of England

Notification addressed to Henry III asking that he bring secular authority to bear on Adam Boleyn of Dunwich, who has remained excommunicate for more than forty days. Norwich, 4 December 1262

A = TNA, C85/130/26. No endorsement; approx. 172 × 67 mm.; tongue torn away.

Excellentissimo domino H. Dei gratia regi Angl' illustri, domino Hibern' et duci Aquit', Simon miseratione divina Norwycensis ecclesie minister humilis salutem cum debita reverentia, obsequio et honore. Cum Adam Boleyn de Dunewyc' nostre diocesis per quadraginta dies et amplius in excommunicatione steterit, et adhuc in salutis sue dispendium et aliorum cum eo communicantium perseveret in eadem, claves ecclesie pertinaciter contempnendo, excellentie vestre supplicamus quatinus, cum ecclesia Dei quid ultra faciat non habeat, precipiatis de eodem iuxta regni vestri consuetudinem iustitie fieri complementum, ut quem Dei timor a malo non revocat secularis saltem coercio cohibeat a peccato. Valeat reverenda dominatio vestra per tempora longa. Dat' apud Norwycum pridie nonas Decembris anno gratie M° CC° sexagesimo secundo.

168. Henry III, king of England

Notification addressed to Henry III asking that he bring secular authority to bear on Bartholomew of Somerton, knight, and Bartholomew his son, who acts as rector of Winterton and Somerton, who have remained excommunicate for more than forty days. London, 10 January 1263

A = TNA, C85/130/28. No endorsement; approx. 167 × 60 mm.; tongue and tie torn away.

Excellentissimo domino H. Dei gratia illustri regi Angl', domino Hybern' et duci Aquit', Simon miseratione divina Norwicensis ecclesie minister humilis salutem cum omni reverentia, obsequio et honore. Cum Bartholomeus de Somerton miles et Bartholomeus filius eius clericus, qui se gerit pro rectore ecclesiarum de Winterton et Somerton nostre diocesis, in excommunicatione iam steterint per quadraginta dies et amplius, et adhuc in salutis sue dispendium et aliorum cum eis communicantium perseverent in eadem, claves ecclesie pertinaciter contempnendo, excellentie vestre supplicamus quatinus, cum ecclesia Dei quid ultra faciat non habeat, iuxta regni vestri consuetudinem precipiatis de eisdem iustitie fieri complementum, ut quos Dei timor a malo non revocat saltem coercio secularis cohibeat a peccato. Valeat reverenda dominatio vestra per tempora longa. Dat' London' .iiii. idus Ianuarii anno gratie M° CC° LX° secundo.

169. Henry III, king of England

Request to Henry III that, whereas master Reginald of Gressenhall, because he had long been excommunicate, was at the king's command captured by the sheriff of Norfolk and imprisoned, since he has sworn before the bishop to obey the church's mandates and has thus received absolution, that the king should order the sheriff to free him without delay.   London, 1 February 1263

A = TNA, C85/130/27. No endorsement; approx. 178 × 52 mm.; tongue and tie torn away.

Excellentissimo domino H. Dei gratia illustri regi Angl', domino Hibern' et duci Aquit', Simon miseratione divina Norwicensis ecclesie minister humilis salutem cum omni reverentia, obsequio et honore. Cum magister Reginaldus de Gressenhal, pro [eo] quod in excommunicatione diutius steterat, claves ecclesie pertinaciter contempnendo, ad mandatum vestrum per vicecomitem Norf' secundum consuetudinem regni vestri captus sit et incarceratus, ac idem magister, prestito coram nobis iuramento de parendo mandatis ecclesie, beneficium absolutionis in forma iuris sit consecutus, excellentie vestre supplicamus quatinus litteris vestris dicto vicecomiti celere precipitis ut dictum magistrum a carcere liberet sine mora. Valete. Dat' London' kalendis Februarii anno Domini M° CC° LX secundo.

On the following day, 2 Feb., a royal writ was despatched to the sheriff ordering Gressenhall's release with immediate effect.

170. Henry III, king of England

Notification addressed to Henry III asking that he bring secular authority to bear on William of Bintree, William of Clavering, Geoffrey Spiget of Stiffkey, William Saltere of Calthorpe, and John Boking, clerk, and Walter Crich of Saxthorpe, who have remained excommunicate for more than forty days.
            Bury St Edmunds [27 March 1263 × 25 February 1264, probably 27 July 1263]

A = TNA, C85/130/29. No endorsement; approx. 188 × 55 mm., bottom left corner torn away; no evidence of sealing method.

Excellentissimo domino illustri principi domino H. Dei gratia rex Angl', domino Hybern' et duci Aquit', Simon eiusdem miseratione Norwicensis ecclesie minister humilis salutem cum omni reverentia, obsequio et honore. Cum Willelmus de Binetre, Willelmus de Claveryng, Galfridus Spiget de Stivekeye, Willelmus Saltere de Calthorp', Iohannes Boking de Saxthorp', clericus, et Walterus Crich de eadem, nostre diocesis, in excommunicatione iam steterint per quadraginta dies et amplius, et adhuc in salutis sue dispendium et aliorum cum eisdem communicantium perseverint in eadem, claves ecclesie pertinaciter contempnendo, excellentie vestre supplicamus quatinus, cum ecclesia Dei non habeat quid ultra faciat, iuxta regni vestri consuetudinem precipiatis de eisdem fieri iustitie complementum, ut quos Dei timor a malo non revocat saltem co[hercio secula]ris cohibeat a peccato. Valeat dominatio vestra per tempora longiora. Dat' apud Sanctum Eadmundum .vi. kalendas ... CC° LX° tertio.

The bp was certainly at Bury St Edmunds on 28 July 1263 (no. 173).

171. Henry III, king of England

Notification addressed to Henry III asking that he bring secular authority to bear on Richard de Musters, who has remained excommunicate for more than forty days.   London [2 April 1263 × 4 March 1264]

A = TNA, C85/130/32. No endorsement; approx. 174 × 54 mm., bottom left corner torn away; no evidence of sealing method.

Excellentissimo domino et illustri principi domino H. Dei gratia regi Angl', domino Hybern' et duci Aquit', Simon divina miseratione Norwicensis ecclesie minister humilis salutem cum omni reverentia, obsequio et honore. Cum Ricardus de Musters nostre dyocesis in excommunicatione iam steterit per quadraginta dies et amplius, et adhuc in salutis sue dispendium et aliorum cum eo communicantium perseveret in eadem, claves ecclesie pertinaciter contempnendo, excellentie vestre supplicamus quatinus, cum ecclesia Dei non [habeat quid] ultra faciat, iuxta regni vestri consuetudinem precipiatis de eodem iustitie fieri [complementum, ut] quem Dei timor a malo non revocat saltem cohercio secularis co[hibeat a peccato. Valeat] excellentia vestra per tempora longiora. Dat' London' .iiii^{to}. nonas .... LX° tertio.

The date of this actum must be between iv nones April 1263 and iv nones March 1264.

173. Henry III, king of England

Notification addressed to Henry III asking that he bring secular authority to bear on John Mayour of Norwich, who has remained excommunicate for more than forty days.   Bury St Edmunds, 28 July 1263

A = TNA, C85/139/30. No endorsement; approx. 185 × 48 mm.; tongue and tie torn away.

Excellentissimo domino et illustri principi domino H. Dei gratia regi Angl', domino Hibern' et duci Aquit', Simon eiusdem miseratione Norwicensis ecclesie minister humilis salutem cum omni reverentia, obsequio et honore. Cum Iohannes Mayour de Norwico nostre diocesis in excommunicatione iam steterit per quadraginta dies et amplius, et adhuc in salutis sue dispendium et aliorum cum eo communicantium perseveret in eadem, claves ecclesie pertinaciter contempnendo, excellentie vestre supplicamus quatinus, cum ecclesia Dei non habeat quid ultra faciat, iuxta regni vestri consuetudinem precipiatis de eodem iustitie fieri complementum, ut quem Dei timor a malo non revocat saltem cohercio secularis cohibeat a peccato. Valeat excellentia vestra per tempora longiora. Dat' apud Sanctum Eadmundum .v. kalendas Augusti anno Domini M° CC° LX° tertio.

174.Henry III, king of England

Notification addressed to Henry III asking that he bring secular authority to bear on William de Ardern and Matilda de Gray, who have remained excommunicate for more than forty days.   London, 10 August 1264

A = TNA, C85/130/35. No endorsement; approx. 165 × 55 mm.; tongue torn away.

Excellentissimo domino H. Dei gratia regi Angl', domino Hybern' et duci Aquit', Simon miseratione divina Norwycensis ecclesie minister humilis salutem cum omni reverentia, obsequio et honore. Cum Willelmus de Ardern' et Matildis de Gray nostre dyocesis in excommunicatione iam steterint per quadraginta dies et amplius, et adhuc in salutis sue dispendium et aliorum cum eis communicantium perseverent in eadem, claves ecclesie pertinaciter contempnendo, excellentie vestre supplicamus quatinus, cum ecclesia Dei non habeat quid ultra faciat, iuxta regni vestri consuetudinem precipiatis de eisdem fieri iustitie complementum, ut quos Dei timor a malo non revocat saltem cohercio secularis cohibeat a peccato. Valeat excellentia vestra per tempora longiora. Dat' London' quarto idus Augusti anno gratie M° CC° sexagesimo quarto.

175. Henry III, king of England

Notification addressed to Henry III asking that he bring secular authority to bear on John of Soham, rector of Naughton, Ralph of Semer, rector of Stanningfield, and Thomas de la Porte of Ipswich, who have remained excommunicate for more than forty days.   Bacton, 7 January 1265

A = TNA, SC85/130/33. No endorsement; approx. 175 × 44 mm.; tongue torn away.

Excellentissimo domino suo H. Dei gratia illustri regi Angl', domino Hibernie et duci Aquitann', Simon miseratione divina episcopus Norwicensis salutem cum obsequio, reverentia, honore. Cum Iohannes de Saham, rector ecclesie de Navelton, et Radulfus de Semere, rector ecclesie de Stanfeud, et Thomas de la Porte de Gypwico, nostre diocesis, in excommunicatione iam steterint per quadraginta dies et amplius, et adhuc in salutis sue dispendium et aliorum cum eis communicantium, claves ecclesie pertinaciter contempnendo, persistant in eadem, excellentie vestre supplicamus quatinus, cum ecclesia non habeat ultra quid faciat, precipiatis iuxta regni vestri consuetudinem de eisdem fieri iustitie complementum, ut quos Dei timor a malo non revocat secularis cohercio cohibeat a peccato. Valeat excellentia vestra in Domino per tempora longiora. Dat' apud Baketon' in crastino Epiphanie Domini anno gratie M° CC° sexagesimo quarto pontificatus nostri anno septimo.

> The form 'Stanfeud' may represent Stansfield and Stanningfield, Sf., and Stanfield, Nf. Since a month later Simon de Presseni was rector of Stansfield (177), and since the other two names signified were men of Suffolk, it is likely that Ralph Semer was rector of Stanningfield.

176. Henry III, king of England

Notification addressed to Henry III asking that he bring secular authority to bear on William [of Badingham], rector of Cransford, who has remained excommunicate for more than forty days.   Norwich, 24 February 1265

> A = TNA, C85/130/36. No endorsement; approx. 171 × 45 mm.; tongue torn away.

Excellentissimo domino H. Dei gratia regi Angl', domino Hybern' et duci Aquit', Simon miseratione divina Norwycensis ecclesie minister humilis salutem cum omni obsequio, reverentia et honore. Cum Willelmus rector ecclesie de Craneford nostre dyocesis in excommunicatione iam steterit per quadraginta dies et amplius, et adhuc in salutis sue dispendium et aliorum cum eo communicantium perseveret in eadem, claves ecclesie pertinaciter contempnendo, excellentie vestre supplicamus quatinus, cum ecclesia Dei non habeat quid ultra faciat, de eodem precipiatis fieri iustitie complementum, ut quem Dei timor a malo non revocat saltem coercio secularis cohibeat a peccato. Valeat excellentia vestra per tempora diuturna. Dat' Norwyc' sexto kalendas Martii anno gratie M° CC° LX^{mo} quarto.

> For William of Badingham, see no. 193 below.

177. Henry III, king of England

Notification addressed to Henry III asking that he bring secular authority to bear on Simon de Presseni, rector of Stansfield, Geoffrey de Pole, Adam de Pole and Richard son of Ranulf of Stansfield, excommunicated at the instance of the executors of the last testament of Thomas de Presseni, who have remained excommunicate for more than forty days.   Norwich, 25 February 1265

> A = TNA, C85/130/34. No endorsement; approx. 175 × 44 mm., bottom cut away; no evidence of sealing method.

Excellentissimo domino H. Dei gratia illustri regi Angl', Symon miseratione divina ecclesie Norwicensis minister humilis salutem cum omni reverentia, obsequio et honore. Cum Symon de Presseny, rector ecclesie de Stanfeud, Galfridus de Pole, Adam de Pole et Ricardus filius Ranullphi de Stanfeud', nostre diocesis, in excommunicatione steterint ad instantiam executorum testamenti Thome de Presseny .xl. dies et amplius, ac in dispendium salutis animarum suarum et aliorum cum eis communicantium, claves ecclesie pertinaciter contempnendo, perseverent in eadem, excellentie vestre supplicamus quatinus cum ecclesia Dei[a] nichil habeat ultra quid faciat, de eis precipiatis iustitie fieri complementum, ut quos Dei timor a malo non revocat secularis saltem cohercio cohibeat a peccato. Dat' Norwic' in crastino sancti Mathie apostoli anno Domini M° CC° LX° quarto.

[a] ecclesia Dei *om.* A

A Robert de Presseni held land of Robert Fitz Walter at Stansfield, Sf., in 1236 (*Bk Fees* 576); cf. no. 175 above.

178. Henry III, king of England

Notification addressed to Henry III asking that he bring secular authority to bear on John Malet, who acts as rector of Sculthorpe and who has remained excommunicate for more than forty days.   Gaywood, 1 April 1265

A = TNA, C85/130/37. No endorsement; approx. 170 × 45 mm.; tongue torn away.

Excellentissimo domino H. Dei gratia illustri regi Angl', domino Hybern' et duci Aquit', Simon miseratione divina Norwycensis ecclesie minister humilis salutem cum reverentia, obsequio et honore. Cum Iohannes Malet, qui se gerit pro rectore ecclesie de Sculthorp nostre dyocesis, in excommunicatione iam steterit per quadraginta dies et amplius, et adhuc in salutis sue dispendium et aliorum cum ipso communicantium perseveret in eadem, claves ecclesie pertinaciter contempnendo, excellentie vestre supplicamus quatinus, cum ecclesia Dei non habeat quid ultra faciat, iuxta regni vestri consuetudinem precipiatis de eodem fieri iustitie complementum, ut quem Dei timor a malo non revocat saltem cohercio secularis cohibeat a peccato. Valeat excellentia vestra per tempora diuturna. Dat' apud Geywod kalendis Aprilis anno gratie M° CC° LX^{mo} quinto.

It is highly likely that Malet was excommuniated for a further breach of his agreement with the monks of Lewes concerning the tithes of Sculthorpe (75–6).

179. Henry III, king of England

Notification addressed to Henry III asking that he bring secular authority to bear on Henry Malebysse, who acts as prior of Spinney, and who has remained excommunicate for more than forty days.   Gaywood, 16 April 1265

A = TNA, C85/130/38. No endorsement; approx. 188 × 49 mm.; tongue torn away.

Excellentissimo domino H. Dei gratia illustri regi Angl', domino Hybern' et duci Aquit', Simon miseratione divina Norwycensis ecclesie minister humilis salutem cum omni reverentia, obsequio et honore. Cum Henricus Malebysse, qui se gerit pro priore de Spineto nostre dyocesis, in excommunicatione iam steterit per quadraginta dies et amplius, et adhuc in salutis sue dispendium et aliorum cum ipso communicantium perseveret in eadem, claves ecclesie pertinaciter contempnendo, excellentie vestre supplicamus quatinus, cum ecclesia Dei non habeat quid ultra faciat, iuxta regni vestri consuetudinem precipiatis de eodem fieri iustitie complementum, ut quem Dei timor a malo non revocat saltem cohercio secularis cohibeat a peccato. Valeat excellentia vestra per tempora diuturna. Dat' apud Geywod' sextodecimo kalendas Maii anno Domini M° CC° LX^{mo} quinto.

> This is the first known occurrence of Henry Malebysse as prior; he still occupied the office in March 1272 (*HRH* ii 462).

180. Henry III, king of England

Notification addressed to Henry III asking that he bring secular authority to bear on Roger son of Richard del Ford of Tasburgh, who has remained excommunicate for more than forty days.   Norwich, 23 February 1266

> A = TNA, C85/130/39. No endorsement; approx. 154 × 48 mm.; tongue and tie torn away.

Excellentissimo domino H. Dei gratia regi Angl', domino Hybern' et duci Aquit', Simon miseratione divina Norwycensis ecclesie minister humilis salutem cum omni reverentia, obsequio et honore. Cum Rogerus filius Ricardi del Feld de Tasburgh nostre dyocesis in excommunicatione iam steterit per quadraginta dies et amplius, et adhuc in salutis sue dispendium et aliorum cum eo communicantium perseveret in eadem, claves ecclesie pertinaciter contempnendo, excellentie vestre supplicamus quatinus, cum ecclesia Dei non habeat quid ultra faciat, iuxta regni vestri consuetudinem precipiatis de eodem fieri iustitie complementum, ut quem Dei timor a malo non revocat saltem secularis cohercio cohibeat a peccato. Valeat dominatio vestra per tempora longa. Dat' apud Norwicum .vii. kalendas Martii anno gratie M° CC° LX^{mo} V.

181. Holme, St Benet's Abbey

Grant by the bishop-elect, with the consent of his chapter, to the monks in proprios usus *of the church of Horning, in the parish of which they were founded, which is vacant and which pertains to their patronage, so that all its revenues shall be distributed by the almoner to the poor at the abbey gate, except for one hundred shillings to be rendered each year by the almoner to the infirmarer for the use of the frail and sick, over and above the revenues hitherto assigned to the infirmarer so the care they receive may be improved. All who divert these revenues to other uses shall incur excommunication. The bishop*

reserves to himself the power to make other arrangements in the future, with the
advice of the abbot and convent, should it appear expedient so to do.

Thorpe, 30 November 1257

B = BL ms. Cotton Galba E ii (St Benet cartulary) fo. 49v (20v). s. xiii ex. C = Bodl. ms.
Norfolk roll 82 (St Benet roll) g. s. xiv in. D = ibid., h (*inspeximus* by prior Roger and
convent of Norwich, 30 Nov. 1257). E = BL ms. Cotton roll iv 57 (St Benet roll) 7. s. xiv.

Omnibus Cristi fidelibus ad quos presens scriptum pervenerit Symon divina
miseratione Norwicensis electus salutem in Domino sempiternam. Addicti
militie regulari, sicut Cristi bonus odor celesti conversatione redolentes, dignis[a]
caritatis operibus dant operam incessanter, ita digne[b] sunt amplioribus beneficiis
honorandi, ut et onus levius ferant ex honore et ad sue liberalitatis imitationem
ceteros animent et invitent; inter quos dilectos filios abbatem et conventum
sancti Benedicti de Hulmo tanto specialius benigno favore prosequi debemus
quanto multipliciter maiorem nostre dilectionis meruerint prerogativam. Optantes
igitur ipsis ex nostri[c] debito officii tanquam dignis[d] et bene meritis benefacere,
ecclesiam de Horninge vacantem et ad eorundem patronatum spectantem, in qua
etiam parochia dicti religiosi fundati noscuntur, eisdem et ecclesie sue in
proprios usus convertendam de voluntate et assensu capituli nostri concedimus et
confirmamus, ita scilicet quod omnes ipsius ecclesie proventus[e] per manus[f]
elemosinarii eiusdem domus ad portam ipsius abbatie pauperibus distribuantur,
excepto centum solidis per manum[g] ipsius elemosinarii infirmario domus
annuatim solvendis et in usus debilium et infirmorum fideliter expendendis, ut
preter proventus in usus infirmorum prius assignatos ex hac nostra concessione
et provisione se solito melius reficiant, gaudeant egrotantes et recreationi sue
sentiant debiles aliquid accrevisse. Omnes autem qui ipsius proventus in alios
usus converterint sententia excommunicationis innodamus, reservata tamen nobis
potestate alio modo ordinandi cum consilio abbatis et conventus si viderimus
futuris temporibus expedire. In cuius rei testimonio presenti scripto sigillum
nostrum fecimus apponi. Hiis testibus: magistro Willelmo archidiacono Norwic',
magistro[h] officiali nostro, Galfrido de Lodenes, magistro Herveo de Fakeham,[j] [k-]
magistro Adam de Wauton',[l] magistro Philippo de Tudeham,[m] magistro Simone
de Netisherde[n] et aliis.[-k] Dat' apud Thorp'[o] die sancti Andree apostoli[p] anno
gratie millesimo ducentesimo quinquagesimo septimo.

[a] dingnis C   [b] dingne C   [c] nostro C   [d] dingnis C   [e] ipsius ecclesie omnes proventus C   [f]
manum C   [g] manus C   [h] magistro interl. C   [j] Facham C   [k-k] *om.* B, *substitutes* etc.   [l]
Vautone B; Wautone E   [m] Thudeham D   [n] Netheshird C; Netlighirde D   [o] Torp' B   [p]
apostoli *om.* D

See no. 69 above. The amount to be allocated to the infirmarer has now been increased from £3
6s 8d to £5.

D represents the first recorded instance of Roger Scarning as prior of Norwich; cf. *Fasti* ii
61; *HRH* ii 55. The archdn of Norwich is almost certainly mr William of Suffield, brother of the
previous bp; *magistro officiali* is strange; this is possibly mr John of Alvechurch, cf. no 197
below.

*182. Lynn, Burgesses of

Grant, with the consent of his cathedral chapter, that the burgesses may elect one of their number as mayor and present him to the bishop and chapter for confirmation. [10 March 1258 × 2 January 1266]

> B = TNA, C53/57 m. 9. s. xiii med. C = King's Lynn Borough Archives, KL/C2/7.
> s. xiii med. D = ibid. KL/C2/8. s. xiii med.
> Pd (calendar) from B in *C Ch R* 1257–1300 92.

cumque S. quondam Norwicensis episcopus et capitulum suum Norwicense concesserint et carta sua confirmaverint prefatis burgensibus quod ipsi per suam electionem creare possint sibi aliquem de suis in maiorem, et maiorem ab eis creatam eidem episcopo et suis successoribus presentare.

> Mentioned in a charter of king Henry III, dated Westminster, 26 March 1268, which recites the liberties granted to the burgesses by king John (*Rot. Chart.* 138) and notes bp Simon's actum as above. The king grants that, in recognition of the good services rendered by the burgesses during the late troubles in the realm, they may henceforth, in lieu of a reeve (*prepositi*), elect and have a mayor without impediment by the crown, and the said mayor shall take distraint of those who take toll or custom from the burgesses of Lynn, saving the city of London.

183. Mendham Priory

Notification that, since the portion of the monks in the church of Mendham is so meagre that nothing without damage can be subtracted from it for a vicar, the bishop, wishing to foster works of charity in their house, has of his special grace granted that they may have their portion served by their own suitable chaplains.
                                                                   Norwich, 20 June 1265

> B = Norfolk R.O., DCN 40/7 (general cartulary) fos. 78v–79r (*inspeximus* by prior Roger and convent of Norwich, 23 June 1265); stained at foot of fo. 78v. s. xiii ex.

Universis sancte matris ecclesie filiis presentes litteras inspecturis vel audituris Symon divina miseratione Norwycensis episcopus salutem in Domino sempiternam. Cum portio prioris et conventus de Mendham quam ª⁻in proprios usus⁻ª optinent in ecclesia de Mendham adeo fuerit exilis quod ex eadem absque .....ᵇ detrimento vicario non valeat resecari, attendentes igitur p....ᶜ prefatis religiosis prospicere quo magis in eorum domo frequentare valeant opera caritatis, [fo. 79r] eisdem priori et conventui concessimus de gratia speciali quod eorum portioni per proprios capellanos ydoneos libere valeant deservire, salvis nobis et ecclesie nostre Norwycensi in omnibus iure et dignitate. In cuius rei testimonium presentibus litteris sigillum nostrum fecimus apponi. Dat' apud Norwycum .xii. kalendas Iulii anno gratie Mᵒ CCᵒ LXᵒ quinto.

> ª⁻ª Reading conjectural   ᵇ Stained, four or five letters   ᶜ Stained, three or four letters

> Mendham was a pre-Conquest minster church (Blair, *Minsters and Parish Churches* 4); its substantial endowment was subsequently divided between the Augustinian canons of Holy

Trinity, Ipswich (fd. *c.* 1133), and the Cluniacs of Mendham priory, a daughter house of Castle Acre (fd. before 1155). In 1254 the Ipswich portion was valued at £30 13s 4d and that of Mendham priory at £16 (rather more than meagre); also listed is a portion of 13s 4d described in various MSS as 'portio de Sechford quam habet H. vicarius' or 'portio Willelmi de Derby', and another portion of F. the vicar, 6s 8d (*VN* 449). In 1291 the canons' portion was valued at £26 13s 4d, the monks' at £11, a vicarage at £4 6s 8d and the portion of the monks of Sées at £5 (*Taxatio* 115b).

184. Norwich Cathedral Priory

Grant in proprios usus *in perpetuity, for the use of the cellar to improve the food of guests, of the church of Blickling. When it falls vacant they may enter into possession by authority of this indult, and they shall cause it to be served by chaplains whom they may themselves appoint and remove.* Hoxne, 20 May 1265

B = Norfolk R.O., DCN 40/5 (cellarer's cartulary) fo. 13v (12v). s. xiii ex. C = ibid. DCN 40/4
(episcopal charters) pp. 122–3. s. xiv in. D = ibid. pp. 303–4.
Pd in *Norwich Cathedral Charters* i no. 217.

Omnibus sancte matris ecclesie filiis presens scriptum visuris vel audituris Simon Dei gratia episcopus Norwicensis[a] salutem in Domino sempiternam. Noverit universitas vestra nos divine intuitu pietatis dedisse, concessisse, assignasse et presenti carta nostra confirmasse dilectis filiis nostris priori et conventui ecclesie sancte Trinitatis Norwic' ecclesiam de Bliclinghe cum omnibus ad eam pertinentibus ad opus celerarie sue in proprios usus perpetuo possidendam ad prebendam hospitium emendandam, salvo nobis et successoribus nostris inperpetuum iure pontificali et parrochiali. Indulsimus etiam eis[b] quod cum istam ecclesiam vacare contigerit, liceat predictis priori et conventui vacuam eiusdem ecclesie possessionem ingredi presenti hac auctoritate a nobis eis indulta; et facient in eadem ecclesia competenter ministrari per capellanos suos pro sua voluntate rationabili amovendos et admittendos. In cuius rei testimonium presenti scripto sigillum nostrum fecimus apponi. Hiis testibus: magistro Ada de Waleton' officiali nostro, magistro Iohanne de Wigorn'[c] cancellario nostro, magistro Iohanne de Wythio, magistro Stephano de Strumeshagh' senescallo nostro, Roberto de Wonecot',[d] Iohanne Tebaud, Iohanne clerico capelle nostre et aliis multis clericis et laicis fidedignis. Dat' apud Hoxn'[e] .xiii. kalendas Iunii anno gratie millesimo ducentesimo sexagesimo quinto, pontificatus nostri anno octavo.

[a] Norwicensis episcopus C, D   [b] eis *om.* C   [c] Wygorton' B   [d] Woneton' B   [e] Hoxne C

The church had originally been granted to the monks by bp Everard (*EEA* 6 no. 39); by an agreement of 1205, it was to be conferred by the consent of the bp and the convent, but shortly afterwards it was granted to the monks *in proprios usus* by bp Gray (ibid. nos. 390–1, 396); in the interim, they received therefrom an annual pension of one mark (*EEA* 21 no. 76). In 1254 the church was valued at £10, *sine portione de Lama* (possibly a portion temporarily assigned to a papal nominee, cf. no. 27 above) (*VN* 397); and in 1291 at £10 13s 4d (*Taxatio* 83).

185. Norwich Cathedral Priory

Confirmation by the bishop of the enfeoffment of the monks by Silvester son of Richard of Combs in his mills in Thornham, the one a watermill and the other a windmill, which he held of the bishop and his predecessors, with the millsoke of all men of the bishop's homage in that vill and with all other appurtenances, saving to the bishop and his successors freedom from multure when the bishop comes there to visit and at the collection of his corn in the autumn, and saving also what his predecessors were accustomed to receive from this tenement.

[*c.* 1 June 1265]

A = Norfolk R.O., DCN 43/49. Endorsed: de molendinis de Thornham (s. xiii); pressmark; approx. 190 × 117 + 16 mm.; parchment tag, seal, brown wax.
B = Norfolk R.O., DCN 40/4 (episcopal charters) pp. 123–4. s. xiv in. C = ibid. pp. 304–5.
Pd in *Norwich Cathedral Charters* i no. 218.

Omnibus Cristi fidelibus presens scriptum visuris vel audituris Symon divina permissione Norwycensis episcopus salutem in Domino sempiternam. Noverit universitas vestra nos donationem, concessionem et feoffamentum quod Silvester filius Ricardi de Cumbes fecit dilectis in Cristo filiis priori et conventui Norwycensibus de molendinis suis, videlicet uno aquatico et alio ad ventum, que de antecessoribus nostris et nobis tenuit et tenet in Thornham, cum tota secta totius homagii nostri in eadem villa ad eadem molendina pertinente et omnibus aliis eorum pertinentiis, confirmasse, salva nobis et successoribus nostris libera multura ad predicta molendina sine prestatione tolneti habenda per nostros adventus et perhendinationes apud Thornham faciendos et ad blada nostra in autumpno colligenda, et salvis nobis et successoribus nostris hiis que nos et predecessores de predicto tenemento percipere consuevimus. In cuius rei testimonium presenti scripto sygillum nostrum fecimus apponi. Hiis testibus: Herveo de Stanhowe et Rogero de Mustroil militibus, Hugone de Kayli, Rogero de Toftes, Thoma filio Willelmi de Hakeford, Gileberto filio Gyleberti de Tychewell', Willelmo de Secheford', Galfrido de Say, Ricardo de Vilechen de Parva Ryngested', Godefrido Suetewater de eadem, Willelmo filio Hugonis de Hulmo et multis aliis.

For the grant to the monks by Silvester, see *Norwich Cathedral Charters* ii nos. 71–2; they paid him £10 and agreed to pay a penny a year at Michaelmas to him and his heirs, and on their behalf £2 a year to the bp; they were also to allow him and his heirs exemption from multure. This last was granted by prior Roger and the convent in a charter dated 1 June 1265 (ibid. no. 79). The lands and rents of the monks at Thornham were valued in 1291 at £5 19s 4d (*Taxatio* 91b).

186. Norwich, Hospital of St Giles

Grant to the master and brethren in proprios usus *of the parish church of Repps with the chapel of Bastwick, of which they hold the advowson, and which they*

*may for their greater profit serve by their own suitable chaplains. Considering,
however, the immense effort, hitherto unremunerated, which William of Rollesby,
clerk, has expended in the service of the hospital and of the bishop and his
church, he has with the consent of the master and brethren conceded to him, for
his lifetime, a portion of the church as a vicarage, which is to consist of all the
tithe of sheaves and all else pertaining to the chapel of Bastwick, all the altarage
of the mother church of Repps and all the land of the church beyond the
messuage of the* persona, *with meadows and the tithe of meadows, mills,
turbaries and fisheries. During his time as vicar William shall discharge all the
customary obligations of the church, and other burdens he and the master and
brethren shall share proportionately. On his death or resignation, the master
and brethren may serve the church by their suitable chaplains and may receive
all the revenues of church and chapel.*   Norwich, 8 December 1261

> A = Norfolk R.O., NCR 25b/604. Endorsed: Confirmatio de Reppys cum Bastwyc; nota
> confirmationem huius scripti de capitulo Nor' inter transcripta de Senges (s. xiii); approx.
> 242 × 147 + 17 mm.; single slit, tag and seal missing.
> B = Norfolk R.O., NCR 25b/3A (*inspeximus* by prior Roger and convent of Norwich, 3 March
> 1265). s. xiii ex. C = ibid. DCN 40/7 (general cartulary of cathedral priory) fo. 75v. s. xiii
> ex. D = ibid. NCR 24/48 (St Giles cartulary) fo. 53r. s. xiii ex.

Universis Cristi fidelibus presentes litteras visuris vel audituris Simon
miseratione divina episcopus Norwycensis salutem in Domino sempiternam.
Cultum divinum ad sustentationem pauperum desiderantes et sperantes augeri,
magistro et fratribus novelli hospitalis sancti Egidii Norwyc' ecclesiam
parochialem de Reppes cum capella de Bastwyk et cum omnibus aliis suis
pertinentiis, in qua ius optinent patronatus, in usus proprios caritatis intuitu
auctoritate pontificali duximus concedendam; et ut predicti magister et fratres ex
hac nostra appropriatione maioris fructus commodum reportent, concessimus
eisdem quod ecclesie de Reppes et capelle de Bastwyk predictis per proprios
capellanos ad hoc ydoneos et competentes valeant deservire. Porro considerantes
et attendentes laborem immensum quem Willelmus de Rollesby clericus in
obsequio predictorum magistri et fratrum necnon et nostro et ecclesie nostre
sustinuit hactenus irremuneratum, de consensu unanimi predictorum magistri et
fratrum portionem nomine vicarie predicto Willelmo suo perpetuo concessimus,
quam in proventibus inferius annotatis consistere ordinamus, videlicet in
omnibus decimis garbarum et aliis omnibus ad capellam de Bastwyk
pertinentibus, et toto altalagio matricis ecclesie de Reppes et tota terra illius
ecclesie extra mesuagium persone, cum pratis et decimis pratorum,
molendinorum, turbarum et piscariarum. Dictus vero Willelmus pro tempore suo
vicarius omnia onera ordinaria et consueta sustinebit; alia autem dicti magister et
fratres et dictus Willelmus pro rata portionum suarum inter se partientur.
Volumus autem et ordinamus quod, cedente vel decedente dicto W. de Rollesby,
predicti magister et fratres concessione nostra superius pretaxata libere utantur,
videlicet quod ecclesie de Reppes et capelle de Bastwyk predictis per proprios
capellanos ydoneos deserviant competenter et omnes proventus ad ecclesiam de

Reppes et capellam de Bastwyk predictas [pertinentes] integraliter percipiant, portione dicti W. de Rollesby cedentis vel decedentis sepedictis magistro et fratribus penitus accrescente, salvis nobis et ecclesie nostre Norwycensi in omnibus iure et dignitate. In cuius rei testimonium presentibus litteris sigillum nostrum fecimus apponi. Hiis testibus: magistro Iohanne de Alvithechyrch' archidiacono Suffolch', magistro Stephano de Strumeshagh', magistro Ada de Wauton', magistro Iohanne de Wygorn', magistro Iohanne de Wychyo, Roberto de Wennecote, Ricardo de Penesaux et aliis. Dat' Norwyc' die conceptionis beate Marie anno gratie millesimo ducentesimo sexagesimo primo.

> The advowson of Repps with Bastwick had been acquired by the Suffield family from St Benet's abbey in the late twelfth century, and Walter, the future bp, and his elder brother sir Roger had litigated in the *curia regis* in 1238 to strengthen their title (Blomefield, *Norfolk* xi 180–3; *CRR* xvi no. 356). The advowson was granted, with land in Repps, by William Suffield, archdn of Norwich, both patron and parson, after the death of his brother the bp, when he chose the hospital as his burial site. His grant was confirmed by Roger Bigod, earl of Norfolk. Eight years after bp Walton's grant of appropriation, in 1269, Hugh de Cailli and Agnes his wife (probably collusively) unsuccessfully challenged the hospital's right in the *curia regis*; they quitclaimed, in return for reception into all the spiritual benefits of the hospital, and issued their own confirmation charter (fos. 52v–53r of D). See Rawcliffe, *Medicine for the Soul* 83.
>
> This is the first occurrence of mr John of Alvechurch as archdn of Suffolk; cf. *Fasti* ii 68, which has 5 Aug. 1262.

187. Norwich, Hospital of St Giles

Induction of the master and brethren into corporal possession of the church of Seething, in accordance with a papal indult which they have presented to him authorising that they might on the death or resignation of the present rector take possession of the church, which had been granted to them in proprios usus *by bishop Suffield. Richard the rector having died, they had out of respect approached the bishop, who now acts by papal authority and his own, in addition permitting them to provide for the service of the church by one of their own chaplains, so long as he is suitable.*   Dereham, 25 October 1264

> A = Bodl. ms. Douce Ch. a. 1 53. No medieval endorsement; approx. 220 × 108 + 18 mm.; seal missing, fragment of parchment tag.
> B = Norwich, Norfolk R.O., DCN 40/7 (general cartulary of Norwich cathedral priory) fo. 75r–v. s. xiii ex.

Universis Cristi fidelibus presentes literas visuris vel audituris Simon miseratione divina episcopus Norwycensis salutem in Domino sempiternam. Accedentes ad nos magister et fratres hospitalis sancti Egidii de Norwyco nobis monstrarunt quod dominus papa eisdem indulsit quod ecclesiam de Scenges, cuius ius patronatus et appropriationem ex collatione bone memorie Walteri predecessoris nostri optinent, cedente vel decedente eiusdem rectore, licite valeant propria auctoritate ingredi et in proprios usus retinere; et licet predicti magister et fratres auctoritate predicta fulti papali possessionem predicte ecclesie possent ingredi, presertim cum Ricardus, tempore predicte indulgentie date rector predicte ecclesie existens, in fata decesserit, volentes tamen in hac parte ob reverentiam nobis deferre, humiliter nobis supplicare curarunt quod prefate indulgentie assensum preberemus et consensum. Nos igitur, predictam concessionem in Domino ratam habentes et commendatam, eandem quantum in nobis est predictis magistro et fratribus concessimus et ratificamus et eosdem in corporalem possessionem predicte ecclesie auctoritate papali et nostra induximus. Et ut de predicto beneficio papali et nostro predicti magister et fratres fructum maiorem optineant in futurum, eisdem concessimus de gratia speciali quod eidem ecclesie per aliquem de propriis capellanis ad hoc ydoneum et competentem valeant deservire, salvis nobis et successoribus nostris in omnibus iure et dignitate. In cuius rei testimonium has literas patentes munimine nostri sigilli fecimus roborari. Dat' et act' apud Derham die sabbati proxima post festum sancti Luce ewangeliste et ante festum apostolorum Symonis et Iude, anno Domini M° CC° LX° quarto et pontificatus nostri anno septimo. Testibus: magistro Ada de Walton', magistro Iohanne de Wygorn', magistro Stephano de Strumeshaye, Willelmo de Wenecote, Iohanne de Norwyco, Iohanne Tebald, Willelmo de Rollesby et aliis.

For the appropriation of the church, see no. 106 above. For papal authority, see pope Alexander IV's confirmation of 10 March 1255 (*Reg. Alex. IV* no. 254, *CPL* i 312; NRO NCR 24b/3), which specifies that on the death or resignation of the incumbents the hospital may enter into full possession of the churches of St Mary's South Walsham, Seething, Hardley and Cringleford, according to the concession of bp Suffield and the chapter of Norwich.

188. Norwich, Hospital of St Giles

Inspeximus *and confirmation of bishop Walter Suffield's second statutes for the hospital [107]. Grant of forty days remission of enjoined penance to those of his diocese, and of others of which the diocesans ratify this indulgence who, confessed and contrite, in any year on the feast of St Giles or within its octave come to the hospital to pray, to visit the sick or to confer any benefit upon its church.*   Norwich, 21 June 1265

A = Norfolk R.O., NCR 24b/4. No medieval endorsement; approx. 372 × 425 + 23 mm.; green cord, seal and counterseal, natural wax.

Universis sancte matris ecclesie filiis presentes literas visuris vel etiam audituris Simon miseratione divina episcopus Norwycensis salutem in Domino sempiternam. Que aguntur in tempore ne per lapsum temporis delabantur solent scriptarum testimonio eternari. Proinde universitati vestre volumus esse notum quod nos literas bone memorie Walteri predecessoris nostri super ordinatione et statutis in hospitali beati Egidii Norwyc', quod fundavit, necnon et collationes eiusdem ipsi hospitali, magistro et fratribus eiusdem hospitalis factis confectas ac suo et capituli sui sigillis munitas, non cancellatas, non abolitas nec in aliqua sua parte viciatas, diligenti examinatione habita inspeximus in hac forma: [no. 107]. Volentes igitur, inspirante gratia divina, per nos consummari et ad debitum effectum produci quod in premissis dedit predicti predecessoris nostri caritas inchoari, ut piorum operum suorum participes fieri mereamur in domo Domini, omnia et singula premissa rata in Domino habentes et firma, ea de verbo ad verbum auctoritate pontificali duximus confirmanda. Et ut fidelium devotio ad ipsum hospitale confluentium ferventius accendatur et laborem eorum leviorem faciat fructus gratie subsequentis, nos de Dei omnipotentis misericordia, gloriose genetricis eius Marie, sancti Egidii abbatis omniumque sanctorum meritis et intercessionibus confidentes, omnibus parochianis nostris et aliis quorum diocesani hanc nostram ratam habuerint indulgentiam, de peccatis suis confessis et contritis, qui causa orationis vel etiam visitationis infirmorum seu alterius beneficii ad ecclesiam ibidem constructam pie devotionis affectu accesserint, singulis annis perpetuo in festo beati Egidii et per octabas, quadraginta dies de iniuncta sibi penitentia misericorditer relaxamus. In cuius rei testimonium has literas patentes impressione [nostri]ᵃ sigilli fecimus communiri. Dat' apud Norwicum die dominica proxima ante festum nativitatis sancti Iohannis Baptiste anno gratie millesimo ducentesimo sexagesimo quinto et pontificatus nostri anno octavo.

ᵃ bottom left corner torn away

189. Peterstone Priory

Grant to the canons in proprios usus, *on account of the great poverty of their house, of the church of West Lexham, which is of their patronage, which is vacant by the death of Nicholas Anglicus, the rector, saving provision for a vicarage. They are to have all the tithe of corn, with half of the land pertaining to the church and with its messuage.*   Creake, 9 August 1259

B = Norfolk RO, DN Reg. 30 (Tanner's index vol. 1) p.144 (insert in Tanner's hand, ex autogr' penes Roger North de Rougham, 1719). s. xviii in.

Symon Dei gratia Norwicensis episcopus dedit priori et canonicis de Petreston, ad relevationem nimie paupertatis qua constricti esse dinoscuntur, ecclesiam de West Lechesham que de ipsorum est patronatu, post mortem Nicholai Anglici vacantem, in proprios usus possidendam, salva vicaria que taxata est etc. Prior habeat omnes decimas garbarum cum medietate terre et mesuagio ad ecclesiam pertinentibus etc. Dat' apud Crec quinto idus Augusti anno pontificatus nostri secundo.

The priory and hospital of St Peter was founded before 1200, possibly by a member of the Chesney family. There were apparently five or six canons caring for poor people. The house's income in 1291 was over £23. In 1449 Peterstone was annexed to the Augustinian priory of Walsingham. Shortly before then John Capgrave, in his treatise on orders under the Rule of St Augustine, described Peterstone as a local order peculiar to Norfolk (*MRH* 170). In 1254 the church was assessed at £2 13s 4d, and in 1291, excluding the portion of £1 10s of the monks of Castle Acre and a vicarage not subject to the tenth, the church appropriated to the canons was valued at £3 6s 8d (*VN* 380; *Taxatio* 79b).

189A. Pinley Priory

Indulgence of twenty days remission of enjoined penance to all those of his diocese, and of others whose diocesans ratify this grant, who, being contrite and confessed, make a contribution from their goods or in any way lend a helping hand to the construction and repair of the nunnery and the maintenance of the nuns.   Pinley, 24 June 1266

B = BL ms. Add. 28564 (R.B. Wheler's Collections for Warwickshire) pp. 109–10. s. xix.

Universis Cristi fidelibus Simon miseratione divina Norwicensis[a] ecclesie minster humilis [p. 110] salutem in Domino sempiternam. De Dei misericordia et beate Marie virginis omniumque sanctorum meritis confidentes, omninus vere prenitentibus et confessis parochianis, videlicet mostris et aliis quorum diocesani hanc nostram indulgentiam ratam habuerint, qui constructioni et reparationi operis monialium de Pineleya et sustentationi[b] earundem ibidem Deo servientium de bonis sibi a Deo collatis aliqua impenderint caritatis subsidia aut quocunque modo congruo manum[c] porrexerint adiutricem, viginti dies de iniuncta sibi penitentia misericorditer relaxamus. Dat' apud Pinneleyam[d] die nativitatis sancti Iohannis Baptiste anno Domini millesimo[e] ducentesimo sexagesimo.

[a] Norwich B   [b] sustentatione B   [c] manu B   [d] Pinneleya B   [e] milesimo B

The Cistercian nunnery of Pinley was founded in the mid-twelfth century by Robert of Pillerton, a tenant of the earl of Warwick, from whose descendant Peter de Montfort acquired the patronage in the mid-thirteenth century, before 1266 (*MRH* 275; *EEA* 13 no. 132). An indulgence of archbp Hubert Walter referred to the poverty of the nuns (*EEA* 3 no. 575). The indulgence issued by bp Walter Cantilupe of Worcester (mentioned *EEA* 13 no. 142) is transcribed in full on p. 109 of B.

190. Henry de Prato

Grant in perpetuity, with the consent of the cathedral chapter, to Henry de Prato of North Elmham, the bishop's sergeant at Thornham, his heirs and assigns, for his homage and service, of all the land which Hervey son of Ralph held in Thornham and of two other parcels there, to be held for an annual rent of four shillings and suit of court at Thornham at Michaelmas.

[10 March 1258 × 2 January 1266]

B = Norfolk R.O., DCN 40/7 (general cartulary of Norwich cathedral priory) fo. 78r; stained at foot. s. xiii ex.
Pd in *Norwich Cathedral Charters* ii no. 78.

Omnibus Cristi fidelibus presens scriptum visuris vel audituris Symon divina miseratione Norwycensis episcopus salutem in Domino sempiternam. Noverit universitas vestra nos de communi assensu et voluntate capituli nostri Norwycensis dedisse, concessisse et hac presenti carta nostra confirmasse Henrico de Prato de Northelmham, servienti nostro de Thornham, pro homagio et servitio suo, totam terram quam Herveus filius Radulfi tenuit in villa de Thornham, unacum duabus acris terre iacentibus apud Sunewyneshyl et tribus acris et dimidia terre que fuerunt de terra Galfridi Seym et Hervei Bunting in eadem villa, habendam et tenendam de nobis et successoribus nostris totam predictam terram cum omnibus suis pertinentiis predicto Henrico et heredibus vel assignatis suis libere, quiete, integre, pacifice et hereditarie in perpetuum, reddendo inde annuatim nobis et successoribus nostris ipse et heredes sui vel sui assignati quatuor solidos sterlingorum ad quatuor terminos anni predicte ville de Thornham censuales pro omni servitio, consuetudine et demanda seculari ad nos vel ad nostros successores pertinentibus, salva nobis et successoribus nostris una secta curie nostre de Thornham que tenetur ad festum sancti Michaelis annuatim facienda. Et ut hec nostra concessio et presentis carte nostre confirmatio omnium predictorum in perpetuum firmitatis robur optineant, presens scriptum et sigillo nostro et sigillo capituli nostri Norwycensis fecimus roborari. Hiis testibus: domino Rogero de Mustroly milite, magistris Stephano de Strumesth', Ada de Wauton', Iohanne de Wygorn', Ada de ...[a] nerel.

[a] three or four letters illeg. B

191. Rumburgh Priory

Grant to the monks, in proprios usus, *for the support of their works of charity, of the church of St Michael, South Elmham, of which they hold the advowson and from which they have long received an annual pension of half a mark, to take effect on the resignation or death of Conan the rector. They may have the church served, according to its resources, by their own suitable chaplains, and when it is vacant they may enter into possession of it by authority of this concession.*

South Elmham, 30 June 1265

B = Norfolk RO, DCN 40/7 (Norwich cathedral priory general cartulary) fo. 79r (*inspeximus* by prior Roger and the convent, 10 July 1265). s. xiii ex. C = Oxford, Bodl. ms. Top. Suff. d. 15 (cartulary of St Michael's, South Elmham) fo. 39r–v (36r–v). s. xv ex.

Universis sancte matris ecclesie filiis presens scriptum inspecturis vel audituris Symon miseratione divina episcopus Norwicensis salutem in Domino sempiternam. Ad universorum notitiam volumus pervenire nos divine religionis intuitu dilectis in Cristo filiis priori et monachis de Rumburg,[a] ut eorum caritatis opera ampliore gaudeant fulcimento,[b] ecclesiam sancti Michaelis de Suthelmham, in qua ius optinent patronatus, de qua dimidiam marcam annuam capiunt et per multa tempora ceperunt nomine pensionis, Conano eiusdem rectore cedente vel decedente, in proprios usus concessisse perpetuis temporibus possidendam, ita quod eidem ecclesie secundum suas facultates per proprios capellanos ydoneos[c] competenter et honeste faciant deservire. Concessimus insuper eisdem priori et monachis quod, decedente vel cedente predicto rectore, possessionem prefate eccesie vacue valeant ingredi et in huiusmodi usus retinere huius nostre concessionis auctoritate, salva[e] nobis et successoribus nostris et ecclesie nostre Norwicensi in omnibus iure et dignitate. In cuius rei testimonium presenti scripto sigillum nostrum fecimus apponi. Dat' apud Suthelmham[f] pridie kalendas Iulii anno gratie M° CC° LX° quinto et pontificatus nostri anno octavo.

[a] Romburg C   [b] incremento C   [c] idoneos C   [d] ecclesie prefate C   [e] salvis C   [f] Southelmham C

In the late twelfth or very early thirteenth century R., both *persona* and *patronus*, notified G[eoffrey], archdn of Suffolk (1188 x1213) that he had granted the church of St Michael to the monks in pure and perpetual alms, and begged him to admit them to the patronage, and Robert Warpeloke of Barsham quitclaimed to them all right in the advowson (fo. 36v of C). The next *persona*, Stephen of Hoxne, in the fifth year of the Interdict (24 March 1212 × 23 March 1213), who had previously from his institution paid an annual pension of one mark, granted to the monks as a pension all the tithes pertaining to the church (ibid. fo. 37r–v). In 1254 the church was valued at £4 (*VN* 461) and in 1291, appropriated to Rumburgh, at £6 13s 4d (*Taxatio* 119).

192. Sibton Abbey

Appropriation to the monks of the church of Rendham, and establishment of their revenues therefrom.   [10 March 1258 × 4 January 1266]

Mentioned in BL ms. Add. 34560 (extent). fo. 19r. s. xiv in.

See no. 122 above.

193. Sibton Abbey

Grant to the monks in proprios usus *of the church of St Peter, Cransford, which is of their advowson, to take effect on the death or resignation of William of Badingham, the rector, saving an adequate vicarage to be taxed by the bishop. This is done for the maintenance of guests and of the poor, formerly received cheerfully by the monks, at a time when hospitality is threatened by the current barrenness of the land.*   Sibton, 12 December 1263

B = Norfolk R.O., DCN 40/7 (general cartulary of Norwich cathedral priory) fo. 80r–v (*inspeximus* by prior Roger and convent of Norwich, 19 Aug. 1265); badly stained at foot of fo. 80r. s. xiii ex.

Pd (calendar) in *Sibton Charters* iv no. 952.

Omnibus Cristi fidelibus presentes litteras visuris vel audituris Symon Dei gratia Norwycensis episcopus salutem in Domino sempiternam. Notum sit ᵃ⁻quod cultaᵃ fide vidimus quatinus hillari wultu et corde iocundo domus de Sybeton' monachorum hospites in aula, pauperes ad portam, nostrisᵇ [fo. 80v] admisit et introduxit temporibus sed, pro dolor, hiis diebus immensa et insolita sterilitas tam piis operibus visa est prestare impedimentum. Cum igitur prefatum monasterium vere domus Dei sit, de sub cuius pede tanquam fons viniis huiusmodi fluunt beneficia, nec processu temporis sterilitatisᶜ morsibus ledi valeat imposterum vel minui, ecclesiam sancti Petri de Cranesford, que de ipsorum dinoscitur esse patronatu, decedente vel recedente Willelmo de Badingham rectore eiusdem ecclesie, ad sustentationem hospitum et pauperum in proprios usus concedimus, salva vicaria competenti per nos ibidem taxanda. Hanc autem donationem et concessionem predictis monachis fecimus salvis in omnibus episcopalibus consuetudinibus et nostre Norwycensis ecclesie dignitate. In cuius rei testimonium presens scriptum sigilli nostri impressione roboravimus. Dat' apud Sibeton' .ii. idus Decembris pontificatus nostri anno sexto. Testibus: magistro A. de Walton', magistro I. de Wilcestr', Roberto de Wlcot', I. de Norwyc', clericis, Rogero de Rhendham et aliis.

ᵃ⁻ᵃ *reading uncertain* B ᵇ nostram B ᶜ sterilitas B

Cransford church was valued at £6 13s 4d, with a portion from separated tithes of £1 held by the monks of Horsham St Faith, in both 1254 and 1291 (*VN* 443; *Taxatio* 119b).

194. Master Stephen of Strumpshaw

Grant, with the consent of the chapter of Norwich, to him, his heirs and assigns, of Thomas son of Adam of Strumpshaw, carpenter, the bishop's villein, with his offspring, chattels, possessions, lands and tenements with appurtenances in Strumpshaw and Braydeston, to be held of the bishop and his successors for an annual render of 2s to be paid at the episcopal manor of Blofield.

[10 March 1258 × 2 January 1266]

B = Norfolk RO, DCN 40/7 (general cartulary of Norwich cathedral priory) fo. 78v. s. xiii ex. C = ibid. fo. 80r (*inspeximus* by prior Roger and the convent). s. xiii ex.

Omnibus Cristi fidelibus presens scriptum visuris vel audituris Symon divina permissioneᵃ Norwycensis episcopus salutem in Domino. Noveritis nos, unanimi assensu et voluntate capituli nostri Norwycensis, concessisse et dedisse magistro Stephano de Strummpishaleᵇ Thomam filium Ade de Strumshale,ᶜ carpentarium, hominem et nativum nostrum, cum tota sequela sua ab eodem procreata et procreanda, rebus, catallis et possessionibus suis, terris et tenementis et pertinentiis que de nobis tenuit in vilenagio in villa de Strumsaleᵈ et de Breyreston'ᵉ pro homagio et servitio suo, illi et heredibus suis vel assignatis tenendum et habendum de nobis et successoribus nostris libere, quiete et hereditarie, reddendo inde annuatim nobis et successoribus nostris duos solidos ad quatuor anni[f] terminos censuales in manerio nostro[g] de Blafeld[h] pro omni servitio, sectis curie, exactione et demanda seculari. In cuius rei testimonium huic scripto sigillum nostrum unacum sigillo capituli Norwycensis fecimus apponi. Hiis testibus: magistris Ada de Wauton'[j] et Iohanne de Wygornia, Roberto de Wlvecot,[k] Willelmo de Gernemuta, Willelmo de Lingwod', [l-] Roberto de Catton, Iohanne Tebaud[-l] et aliis.

[a] miseratione C [b] Strumpishale C   [c] de eadem C   [d] Strumishale C   [e] Bregeston C   [f] anni *om.* C [g] nostro *om.* B [h] Blafeud C [j] Wauston B [k] Wyvecot B [l-l] *om.* C

Mr Stephen of Strumpshaw, the bp's seneschal, attests mid to late thirteenth-century charters relating to Thornham, Plumstead and Postwick (*Norwich Cathedral Charters* ii nos 78, 209, 221).

195. Walsingham Priory

Grant to the canons in proprios usus, for the increase of works of piety, of the church of St Peter, [Great] Walsingham, which is of their patronage, to take effect upon the death or resignation of Bartholomew of Ferentino, the rector, with reservation to the bishop and his successors of the ordination, at the appropriate time, of a vicarage.   Gaywood, 10 October 1264

B = BL ms. Cotton Nero E vii (Walsingham cartulary) fo. 31r (26r). s. xiii ex.

Omnibus Cristi fidelibus presentes litteras inspecturis vel audituris Simon divina miseratione Norwicensis episcopus salutem in Domino sempiternam. Religionis honestas et hospitalitatis eminentia quibus dilecti[a] filii canonici beate Marie de Walsingham vigere dinoscuntur nos excitant et hortantur ut eorum personas et ecclesiam beneficiis amplioribus prosequamur. Ut igitur in domo prefata uberius excerceantur opera pietatis, predictis religiosis ecclesiam beati Petri de Magna Walsingham, in qua ius optinent patronatus, cedente vel decedente Bartholomeo de Ferentino eiusdem ecclesie rectore, in proprios usus perpetuis temporibus concessimus possidendam, reservata nobis aut successoribus nostris facultate vicariam taxandi in eadem cum viderimus oportunum. In cuius rei testimonium presentibus litteris sigillum nostrum fecimus apponi.[b] Dat' apud Geywod' sexto idus Octobris anno gratie M° CC° sexagesimo quarto, pontificatus nostri anno septimo.

[a] dicti B   [b] apponi *interlined* B

For the long-running dispute, stretching back to the time of Henry I, concerning a mediety of this church, which the monks of Binham claimed against the lords of Clare, see *EEA* 6 nos 25, 324, 371A. The grant of the church to the canons by Richard, earl of Hertford, was confirmed by bp-elect Pandulph in 1221 × 1222 (*EEA* 21 no. 26); the king nevertheless claimed in 1237 the right to present to the church during the minority of Richard, heir of Gilbert, earl of Gloucester and Hertford, and it is from this litigation that the early history of the church can be reconstructed (*Bracton's Notebook* iii no. 1238). Bartholomomew of Ferentino was one of the many clerks from that city beneficed in the diocese in the early and mid thirteenth century (Harper-Bill, 'The Diocese of Norwich and the Italian Connection, 1198–1261' 82–3). He was a canon of Meaux, resident in Paris in 1240 (*Reg. Gregory IX* no. 5259). In 1254 the church was valued at £10, the separated tithes of Binham priory at 15s, and (strangely) a vicarage at 10s (*VN* 374); in 1291 the church apart from the portion at £10, and Binham's portion 15s (*Taxatio* 81).

196. Wymondham Priory

Notification to J[ohn], abbot of St Albans that, since he had recently promised W[illiam], prior of Wymondham, that he would, for the increase of hospitality to the sick and poor, grant to him in proprios usus *an ecclesiastical benefice which was of the monks' patronage, he has conceded to them the church of Besthorpe, vacant by the death of master Roger de Cantilupe, so that the monks should receive fifteen marks a year from certain tithes as the rectory, the residue being assigned to a vicarage to which they shall freely present the vicar. He has already instituted and admitted a vicar at their presentation. He asks the abbot that he should commend the prior for his diligence and should not impute blame to him for preferring the good of his own church to the profit of another.*

[30 March 1258 × 12 March 1262, probably 1259]

B = BL ms. Cotton Titus C viii (Wymondham cartulary) fo. 84r (95r). s. xiii med.

Venerabili viro et amico in Cristo karissimo domino I. Dei gratia abbati de sancto Albano Symon eadem gratia episcopus Norwicensis salutem, gratiam et benedictionem. Cum dudum promiserimus domino W. priori de Wymundham, quem interne brachio dilectionis amplectimus, beneficium ecclesiasticum quod sui fuerit patronatus cum vacare contigerit, ad hospitalitatis prioratus sui augmentum que egris[a] et pauperibus iugiter exhibetur ibidem, in proprios usus assignare, ecclesiam de Besthorp', per mortem magistri Rogeri de Cantilupo vacantem, ob amorem quem erga vos et erga domum vestram habemus dicto priori et conventui suo concessimus in forma subscripta, videlicet quod dicti prior et conventus quindecim marcatas redditus in certis decimis sibi assignandas nomine personatus percipient annuatim, residuo autem dicte ecclesie vicarie deputato, ad quam vicariam dictus prior et eius successores libere presentabunt, et ad eiusdem prioris presentationem quendam iam admisimus et instituimus in eadem. Cum igitur ad specialem interpellationem capituli nostri et aliorum specialium[b] amicorum nostrorum ecclesie vestre prospicientes, taliter in hoc facto duximus procedendum, venerandam discretionem vestram requirimus et rogamus affectione qua possumus ampliori quatinus personam dicti prioris pro diligentia sua commendatam habentes, eidem minime imputetis si commodum ecclesie sue preferre voluit utilitati aliene.

[a] egeriis B   [b] *reading uncertain, possibly* spiritualium

William of St Albans, prior of Wymondham, first occurs Oct. 1256 × Oct. 1257, and died 12
March 1262 (*HRH* ii 136). The abbot is John of Hertford. For mr Roger de Cantilupe see *BRUO*
347, also *Fasti* 1 37; 5 27. He had served as a papal judge-delegate as early as 1222, was a
king's clerk, and represented Henry III at the *curia* in 1231 and 1243; he was a canon of St
David's and St Paul's London, and also of Chichester, although appearing only by proxy. He
last occurs on 30 May 1258 and was dead by 15 June 1259.

197. Wymondham Priory

Grant in proprios usus *of the church of Besthorpe, which is of the monks'*
patronage and is vacant by the death of master Roger de Cantilupe, saving a
vicarage, to which when vacant they shall freely present to the bishop a suitable
persona. *For the avoidance of future conflict over their value, he has made this*
division between personatus *and vicarage: the prior and convent shall receive as*
the personatus *the fruits and tithes of various lands [listed], valued by the*
assessment of chosen law-worthy men under oath at fifteen marks. The
remainder shall be held by the vicar and his successors, who shall discharge all
the ordinary obligations of the church to bishop and archdeacon.

[10 March 1258 × 8 December 1261]

B = Bodl. ms. Ch. Norfolk ch. (a. 5) 585 (*inspeximus* by prior Roger and the convent of
Norwich, 9 March 1260). s. xiii med. C = BL ms. Cotton Titus C viii (Wymondham
cartulary) fo. 84r–v. s. xiii med. D = Bodl. ms. Gough Norfolk 18 (Thetford Priory
register) fos. 35v–36r. s. xv ex.

Universis Cristi fidelibus presentes literas[a] inspecturis Symon Dei gratia
Norwicensis episcopus salutem in Domino sempiternam. Ut ex dilectione sincera
quam habemus erga priorem et conventum de Wymundham nostre diocesis ob
sue religionis sanctitatem et caritatis habundantiam fervor quem habemus eis
benefaciendi in lucem prodeat et sic aliquem sortiatur effectum, universitati
vestre notum facimus nos divine caritatis intuitu ecclesiam de Bestorp[b], que de
ipsorum patronatu esse dinoscitur, per mortem magistri Rogeri de Cantilupo
vacantem, eisdem in proprios usus duximus concedendam perpetuis temporibus
possidendam, salva vicaria in eadem per nos in forma subscripta taxata, ad quam
dicti prior et conventus quotiens vacaverit nobis et successoribus nostris idoneam
personam libere presentabunt. Et ne de estimatione personatus seu vicarie
hesitatio seu contentio oriatur in futurum, personatum a vicaria sic duximus
distinguendum, videlicet quod dicti prior et conventus nomine personatus fructus
et decimas de terris subscriptis provenientes, que per viros fidedignos ad hoc
electos et iuratos ad quindecim marcas annuatim valere dinoscuntur, percipiant et
habeant infuturum; scilicet de quindecim acris terre quas Andreas Ode tenet in
una crofta, et de tresdecim acris quas idem Andreas tenet apud Thweit,[c] de tribus
acris et dimidia quas Robertus Anger[d] tenet in crofta Godard cum tofta, de tribus
acris in eadem crofta quas Rogerus Sprunt[e] tenet, de quindecim acris in crofta
Bret[f] quas Hugo de[g] Bavent tenet, de viginti una acris apud Millehowe, de
undecim acris apud Rulpic[h], de sex acris apud Godwinescroft,[j] et de duabus acris

et dimidia apud Elebaldescroft[k] quas supradictus Hugo Bavent tenet, et de triginta quinque acris quas prior de Wymundham tenet in Brectescroft,[l] et de septemdecim acris quas idem prior tenet apud Milleshowe,[m] et de decem acris dicti prioris sub bosco Veske et septem acris dicti prioris apud Reinaldescroft,[n] de tresdecim acris et dimidia eiusdem prioris apud Rulpik,[o] de decem acris eiusdem apud Parcroft,[p] de octo acris quas Willelmus de Illeye tenet apud Millehowe, et[r] de septem acris quas idem tenet apud Kymescroft[s] et de sex acris quas Ricardus Botild tenet apud Umfreiscroft,[t] et de octodecim acris quas Willelmus le Chamberleng[u] tenet apud Veskescroft,[v] de sex acris quas idem tenet apud Thweit,[w] de tribus acris quas moniales de Marham tenent in Holt, de dimidia acra Ricardi de Fossa in Thweit,[w] et de una acra et dimidia Andree Wilekyn[x] in Thweit,[w] et de dimidia acra Henrici Wilekyn[x] in Thweit,[w] et de duodecim acris de terra Wodehind[y] apud Thweit,[w] de quatuor acris Radulfi Chikeit[z] ibidem, de septem acris Hugonis Godman[aa] ibidem, [bb-]et de quatuor acris Rogeri Botild ibidem et de una acra Avicie filie[-bb] Herberti ibidem, de duodecim acris Emme filie Herberti, de tribus acris et dimidia Willelmi Colevil'[cc] ibidem, de septem acris Helebandi,[dd] de dimidia acra Angnetis Holt in Thweit,[w] de una acra et dimidia Iohannis filii Alexandri ibidem, de tribus rodis Rogeri Sprunt[e] ibidem, de dimidia acra Iohannis Coman[ee] ibidem, de una acra Roberti de Mortemer que fuit Ade Cukewald,[ff] de viginti acris Baldewyni de Mell' in crofta Reginaldi, de quinque acris iuxta Levedeisacre quas Radulfus Charun tenet, de tribus acris Iohannis de Holt ibidem, de tribus acris Rogeri Botild ibidem, de quatuor acris Radulfi Elebaud[gg] ibidem, de una acra et dimidia Radulfi filii Galfridi ibidem, de novem acris Iohannis Mengi[hh] ibidem, de duabus acris apud Holebec quas dictus Iohannes tenet, de sex acris et dimidia quas Rogerus Kempe tenet in Herolfiscroft,[ji] de septem acris et dimidia Ricardi Bele[kk] ibidem, de tribus acris et dimidia Willelmi Mengy ibidem et quatuor acris Willelmi Bumbel[ll] ibidem, de tribus acris eiusdem in Kergate, de viginti et sex acris in crofta Mengy, de tribus acris et dimidia Willelmi Rigald in Bareliscroft, in crofta Kempe de tresdecim acris, et de tribus acris Radulfi de Peco,[mm] de viginti acris Willelmi Rigald[nn] et Rogeri burgens', de una acra Willelmi Toly in Pictel, de novem acris Ricardi Anketel in crofta, de viginti acris in Wodecroft, de decim acris in Bulescroft,[oo] de quinque acris et dimidia Iohannis Buk,[pp] de septem acris Milleres, de viginti novem acris in Ketelescroft,[rr] de viginti quinque acris in Credescroft, de viginti septem acris in crofta Simonis dispensatoris, de novem acris in crofta Nicholai quas idem Symon tenet, in crofta Roche de septem acris, in crofta Breite[ss] et Quyte[tt] de septem acris et dimidia et una roda, de decem acris et dimidia Walteri Dune,[uu] de decem acris Roberti Eylward,[vv] de octodecim acris Rogeri Hardi, de tresdecim acris Ricardi filii fabri, de sex acris Willelmi Picard,[ww] de triginta acris Willelmi Plasseys. Residuum autem, fructus, proventus et obventiones omnes totius dicte parochie cum dominico eiusdem ecclesie et capitali mesuagio vicarie et vicario qui pro tempore fuerit ibidem ministraturus deputavimus, concedimus et confirmavimus, qui vicarius onera ordinaria episcopalia et archidiaconalia sustinebit. Et ut hec omnia perpetue

firmitatis robur optineant, presenti scripto sigillum nostrum duximus
apponendum. Hiis testibus: magistro Willelmo de Dunton' tunc archidiacono
Suff', magistro Iohanne de Alvirhescherch'[xx] tunc officiali domini Norwicensis
episcopi, magistro Herveo de Fakenham tunc officiali consistorii Norwicensis,
magistro Stephano de Strumeshae, magistro Adam de Wauton' magistro Thoma
de Ingelesthorp'[yy] et aliis.

[a] litteras C   [b] Besthorp C   [c] Tueyt C; Tweyt D   [d] Angot B C   [e] Sprot D   [f] Breet D   [g] de *om.*
C   [h] Rulpik C; Rulpyttis D   [j] Godwynescroft D   [k] Elebwdiscroft B; Eldalaldescroft D
[l] Brectescroft D   [m] Millehowe C   [n] Reynaldiscroft D   [o] Rulpik C; Rulpittis D   [p] Parscroftis
D   [r] et *om.* C   [s] Lymescroft B; Kemescroft D   [t] Umfreyescroft D   [u] Chamberleyn D
[v] Veskecroftis D   [w] Tweyt C   [x] Walekyn D   [y] Wodehunt C   [z] Chikeyt C; Cheheyt D
[aa] Todeman C   [bb-bb] *om.* D   [cc] Colvil D   [dd] Elebaud C; Helebaud D   [ee] Seman D
[ff] Tukewald D   [gg] Helebalt D   [hh] Mangy D   [jj] Herolfescroft D   [kk] Bese D   [ll] Bunbel D
[mm] de Peke D   [nn] Reguld D   [oo] Bukescroft C   [pp] Vuk D   [rr] Kertellescroft D   [ss] Brodie
D   [tt] Qwythe D   [uu] Daune D   [vv] Aileward D   [ww] Pykard D   [xx] Alvireschirc D
[yy] Ingoldecest' C

Mr John of Alvechurch was archdn of Suffolk by 8 Dec. 1261 (186). In 1254 the church of
Besthorpe was valued at £13 6s 8d, and the separated tithes of the dean of Thetford at 15s (*VN*
393); in 1291 the church was assessed at £6 13s 4d, the vicarage at £8, and the portion of the
monks of Thetford at 15s (*Taxatio* 87).

*198. Last Testament

The will of the bishop.

Mentioned in a royal writ, dated 13 January 1266, to the keepers of the temporalities *sede
vacante*, ordering them to allow the bishop's executors free administration of his goods, after
they had given security for the payment of any debts due to the king.

Pd in *Cl. R. 1264–68* 166.

APPENDIX 1

ADDITIONAL ACTA OF THE BISHOPS OF NORWICH, 1070–1243

WILLIAM TURBE

*1. Butley Priory

Confirmation for the canons of a quarter part of the church of [South] Glemham.
[1171 × 17 January 1174]

Mention of charter, from a 'kalendar of evidences' of Butley priory, fo. 46, in Norfolk R.O., DN Reg. 31 (Tanners's index vol. 2) p. 1098. s. xviii in.

The 'kalendar' is certainly that which Tanner, in his *Notitia Monastica*, cites as being in 1715 in the possession of Robert Hawes of Framlingham (Davis, *Medieval Cartularies* no. 139). This quarter of the church, subsequently increased to a mediety (below no. 3), was the gift of Ranulf de Glanvill, the founder (*Leiston Cartulary* no. 120).

JOHN OF OXFORD

2. Bury St Edmunds Abbey

Institution of Geoffrey de Say, clerk, to the perpetual vicarage of the church of All Saints, Chelsworth, at the presentation of master Jordan de Ros, persona, with the consent of abbot Samson, the patron. The vicar shall pay to the persona, at the Easter synod at Hoxne, an annual pension of 2s. [1188 × 2 June 1200]

B = BL ms. Add 7096 (register of abbot Curteys, vol. 2) fos. 98v-99r (29v-30r). s. xv med.

Omnibus Cristi fidelibus ad quos presens scriptum pervenerit Iohannes Dei gratia Norwicensis episcopus salutem in Domino. Ad universorum volumus pervenire notitiam nos concessisse et dedisse Galfrido de Sai clerico perpetuam vicariam ecclesie omnium sanctorum de Cheleswurth, et ipsum in illa ecclesia canonice perpetuum vicarium instituisse ad presentationem magistri Iordani de Ros eiusdem ecclesie persone, assensu venerabilis viri domini Sampsonis abbatis de sancto Edmundo iam dicte ecclesie patroni, solvendo annuatim de illa ecclesia persone [*fo. 99r*] eiusdem ecclesie duos solidos nomine pensionis ad sinodum de Hoxe proximam post Pascha. Hanc itaque vicariam cum omnibus ad memoratam ecclesiam pertinentibus prenominato G. clerico confirmamus. Et ut hec nostra concessio et institutio perpetuam obtineat firmitatem, eam presenti scripto et sigilli nostri patrocinio communimus. Testibus Thoma archidiacono, Eustachio, Willelmo capellanis, Roberto de Chipenham, magistro Lamberto.

> Mr Jordan de Ros was at one time in dispute with the abbot both over the church of Hopton, of which he claimed to be *persona*, and over land in Harlow (*Jocelin* 61–2). In 1206 he held the perpetual vicarage of St Andrew's, Great Saxham (*EEA* 6 no. 334).
>
> The near-contemporary valuation of the church of Chelsworth was £5 (*Jocelin* 64). In 1254 the portion of the *persona* was valued at £6 13s 4d and that of the hospital of St Saviour at 30s (*VN* 436). In 1291 church was valued at £8 (*Taxatio* 122).

*3. Butley Priory

Confirmation for the canons of the grant by Ranulf de Glanvill, their founder, of a mediety of the church of South Glemham.   [14 December 1175 × 1190]

> Mention of charter in Norfolk R.O., DN Reg.31 (Tanners index vol. 2) p. 1098 (from lost Butley cartulary fo. 47)

> This confirmation was probably issued before Glanvill's death at the siege of Acre in 1190. In 1254 the church of South (or Little) Glemham was valued at £6 (*VN* 442); in 1291 Butley's part of the church was assessed at £3 6s 8d and the portion of the abbot of Colchester at 10s (*Taxatio* 119).

*4. Butley Priory

Grant to the prior and canons in proprios usus *of the church of North Glemham, to take effect when it shall fall vacant.*   [14 December 1175 × 2 June 1200]

> Mention of charter in Norfolk R.O., DN Reg.31 (Tanner's index vol. 2), p. 1099 (from lost Butley cartulary fo. 46).

> In 1254 the church of North (or Great) Glemham was assessed at £10 and the separated tithes of Horsham St Faith priory at £1; in 1291 the church, appropriated to Butley, was still valued at £10 (*VN* 443; *Taxatio* 119). See also no.12 below.

*5. Butley Priory

Assignment to the vicar of North Glemham of an annual pension of 20s.
                                            [14 December 1175 x 2 June 1200]

> Mention of charter in Norfolk R.O., DN Reg.31 (Tanner's index vol. 2), p. 1099 (from lost Butley cartulary fo. 47).

> See no. 4 above.

6. Horsham St Faith Priory

Confirmation for the monks of the church of Tibenham, as they canonically acquired it from the patrons in the time of bishop William [Turbe], and grant to them of the same church in proprios usus *in perpetuity, saving honourable provision for a vicar who shall be instituted by the bishop at their presentation.*

[13 November 1188 × 2 June 1200]

B = Norfolk R.O., DN Reg. 31 (Tanner's index vol. 2) p. 1745 (*ex originali penes Clem' Hern de Heverland armiger'* 1714). s.xviii in.

Omnibus Cristi fidelibus ad quos presens scriptum pervenerit Iohannes permissione divina Norwicensis ecclesie minister salutem in Domino. Universitati vestre notum esse volumus nos confirmasse dilectis filiis nostris viris religiosis monachis sancte Fidis de Horsford ecclesiam de Tibenham cum omnibus pertinentiis suis, sicut eam tempore predecessoris nostre bone memorie Willelmi episcopi canonice sunt adepti et sicut eis ab advocatis concessa est. Concessimus igitur pietatis intuitu ut predictam ecclesiam in sue sustentationis usus habent in perpetuum, salva honesti et sufficienti sustentatione vicarii, quem[a] nobis vel successoribus nostris presentabunt et, auctoritate episcopali in memorata institutus[b] ecclesia ut curam et regimen habeat animarum, qui nobis et officialibus nostris de spiritualibus et debitis consuetudinibus respondet in omnibus. Et ut hec nostra confirmatio et concessio plenam et perpetuam obtineat firmitatem, eam presenti scripto et sigilli nostri appositione communimus. Dat' anno ab incarnatione Domini M IC XI XII[c]. Testibus: Gaufrido et Rogero archidiaconis, Thoma Brit', magistro Roberto de Wacston', Eustacio capellano, magistro Lamberto, magistro Rogero, Roberto de Cipeham.

[a]qui B   [b] instituetur B   [c]sic *transcript, obviously in error*

The dating limits are established by the last occurrence of archdn Geoffrey (presumed to be of Suffolk, a frequent witness — see *EEA* 6 pp. lxxxvi–vii) without title, and the bp's death. In 1254 the church was valued at £13 6s 8d and the vicar's portion at £3 6s 8d (*VN* 411). In 1291 the church was valued at £15 6s 8d, with portions held by the priories of Lewes and St Olave's, Herringfleet, assessed at 6s 8d each; the vicarage was not subject to the tenth (*Taxatio* 84).

JOHN DE GRAY

7. Bury St Edmunds Abbey

Institution of Ernald of Saxham, clerk, to the church of St George, Bradfield, at the presentation of abbot Samson.   London, 12 October 1204

B = BL ms. Add. 7096 (register of abbot Curteys) fo. 101v (32v). s. xv med.

Omnibus ad quos presens scriptum pervenerit Iohannes Dei gratia Norwicensis episcopus salutem in Domino. Noverit universitas vestra nos divine pietatis

intuitu, ad presentationem Sampsonis abbatis sancti Edmundi, patroni ecclesie
sancti Georgii de Bradefeld, dedisse, concessisse et presenti carta confirmasse
Ernaldo de Saxham clerico predictam ecclesiam de Bradefeld cum omnibus ad
eam pertinentibus, ipsumque in eadem personam canonice instituisse, salvo
nobis et successoribus nostris imperpetuum iure pontificali et parochiali. Hiis
testibus: Hugone archidiacono Wellensi, Iohanne archidiacono Wygornensi,
Roberto de Rudebi et Iordano capellanis, magistro Roberto de Tywe, Iohanne de
Offinton, Alano clerico et aliis. Dat' per manum G. de Derham apud London'
quarto idus Octobris pontificatus nostri anno quinto.

> The church was valued at £8 in 1254 and at £10 13s 4d in 1291 (*VN* 426; *Taxatio* 120). Ernald
> of Saxham was again instituted as *persona* of St Andrew's, Great Saxham on 6 Oct. 1206,
> saving the perpetual vicarage of mr Jordan de Ros, who was to render him an annual pension of
> one *aureus* (*EEA* 6 no. 334).

*8. Butley Priory

Grant to the canons in proprios usus *in perpetuity of a mediety of the church of
Bredfield.*   [20 September 1200 × 18 October 1214]

> Mention of charter in Norfolk R.O., DN Reg.31 (Tanner's index vol. 2), p. 1172 (from lost
> Butley cartulary fo. 45).

> The church of Bredfield was the gift of William de Glanvill (*Leiston Cartulary* 9). In 1254 it
> was assessed at £6 13s 4d (*VN* 454). In 1291 the church was divided into the medieties of
> Butley and Capes, the latter presumably the secular rector of the other mediety; the whole was
> again valued at £6 13s 4d, apart from the portion of Sutton Hoo chapel, worth £2 13s 4d
> (*Taxatio* 117).

*9. Butley Priory

*Charter recording the bishop's acceptance of the resignation of a mediety of the
church of Bredfield by Robert Mautalent,* persona *thereof.*
                                                [20 September 1200 × 18 October 1214]

> Mention of charter in Norfolk R.O., DN Reg. 31 (Tanner's index vol. 2), p. 1172 (from lost
> Butley cartulary fo. 45).

> See above no.8.

THOMAS BLUNDEVILLE

10. Battle Abbey

Institution of master Odard, clerk, as persona *of the church of [Great] Thurlow,
at the presentation of abbot Richard, the true patron as is claimed, saving to the*

abbot an annual payment and benefice of two and a half marks to be received at the two Suffolk synods, and hospitality for two nights twice yearly when he comes to the region.   London, 5 October 1234

B = San Marino, California, Huntingdon Library, HEH/BA 29 (Battle cartulary) fo. 91v (80v). s. xiii ex.

Omnibus Cristi fidelibus ad quos presens scriptum pervenerit Thomas Dei gratia Norwicensis episcopus salutem in Domino. Ad universorum notitiam volumus pervenire nos ad presentationem venerabilis viri Ricardi Dei gratia abbatis de Bello, veri ut dicitur patroni ecclesie de Trillawe admisisse Odardum clericum ad predictam ecclesiam de Trillawe cum omnibus ad ipsam pertinentibus, ipsumque Odardum clericum personam in eadem canonice instituisse, salva dicto abbati annua prestatione et beneficio duarum marcarum et dimidie ad duos sinodos Suff' percipiendas. Insuper etiam dua hospitia duarum noctium per singulos annos abbati cum in provinciam venerit ex consuetudine predictus Odardus persolvet, salvis etiam in omnibus reverentia et obedientia nobis et successoribus nostris et sancte Norwicensis ecclesie consuetudinibus debitis vel consuetis. In cuius rei testimonium presentes literas fieri fecimus et sigillo nostro muniri. Dat' London' quinto die Octobris pontificatus nostri anno octavo.

There was a long standing dispute between the abbey and the Pecche family over the patronage of this church. For the conflict in the twelfth century, see *EEA* 6 nos. 58n, 166n (where *for* Sumeneio *read* Funteneio). In 1230 the abbot successfully brought an action against Hamo Pecche in the *curia regis* for recovery of the advowson, and mr Odard is the next recorded incumbent. In 1236 the abbot and convent granted the advowson to the hospital of St Auxentius in Anagni, founded by pope Gregory IX, while still a cardinal, as a dependency of the hospital of Altopascio near Lucca, but Battle was to retain presentation to a newly established vicarage, and also its customary pension and procuration; for the subsequent history of the church in the late thirteenth century, see Harper-Bill, 'Battle Abbey and its East Anglian Churches' 163–67.

11. Bury St Edmunds

Institution of John of St Edmunds, clerk, to the church of St Leonard, [Great] Horringer, at the presentation of abbot Hugh [Northwold], stated to be the true patron.   London, 10 February 1227

B = BL ms. Add. 7096 (register of abbot Curteys) fo. 102r (33r). s. xv med.

Omnibus Cristi fidelibus ad quos presens scriptum pervenerit Thomas Dei gratia Norwicensis episcopus salutem in Domino. Ad universorum notitiam volumus pervenire nos admisisse Iohannem de sancto Edmundo clericum ad ecclesiam sancti Leonardi de Hornyngesherd ad presentationem venerabilis viri Hugonis abbatis de sancto Edmundo, eiusdem ecclesie ut dicitur veri patroni, et ipsum I. in eadem canonice instituisse, salvis in omnibus reverentia et obedientia nobis et successoribus nostris et sacrosancte Norwicensis ecclesie consuetudinibus debitis vel consuetis. In cuius rei testimonium presentes litteras fieri fecimus et sigillo nostro muniri. Dat' London' .iiii. idus Februarii pontificatus nostri anno primo.

In 1254 the church was valued at £13 6s 8d and the hospital of St Saviour had a portion worth 15s (*VN* 434). In 1291 the church was valued at £15 (*Taxatio* 120b).

*12. Butley Priory

Grant to the canons in proprios usus *in perpetuity of the church of North Glemham.*   [20 December 1226 × 16 August 1236]

> Mention of charter in Norfolk R.O., DN Reg. 31 (Tanner's index vol. 2), p. 1099 (from lost Butley cartulary fo. 46).
>
> See nos. 4–5 above.

*13. Butley Priory

Confirmation for the canons of the grant by William de Coleville of land at Kenton, together with the advowson of the church.
                                    [20 December 1226 × 16 August 1236]

> Mention of charter in Norfolk R.O., DN Reg. 31 (Tanner's index vol. 2), p. 1074 (from lost Butley cartulary, fo. 41).
>
> See below no.14.

*14. Butley Priory

Grant to the canons in proprios usus *in perpetuity of the church of Kenton.*
                                    [20 December 1226 x 16 August 1236]

> Mention of charter in Norfolk R.O., DN Reg. 31 (Tanner's index vol. 2), p. 1074 (from lost Butley cartulary, fo. 41).
>
> In 1254 the church was valued at £10, and in 1291 the rectory, appropriated to Butley, at £8 (*VN* 466; *Taxatio* 117).

15. Sempringham Priory

Grant to the canons and nuns in proprios usus *of the church of St Andrew, Buxton, saving to Richard of Kirkby a vicarage valued at £5, which shall consist of all the altarage, all the free land of the church with a messuage assigned to the vicar, the tithe of the hall, this being a third of the great tithe due to the church, the tithe from the croft of Hervey of Lynn, this consisting of twenty acres, and all the tithe of hay of the hall and of the parishioners. To this vicarage, whenever it falls vacant, the canons and nuns shall present that suitable* persona *on whom the bishop or his successors decide and whom they will admit; and if they fail to present the bishop may nevertheless institute such a* persona *without* consultation.   [North or South] Elmham, 9 October 1232

B = Norfolk R. O., DCN 31 (Tanner's index vol. 2) p. 1489 (*ex libro antiquo collect' ex registris episcoporum Norwic' penes Thomam Batcheler LL.B.*). s. xviii in.

Omnibus Cristi fidelibus ad quos presens scriptum pervenerit Thomas Dei gratia Norwicensis episcopus salutem in Domino. Ad universorum[a] notitiam volumus pervenire nos Dei causa et gratia in religionis favore concessisse et presenti carta confirmasse dilectis nobis in Cristo canonicis et monialibus de Simplyngham ecclesiam sancti Andree de Buxton cum omnibus ad ipsam pertinentibus, habendam et tenendam [et] in proprios usus perpetuo possidendam, [salva] Richardo de Kirkeby vicaria centum solidorum in eadem, subscriptis portionibus taxata[b] in hunc modum, videlicet quod dictus Richardus habebit totum alteragium prefate ecclesie et totam liberam terram ecclesie cum messuagio ad vicariam assignato, et decimam provenientem de aula, scilicet tertiam garbam spectantem ad ecclesiam predictam, item decimam provenienem de crofto Hervei[c] de Lenn, scilicet de .xx. acris terre, item totam decimam feni provenientem de aula et parochianis in eadem villa; ad quam vicariam, quotiens vacare contigerit, dicti canonici et moniales de Symplyngham personam idoneam quamcumque voluerimus nobis et successoribus nostris presentabunt, et presentatam admittemus; et si forte omiserint vel neglexerint presentare, nos et successores nostri nihilominus personam quamcumque voluerimus, dictis canonicis et monialibus irrequisitis, vicarium in eadem instituemus. Dictus autem vicarius pro tempore onera ordinaria debita et consueta dicte ecclesie sustinebit, salvis etiam in omnibus reverentia et obedientia nobis et successoribus nostris et sacrosancte ecclesie Norwicensis consuetudinibus debitis et consuetis. In cuius rei testimonium presentes litteras fieri fecimus et sigillo muniri. Dat' apud Elmham die sancti Dionisii sociorumque eius pontificatus [nostri] anno sexto.

[a] universitati B   [b] taxatis B   [c] Hervy B

In 1254 the *personatus* was valued at £10 and the vicarage at £1; the monks of Norwich had a portion, consisting of tithes of £4 (*VN* 366–7, 503). In 1291 it was valued at £14 13s 4d, apart from the portion and the vicarage, which was not subject to the tenth (*Taxatio* 82b).

WILLIAM RALEIGH

16. Horsham St Faith Priory

Grant to the monks in proprios usus, *out of concern for their poverty and with the consent of prior Simon and the convent of Norwich, of the church of Hor'* [probably *Horsford*], *which is of their advowson, and the revenues of which they obtained* de facto *during the vacancy of the see by order of [Anger] abbot of [West] Dereham, vicegerent of the archbishop of Canterbury, saving a vicarage, to which the monks shall always present a suitable* persona *chosen by the bishop or his successors. The vicarage shall consist of all the altarage, the tithe of the mill and of hay and of all legally tithable things, all the free land of the church with its tithe, a suitable manse adjacent to the church, and all pertaining to the church, apart from the monks' grange and the tithe of sheaves; and also two marks a year to be received in perpetuity from the monks at the two Norwich synods. The vicar shall discharge all obligations of the church to bishop and archdeacon.*   Norwich, 1 December 1240

B = Norfolk R. O., DN Reg. 31 (Tanner's index vol. 2) p. 1745 (*ex originali penes Clem' Hern de Heverlond armiger'* 1714). s. xviii in.

Omnibus sancte matris ecclesie filiis presens scriptum visuris Willelmus Ralegh Dei gratia episcopus Norwicensis salutem in Domino. Nimia paupertas dilectorum filiorum prioris et conventus sancte Fidis de Horsham et eorum grata devotio nos vehementius exhortantur ut gratie ianuam, quam frequentius extraneis aperimus, misericorditer pandamus eisdem. Ipsorum igitur necessitati[a] pie compatientes, de dilectorum in Cristo filiorum Simonis prioris et conventus nostri Norwicensis assensu, dedimus et concessimus predictis priori et conventui sancte Fidis ecclesiam de Hor', ad eorum advocationem spectantem, in proprios usus suos imperpetuum possidendam, cuius etiam possessiones vacante sede Norwicensi per abbatem de Derham vices domini Cantuariensis tunc gerentem de facto fuerant assecuti; salva ipsius ecclesie perpetua vicaria per nos sub forma subscripta taxata, ad quam iidem monachi personam idoneam quamcumque[b] nos et successores nostri voluerimus perpetuo presentabunt. Consistit autem ipsa vicaria in toto altaragio eiusdem ecclesie et decimis molendini et feni et in omni genere legali, et in tota libera terra ipsius ecclesie cum decima eiusdem, et in manso competenti iuxta ecclesiam, et in omnibus ad ipsam ecclesiam pertinentibus, preter grangiam monachorum et decimam garbarum, et in duabus marcis annuis percipiendis in perpetuum in duabus synodis Norwicensibus a predictis priore et conventu. Vicarius vero onera ipsius ecclesie tam episcopalia quam archidiaconalia debita et consueta perpetuo sustinebit. Quod ut perpetuam obtineat firmitatem presens scriptum tam sigilli nostri quam capituli nostri Norwicensis munimine duximus roborandum. Hiis testibus: magistris Rogero archidiacono Sudburie, Willelmo de Clara et Waltero de Exon', Iohanne de Chelebauton, Iohanne de Leominster, Ricardo de Fretun, Thoma de Breccles et Willelmo de Dunkeswell clericis, et aliis. Dat' per manum Philippi de Sydeham capellani nostri apud Norwicum, kalendis Decembris pontificatus nostri anno secundo.

[a]reading uncertain   [b]qualem B

The priory was founded by Robert Fitzwalter in 1105 at Kirkscroft, but soon afterwards was moved to Horsham (*MRH* 68). It is likely that the church there was given to them in its entirety at an earlier date, and that the abbreviation *Hor'* therefore here refers to nearby Horsford, valued in 1254 at £5 6s 8d and in 1291, appropriated to the monks and apart from the vicarage not subject to the tenth, at £6 (*VN* 364; *Taxatio* 78b).

17. London, St Paul's Cathedral

Remission of thirty days enjoined penance granted to those, contrite and confessed, of his diocese, and to others whose diocesans ratify this indulgence, who visit the cathedral to pray on the anniversary of its dedication or within its octave, or who make a grant towards the fabric. This grant of remission shall be valid in perpetuity. London, 11 September 1241

> A = London, Guildhall Library, ms. 25124/16. No medieval endorsement; approx. 150 × 108 + 18 mm.; tag and seal missing.

Omnibus Cristi fidelibus ad quos presens scriptum pervenerit Willelmus Dei gratia episcopus Norwicensis salutem in Domino. Cum inter caritatis opera sacrasanctorum limina visitare in conspectu altissimi non immerito sit acceptum, nos de Dei misericordia, gloriose virginis genetricis eius et beati Pauli apostoli necnon et omnium sanctorum meritis confidentes, omnibus parrochianis nostris, et aliis quorum diocesani id ratum habuerint, vere contritis et confessis, qui ecclesiam cathedralem sancti Pauli London' anniversario dedicationis ipsius die vel aliquo die octavarum orationis causa pro devotionis affectu visitaverint vel ad eiusdem ecclesie fabricam aliquid de bonis a Deo sibi collatis contulerint, triginta dies de iniuncta sibi penitentia misericorditer relaxamus, concedentes hanc nostram relaxationis gratiam perpetuo duraturam. Dat' London' tertio idus Septembris anno Domini M° CC° quadragesimo primo.

18. London, St Paul's Cathedral

Letters directed to all clergy of the diocese, urging them to receive favourably the proctors of the cathedral seeking alms for its fabric. Those ministering in churches should recommend their quest to their parishioners for three Sundays or feast days, and should pass everything collected without any deduction to the bearers of these letters. Grant of remission of twenty days enjoined penance to benefactors, being contrite and confessed, from his diocese, and to others whose diocesans ratify this indulgence, which in his diocese shall be valid in perpetuity.
London, 8 June 1243

> A = London, Guildhall Library, ms. 25124/18. Endorsed: Willelmus Norwycen' .xx. dies et perquirendi in sua diocesi; approx. 27 × 65 + 11 mm.; brown cord, two strands, fragments of seal, dark green wax, counterseal.

Willelmus Dei gratia episcopus Norwicensis dilectis in Cristo filiis abbatibus, prioribus, archidiaconis, officialibus, decanis, personis, vicariis, capellanis et ceteris tam clericis quam laycis per Norwicensem diocesim constitutis, salutem, gratiam et benedictionem. Universitatem vestram rogandam duximus ac attentius in Domino exhortandam quatinus cum nuntii nobilis ecclesie sancti Pauli Lond' ad vos venerint ad ipsius fabricam, que sine largitione fidelium vix aut numquam poterit consummari, vestras elemosinas petituri, eos ob reverentiam beati apostoli Pauli benigne recipientes, ad prefatam fabricam pia caritatis subsidia de bonis a Deo vobis collatis per eosdem taliter transmittere studeatis, ut per eadem ac alia bona opera, ipsius apostoli intervenientibus meritis, eternam remunerationem recipere valeatis. Vos autem capellani hoc eorundem negotium vestris parochianis per tres dies dominicos aut sollempnes taliter exponere satagatis ut vestram diligentiam in hac parte debeamus merito commendare. Et quicquid collectum fuerit sine aliqua diminutione latori presentium fideliter tradi permittatis. Nos autem, de Dei misericordia, gloriose virginis genetricis eius, ipsiusque beati apostoli et omnium sanctorum meritis confisi, omnibus dicti loci benefactoribus nostre diocesis, et aliis quorum diocesani id ratum habuerint, vere contritis et confessis, viginti dies de iniuncta sibi penitentia misericorditer relaxamus, concedentes hanc nostram gratiam in nostra diocesi inperpetuum duraturam. Dat' London'; .vi. idus Iunii pontificatus nostri anno quinto.

WILLIAM RALEIGH OR WALTER SUFFIELD

19. Holme-next-the- Sea Church

Notification that when a vacancy occurred in the vicarage through the death of John of Happisburgh, chaplain, and by inquisition it was discovered that the bishop's predecessor, Thomas Blundeville, had collated the vicarage de facto *to the said John, for this reason alone he considered the vicarage to pertain to his collation and collated it to Thomas of Norwich, chaplain. W. de Tregoz, the rector, approached him several times both before and after this collation, on his own behalf and that of the lord John Lestrange, the patron, arguing that this collation did not pertain to the bishop* de iure, *and urgently requesting that the vicarage should be consolidated with the* personatus. *Eventually, considering these arguments to be in accordance with he law, the bishop agreed that, with the consent of rector and patron, Thomas should retain for his lifetime the vicarage, apart from the houses of the church which, by the bishop's consent, the rector should himself retain; but whensoever this chaplain vacates the vicarage, by death either natural or civil, the vicarage should accrue to and be consolidated with the* personatus *in perpetuity, without contravention by he bishop or any of his successors. In the meantime the vicar shall discharge all obligations of the church to bishop and archdeacon.*

Gaywood, 29 July [1243 or 1248]

A = TNA, E326/11317. No medieval endorsement; approx. 187 × 94 mm.; tongue and seal missing, parchment tie remains.
Pd in *Formulare Anglicanum* no. 539.

Omnibus Cristi fidelibus presentes literas inspecturis W. Dei gratia Norwicensis episcopus eternam salutem in Domino. Noverit universitas vestra quod cum vicaria de Hulmo per mortem Iohannis de Hapisburg' capellani vacare cepisset et nobis per inquisitionem factam constaret dominum Thomam de Blunvill' predecessorem nostrum dictam vicariam iam dicto Iohanni capellano de facto contulisse, nos ob hoc solum attendentes dictam vicariam ad nostram pertinere donationem, ipsam Thome capellano de Norwich' pietatis intuitu contulimus. Accedens vero ante dictam collationem et postea sepius coram nobis dominus W. de Tregos, rector dicte ecclesie de Hulmo, pro se et pro patrono suo domino Iohanne Extraneo, rationes inducens quod ad nos dicta collatio de iure non spectabat, pro se et pro patrono suo appellans et instanter petens dictam vicariam personatui suo consolidari, demum ponderatis rationibus ut iuri consonis, in hoc convenimus amicabiliter, quod dicto Thome capellano de consensu dictorum rectoris et patroni remaneat dicta vicaria toto tempore suo, preter domos ecclesie quas ex ordinatone nostra dictus rector sibi retinet, ita tamen quod quandocumque dictus capellanus dictam vicariam per mortem naturalem seu civilem dimiserit, absque omni contradictione vel a nobis vel ab aliquo successore nostro plene accrescat et consolidetur libere dicta vicaria dicto personatui in perpetuum. Sustinebit autem dictus vicarius dum ibidem fuerit omnia honera dicte ecclesie episcopalia et archidiaconalia. In huius vero rei testimonium presentibus literis sigillum nostrum apposuimus. Dat' apud Gaywud' .iiii°. kalendas Augusti pontificatus nostri anno quarto. Valete semper in Domino.

It appears impossible to determine by which of the two bps this *actum* was issued; the place and date are compatible with the itinerary of either. It is unique among the beneficial acta of both bps in being sealed on the tongue, rather than with a tag.

A dispute between an earlier John Lestrange and the monks of Ramsey concerning the advowson was terminated by a final concord of 13 Nov. 1188, by which the abbot and convent conceded the advowson to John and his heirs, and bp John of Oxford (one of the judges in the *curia regis*) granted the monks an annual pension of one mark (*Ramsey Cartulary* ii no. 494; *EEA* 6 no. 272). In 1254 the church, with the vicarage, was valued at £22 13s 4d, with portions pertaining to Ramsey (13s 4d), the prior of Sporle (£2) and Ralph de Berri (£1 6s 8d) (*VN* 406); in 1291 the church, including the former vicarage, was valued at £40, excluding portions therein (*Taxatio* 89). Some time after the issue of this actum the advowson was granted by a John Lestrange to the canons of Lilleshall (BL ms. Add. 50121 (Lilleshall cartulary) fo. 28r), to whom the church was eventually appropriated in 1398 by bp Henry Despenser (*HMC Various Collections* v 450).

APPENDIX 2

REFERENCES TO ACTS, PRIVATE DEEDS AND USE OF SEAL

Where there are clear references to a lost episcopal charter, these have been included in the main text of the *acta*. Where, however, the bishop's actions are recorded without any clear indication whether or not there was an evidentiary document, these instances are listed below, together with references to the appending of the episcopal seal to a document issued in the name of another person or institution, and a few letters and charters issued by bishop Walton in a private capacity.

WALTER SUFFIELD

1. Request to pope Innocent IV for advice; in his diocese there are parish churches held by religious and others, in some of which vicarages are not yet taxed or are unsuitably taxed, from which arises spiritual damage. Mentioned in the reply of the pope (Lyons, 8 Aug. 1245) who, having confidence in the bp, and following the example of his predecessor pope G[regory IX], instructs that he should proceed as the law and custom of the English church requires, deciding as seems best to him for the utility of those churches and for the worship of God, saving objection and appeal by any person [19 Feb. × 8 Aug. 1245] (*Norwich Cathedral Charters* i no. 299).

2. Consolidation of the rectory and vicarage of Hedenham (*Hedeam*); the vicar, Walter of Woodton (*Wudeton*) being dead, no new vicar shall be appointed, and in future the church shall be served by the rector. Mentioned in confirmation of pope Innocent IV (Lyons , 12 Oct. 1246) for John, the rector [19 Feb. 1245 × *c*. Sept. 1246] (Sayers, *Original Papal Docs*. no. 317).

3. Assent to the grant in perpetuity to the monks of Sibton by William son of Roger of Ketteringham, for the maintenance of a lamp in the abbey church, of an annual rent of 3s from the messuage and tenement which Robert son of Walter of Henley used to hold of him in Henley, to be paid henceforth by Robert and his heirs to the monks, saving to the bp of Norwich their homage, reliefs, wardships and other forinsec services owed from this land [19 Feb. 1245 × 19 May 1257] (*Sibton Charters* ii no. 145).

4. Mandate to mr Edmund of Walpole, official of the archdn of Sudbury, to conduct an inquisition into the vacancy of the church of Cockfield; mentioned in the official's return, reporting that the inquisition was taken on 13 May 1246 and that it was found that the church was vacant by the death of mr John of Houghton

(*Hoveton*) on 18 Apr. and that the abbot of Bury was the legitimate patron. On 17 May Hugh de Vere notified the bp that, while he had recently presented one of his clerks to the church, thinking that the presentation pertained to him, he had now discovered that Cockfield was of the abbot's advowson and revoked his presentation [18 Apr. × 13 May 1246] (PRO, DL 42/5 fo. 81r (97r); CUL ms. Gg iv 4, fos 391v–92r).

5. Confirmation for the monks of Hailes (*Hyales*), O. Cist., of the grant by Richard earl of Cornwall of the church of Haughley (*Hagelee*) and licence that they may hold it *in proprios usus* (mentioned in papal confirmation) [17 July 1246 × 2 Jan. 1248] (*Reg. Inn. IV* i no. 3524; *CPL* i 240).

6. Agreement made in the bp's presence between the monks of Sibton, as rector of the parish church of Sibton with the chapel of St Michael, Peasenhall, and mr Adam of Bromholm, rector of Heveningham, concerning various tithes (detailed) over which there had been prolonged litigation. Mr Adam has, for himself and his successors, granted these tithes to the monks, who in return have granted nine acres and a toft (detailed). Both parties submit themselves entirely to the jurisdiction of the bp and his successors for the enforcement of this agreement, which was reached with the consent of the chapter of Norwich and the monks of St Neots, patrons of Heveningham church. Sealed by the bp, both parties and the prior and convent of St Neots. Hoxne, 26 Aug. 1246 (*Sibton Charters* iii no. 745).

7. Agreement between prior Adam and the convent of Castle Acre on one part and John of Pakenham (*Pakeam, Pakeham*) on the other, whereby the monks have leased at farm to John two parts of the demesne tithes of Robert de Freville (*Frivill'*) in the vill of Fouldon (*Fugeldun'*), which they have been accustomed to have collected for their own use, for four marks *p.a.* to be paid in two instalments at the Norwich synods. Should he default in payment at any term, the tithes shall revert to the monks without contradiction, and they shall have possession as hitherto. John also agreed that in case of default at any term he should within eight days thereafter pay the monks 20s as recompense for damages, interest and expenses incurred in recovery. Both parties swore on oath to observe this agreement and submitted themselves to the jurisdiction of the bp of Norwich who might, after issue of one warning, enforce observance by sentence of interdict and excommunication and without formal hearing; and they renounced all legal remedy in any court, apostolic letters obtained or to be obtained, all exceptions relating to persons or property, and anything to the detriment of the agreement. After John's death or resignation the tithes shall revert to the monks. This agreement was made in the presence and with the consent of the bp, and recorded in a chirograph sealed by him and the parties. Witnessed by William of Horham, archdn of Suffolk, Robert de Insula, archdn of Colchester, John of Holkham and Thomas of Tew (*Theie*), chaplains, William of Whitwell, Thomas of Walcott, Willam of Acle, William of Ludham and others [24 Feb. 1247 × Oct. 1253, probably 1247 × 48, as all other attestations by William of Acle are Oct.1248] (BL ms. Harley 2110 fo. 127v (134v).

8. Agreement between prior Adam and the convent of Castle Acre on one part and the prior and convent of Coxford on the other whereby the monks have leased at perpetual farm to the canons of Coxford two parts of the demesne tithes of Baldwin de Rosei (*Rosey*), Hugh son of Richard and William de Cailly (*Kaylly*) in the vill of Houghton on the Hill (*Houtun'*) which pertain to Castle Acre, for 36s *p.a.* to be paid to the monks' sacrist in two instalments at the Norwich synods. Should the canons at any term default in payment they shall, unless they have been impeded by just and evident cause, forfeit the farm and any right which they might claim in these tithes, which shall revert to the monks without contradiction. The canons also agreed that in case of default at any term they should within eight days thereafter pay the monks 20s as recompense for damages, etc. Further provisions as no.7 above. Made in the presence and with the consent of the bp, and recorded in the form of a chirograph sealed by the bp and the parties. Witnesses as no.7, with William of Whitwell described as mr [24 Feb. 1247 × Oct. 1253, probably 1247 × 48, as all other attestations by William of Acle are Oct. 1248] (BL ms. Harley 2110 fo. 127r (134r).

9. Delivery in the royal wardrobe to its keeper of £40 by deposition of a deceased person in their last will, 18 May 1247 (*CPR 1232–47* 501).

10. Approves and sets his seal, alongside that of the abbot of St Benet of Holme, to a charter of Reginald le Gros recording an exchange of lands (detailed) between himself and mr Peter de Arc(e), rector of Stalham. Norwich, 28 June 1247 (Norfolk RO, DN Reg. 31 p. 823).

11. Payment, at the king's command, of twelve marks to Wibert of Kent, keeper of the issue of the royal seal, which he owed for a charter allowing him to have two markets. Royal order to barons of Exchequer to acquit him of this sum, Clarendon, 14 July 1247 (*Cl. R. 1242–47* 523).

12. Testimony to the merits of J[ohn] le Bigod, rector of Settrington (*Setherington*) [YE], mentioned in an *actum* of archbp Walter Gray of York, whereby he consolidated the vicarage and *personatus* and made various provisions for the effective service of the church despite Bigod's infirmities and absence [shortly before 5 April 1248] (*Reg. Gray* 103).

13. Question directed to pope Innocent IV concerning the legitimacy of Thomas of Raveningham, whose father, also named Thomas, had married a certain Cassandra and, having had by her a son and heir, died. Hugh, a layman and the younger Thomas's paternal uncle, had attempted to exclude him from inheritance, asserting that the older Thomas could not have been Cassandra's husband, inasmuch as William, their brother, had espoused her, although the marriage had not been consummated, and that therefore the younger Thomas could not be his father's legitimate son. Against this the younger Thomas argued that Cassandra was under seven years of age when espoused to William, and as he himself was born of a marriage contracted *in facie ecclesie*, and no doubt had been cast on his legitimacy during his father's lifetime, he should be adjudged legitimate. The uncle responded that Cassandra, when espoused to William, must be presumed to have been of age, unless the contrary could be proved, witnesses on both sides being unable to determine this point. The pope replied that, to deprive the younger Thomas of his inheritance, not only must it be proved that Cassandra, when William espoused her, was seven years old, or that the betrothal was extended beyond that age by the will of the parties, but also that the older Thomas knew this when he married her, of which Hugh produced no proof. Lyons, 27 April 1248 (*Reg. Inn. IV* no. 4468; *CPL* i 254–5).

14. Request to the king that he should cause the removal of the secular power now occupying the church of Bexwell (*Bekeswell'*). Mentioned in mandate to the sheriff of Norfolk that he should put an end to this occupation. 1248 (shortly before 2 July) (*Cl. R. 1247–51* 120).

15. Agreement between the prior and convent of Castle Acre on one part and Bartholomew, rector of Wiveton (*Wyvetun'*) on the other that, whereas the monks have two parts of the great tithe of all 'Bernard's land' at Wiveton and Blakeney (*Sniterle*) and two parts of the great tithe of the demesne of Robert Aiguillon (*Agylyun*) of the fee of Branche at Wiveton, they have leased these at perpetual farm to the rector and his successors for 20s *p.a.* payable in equal instalments at the two Norwich synods. If the rector should at any term default in payment for more than eight days, he shall immediately forfeit in perpetuity possession of the tithes and the right to their farm, and they shall revert irrevocably to the monks; the rector who has so defaulted shall nevertheless, at the simple complaint and appeal of the monks or their proctor, be compelled by the bp, by sentence of excommunication, to pay the sum due. This agreement was ratified and confirmed by the bp and recorded in the form of a chirograph sealed by him and alternately by the parties. Witnessed by William Suffield, archdn of Norwich, Robert de Insula, archdn of Colchester, *domini* John of Holkham, William of Whitwell and William of Pakenham, masters John of Palgrave, Robert of Hempnall (*Hemmenhale*) and Geoffrey of Dereham, Drogo of Acre and others. Castle Acre, 15 Aug. 1248 (BL ms. Harley 2110 fo. 126r (133r)).

16. Announcement by the bp in the presence of the pope that he intends to dedicate soon the cathedral church of Norwich, to which Innocent IV responds by granting to visitors on the day of consecration and its anniversary each year, who are contrite and confessed, one year and forty days of enjoined penance. Lyons, 28 March 1249 (*Norwich Cathedral Charters* i no. 301).

17. Grant in free and perpetual alms to the hospital of St Giles, Norwich, of all the land which the bp held of Roger Bigod, earl of Norfolk, in the vill of Hethel, to be held for an annual rent of 5s payable to the earl in equal instalments at Michaelmas and Easter for all customs and services; mentioned in the earl's confirmation charter [1249 × 19 May 1257] (BL Add. ch. 7207).

18. Sequestration of all the ecclesiastical goods of Stephen, *persona* of West Bradenham, who had failed to appear before the king's justices when impleaded by Osbert de Cailli (*Kayli*) as to why he had heard a plea concerning chattels not relating to testamentary business [12 Nov. 1249 × 20 Jan. 1250] (*CRR* xix no. 1260).

19. Concession made by Walter (de Salerne, *alias* of London), archdn of Norfolk, with the assent and according to the will of the bp and chapter of Norwich, to the prior of Wymondham and the vicars of Wymondham, Happisburgh and Snettisham, that he and his successors as archdn will be content with a procuration of three marks, that is one from each vicar, for visitation, and that they may demand no more than this. In case of default the archdn may not sequestrate the portions or any other goods of the prior and convent, but only the vicars' portions, neither may he impose interdict upon the churches; if he should act thus, his action shall be void at law; saving to the archdn and his successors jurisdiction over those churches, as contained in the pope's judgement (*Reg. Inn. IV* nos 4645–6; *CPL* i 258). Sealed by the archdn, the bp and the chapter, Norwich, 20 June 1251 (BL ms. Cotton Titus C viii fos 71v–72r).

20. Renunciation by Walter, archdn of Norfolk, at the instance of the bp and prior of Norwich and of the archdn of Colchester, of his action for damages against the prior and convent of Wymondham and the vicars of Wymondham, Happisburgh and Snettisham, Norwich, 20 June 1251 (BL ms. Cotton Titus C viii fo. 72r).

21. Consecration of an altar when Walter Cantilupe, bp of Worcester, dedicated the abbey church of Hailes, assisted by thirteen other bps, 5 Nov. 1251 (*Ann. mon.* ii 343; *HMC Wells* ii 563).

22. The bp is party to the resolution by the suffragans of Canterbury to send mr John of Cheam to the papal *curia* to obtain letters of grace concerning the visitation which the archbp recently attempted in London and the associated procurations, which visitation was likely to be repeated elsewhere; and also to obtain papal letters compelling all suffragan bps, non-exempt religious and clergy of the province to contribute to the subsidy to the apostolic see; and to act in the matter of the grace lately made to the archbp in regard to first fruits. Winchcombe, 6 Nov. 1251 (*HMC Wells* ii 563).

23. Attestation as first witness of a charter of John de Warenne, earl of Surrey, by which he granted to the nuns of Marham the service of all free tenants and villeins pertaining to the honour of Warenne in the vill of Marham, with all appurtenances etc. [*c.* Aug. 1252 × 19 May 1257] (BL Harley ch. 57 E 31).

24. Arbitration, with Walter Cantilupe, bp of Worcester, in the dispute between archbp Boniface of Canterbury and Aylmer de Valence, elect of Winchester, concerning the appointment of a prior of St Thomas's hospital, Southwark; mentioned in a letter of Adam Marsh (*Monumenta Franciscana* i 188); shortly before the provincial council which, Matthew Paris implies, met at London on 13 Jan. 1253 primarily for the absolution of Aylmer and his formal reconciliation with the archbp (*Chron. Maj.* v 359; *C & S* II i 467).

25. Agreement between the prior and convent of Castle Acre on one part and master Ralph, rector of Elsing (*Ausinge*) on the other, made with the express consent of lord William de Stuteville, patron of the church, whereby the monks have leased at perpetual farm to the rector and his successors two parts of William's demesne tithes in the vill of Elsing, for two marks *p.a.* payable in equal instalments at the two Norwich synods. If any rector should at any term default in payment for more than fifteen days, he shall immediately forfeit in perpetuity the tithes and the right to farm them, and they shall revert irrevocably to the monks; the defaulting rector shall nevertheless, at the simple complaint and appeal of the monks or their proctor, be compelled by the bp to pay the sum due, by sentence of excommunication. This agreement was ratified and confirmed by the bp and recorded in the form of a chirograph sealed by the bp and chapter of Norwich and alternately by the parties. Witnessed by William Suffield, archdn of Norwich, Robert de Insula, archdn of Colchester, mr John of Palgrave, Ralph Burd' and others, 24 Feb. 1253 (BL ms Harley 2110 fo. 127r (134r)).

26. With the king and others, the bp appends his seal to letters of P[eter] of Savoy (*Sabaudia*), in which he promises to go to the Holy Land with the king, if he is still alive then and has been provided with the aid which the king has promised. Westminster, 18 Apr. 1253 (*CPR 1247–58* 188).

27. The bp, with the bp of Chichester and the abbot of Westminster, in the presence of the king's council, make arrangements for the allocation of their separate responsibilities as collectors of the tenth, being the Holy Land subsidy conceded to the king; bp Walter is assigned London diocese (excluding the archdeaconry of Middlesex), Ely, Norwich, Lincoln and Coventry dioceses and the whole province of York, and is assigned 500 marks for expenses. 17 May 1254 (*CPR 1247–58* 370).

28. The bp, with the bp of Chichester and the abbot of Westminster, publish their commission from pope Innocent IV to collect the tenth, 12 Sept. 1253 (*Reg. Inn. IV* no 6989; *CPL* i 290) in London. 4 July 1254 (*Chron. Maj.* vi 296–7).

29. The bp is engaged in litigation against William of Wiggenhall (*Wighal'*) and Isabelle his wife, who have obtained against the bp and others an assize of *novel disseisin* concerning tenements in Holme, Hunstanton and Burnham Thorpe; W. le Bretun is appointed to take the assize, 12 Oct. 1254 (*Cl. R. 1253–54* 160).

30. The bp has claimed as wreck a great and monstrous fish recently taken on the land of a boy in his custody; the sheriff of Norfolk is to have it sold at the best price possible and to appear with the money before the Council three weeks after Easter, 19 Feb. 1255 (*Cl. R. 1254–56* 44; cf. Powicke, *Henry III and the Lord Edward* 334 and refs. there given).

31. Payment by the bp of 5500 marks, out of the tenth collected by him for the business of the realm, made to Ventura Fornarii, Reyner Barboti, Hereminus Herminii and James Tecii, citizens and merchants of Siena, at the mandate of mr Rostand [Masson], papal subdeacon and chaplain, executor of the business of the cross in England and other lands subject to the king, deputed by the apostolic see to make payments to various merchants for the business of the realm of Sicily; mentioned in an acquittance of the bp and his church in respect of this payment and any other made at mr Rostand's command, Windsor, 4 Dec. 1255 (*CPR 1247–58* 508–9).

32. Request to the king for respite of knighthood for William of Calthorpe (*Calethorp*), granted for three years from the feast of Holy Trinity, 5 June 1256 (*CPR 1247–58* 477).

33. Indulgence (number of days of remission unspecified) granted to those who might come to venerate the newly discovered tomb of St Alban at his abbey [26 Dec. 1256 x 19 May 1257] (*Chron. Maj.* vi 495).

SIMON WALTON

34. Petition to the king by the bp-elect for the exemption for life of Adam of Redmarley from taking part in assizes, juries and recognitions, and from being made sheriff etc. 4 June x 25 Sept. 1257. Mentioned in grant of exemption, 25 Sept. 1257 (*CPR 1247–58* 579).

35. Confirmation of the grant in alms by Nicholas son of William le Cuntur, as confirmed by Thomas his son, of various messuages to the Dominican friars of Lynn; these properties are on the east side of the road which leads northwards from Blackfriars. 10 Mar. 1258 × 2 Jan. 1266. Mentioned in a list of tenants in Newland in Lynn in a rental, before 1296 (*King's Lynn* 181, no. 174).

36. Grant to Matilda, daugher of Roger of Pershore (*Persher'*), for her lifetime, of an annual rent of £10, in two instalments, from all the land which bp Simon had purchased from the lord William Bagot in the vill of Loxley (*Lockesleye*) [Wa.]. [10 Mar. 1258 × 2 Jan. 1266] (*Reg. Giffard, Worcester* 475).

37. Enfeoffment of Ralph son of James of Ettington (*Etindon'*) of the manor of Barnham (*Bernham*) with appurtenances, and appointment, as he was under age, of Robert de Wivecot as his guardian. Mentioned in a royal writ, dated 18 Jan. 1266, to the keepers of the temporalities *sede vacante* to restore this manor, which had been taken into the king's hands on the bp's death by the king's eschaetor in Suffolk, to Ralph or his guardian, if it had, as alleged, never been part of the episcopal demesne [10 Mar. 1258 × 2 Jan. 1266] (*Cl. R. 1264–68* 231–2).

38. (Probable) indulgence issued for the benefactors of Salisbury cathedral. Bp Walton was present with archbp Boniface and eight other bps at the dedication 29 Sept. 1258 (*Ann. mon.* i 166). The Salisbury statutes state that various prelates gave indulgences for the anniversary of the dedication to its octave totalling twenty-two years 112 days (*C. & S.* II i 563).

39. Petition to pope Alexander IV for confirmation of the ancient, approved and hitherto observed custom that the bp should receive the first year's revenues of benefices in his diocese in which on Easter day there was no rector instituted; the confirmation was granted at Anagni, 27 June 1260 (*Norwich Cathedral Charters* i no. 306).

40. Coercion exercised against Simon Passelewe in his benefices of Barningham (*Bruningham*) [unid.] and Bardwell for arrears of payment of his portion of the tenth conceded by the pope to the king. Mentioned in a royal writ, 26 Jan. 1261, ordering the bp to desist from the coercion he has rightly applied, because the king cannot provide enough for Simon for his services, expenses and honour, and has therefore remitted the arrears of the tenth (*Cl. R. 1259–61* 456–7).

41. Complaint by the bp to the king that, whereas William of Measham (*Meysham*) had granted him the manor of Measham [Lei.] at farm for twenty-six years, the said William came and maltreated his men there, carried away and destroyed his cups and other goods, extorted rents from the tenants, depastured the crops growing on the lands and meadows pertaining to the manor with his beasts, trod them down and did other damage. Mentioned in a writ appointing Adam de Greynville to enquire and do justice, 26 Mar. 1261 (*CPR 1258–66* 185; cf. ibid. 186).

42. Notification by Robert , perpetual vicar of Woolpit, of an agreement made on 17 March 1261 in Pakenham church, in the bp's presence, between himself and the abbot and convent of Bury St Edmunds; whereas the vicar has defaulted for more than two years in payment of the annual pension of twenty marks from the church, as ordained by Walter, late bp of Norwich (9), eventually the abbot and the prior and convent , taking pity on his poverty, remitted these arrears apart from fifteen marks, which the vicar should pay in two instalments of £5 at the next Easter synod at Ipswich and the feast of the nativity of St John the Baptist (24 June) next, and thereafter should faithfully render the pension in full, to the fulfilment of all of which he took an oath on his honour as a priest, submitting himself humbly to the jurisdiction of the bp, who might coerce him to observance by sentence of interdict and excommunication and by confiscation and deprivation of his benefice, if need be, without formal judicial process. The notification was sealed both by Robert and by the bp at Thornage, 28 March 1261 (*Memorials of St Edmunds* iii 83–4).

43. Letter of the bp to W[alter] of Merton, the king's chancellor, relating that his previous complaints to the king on behalf of the lady Margery de Comyn against William of Measham (*Meisham*), knight, have had no effect, and imploring the chancellor that he should issue, as quickly as possible, royal letters patent for the benefit of the said lady, who has been ejected by William from the manor of Measham and despoiled of her goods, so that the lords Giles of Erdington and Adam de Greynville should enquire into this wrongdoing and deliver her swift justice. 19 Aug. 1261 (TNA, SC1/7/205; cf. *CPR 1258–66* 230, 232–3).

44. Grant in heredity and in perpetuity to John of Walton [his son, as noted on endorsement], for his homage and service, of all his manor of Walton Mauduit (*Wauton Mauduth*), which he had purchased from William Mauduit, earl of Warwick, with all appurtenances and liberties within the vill and without, to have an to hold of the bp and his heirs or assigns, rendering on their behalf to the capital lords of the fee the services due for a twentieth part of a knight's fee. Warranty is granted. 4 Apr. [1263 × 2 Jan. 1266] (Warwick County R.O., CR 133/4).

45. License granted to John Walton to do homage to the capital lords for land in Walton Mauduit (*Walton Inferior*), Walton Deyville (*Walton Superior*) , Loxley (*Lochesl'*) [Wa.], Bradley (*Bradle*) [Wo.], *Aucrinton* [unid.] and elsewhere in the

counties of Warwickshire, Worcestershire, Gloucestershire and Oxfordshire, so
that neither the bp or his heirs may demand from the said lands homage, service
or other secular exactions [4 Apr. 1263 × 2 Jan. 1266] (*Reg. Giffard, Worcester*
443–4).

46. Distraint on the churches of Lavenham and Aldham, benefices of Godfrey de
Merk, because of his failure to contribute to the tenth due to the king. Mentioned
in a royal writ to the bp, dated 21 Jan. 1265, to relax sequestration if there was
truth in Godfrey's complaint that he had incurred great expense preparing for the
defence of these two churches against potential enemy attack, and that the bp had
distrained upon him as on other rectors of the diocese who had not paid the tenth
but had not either incurred such expense (*Cl. R. 1264–68* 92; cf. Powicke, *Henry
III and the Lord Edward* 483–4).

APPENDIX 3

FINAL CONCORDS

Below are calendared fines made before the king's justices to which one of the bishops was a party.

WALTER SUFFIELD

1. Final concord made in the king's court before the justices in eyre at Norwich, 3 Apr. 1247, between bp Walter, *persona* of Hoxne, plaintiff, and Richard of Ling (*Lyng*) and Margery hs wife, defendants, concerning nine and a half acres of land with appurtenances in Yaxley (*Iakele*), Thrandeston (*Randeston*) and Mellis (*Melles*), and between the bp and the same Richard and Margery, who were called to warrant and granted warranty for Henry de la Howe for an acre and three roods of land with appurtenances in Yaxley; Richard the smith (*faber*) for an acre etc. in Yaxley; William Acher, for three acres etc. in Yaxley; William de Gosewald for two acres and a rood etc. in Yaxley; Katherine daughter of Gervase for half an acre etc. in Yaxley; Robert le Fraunceys for half an acre of meadow in Yaxley; William Joze for half an acre of land in Yaxley; Richard son of Gervase for three acres etc. in Yaxley; Richard son of Reginald for one acre etc. in Yaxley; Gervase of Thrandeston for two acres etc. in Thrandeston. An assize *utrum* was summoned between them in the same court, whereby Richard of Ling and Margery recognised all the foresaid tenements with appurtenances to be the right of the bp and his church of Hoxne; and for this recognition and final concord the bp granted to Richard and Margery and to Margery's heirs all the foresaid tenements and appurtenances, to have and to hold of the bp and his successors as *persone* of Hoxne in perpetuity for an annual rent of 8s in two instalments at Michaelmas and Easter for all service etc, whereas hitherto they had paid only 5s *p.a.*(TNA, CP25/1/214/19/26).

2. Final concord made in the king's court before the justices in eyre at Bedford, 13 × 19 Oct. 1247, between bp Walter, *persona* of Hoxne, plaintiff, and mr William of Horham, defendant, concerning thirty acres of land with appurtenances in Chickering in Hoxne. An assize *utrum* was summoned between them in the same court, whereby the bp conceded the land with appurtenances to mr William, to have and to hold to him and his heirs in perpetuity of the bp and his succcessors as *persone* and of the church of Hoxne for an annual rent of 28s in two instalments at the feasts of the Purification and of St John the Baptist for all services etc. Warranty is granted in perpetuity (TNA, CP25/1/214/19/23).

3. Final concord made in the king's court before the justices in eyre at Bedford, 13 × 19 Oct. 1247, between bp Walter, *persona* of Hoxne, plaintiff, and William le Flemeng, defendant, concerning five and a half acres of land with appurtenances in Denham, and between the bp and the same William, who was called to warrant and granted warranty for Hubert of Bedingfield (*Bedingfeud*) and Martine his wife, concerning six acres of land with appurtenances in the same vill; whereby William recognised all the foresaid land with appurtenances to be the right of the bp and his church of Hoxne; for this recognition and final concord the bp granted all this land to William and his heirs, to have and to hold of the bp and his successors as *persone* and of the church of Hoxne in perpetuity, rendering 3s 4d *p.a.* in two instalments at Easter and Michaelmas for all service etc. (TNA, CP25/1/214/19/27).

4. Final concord made in the king's court before the justices in eyre at Bedford, 13 × 19 Oct. 1247, between bp Walter, *persona* of Hoxne, plaintiff, and mr Henry of Mellis (*Melles*), defendant, concerning four acres of land with appurtenances in Yaxley (*Iakele*). An assize *utrum* was summoned between them in the same court, whereby mr Henry recognised this land to be the right of the bp and of his church of Hoxne; for this recognition and final concord the bp granted this land to him and his heirs, to hold of the bp and his successors as *persone* of Hoxne in perpetuity, for an annual rent of 12d at Michaelmas, whereas he had hitherto paid only 10d *p.a.* (TNA, CP25/1/214/19/28).

5. Final concord made in he king's court before the justices in eyre at Cambridge, 20 × 26 Oct. 1247, between bp Walter, plaintiff, represented by William of Pakenham, and Peter of Hautbois (*de Alto Bosco*), defendant, represented by Peter of Lammas (*Lammesse*), concerning one quarter of a knight's fee in Calthorpe (*Kaletorp'*). A *placitum conventionis* was summoned in that court, whereby Peter recognised this quarter fee to be the right of the bp and his successors and of his church of Norwich by Peter's gift, to have and to hold in perpetuity by the services pertaining thereto. Warranty is granted. For this recognition etc. the bp gave Peter forty marks (TNA, CP25/1/157/70/907).

For Peter de Hautbois, or Obys, see Rawcliffe, *Medicine for the Soul* 18, 74.

6. Final concord made in the king's court before the justices in eyre at Chelmsford, 14 Jan. 1248, between bp Walter, plaintiff, represented by William of Pakenham, and Peter of Hautbois, defendant, represented by Peter of Lammas, concerning seven acres of land, twelve acres of woodland and eighteen acres of pasture, with appurtenances, in Calthorpe (*Kalethorp'*), and the advowson of the church there. A *placitum conventionis* was summoned in that court, whereby

Peter recognised all the foresaid to be the right of the bp for his lifetime by Peter's gift, to have and to hold of Peter and his heirs for an annual rent of 15d at Michaelmas for all service etc. After the bp's death all the foresaid shall remain to William of Calthorpe and his heirs, to be held in the same manner in perpetuity. Warranty is granted. This is done with the reservation to Matilda, widow of Peter of Hautbois the donor's father, of a third part of the woodland and pasture, which she shall hold in dower for her lifetime, and which after her death shall revert to the bp or to William of Calthorpe and his heirs in perpetuity; she, being present, assented to this and to the making of this final concord. For this grant etc. the bp has given Peter one hundred marks (TNA, CP25/1/157/71/927)

7. Final concord made in the king's court before the justices in eyre at Chelmsford, 27 Jan. × 2 Feb. 1248, between bp Walter, plaintiff, represented by William of Pakenham, and Walter Leffort and Matilda his wife, defendants, concerning 29s 8d annual rent with appurtenances in Lynn. There was a plea between them in the same court, whereby William and Matilda recognised the rent etc. to be the right of the bp and his church of Norwich and quitclaimed for themselves and their heirs. For this recognition etc. the bp gave them twenty-three marks (TNA, CP25/1/157/71/934).

8. Final concord made in the king's court before the justices in eyre at Ipswich, 20 × 26 Jan. 1251, between Geoffrey of Loddon (*Lodnes*), plaintiff, and bp Walter, defendant, represented by William of Pakenham, concerning ten marks annual rent with appurtenances in Lynn. There was a plea between them in the same court, whereby the bp conceded for himself, his successors and his church of Norwich that Geoffrey should for his lifetime receive this rent at the feast of St Margaret (20 July) by the hands of the bailiff and warden of the bp's tolbooth on behalf of the bp and his successors, who after Geoffrey's death shall be quit in perpetuity of this payment. For this recognition etc. Geoffrey gave the bp a sore goshawk (TNA, CP25/1/157/78/1110).

9. Final concord made in the king's court at Westminster before the king's justices, 27 Jan. x 2 Feb. 1253, between bp Walter, plaintiff, and John Hereman and Agnes his wife, defendants, concerning twenty-three acres of land with appurtenances in Sprowston (*Sprouston'*), and between the bp, plaintiff, and Adam Gernun and Alice his wife, defendants, concerning eighteen acres of land with appurtenances in the same vill. There was a plea between them in the same court , whereby the defendants recognised all the foresaid land etc. to be the right of the bp and his church of Norwich; for this recognition and final concord the bp granted that which they claimed, being that they, and after them the heirs of Agnes and Alice, should have and hold these lands of the bp and his successors and the church of Norwich for an annual rent of 8s payable at Michaelmas for all service etc., of which 7s 6d shall be paid by Adam Gernun, Alice and her heirs,

and 6d by John Hereman, Agnes and Agnes's heirs. For this recognition, warranty and final concord, John and Agnes at the bp's petition granted and conceded to Hamo, master of the hospital of St Giles in Norwich, and his successors and to the brethren thereof an acre of meadow with appurtenances in Norwich, lying adjacent to the hospital to the east, and also the homage and service of John the smith (*faber*) and his heirs for the tenement held of them, to be held in perpetuity of John, Agnes and Agnes's heirs, rendering on their behalf the services due to the capital lords of the fee. Warranty is granted to the hospital (TNA, CP25/1/157/82/1207; cf. Rawcliffe, *Medicine for the Soul* 46-7, 78).

SIMON WALTON

10. Final concord made in the king's court at Westminster before the king's justices, 25 June 1260, between bp Simon, plaintiff, and William Sprot and Mariota his wife, defendants, concerning one and a half acres of land at Ipswich. A *placitum conventionis* was summoned in that court, whereby William and Mariota recognised this tenement with appurtenances to be the right of the bp and his church of Norwich, and they restored (*reddiderunt*) it to him in court and quitclaimed for themselves and Mariota's heirs to the bp, his successors and his church in perpetuity. For this recognition etc. the bp gave them a mewed sparrowhawk (TNA, CP25/1/214/26/25).

APPENDIX 4

ROYAL PRESENTATIONS TO BENEFICES

Listed below are royal writs of presentation which almost certainly resulted in action by the bishops, and most probably in the issue of letters of institution.

WALTER SUFFIELD

1. Royal presentation of Henry of Canterbury (*Cantuaria*), king's chaplain, to the church of Chelmondiston (*Chelmodestun'*), directed to the bp-elect in substitution for mr Hugh Mortimer (*de Mortuo Mari*), official of the elect of Canterbury. 9 July 1244 (*CPR 1232-47* 431).

2. Royal presentation of Osbert of Maidstone (*Maidenestan*), king's chaplain, to the church of Alburgh (*Aldeburg'*), in the king's gift by reason of custody of the lands and heir of the late W[illiam] de Warenne; the bp is directed to do his part. 7 Apr. 1245 (*CPR 1232-47* 450).

3. Royal presentation of mr Henry of Campden to the church of Gosbeck, in the king's gift by reason of his seisin of the manor of Gosbeck because Richard of Gosbeck, lord of the vill and rector of the church, ravished (*rapuit*) her who was the wife of William le Bretun against the king's peace and married her (*cum ea contraxit*); directed to the bp. 17 Oct. 1246 (*CPR 1232-47* 489).

4. Royal presentation of John of Southwark (*Sutwerk*) to a mediety of the church of Ingworth, directed to the bp. 20 Jan. 1247 (*CPR 1232-47* 496).

5. Royal presentation of Reginald Herlizun, king's proctor at the court of Rome, to the church of Withersfield (*Whitherfeld*), directed to the bp. 8 Mar. 1247 (*CPR 1232-47* 499).

6. Royal presentation of Nicholas de Bleys to the church of Tattingstone (*Tadingeston*), directed to the bp. 23 May 1247 (*CPR 1232-47* 502).

7. Royal presentation of Richard le Salvage to the church of Weston [Sf.], directed to the bp. 25 Jan. 1250 (*CPR 1247-58* 58).

8. Royal presentation of Peter de Aubusson (*Abezun*) to the church of *Hemngton* [unid., possibly Hemingstone, Sf.], directed to the bp. 6 Feb. 1250 (*CPR 1247-58* 59

9. Royal presentation of mr John Luvel to the church of St John, Ipswich, directed to the bp. 12 Oct. 1251 (*CPR 1247-58* 111)..

10. Royal presentation of Raymond de Boyvill to the church of Kirtling (*Kerlling*), in the king's gift by reason of the custody of the lands and heir of Ralph de Tosny (*Thoeny*), directed to the bp. 20 Dec. 1251 (*CPR 1247-58* 121).

11. Royal presentation of Peter de Aubusson (*Abuson*) to the church of Necton, directed to the bp. 20 Dec. 1251 (*CPR 1247-58* 121).

12. Royal presentation of Amauri de Rochecorbon (*Rupe Cavardi*) to the church of Willingham St Mary (*Wilingham*), directed to the bp. 13 May 1252 (*CPR 1247-58* 138).

13. Royal presentation of William of Blythburgh (*Bliburgh*), chaplain, to the mastership of God's House, Dunwich, directed to the bp. 16 May 1252 (*CPR 1247-58* 139).

14. Royal presentation of Nicholas Gacelin to the chuch of *Wycham* [unid., probably Wickham Market or Wickham Skeith, Sf.], directed to the bp. 11 Apr. 1253 (*CPR 1247-58* 187).

15. Mandate to the bp to admit John de Sancta Maria as warden of the *Domus Dei*, Dunwich. 10 Jan. 1256 (*CPR 1247-58* 457).

16. Royal presentation of John Wallerand to the church of Outwell (*Wywell*), in the king's gift by reason of the voidance of the see of Ely, directed to the bp. 29 Oct. 1256 (*CPR 1247-58* 528).

17. Royal presentation of mr Rostand [Masson], papal subdeacon and chaplain, to a quarter part of the church of Dickleburgh (*Sceburg*), in the king's hands by the voidance of the abbey of Bury, directed to the bp. 8 Jan. 1257 (*CPR 1247-58* 536).

18. Royal presentation of Arnold Coceti, kinsman of mr Rostand, to a quarter part of the church of Dickleburgh, directed to the bp. 22 Feb. 1257 (*CPR 1247-58* 543).

19. Royal presentation of Adam of Filby (*Fileby*) to the church of Chelmondiston, vacant by the resignation of Henry of Malling, rector, directed to the bp. 2 Mar. 1257 (*CPR 1247-58* 544).

20. Royal presentation of mr Henry of Wingham (*Wengham*) to the church of Rougham (*Ruham*), vac. by the resignation of Henry of Wingham, directed to the bp. 23 Mar. 1257 (*CPR 1247-58* 546).

21. Royal presentation of Raymond Masson to the church of Elveden, in the king's gift by the voidance of the abbey of Bury, directed to the bp. 8 Apr. 1257 (*CPR 1247-58* 548).

22. Royal presentation of mr Rostand to the church of Barking (*Berkinng*), in the king's gift by reason of the voidance of the see of Ely; directed to the bp, but cancelled because the church is not vacant. 21 Apr. 1257 (*CPR 1247-58* 550).

SIMON WALTON

23. Royal presentation of John of Salisbury (*Sarresburia*) to a mediety of the church of Ingworth, vacant by the death of John of Southwark (*Suwerc*), directed to the bp-elect. 8 Oct. 1257 (*CPR 1247-58* 581).

24. Royal presentation of William de Chavent (*Chauvent*) to the church of Palgrave, in the king's hands by reason of the voidance of the abbey of Bury, directed to the bp-elect. 2 Nov. 1257 (*CPR 1247-58* 603).

25. Royal presentation of Arnald de Saltu, chaplain, to the church of Saxham, in he king's hands by reason of the voidance of the abbey of Bury, directed to the bp-elect. 5 Nov. 1257 (*CPR 1247-58* 604).

26. Royal presentation of mr Rostand to the church of Gislingham (*Giselingham*), in the king's hands by reason of the voidance of the abbey of Bury, directed to the bp- elect. 18 Nov. 1257 (*CPR 1247-58* 606).

27. Royal presentation of Henry of Merrington (*Mereynton*) to the church of Brandon Ferry, in the king's hands by reason of the voidance of the see of Ely, directed to the bp-elect. 15 Dec. 1257 (*CPR 1247-58* 608).

28. Royal presentation of Robert of Necton to the church of Tittleshall (*Tisteshall*), vacant by the resignation of William of Necton, in the king's hands by reason of the voidance of the abbey of Bury, directed to the bp-elect. 15 Dec. 1257 (*CPR 1247-58* 608).

29. Royal presentation of Adam of Chesterton (*Cestreton*) to a mediety of the church of Ingworth, vacant by the death of John of Salisbury (*Sarr'*), in the king's hands by reason of the voidance of the abbey of Bury, directed to the bp-elect. 1 Jan. 1258 (*CPR 1247-58* 614).

30. Royal presentation of mr Luke of Paignton (*Peynton*) to the church of North Cove (*Cove*), vacant by the resignation of Martin de Sancta Cruce, directed to the bp-elect. 16 Feb. 1258 (*CPR 1247-58* 614).

31. Royal presentation of Vincent de Malo Lacu to a mediety of the church of Ingworth, vacant by the resignation of Adam of Chesterton, in the king's hands by reason of the voidance of the abbey of Bury, directed to the bp. 30 March 1258 (*CPR 1247-58* 621).

32. Royal presentation of Simon of Canterbury (*Cantuaria*), chaplain, to the church of *Brandeston* [unid., Brandeston, Sf., or Brandiston, Nf.], directed to the bp. 4 May 1259 (*CPR 1258-66* 21).

33. Royal presentation of Giles of Tuddenham to the church of *Blakeham* [probably Great Blakenham, Sf.], directed to the bp. 1 Oct. 1260 (*CPR 1258-66* 94).

34. Royal presentation of Roger of Evesham to a mediety of the church of Ingworth, vacant by the death of Vincent de Malo Lacu, in the king's hands by reason of the voidance of the abbey of Bury, directed to the bp. 15 Feb. 1261 (*CPR 1258-66* 141).

35. Royal presentation of Nicholas de Villa to the church of Bodham (*Bodeham*), by reason of the lands of William of Bodham being in the king's hands. 18 Feb. 1262 (*CPR 1258-66* 201).

36. Royal presentation of Robert Fulconis *alias* Fulton, of Reading, to the church of Hintlesham, directed to the bp. 15 July 1264 (*CPR 1258-66* 337).

37. Mandate to the bp that, whereas the king by right of the crown presented Robert Fulton, king's clerk, to the church of Hintlesham, concerning the advowson of which there was litigation in the *curia regis* between the king and William Pipard, tenant in chief, who died before a decision was reached, after which the wardship of his land and heirs was in the king's hands and the right of presentation to the church, if William had such, pertains to the king, the bp should now admit the said clerk at the king's presentation, saving the rights of the king and of William's heirs when they come of age, if they have such in the advowson. 29 Nov. 1264. Note that the king presented the last *persona* to this church in the eighteenth or the thirtieth year of his reign (*CPR 1258-66* 451).

38. Royal presentation of Simon of Creeping (*Creppinges*) to the church of Hengrave (*Hemmegrave*), in the king's gift by reason of the land and heirs of Thomas of Hengrave, tenant in chief, being in his hands, directed to the bp. 25 Oct. 1265 (*CPR 1258-66* 471).

APPENDIX 5

ITINERARIES OF THE BISHOPS OF NORWICH, 1244–1266

Dates for attendance at councils, taken from *C. & S.* II i, distinguish between references to 'all' or 'almost all' bishops, and definite notices that the bishop of Norwich was present. Starred entries denote the bishop mentioned as a witness only.

WALTER SUFFIELD

1244

December	Terling	actum no. 17A

1245

2 January	Ipswich	actum no. 11
19 January	Thorpe	actum no. 44
19 February	Norwich, Carrow priory (consecration)	*Chron Bury* 13 (correcting *Fasti* ii 57)
20 February	Norwich	actum no. 17B
23 February	Westminster, Great Council	*C. & S.* II i 388; *Ann. mon.* iii167
22 March	Norwich	actum no. 110
26 March	Terling	actum no. 14
30 March	Norwich	acta nos. 136–7
31 March	South Elmham	actum no. 123
7 April	Blythburgh	actum no. 74
11 April	Sibton	actum no. 127
21 April	Norwich	actum no. 2
29 April	North Elmham	acta nos. 88–9, 109
1 May	Coxford	actum no. 35
6 May	Pentney	actum no. 40
8 May	Gaywood	actum no. 20
14 May	Ipswich	actum no. 66
24 June – 17 July	Lyons, general council	*C. & S.* II i 402

1246

4 February	Blofield	actum no. 90
9 February	Rollesby	actum no. 21

19 February	North Elmham	actum no. 22
21 February	Norwich	actum no. 91
18...24 March	London, great council (prelates attend)	*Chron.Maj.* iv 557; actum no. 119
12 April	Thorpe	actum no. 9
19 April	Happisburgh	actum no. 92
28 April	North Elmham	actum no. 23
10 August	Broome	actum no. 49
26 August	Hoxne	actum no. 124; Appx 2. 6
29 September	South Elmham	actum no. 115
10 December	Gaywood	actum no. 75
13 December	Lynn	actum no. 77

1247

24–25 February	Norwich	acta nos. 93, 109
11 March	Gaywood	actum no. 113
9 April	Thetford	actum no. 52
11 May	Bacton, Sf.	actum no. 41
28 June	Norwich	Appx. 2.10
28 June	Thornage	actum no. 42
16 September	London	actum no. 53
6 October	protection granted until feast of Purification [2 Feb. 1248] to go on pilgrimage to St Gilles en Provence	*CPR 1247–58* 28
13 October	Westminster, preaches at translation of the Holy Blood relic	*Chron. Maj.* iv 642

1248

1–2 January	Hadham	acta nos. 131–32
8 February	Westminster, great council	*C. & S.* II i 418–9
7 March	Hertford	actum no. 54
13 April	North Elmham	actum no. 25
29 April	Norwich	actum no. 3
1 June	Thornham	actum no. 56
15 August	Castle Acre	Appx 2. 15
21 August	Thornham	actum no. 37
23 August	*Dunham*	actum no. 57
1 October	Thorpe	actum no. 69
6 October	Norwich	actum no. 94

24 October	Terling	actum no. 118
after Michaelmas	sets out for court of Rome	*Historia Minor* iii 36

1249

28 March	Lyons	Appx 2. 16
Autumn	returns from court of Rome	*Chron. Maj.* v 638; *Historia Minor* iii 58
10 October	Westminster*	*C.Ch.R 1300–26*, 480
15 October	Stoke-by-Clare	actum no. 78
27 December	Marham	actum no. 26
30 December	Eccles	actum no. 70

1250

20 January	Ipswich	actum no. 79
c.20 April	Oxford, provincial council (*convenerunt episcopi*)	*C. & S.* II i 445–6; *Chron. Maj.* v 100
21 July	Hoxne	actum no. 112
7 October	London	actum no. 81A

1251

24 February	Dunstable, meeting of suffragans of Canterbury (specifically mentioned)	*C. & S.* II i 447–8; *Chron. Maj.* v 225–6; *Ann. mon.* iii 181
15 March	[Great] Barton	actum no. 10
25 March	[Great] Snoring	actum no. 4
2 April	Thorpe	actum no. 83
4 April	? Oxford	*C. & S.* II i 447–8
10 April	? London (*per tractatum episcoporum Anglie*	*C. & S.* II i 447–8
20 May	Bacton	actum no. 116
26 July	Cressingham	acta nos. 96, 135
9 September	North Elmham	acta nos. 85–6
1 October	Norwich	actum no. 105
5 November	Hailes, dedication of abbey	Appx 2. 21
6 November	Winchcombe, meeting of bps in king's presence	Appx 2. 22

1252

24 February	North Elmham	acta nos. 27–8
April	? London, great council (suffragans of	*C. & S.* II i 449–50

	Canterbury, not specifically mentioned)	
25 June	Hevingham	actum no. 111
25 August	[Great] Snoring	actum no. 43
27 August	Shouldham	actum no. 121
13 October	? London, meeting (*totius Anglie prelati fere universi*, absentees specified)	*C. & S.* II i 451
19 October	Stratford-atte-Bowe	actum no. 76
8 December	Weasenham	actum no. 36
15 December	Gaywood	actum no. 58
20 December	Thornham	actum no. 29

1253

before 13 January	London	Appx 2. 24
13 January	London, council of province of Canterbury (*omnes episcopi*)	*C. & S.* II i 467–8
15 January	London	actum no. 60
2–3 February	London	acta nos. 67–8
12 March	Hevingham	actum no. 128
18 April	Westminster	Appx 2. 26
4–13 May	Westminster, great council (*episcopi Anglie fere omnes*)	*C. & S.* II i 474–9; actum no. 61
17 May	London	Appx 2. 27
4 July	London	Appx 2. 28
12 July	Hevingham	actum no. 71
28 July	Norwich	actum no. 97
13 October	granted simple protection on going overseas	*CPR 1247–58* 223
20–21 October	Lambourne	acta nos. 29, 106

1254

27 January	Westminster, council summoned by regents (all bishops, not among named exceptions)	*C. & S.* II i 481–3; *Chron. Maj.* v 423
26 April	? Westminster, council summoned by regents (not specifically mentioned)	*C. & S.* II i 481–3

c. 21 May	Northamptonshire	*Cl.R. 1253–54* 66
20 June	Norwich	actum no. 87
11 July	St Albans	*Chron. Maj.*. v 4512;
		Historia Minor iii 326;
		Gesta Abbatum i 368
18 July	Eynsham	actum no. 34
13 August	Cambridge	actum no. 15
8 September	Durham	acta nos. 38–9
13 October	? London	actum no. 62
22 October	Terling	actum no. 33
11 November	Sulby	actum no. 16
17 December	Ipswich	actum no. 129

1255

20 July	Blofield	actum no. 64
4 October	Norwich	actum no. 102
13 October	London, council to meet	*C. & S.* II i 501–3;
	mr Rostand Masson	*Chron. Maj.* v 524
	(*universos Anglie*	
	prelatos)	

1256

18 January	? London, New Temple,	*C.& S.* II i 504–8
	council	
	(*episcopi Anglie et*	
	archidiaconi)	
20 January	Wicks Bishop	actum no. 65
25 February	Coxford	actum no. 30
6 March	Eccles	actum no. 80
24–5 March	Westminster*	*C.Ch.R. 1257–1300,*
		315, 402
1 April	Norwich	actum no. 98
15 April	Westminster*	*C.Ch.R. 1257–1300* 402
20 April	Westminster*	*C.Ch.R. 1257–1300* 315
19 June	Hoxne	actum no. 138
25 July	Norwich	acta nos. 99–101
2 September	Norwich	actum no. 72

1257

7 January	London, St Paul's,	*Canterbury Professions*
	consecration of William	no. 193; cf. *Llandaff*
	of Radnor as bp of	*Acta* p. xviii
	Llandaff	
11 March	Canterbury, Christ	*Canterbury Professions*

	Church, consecration of Giles of Bridport as bp of Salisbury	no. 194; cf. *Fasti* iv 5 and n. 2
16–25 March	? London, great council	*C. & S.* II i 524
25 April	Hevingham	actum no. 6
6 May	? London, clerical assembly	*C. & S.* II i 524
19 May	dies at Colchester	*Chron. Maj.* v 638

SIMON WALTON

1257

30 November	Thorpe	actum no. 181
23 December	Hertford	actum no. 155

1258

10 March	Canterbury, Christ Church, consecration as bp	actum no. 139
6 June	? Merton, ecclesiastical council (*congregatis ...suis suffraganeis*)	*C. & S.* II i 568–72 esp. 569 n.1
8 June	? Westminster, ecclesiastical council	*C. & S.* II i 568–72
July or August	? Oxford (specifically mentioned by Paris, but meeting itself doubtful)	*C. & S.* II i 572
29 September	Salisbury, dedication of cathedral	*Ann. mon.* i 166
3 November	Canterbury, Christ Church, consecration of Richard Gravesend as bp of Lincoln	*Canterbury Professions* no. 199; cf. *Fasti* iii 4
4 December	Eccles	actum no. 158

1259

5 January	? North Elmham	actum no. 144
9 August	(?North) Creake	actum no. 189
23 August	Colchester	actum no. 149
9 September	granted protection on going as envoy to king of France	*CPR 1258–66* 42

1260

15 February	Southwark, St Mary Overy, consecration of Henry of Wingham as bp of London	*Canterbury Professions* no. 200; cf. *Fasti* i 3
(? 2) May	Gaywood	actum no. 140
24 June	Pinley	actum no. 189A
4 December	Norwich	actum no. 160

1261

26 January	Westminster	*EEA* 29 no. 123
17 March	Pakenham	Appx 2 42
20 March	Hoxne	actum no. 161
27 March	Thornage	Appx 2 42
8–13 May	Council of Lambeth (specifically named)	*C. & S.* II i 668–9
17 May	London	actum no. 162
5 October	*London	*Beauchamp Cart.* no. 309
8 December	Norwich	actum no. 186
24 December	Norwich	actum no. 150

1262

24 February	Norwich	actum no. 163
9 May	London	actum no. 164
30 September	ordered to be at ford of Montgomery as arbitrator	*CPR* 1258–66 227
4 December	Norwich	actum no. 167

1263

10 January	London	actum no. 168
1 February	London	actum no. 169
23 March	Ipswich	actum no. 151
21 June	London	actum no. 172
27–28 July	Bury St Edmunds	acta nos.170, 173
12 December	Sibton	actum no. 193

1264

5 January x 24 March	Ipswich	actum no. 147
15 May	Gaywood	actum no. 145
10 August	London	actum no. 174
10 October	Gaywood	actum no. 195
25 October	(?West) Dereham	actum no. 187

1265

4 January	Hoxne	actum no. 152
7 January	Bacton	actum no. 175
23–25 February	Norwich	acta nos. 180, 176–7
1 April	Gaywood	actum no. 178
16 April	Gaywood	actum no. 179
20 May	Hoxne	actum no. 184
20–21 June	Norwich	acta nos.183, 188
30 June	South Elmham	actum no. 191
25 July	Gaywood	actum no. 142
31 July	Gaywood	actum no. 143
18 August	Gaywood	actum no. 153

1266

2 × 4 January	dies	*Fasti* ii 57

INDEX OF PERSONS AND PLACES

Arabic numerals refer to the numbers of the *acta* in this edition. These are followed, where appropriate, by references to the first four appendices (Appx 1, 2, 3 or 4, followed by the number of the entry therein), to the fifth appendix (Appx 5, followed by page reference therein), and finally to the Introduction, indicated by the page number in Roman numerals. The bishops whose *acta* are edited in this volume are indexed only when referred to outside the section devoted to their *acta*.

The following abbreviations for counties and religious orders have been used:

Bd.	Bedfordshire	Sa.	Shropshire
Bk.	Buckinghamshire	Sf.	Suffolk
Brk.	Berkshire	So.	Somerset
Ca.	Cambridgeshire	St.	Staffordshire
Db.	Derbyshire	Sx	Sussex
De.	Devon	Sy	Surrey
Do.	Dorset	Wa.	Warwickshire
Du.	Durham	Wlt.	Wiltshire
Ess.	Essex	Wo.	Worcestershire
Gl.	Gloucestershire	Yk. (ER)	Yorkshire (East Riding)
Glam.	Glamorgan	Yk. (NR)	Yorkshire (North Riding)
Ha.	Hampshire	Yk. (WR)	Yorkshire (West Riding)
He.	Herefordshire	Aug.	Augustinian canons
Hrt.	Hertfordshire	Ben.	Benedictine
Hu.	Huntingdonshire	Cist.	Cistercian
Li.	Lincolnshire	Clun.	Cluniac
Mx	Middlesex	Font.	Order of Fontevrault
Nb.	Northumberland	Gilb.	Gilbertine
Nf.	Norfolk	OFM	Franciscan
Np.	Northamptonshire	OP	Dominican
Ox.	Oxfordshire	Prem.	Premonstratensian

Aagas, William, 43W
Abezun, Abuson, *see* Aubusson
Achonry (Ireland), bp of, 84n
Acle, Akel, Hakel (Nf.), Alice of 172
−William of, clerk, 69W, 94W, 118W; Appx 2. 7W, 8W; xlvii
Acolt, Acout, *see* Occold
Acre, Castle, *see* Castle Acre
Acre, South, Sutacra (Nf.), tithes from, 143
Acre, West, *see* Westacre
Acre, Drogo of, Appx 2. 15W
Adam, the groom, 138
−prior of Castle Acre, Appx 2. 7–8
−seneschal of bp at Lynn, 138
−warrener of Eccles, 138
−son of Roger, 57
Adelum, Martin, 146n
Agnes, tenant at Kempstone, 22

Aigueblanche, Peter d', bp of Hereford, 61, 78n; xlv
Aiguillon, Agylyun, Robert, Appx 2. 15
Akel, *see* Acle
Aker, Alice del, 157
Alan, the clerk, Appx 1. 7W
−the constable, 101W
−servant of Adam Talbot, 58
−the villein, 43
−son of Brian, demesne tithe of, 143
−son of Roger, demesne tithe of, 143
Albert, prior of Lewes, 76
Albini, Hugh d', earl of Arundel, 85n
Alburgh, Aldeburg' (Nf.), rector of, *see* Maidstone, Osbert of
Aldborough (Nf.), 64n
Aldeburg' (unid.), 64
Aldeburgh (Sf.), 64n

Ingworth, Appx 4. 23
–Roger of, bp of Bath and Wells, 32n
Salle, *see* Aula
Salmon, John, bp of Norwich, 131n
Saltere, William, 170
Saltu, Arnald de, rector of Saxham, Appx 4.
  25
Salvage, Richard le, rector of Weston, Sf.,
  Appx 4. 7
Samson, Sampson, 101W
–abbot of Bury St Edmunds, Appx 1. 2, 7
Sancta Cruce, Martin de, rector of North Cove,
  Appx 4. 30
Sancta Maria, John de, master of God's
  House, Dunwich, Appx 4. 15
Sancto Martino, Reginald de, demesne tithe
  of, 143
'Sandhil' (unid., Sf.), Cecilia of, 65
Sandon (Ess.), church, 5
Sandra, 138
Sandwich (Kent), Nicholas of, prior of Christ
  Church, Canterbury, 18, 114
Santon, Santun' (Nf.), tithes from, 143
Sarresburia, *see* Salisbury
Sarsden, Cercedene (Ox.), rector of, *see* J., mr
Saul, son of, *see* Bundon; Geoffrey; Godwin
Savigny (Manche), Cist. abbey, 148n; xlix
Savoy, Sabaudia, Boniface of, archbp–elect of
  Canterbury, 1, 17n, 18; archbp, 61, 67–8,
  133n, 139; Appx 2. 22, 24, 38; xxix–xxx,
  xxxviii, lxi
——official of, *see* Mortimer, Hugh de
–Peter of, Appx 2. 26
Saxham, Great (Sf.), church of St Andrew,
  rector of, *see* Saltu, Arnald de; Saxham,
  Ernald of
——vicar of, *see* Ros, Jordan de
Saxham, Ernald of, *persona* of Bradfield St
  George, Appx 1. 7; of Great Saxham, Appx
  1.7n
Saxthorpe, Saxthorp' (Nf.), inhabitant of, *see*
  Bocking, John; Crich, Walter
Say, Sai, Geoffrey de, vicar of Chelsworth,
  Appx 1. 2
–Geoffrey (another), 185W
Scales, Scal', Scalis, Robert (son of Robert)
  de, 5–6; liv; chantry for, 5; obit of, 6;
——wife of, *see* Clementia; Isabelle
–Robert son of Roger de, 5n
——wife of, *see* Alice
Scarlet, Roger, 120
Scarning, Skerninge, Skerninges (Nf.), fee in,
  40n
–tithes from, 88, 143
Scarning, Roger, prior of Norwich, 185n; bp

of Norwich, 37n, 43n, 81n; xlvi, li
–clerk of, *see* Deopham, Thomas of
Scenges, *see* Seething
Schecheford, *see* Sedgeford
Schouldham, *see* Shouldham
Scot, 'bare', 138; xlviii
Scotland, papal collector in, *see* Frosinone,
  John de
Scottow, Scothoe (Nf.), church, 70; xxxii, liii
–fee in, 42n
Scratby, Scroutebi, Scrouteby, Scrowtebi
  (Nf.), church, 100
Sculthorpe, Sculphord', Sculthorp (Nf.),
  church, 75–6; lv
—patron of, *see* Pavillia, Eustachia and
  Theophania de
—rector of, *see* Crowele, Martin de; Dunton,
  Henry of; Malet, John; Nicholas; Pavelli,
  William de; Richard son of John
–demesne tithe from, 75–6
Sedgeford, Secheford, Sechford (Nf.), church,
  100; portion of in Mendham church, 183n
Sedgeford, William of, 185W
Seething, Scenges, Senges, Sengis (Nf.),
  church, 103, 106–7, 187; li, liii;
—rector of, *see* Richard, mr; vicarage of, 106
Seething, Walter of, lord, 43W
–William of, lord, 43W; 105n
Séez (Orne), Ben. abbey, portion of in
  Mendham church, 183n
Seman of the kitchen, 138
Semer, Semere (Nf. or Sf.), Ralph of, rector of
  Stanningfield, 175
Sempringham, Simplyngham (Li.), Gilb.
  priory, Appx 1. 15; master of, 138
Senges, *see* Seething
Settrington, Setherington (YE), rector of, *see*
  Bigod, John
Sewal, tenant at Kempstone, 22
'Shaprescroft', *see* Loddon
Shipdham, Sypedeham (Nf.), tithes from, 143
Shipton-under-Wychwood, Siptona (Ox.),
  vicar of, *see* Robert
Shotesham, Sotesham (Nf.), tithes from, 88
'Shoteshomesacre', *see* Raveningham
Shouldham, Schouldham, Shuldham, Suldham
  (Nf.), 121; Appx 5. p. 239
–inhabitants of, lviii; *see also* Alan the
  servant; Brun, Roger; Cusin, Robert; Erl,
  Richard; Geoffrey the deacon; Geoffrey the
  smith; Hogger, William; Matthew son of
  Matilda; Richard the cobbler; Shouldham,
  Alan of; Talbot, Adam and Samson
–tithes from, 143
Shouldham, Alan of, 58

SUBJECT INDEX

Advice
–of abbot and convent, 181
–of men learned in the law, 24
–of religious men, 151
advowson (*ius patronatus*), 21, 27, 33, 35–6,
37n, 41, 70, 72, 91n, 94, 97, 103–7, 110–
11, 116n, 118n, 122n, 129, 141, 144, 146,
181, 186–7, 189, 191, 193, 195–7; liii–liv
–dispute concerning, 5, 92; Appx 1. 13; Appx
3. 6; Appx 4. 37; xxxii, lvi
–purchase of, 104n, 106n
–quitclaimed, 5, 95n
agreement, *compositio, concordia, forma
pacis, pax, via concordie*
–amended by bp, 75
–breached, 76
–reached before bp, 5, 11, 23, 78, 116, 123,
135n, 153n; Appx 2. 6–8, 15, 25, 42; lvi
see also arbitration
–reached before papal judges delegate, 3
alms, 106, 138; l; *see also* charity
almoner, monastic, 69, 181
almsgiving, monastic, 151
altar
–bequest for lighting of, 138
–of St Mary, 5
altarage, 6, 22–3, 33, 83, 98–9, 128, 141, 145–
6, 186; Appx 1. 15–16
anathema, 143
anchorite, 130, 138; xxxv
animals, bequeathed, 138
anniversary, celebration of, 6, 33, 106, 138; li–
lii
apostolic see, *see* papacy
appeal
–for murder, 154
–permitted, Appx 2. 1
appropriation (grant *in proprios usus*), 5–6,
12, 21, 33, 35–7, 41, 69–70, 72, 77, 83, 94,
100, 103–7, 118n,122, 127, 129, 144, 146,
152, 191–3, 195–7; Appx 1. 4, 6, 12, 14–
16; Appx 2. 5; xxviii, xxxi, xxxiv, xli, l–lvi,
lxi–lxii
–by previous bps, 21n, 30n; lii
—confirmed, 25–6, 100, 143; lii
–by papal mandate, 141, 144–5; xl, lii–liii
–because of increase in religious observance,
94; lii
–because of poverty of house, 144; lii

–for celebration of obit, 6
–for commemoration of St Richard Wich, 33
–for increase of works of piety, 195
–for maintenance of charity, 191
–for maintenance of hospital, 105, 193
–for maintenance of hospitality, 35, 127, 196;
lii–liii
–for maintenance of sick priests, 104
–for *mensa* of prior, 98
–for repair of conventual church, 41; lii
–for use of almoner and infirmarer, 69, 181
–in compensation for losses, 70, 72; lii
–of mediety of church, Appx 1. 8; li
–of tithes, 87
–out of devotion for Cluniac order, 77; lii
arbitration by bp, 5, 11, 23, 78, 123; Appx 2.
24; xxxiv, lv–lvii, lxii–lxiii; *see also*
agreement
archdeacon, 5, 9, 22, 67, 83, 90–1, 103, 107,
122, 128, 145–6, 197; xxxiv, xli–xlvi; *see
also* Alvechurch, John of; Clare, William
of; Dunton, William of; Ferentino, John of;
Geoffrey; Horham, William of; Hugh (of
Wells); Ingoldisthorpe, Thomas of; Insula,
Robert de (of Colchester); John (of
Worcester); Plympton, Nicholas of; Roger;
Salerne, Walter de; Suffield, William
–vice-archdn, *see* Insula, Ralph de
arenga, lx–lxi
armour, bequeathed, 138
assarts, tithe of, 75, 108–9
assessment, by view of trustworthy men, 197
assize
–of darrein presentment, xxxii
–of novel disseisin, Appx 2. 29
–utrum, Appx 3. 1–2, 4
attorney, *see* proctor
Augustine, St, Rule of, 103, 107, 149–51,
189n

baker, *see* Geoffrey; Peter
bed, bequeathed, 138
belt, bequeathed, 138; xlvi
benediction, 138
benefice, 27, 71, 78–9, 97, 100, 107, 126, 152,
196; Appx 1. 10; xliv, lvii–lviii
–within parish church, 14, 24, 27–9, 36, 110–
11, 120, 127, 136–7; Appx 1. 10; liii, lv–lvi

103, 107, 149–51
office, divine, 103, 149
–according to rite of Sarum, 107
–shorter form of, for nuns, 150
–*see also* mass
official
–of archdn, xxxii; *see also* Walpole, Edmund
   of
–of bp of Chichester, *see* Somercotes,
   Lawrence of; Wich, Richard
–of bp of Norwich, 20, 43n, 103, 107, 123,
   132, 154, 197; xlii–xlii; xlv; xlix; *see also*
   Alvechurch, John of; Horham, William of
–of bp of Rochester, *see* Salerne, Walter de
–of consistory, 103, 107; xlii–xliii; *see also*
   Fakenham, Hervey of
officiality *sede vacante*, exercised by Walter
   Suffield, 138
oratory
–in canons' house, 113
–in hospital, 103, 107
–in monks' manor, 115
–*see also* chapel
ordination of vicars, xxxiv
ornaments
–of chapel, 98–9
–of church, 128

packhorse, keeper of, *see* Banigham
page, bp's, *see* Nicholas; William
palfrey, bequeathed, 138
papacy, pope
–*camera* of, xxv
—clerk of, *see* Martin, mr
–chaplain of, *see* Canterbury, Adam of;
   Frosinone, John de; Masson, Rostand;
   Spata, John
–confirmation by, 68n, 98n, 103n, 107n, 128n;
   xxxi, xl
–*curia*, 9n, 31n; Appx 5. p. ; xxviii–xxix,
   xxxi–xxxii, xxxiv–xxxvii, xxxix, xliii–xlv
—delegation from English church to, 68n
—envoys of suffragans of Canterbury to,
   Appx 2. 22
—lawyers of, *see* Peronti, Jordan; Spata, John
—decretal issued by, Appx 2. 13
–executors of business of the Cross appointed
   by, 8, 16, 31, 34, 63A, 82, 84, 126, 133;
   Appx 2. 28
–grant of taxation to English crown by, 63–A,
   84
–judges-delegate appointed by, 3, 17n, 75n;
   xlv, xlix
–legate of, *see* Otto; Ottobuono

–letters issued by, 9n, 17n, 18n, 27, 31n, 63A,
   67n, 70n, 71, 75n, 78–9, 84, 97n, 103n,
   107n, 119, 128n, 133n, 134n, 141, 144,
   145n, 184n, 187; Appx 2. 1–2, 13, 16, 28,
   39
–*nuncio* of, *see* Masson, Rostand; Plympton,
   Nicholas of
–petitions to, Appx 2. 1, 13, 39
–provision for clerks by, 27, 71, 78–9, 184n;
   xxx–xxxi, xxxiii, xl, liii, lv, lvii
–*scriptor* of, *see* Linasius; Nimpha, Berard de
–subdeacon of, *see* Plympton, Nicholas of;
   Somercotes, Lawrence of
–subsidy granted by English church to, 68,
   119
–*see also* Alexander III and IV; Celestine III;
   Clement IV; Gregory IX; Honorius III;
   Innocent III and IV; Urban IV
park, le parc, 43
parliament, xxxix
pasture, Appx 3. 6
patron, of hospital, 103, 105, 107
–of monastery, 74, 149–51
–of parish church, 5, 24, 75n, 76, 92, 116,
   153n
—consent of, 42, 85, 87, 118; Appx 1. 2;
   Appx 2. 25
peace, breach of, xxxii
penalty for breach of agreement, 3, 5, 11, 24,
   29, 33, 75–6, 79, 98 110–11; Appx 2. 7–8,
   15, 25, 40, 42; *see also* fine; forfeiture;
   sequestration; suspension
penance, remission of, lviii
pension annual
– from parish church to monastery, 9, 29–30,
   33, 72n, 91n, 95n, 114, 136n, 141, 143;191;
   Appx 1. 19n; liii, lvi
—ancient, 27, 79, 120, 143, 184n, 191
—resignation of, 127
—arrears of remitted, Appx 2. 42
—assigned to monastic almonry, 92
—assigned to monastic infirmary, 92
—restitution of, 96
–paid to individuals
–as part of vicarage, 13, 141; Appx 1. 5, 16
–as security for future benefice, 27–9, 71, 78–
   9
–as security for specified benefice, 80
–in return for surrender of benefice, 79n
–to papal chaplain, 79; lv
–to rejected presentee, 29
–to *persona* from vicar, Appx 1. 2
–to rector from religious, for tithes, 11
–various, from church, 128
   see also benefice; portion